'The Age-Old Struggle'

Irish republicanism from the Battle of the Bogside
to the Belfast Agreement, 1969–1998

'The Age-Old Struggle'

Irish republicanism from the Battle of the Bogside to the Belfast Agreement, 1969–1998

Jack Hepworth

LIVERPOOL UNIVERSITY PRESS

First published 2021 by
Liverpool University Press
4 Cambridge Street
Liverpool
L69 7ZU

British Library Cataloguing-in-Publication data
A British Library CIP record is available

ISBN 978-1-80085-539-7 cased

Typeset by Carnegie Book Production, Lancaster
Printed and bound by CPI Group (UK) Ltd, Croydon CR0 4YY

Contents

Acknowledgements

This book would not have been possible without the assistance and goodwill of very many people, so it is a pleasure to record my gratitude. *'The age-old struggle'* originated in a doctoral study at Newcastle University, where the acuity, diligence, and encouragement of my supervisors, Dr Sarah Campbell and Dr Matt Perry, was exceptional. Sarah and Matt set and maintained the highest standards, and my greatest intellectual debt is to them. I am especially grateful for the Research Excellence Academy award which funded my doctoral work at Newcastle, and for supplementary grants from the British Association for Irish Studies and the Society for the Study of Labour History.

The camaraderie of colleagues and friends in Newcastle and beyond underpinned three exhilarating years of research and writing. The friendship and intellectual stimulation of colleagues in Newcastle University's Oral History Unit and Collective was vital. Special thanks to Dr Alison Atkinson-Phillips, Sue Bradley, Rosie Bush, Dr Andy Clark, Silvie Fisch, Professor Graham Smith, and the wider network and reading group. Seminars, workshops, and conversations with colleagues in Newcastle's Labour and Society Research Group, and across the School of History, Classics and Archaeology, played a formative role: thanks to Dr Joan Allen, Dr Richard Allen, Professor Claudia Baldoli, Professor Máire Cross, Dr Ben Partridge, Dr Alex Quiroga, Dr Felix Schulz, Dr Jemima Short, and Professor Annie Tindley. All work and no play would have made for a humdrum experience, so it is a pleasure to thank my Classics colleague Dr Susanna Phillippo for organising the weekly Friday five-a-sides at Eldon Square: the perfect start to a weekend. The unrivalled hospitality of the Tyneside Irish Centre was the natural successor.

While the majority of research and writing took place in Newcastle, I also benefited enormously from time spent at the University of Durham and the University of Central Lancashire. Early academic inspiration came from Martin Barrett, Dr Luke McMahon, Jonathan Morgan, and Jo Venn. In Durham, I was especially fortunate to be taught by Dr Alex Barber,

Dr Matthew Johnson, Professor Ludmilla Jordanova, Professor Christian Liddy, Dr Andrzej Olechnowicz, and Dr Gabriella Treglia. At St John's College, the encouragement and support of Dr Mark Ogden, Dr Sue Trees, and the Reverend Professor David Wilkinson constituted a first-rate foundation. In Preston, I enjoyed the collegiality of Dr Jonathan Colman, Dr Billy Frank, Dr Alexandros Koutsoukis, Dr Stephen Meredith, Dr Máirtín Ó Catháin, Dr Jack Southern, Dr David Stewart, and Dr Keith Vernon.

Teaching more than 350 undergraduates and postgraduates at UCLan and Newcastle contributed inestimably to this project's journey. Particular thanks to the Newcastle special-subject group, the MA cohort, and the 22 dissertation candidates I have had the pleasure of supervising. Sections of this book formed the basis of papers presented to conferences of the American Conference of Irish Studies, Oral History Network of Ireland, and Oral History Society. I am grateful for the comments and ideas of many scholars, including Dr Paul Burgess, Dr Sophie Cooper, Professor Graham Dawson, Dr Niamh Dillon, Dr Seán Donnelly, Professor Richard English, Dr Darragh Gannon, Dr José Gutiérrez, Dr Brian Hanley, Dr Roisín Higgins, Dr Erin Hinson, Dr Brian Hughes, Dr Erin Jessee, Struan Kennedy, Dr Dianne Kirby, Dr Martin Maguire, Dr Eve Morrison, Professor Marc Mulholland, Dr Dieter Reinisch, Dr Chris Reynolds, Eimear Rosato, and Dr Tony Varley, and Siobhan Warrington.

The research for this book would have been impossible without the generosity of many people. First and foremost, my thanks to the interviewees for their time, goodwill, and candour: Albert Allen, Mickey Brady, Don Browne, Charlie Casey, Gerry Foster, Fra Halligan, Kevin Hannaway, Peadar Lagan, Eamonn MacDermott, Gerry MacLochlainn, Patrick Magee, Raymond McCartney, Francie McGuigan, Seamus McHenry, Tommy McKearney, Danny Morrison, Conor Murphy, Nuala Perry, and Seánna Walsh. Thanks also to those anonymous interlocutors who are, of course, not named here, but whose time, thoughts, and reflections are appreciated. The staff and volunteers of the Linen Hall Library in Belfast, Ex-Prisoners Outreach Programme in Derry, Teach na Fáilte, and Coiste na nIarchimí were extremely helpful and gave invaluable assistance. At the Eileen Hickey Irish Republican History Museum in west Belfast, I am particularly grateful to Johnny Haddock, who went above and beyond to facilitate research visits. I am also thankful to Philomena Gallagher, Fra Halligan, Peter Heathwood, Jim McIlmurray, Seán McMonagle, Nuala Perry, and Hilary Rock-Gormley for their munificent support. The genial hospitality of Ruth Quigley at Farset International and the Rosato and Trainor families will live long in the memory. I am delighted that Peter Denton, Bobbie Hanvey, Kaveh Kazemi, Rory Nugent, and Dr Jeff Sluka gave permission for their evocative photographs to enrich this book. Working with Christabel Scaife (Liverpool University Press) and Sarah Warren (Carnegie) has been a pleasure.

Valued friendships have sustained this book's journey over the years. My heartfelt thanks especially to Mark, Amanda, Jennie, Connal, John, Jamie, Steven, Chris, Susan, Andy, Paola, Enya, Ian, Julia, Georgie, Andrew, Ally, Francis, Sally, David, Emma, Luke, Sam, Chris, Steve, June, Lily, and Tom. Coaches, players, and committee members at Chorley and Wallsend provided the best possible diversion from researching and writing: it has been a privilege to work with Rammy, Jan, Geoff, Shaun, Abi, Aldo, Carl, Reece, and Bex. Barbara is very sadly missed, and will never be forgotten. At Chorley, the heroics of Jamie, Smudge, and the entire 'class of 2019' provided brilliant inspiration in the final throes of the PhD.

Finally, it is a delight to thank Mary Celine, who first awakened my curiosity towards all things Irish; my family and friends across the Irish Sea, especially those in Donegal, where my fascination with Irish history took root; and Joan, Bob, and Gerry, for encouraging me to think critically and question everything. My deepest gratitude goes to my parents, whose unwavering support and belief made this project possible. I dedicate this book to them.

Abbreviations

ANC	African National Congress
CCDC	Central Citizens' Defence Committee
CESA	Catholic Ex-Servicemen's Association
DCDA	Derry Citizens' Defence Association
EEC	European Economic Community
INLA	Irish National Liberation Army
IRA	Irish Republican Army (pre-1970)
IRSP	Irish Republican Socialist Party
LCR	League of Communist Republicans
MLA	Member of the Legislative Assembly
NHBAC	National H-Block/Armagh Committee
NICRA	Northern Ireland Civil Rights Association
OC	Officer Commanding
OIRA	Official Irish Republican Army
OSF	Official Sinn Féin
PD	People's Democracy
PIRA	Provisional Irish Republican Army
RSF	Republican Sinn Féin
RUC	Royal Ulster Constabulary
SDLP	Social Democratic and Labour Party

Glossary

Ard Comhairle	Governing body or national executive
Ard Fheis	Annual conference (plural: *ard fheiseanna*)
Comhairle Ceantair	District committee or area council
Cumann	Local party branch (plural: *cumainn*)

Key to archives

EHI	Eileen Hickey Irish Republican History Museum, Belfast
HVA	Heathwood Video Archive
ILA	Irish Left Archive (https://clririshleftarchive.org/)
LHL NIPC	Northern Ireland Political Collection, Linen Hall Library, Belfast
NAI	National Archives of Ireland, Dublin
PRONI	Public Record Office of Northern Ireland, Belfast

'The Age-Old Struggle'

Introduction

Historical background

Asking Irish republicans to explain the origins of the conflict in and about Northern Ireland elicits a wide range of responses. Some talk first about 1969, when the north's two major cities, Belfast and Derry, experienced intense rioting and the British Army arrived. Others refer to 1919, when revolutionary separatists gathered in Dublin's Mansion House to assemble Dáil Éireann, the all-Ireland parliament. Many republicans would tell a longer story, insisting their struggle can only be understood with reference to the Elizabethan 'plantations' of the late sixteenth century; others trace their political origins to 1169, when Anglo-Norman mercenaries landed in Ireland. In microcosm, these diverse responses reflect the variations in Irish republicanism that are the subject of this book.

In 1969, when loyalist counter-demonstrators and members of the Ulster Special Constabulary violently suppressed civil rights protests in Northern Ireland, riots ensued. Home Secretary James Callaghan swiftly deployed the British Army. For neither the first nor the last time, Irish republicans mobilised in pursuit of Irish unity and independence. In the political tumult of 1969, republicans reorganised. When the republican movement split that winter, two factions emerged, soon becoming knowns as Officials and Provisionals. Both demanded a united Ireland and fought the British presence.

Through the next three decades, republican militants – constituted chiefly in the Provisional IRA (PIRA) – waged guerrilla warfare and a political campaign. In the subsequent conflict, more than 3,500 people were killed, the majority of whom were civilians. Republicans killed more than 2,000 people. The Good Friday Agreement of 1998 – between the British and Irish governments, and most political parties in Northern Ireland – was an epochal moment in Ireland's recent history. The Agreement stipulated that Northern Ireland's constitutional status could change only with the consent of the majority. Momentously, the major republican party, Sinn Féin, supported the Agreement, and its military partner, the PIRA, eventually announced the end of its armed campaign in July 2005.

Since 1969, thousands of Irish republicans have participated in guerrilla struggle against British rule in Ireland, with the support of thousands more. Historians have acknowledged that this enduring and evolving politics is not hermetically sealed. Writing in 2004, Jonathan Tonge highlighted the capaciousness of Irish republicanism, spanning 'militant nationalists, unreconstructed militarists, romantic Fenians, Gaelic Republicans, Catholic sectarians, Northern defenders, international Marxists, socialists, libertarians and liberal Protestants'.[1] Richard English, among the foremost historians of modern republicanism, has highlighted the diversity of its political ideas.[2] Republican activists are aware of the variety of their tradition. Writing in 1998, Des O'Hagan, a former Official republican interned in the early 1970s, identified four distinct tendencies within Irish republicanism: democratic, internationalist, secular, and socialist.[3]

Writing the history of Irish republicanism

Historians, political scientists, security studies experts, sociologists, ethnographers, journalists, and commentators have all contributed to making Northern Ireland, relative to its size, the most intensively studied place in the world. Yet, until recently, only a few book-length treatments suggested the polyvocality of republicanism's internal dynamics.

Ed Moloney's *A secret history of the IRA* (2002) depicted a Provisional republican movement shifting politically leftward in the 1970s. Moloney also alluded to republicans dissenting against the electoral path of Gerry Adams and Martin McGuinness from the mid-1980s.[4] Scholars have often echoed these themes, but have seldom empirically tested or complicated them. For instance, Moloney's interpretations rested upon a particular reading of rising 'northern radicals', and neglected socialist tendencies earlier in the Provisionals' history.

[1] Jonathan Tonge, '"They haven't gone away, you know": Irish republican "dissidents" and the armed struggle', *Terrorism and Political Violence*, 16 (2004), p. 672.

[2] Richard English, *Armed struggle: the history of the IRA* (London: Pan Books, 2012) [First edition London: Macmillan, 2003], p. 166.

[3] Des O'Hagan, 'The concept of republicanism', in Norman Porter (ed.), *The republican ideal: current perspectives* (Belfast: Blackstaff, 1998), p. 84.

[4] Ed Moloney, *A secret history of the IRA* (London: Penguin, 2002), pp. 185, 242.

While academics have not ignored the processes that Moloney charted, much of the debate has revolved around superficial treatment of republican factions. Brendan O'Brien posited that electoral tactics in the 1980s divided the Provisionals straightforwardly between a presumably pro-electoral 'Sinn Féin versus the IRA'.[5] Dawn Walsh and Eoin O'Malley suggested that the Provisionals 'moved to moderate public statements to make them more acceptable to the broader nationalist community'.[6] Yet the micro-dynamics of these processes remained unexamined. Richard English has helpfully argued that even Provisionals endorsing electoral experimentation in the early 1980s still distrusted and deplored the process.[7] For the most part, agency and division within the movement on such issues has remained unclear.

Due perhaps to practical research challenges, analysts have often reified networks within republicanism. Divisions have been demarcated without explaining how milieux and allegiances emerged. For example, Henry Patterson, Ed Moloney, and M. L. R. Smith have highlighted debates concerning the 'Éire Nua' proposals that underpinned Provisional republican policy from 1971 to 1982.[8] Former Sinn Féin president Ruairí Ó Brádaigh's position became untenable after the party *ard fheis* voted to drop 'his' proposals for a federal Ireland.[9] It is incumbent upon scholars to unpack how that political programme, over time, became synonymous with Ó Brádaigh's leadership cadre – and, by implication, how opposition to Éire Nua was identified with a leadership milieu around Gerry Adams and his supporters.

Rogelio Alonso's *The IRA and armed struggle* (2007) drew upon oral history interviews with a range of republican ex-combatants, spanning supporters and opponents of Sinn Féin's constitutional strategy, and including 'second-generation' republicans who mobilised as late as the 1990s. Alonso also insightfully discussed how leftist PIRA prisoners were ostracised in the late

---

[5] Brendan O'Brien, *The long war: the IRA and Sinn Féin* (Dublin: O'Brien Press, 1999), p. 122.

[6] Dawn Walsh & Eoin O'Malley, 'The slow growth of Sinn Féin: from minor player to centre stage?', in Liam Weeks & Alistair Clark (eds.), *Radical or redundant? Minor parties in Irish politics* (Dublin: History Press Ireland, 2012), p. 206.

[7] English, *Armed struggle*, 207.

[8] Henry Patterson, *The politics of illusion: republicanism and socialism in modern Ireland* (London: Hutchinson Radius, 1989), p. 162; Moloney, *Secret history*, 181; M. L. R. Smith, 'Fin de siècle, 1972: the Provisional IRA's strategy and the beginning of the eight-thousand-day stalemate', in Alan O'Day (ed.), *Political violence in Northern Ireland: conflict and conflict resolution* (Westport, Connecticut: Praeger, 1997), p. 23.

[9] Robert W. White, *Ruairí Ó Brádaigh: the life and politics of an Irish revolutionary* (Bloomington, Indiana: Indiana University Press, 2006), p. 293.

1980s. However, the focus of his work was initial mobilisation and motivations. Noting patterns in how republicans justified past activism, Alonso implied homogenising tendencies in republican memory.[10]

J. Bowyer Bell, Paul Gill, and John Horgan are undoubtedly justified in characterising republicanism's popular base as young, working-class, and male, in urban housing estates and small rural farms.[11] It remains for scholars to explain cultural influences and subjectivities propelling this mobilisation. If republicans enjoyed popular status as community defenders, how did they sustain this reputation locally, given their manifest inability in real terms to shield Catholic civilians from brutal state repression and loyalist paramilitarism? From 1969 to 1998, loyalists killed 506 Catholic civilians.[12] Probing the Provisional movement's foundational myths – most familiarly the nascent PIRA's role in repelling loyalist incursions in west Belfast from August 1969 – Stephen Hopkins has adroitly noted that the refrain's mobilising power and meaning goes beyond the geographical immediacy.[13] Martyn Frampton's detailed analysis of Sinn Féin policy statements demonstrated that the Provisional leadership's international politics were highly malleable,[14] begging further questions. How did the grassroots interpret and refract these international perspectives? To what extent did such policy statements affect or interest republicans on the ground?

The Provisional republican movement's strategic changes from the 1980s and the consequent emergence of 'dissenting' and 'dissident' republicanism has provoked considerable interest among academics, commentators, and activists alike. Laurence McKeown's *Out of time* (2001) elucidated clannish tendencies between republican prisoners from different parts of Ireland, and highlighted prisoners' differentiated interactions with education in the movement.[15]

---

[10] Rogelio Alonso, *The IRA and armed struggle* (Abingdon: Routledge, 2007), pp. 4, 60–62, 67, passim.

[11] J. Bowyer Bell, *The IRA, 1968–2000: analysis of a secret army* (London: Frank Cass, 2000), p. 97; Paul Gill & John Horgan, 'Who were the volunteers? The shifting sociological and operational profile of 1240 PIRA members', *Terrorism and Political Violence*, 25 (2013), pp. 435–456.

[12] Human Rights Watch, *Human rights in Northern Ireland* (New York: Human Rights Watch, 1991), p. 108.

[13] Stephen Hopkins, *The politics of memoir and the Northern Ireland conflict* (Liverpool: Liverpool University Press, 2013), p. 28.

[14] Martyn Frampton, '"Squaring the circle": the foreign policy of Sinn Féin, 1983–1989', *Irish Political Studies*, 19 (2004), pp. 43–63; Martyn Frampton, 'Sinn Féin and the European arena: "ourselves alone" or "critical engagement"?', *Irish Studies in International Affairs*, 16 (2005), pp. 235–253.

[15] Laurence McKeown, *Out of time: Irish republican prisoners in Long Kesh, 1972–2000* (Belfast: Beyond the Pale Publications, 2001), pp. 31–32, 38, 47, 132, 161.

Diachronic sophistication and appreciation of how shifting international contexts affected Provisional republicanism set the work of Mark Ryan and Kevin Bean apart. For Ryan, Sinn Féin's move towards constitutionalism and 'conciliatory' politics had to be situated among global transformations: the Soviet Union's disintegration had discredited 'oppositional' politics worldwide.[16] Bean looked closer to home to explain the Provisionals' tactical changes. The Provisionals had always been a hybrid of factions, Bean argued, and Sinn Féin's increasing entanglement in state structures, electoral politics, and community populism had produced reformism.[17]

Similarly, Stephen Hopkins has argued that republicanism since the late 1980s ceded its outward-facing revolutionary aims and gradually settled for a rights-based discourse of cultural freedom within Northern Ireland.[18] Former PIRA prisoners Anthony McIntyre and Tommy McKearney have criticised a perceived populist drift in Provisional republicanism.[19] Martin J. McCleery's study of internment's impact on four provincial towns moved the object of research beyond the routine focus upon Northern Ireland's two largest cities.[20]

Happily, rigorous academic analyses of Irish republicanism continue to appear, constituting a major field of study. Important recent works by Robert W. White, Marisa McGlinchey, and Daniel Finn have done much to illuminate the historical origins of contemporary divisions. White's substantial oeuvre has highlighted the dynamism and complexity of individual republican trajectories.[21] *Out of the ashes* (2017) synthesised interviews with Provisional republican activists

---

[16] Mark Ryan, *War and peace in Ireland: Britain and the IRA in the new world order* (London: Pluto Press, 1994), pp. 7, 9, 16.

[17] Kevin Bean, *The new politics of Sinn Féin* (Liverpool: Liverpool University Press, 2007), pp. 6, 84–85, 93, 172, 251, 254, 259.

[18] Stephen Hopkins, '"Our whole history has been ruined!" The 1981 hunger strike and the politics of republican commemoration and memory', *Irish Political Studies*, 31 (2016), p. 50.

[19] Anthony McIntyre, *Good Friday: the death of Irish republicanism* (New York: Ausubo Press, 2008); Tommy McKearney, *The Provisional IRA: from insurrection to parliament* (London: Pluto Press, 2011).

[20] Martin J. McCleery, *Operation Demetrius and its aftermath: a new history of the use of internment without trial in Northern Ireland, 1971–1975* (Manchester: Manchester University Press, 2015).

[21] Robert W. White, 'From peaceful protest to guerrilla war: micromobilisation of the Provisional Irish Republican Army', *American Journal of Sociology*, 94 (1989), pp. 1277–1302; Robert W. White, *Provisional Irish republicans: an oral and interpretive history* (Westport, Connecticut: Greenwood Press, 1993); White, *Ó Brádaigh*; Robert W. White, 'Structural identity theory and the post-recruitment activism of Irish republicans: persistence, disengagement, splits, and dissidents in social movement organizations', *Social Problems*, 57 (2010), pp. 341–370.

conducted across three phases in the mid-1980s, mid-1990s, and late 2000s. White's study unravelled simplistic binaries in the movement's composition and raised vital questions concerning how to understand the Provisional movement's evolution.[22] Drawing upon 90 interviews with republicans, McGlinchey's *Unfinished business* (2019) highlighted moments of rupture for individual republicans leaving their erstwhile organisations.[23] Engaging hitherto unused activist literature, Finn charted shifted loci of power and contextualised tactical and strategic departures in the movement.[24]

Burgeoning inquiries into the internal dynamics of radical groups, especially in Northern Ireland, have increasingly applied the conceptual frameworks and analytical categories associated with social movement theory. Several essays in Lorenzo Bosi and Gianluca de Fazio's edited volume *The troubles in Northern Ireland and theories of social movements* (2017) examined micro-mobilisation between civil rights protest and republican armed struggle in the early 1970s.[25]

'Insider accounts' have also prompted historiographical discussions of power relations within republican organisations. As Stephen Hopkins has noted, republican memoirists have often reflected critically on the movement to which they belonged.[26] This confessional genre negotiates hindsight and grapples with the profound changes in republicanism's composition. For example, former PIRA prisoner Anthony McIntyre's critique of the Provisional movement traced its shifting strategies from the early 1970s.[27] Another longstanding PIRA volunteer who later became disillusioned with the movement, Gerry Bradley documented dissent among his comrades in north Belfast against the Belfast Brigade's leadership. Bradley remembered his milieu protesting against the ceasefire of 1972 and Sinn Féin's electoral initiatives in the early 1980s.[28] McIntyre's and Bradley's contributions crucially pinpointed locality and networks as important factors in intra-republican disputes.

---

[22] Robert W. White, *Out of the ashes: an oral history of the Provisional Irish republican movement* (Newbridge: Merrion, 2017).

[23] Marisa McGlinchey, *Unfinished business: the politics of 'dissident' Irish republicanism* (Manchester: Manchester University Press, 2019).

[24] Daniel Finn, *One man's terrorist: a political history of the IRA* (London: Verso, 2019).

[25] Lorenzo Bosi & Gianluca de Fazio (eds.), *The troubles in Northern Ireland and theories of social movements* (Amsterdam: Amsterdam University Press, 2017).

[26] Stephen Hopkins, 'Sinn Féin, the past and political strategy: the Provisional Irish republican movement and the politics of "reconciliation"', *Irish Political Studies*, 30 (2015), p. 89.

[27] Anthony McIntyre, 'Modern Irish republicanism: the product of British state strategies', *Irish Political Studies*, 10 (1995), pp. 97–122.

[28] Gerry Bradley & Brian Feeney, *Insider: Gerry Bradley's life in the IRA* (Dublin: O'Brien Press, 2009), pp. 34, 131, 194–200.

A similar partisanship pervaded the in-depth interviews with former PIRA commander Brendan Hughes that spanned half of Ed Moloney's momentous *Voices from the grave* (2010). Although the project was later subsumed in controversy, Hughes's interviews illuminated schisms within the Provisional movement regarding military tactics and creeping sectarianism in the mid-1970s.[29]

Retrospective discussions of divisions within republicanism often reduce historical contingency. Assessing fissures within the movement, scholars have employed binaries of 'moderates' and 'hardliners', 'leftists' and 'traditionalists'. For Emmet O'Connor, the republican movement split between 'a "red" faction, the Officials, and the "green" Provisionals'.[30] Graham Spencer's perceptions of 'notable differences' between militaristic Provisionals and more politically inclined New Leftist Officials may hold for the organisations' leaderships, but the extent to which the same can be said of the grassroots is subject to debate:[31] in the chaos of 1969 and 1970, Derry republicans Martin McGuinness and Mitchel McLaughlin, for instance, both transferred allegiance to the Provisionals, having initially sided with the Officials at the time of the split.[32] Henry Patterson and Ed Moloney have described the pivotal Sinn Féin *ardfheis* (annual conference) of 1986 in terms of divisions between 'traditionalists' and 'militarists' and younger, pro-electoral, northern Provisionals.[33]

These bifurcated terms are usually the product of hindsight's inordinate influence, doing little to explain how allegiances and subjectivities within republicanism have evolved. Rigid categories lend undue clarity to boundaries within republicanism, and obscure more sophisticated patterns of difference. Anthony McIntyre's critique of scholarship dichotomising 'military' and 'political' dimensions of republicanism is to be welcomed.[34]

---

[29] Hughes's testimony was part of the Boston College project, which was subsequently discredited for its disregard for ethical protocols: at interview, researchers 'guaranteed' loyalist and republican ex-combatants anonymity and secure storage of their recordings for as long as they lived. The promise could not be kept in 2013, when the Police Service of Northern Ireland (PSNI) subpoenaed tapes for ongoing investigations. Ed Moloney, *Voices from the grave: two men's war in Ireland* (London: Faber & Faber, 2010).

[30] Emmet O'Connor, 'Labour and left politics', in Arthur Aughey & Duncan Morrow (eds.), *Northern Ireland politics* (Harlow: Longman, 1996), pp. 48–55.

[31] Graham Spencer, *From armed struggle to political struggle: republican tradition and transformation in Northern Ireland* (London: Bloomsbury, 2015), pp. 4–5, 46.

[32] White, *Provisional Irish republicans*, 45; John Morrison, 'Why do people become dissident Irish republicans?', in P. M. Currie & Max Taylor (eds.), *Dissident Irish republicanism* (New York: Continuum, 2011), p. 27.

[33] Patterson, *Politics of illusion*, 186; Moloney, *Secret history*, 293.

[34] McIntyre, 'Modern Irish republicanism'.

Where analysts have explained popular support for republicanism, the emphasis has typically been around specific events, most notably Bloody Sunday in 1972 and the hunger strikes of 1980 and 1981.[35] These acutely important moments in contemporary republicanism conform to what James M. Jasper and Jane D. Poulsen term 'moral shocks' of such seismic significance that they extend mobilisation.[36] This causality is well-established and often substantiated in republicans' oral history interviews and written testimonies. But in explaining mobilisation uniformly, there is a risk of homogenising republicanism.

Recent inquiries have illuminated shifts in how the republican grassroots responded to the movement's changing repertoires of contention. F. Stuart Ross investigated how the Provisional movement's campaigns developed during the prison protests from 1976.[37] Tony Craig considered the PIRA ceasefire of 1975 and 1976 a watershed for the movement, triggering Sinn Féin's growing involvement with tenants' associations and urban advice centres.[38]

Scholarship questioning republicanism's social orientation since the early 1970s – *before* the prison protests and Sinn Féin's electoral experimentation – has stressed Northern Ireland's differentiated geography. Rachel Monaghan and Andrew Silke have discussed republican vigilantism and informers, and the movement's relationship with its host communities.[39] Jeffrey Sluka's pioneering ethnographic perspectives refined perceptions of republicanism's complex interactions with its support base. During extensive field research in Belfast's Divis Flats in 1981, Sluka found multi-layered popular responses to republican paramilitaries, with guerrillas cast simultaneously as community defenders and social burdens, as heroic patriots and escalators of a nightmarish war. A

---

[35] Patrick Bishop & Eamonn Mallie, *The Provisional IRA* (London: Heinemann, 1987), p. 160; Brian Feeney, *Sinn Féin: a hundred turbulent years* (Madison, Wisconsin: University of Wisconsin Press, 2002), p. 270; Peter Taylor, *Provos: the IRA and Sinn Féin* (London: Bloomsbury, 1997), p. 113.

[36] James M. Jasper & Jane D. Poulsen, 'Recruiting strangers and friends: moral shocks and social networks in animal rights and anti-nuclear protests', *Social Problems*, 42 (1995), pp. 493–512.

[37] F. Stuart Ross, 'Between party and movement: Sinn Féin and the popular movement against criminalisation, 1976–1982', *Irish Political Studies*, 21 (2006), pp. 337–354; F. Stuart Ross, *Smashing H-block: the rise and fall of the popular campaign against criminalisation, 1976–1982* (Liverpool: Liverpool University Press, 2011).

[38] Tony Craig, 'Monitoring the peace? Northern Ireland's 1975 ceasefire incident centres and the politicisation of Sinn Féin', *Terrorism and Political Violence*, 26 (2014), pp. 307–319.

[39] Rachel Monaghan, 'An imperfect peace: paramilitary "punishments" in Northern Ireland', *Terrorism and Political Violence*, 16 (2004), p. 440; Andrew Silke, 'Rebel's dilemma: the changing relationship between the IRA, Sinn Féin and paramilitary vigilantism in Northern Ireland', *Terrorism and Political Violence*, 11 (1999), p. 81.

significant majority of Sluka's sample of interviewees (76.9 per cent) thought that PIRA and Irish National Liberation Army (INLA) volunteers crucially maintained the local social order.[40]

This analysis of republicanism's internal dynamics engages a central research question: how and why did republicans historicise, spatialise, frame, and adapt their struggle in different ways? Explaining variations within Irish republicanism, this book posits three interconnected factors that simultaneously sustained, complicated, and fragmented republican politics: class, space, and networks within republicanism. Republicans experienced class and interacted with class politics differently, and spatialised and historicised their struggle locally, nationally, and internationally. At moments of crisis and transformation in their campaign, activists mobilised in networks that either advocated or eschewed 'new departures' from long-held orthodoxies.[41] These competing milieux mediated subjective responses to power relations and strategic changes in the movement. These findings have implications for qualitative analyses of radical movements beyond Ireland, and for understandings of republicanism today.

Sources, methods, and concepts

This book draws together a wide range of archival material alongside oral histories to explore the diversity of Irish republicanism and republican memory since 1969. Its sensitivity to the significance of place, class politics, and networks within republicanism explains the complexity of Irish republicanism. Yet the centripetal forces that have cohered republican groups through decades of struggle also command attention. Examining these contrasting processes that have simultaneously splintered and galvanised Irish republican organisations, the book illuminates power dynamics within this heterogeneous political tradition. It analyses the variety of influences working within Irish republicanism, and wide-ranging republican responses to crucial moments in the conflict.

Geographically, the primary focus is republicanism in Northern Ireland and, to a slightly lesser degree, in the five border counties of the Republic of Ireland: Cavan, Donegal, Leitrim, Louth, and Monaghan. The emphasis is on republicanism as a lived experience among its supporters. Inevitably, those areas of 'the north' where republicanism was most significant receive most attention, both in urban strongholds such as west Belfast and Derry's Bogside, as well

[40] Jeffrey A. Sluka, *Hearts and minds, water and fish: support for the IRA and INLA in a Northern Irish ghetto* (Greenwich, Connecticut: JAI Press, 1989), pp. 119–120.

[41] Kevin Bean, 'The new departure? Recent developments in republican strategy and ideology', *Irish Studies Review*, 10 (1995), pp. 2–6.

as rural heartlands such as south Armagh and east Tyrone. The considerable republican presence in numerous 'border towns' like Bundoran, Dundalk, and Monaghan in the Republic's five border counties justifies extending this study beyond Northern Ireland.

The geographical demarcation supports an analytical discussion. There are, of course, occasional allusions to republicans outside these geographical confines, across the island of Ireland and beyond. The vast majority of republican organisations discussed in this book enjoyed support beyond the north and the Republic's border counties: for example, from its foundation, the Irish Republican Socialist Party (IRSP) had active *cumainn* in Wicklow, Limerick, and Cork,[42] while the Provisional republican movement's 'southern' support base included elements in Ireland's agricultural west in Mayo, Galway, and Roscommon – home of Ruairí Ó Brádaigh, the movement's long-serving leader. Necessarily, this book largely bypasses a further 21 Irish counties, not to mention republicanism in Britain or the United States of America. Thanks to the pioneering work of Brian Hanley and Gearóid Ó Faoleán, republicanism across the Republic is now receiving greater attention.[43]

Whereas many accounts of republicanism focus predominantly on the conflict's outbreak in the late 1960s and early 1970s,[44] or the prison protests from 1976 to 1981,[45] this book includes vast new material on republicanism throughout these decades. Sources ranging from local newspapers to community bulletins and pamphlet literature elucidate new understandings of republicanism in the first years of conflict after 1969. In particular, this material complexifies analyses of the interactions of leftism, international politics, religion as a signifier

---

[42] 'I.R.S.P. grows', *The Starry Plough/An Camhchéachta*, Volume 1, Number 9 (December 1975).

[43] Brian Hanley, *The impact of the troubles on the Republic of Ireland, 1968–1979: boiling volcano?* (Manchester: Manchester University Press, 2018); Gearóid Ó Faoleán, *A broad church: the Provisional IRA in the Republic of Ireland, 1969–1980* (Newbridge: Irish Academic Press, 2019).

[44] Simon Prince & Geoffrey Warner, *Belfast and Derry in revolt: a new history of the start of the troubles* (Dublin: Irish Academic Press, 2011); Thomas Hennessey, *The evolution of the troubles, 1970–1972* (Dublin: Irish Academic Press, 2007); Brian Hanley, '"I ran away"? The IRA and 1969 – the evolution of a myth', *Irish Historical Studies*, 38 (2013), pp. 671–687.

[45] Ross, *Smashing H-block*; David Beresford, *Ten men dead: the story of the 1981 Irish hunger strike* (London: HarperCollins, 1994) [First edition London: Grafton, 1987]; Brian Campbell, Laurence McKeown, & Felim O'Hagan (eds.), *Nor meekly serve my time: the H-block struggle, 1976–1981* (Belfast: Beyond the Pale Publications, 1994); Liam Clarke, *Broadening the battlefield: the H-blocks and the rise of Sinn Féin* (Dublin: Gill & Macmillan, 1987); Tim Pat Coogan, *The H-block story* (Dublin: Ward River Press, 1980).

of identity, and the cultural significance of place in shaping republicanism during the 1970s.

'*The Age-Old Struggle*' draws upon more than 500 political ephemera and periodicals, emerging from activists throughout the ranks of diverse republican organisations. Sources such as *An Eochair* (the internal prison journal of Official republican prisoners in the early 1970s), *Socialist Republic: Paper of People's Democracy*, and *The Starry Plough/An Camchéachta* afford valuable insights into discussions beyond the Provisional movement. Additionally, occasional publications that emerged in the 1980s – including *The Captive Voice*, *Iris Bheag*, *Women in Struggle*, and *Congress '86* – encompass wide-ranging critiques from the republican rank-and-file. Often, these alternative voices depart from analyses presented in 'official' organisational publicity. In Belfast, holdings of local citizens' committees and republican organisations in the Linen Hall Library's Northern Ireland Political Collection and the Eileen Hickey Irish Republican History Museum are essential reading for place-based identities and radical formulations of community.

No local newspaper in Northern Ireland or the Republic's border counties explicitly supported republican armed struggle: west Belfast's *Andersonstown News* came closest, with its pronounced nationalist emphasis. Nevertheless, such outlets are valuable for episodic research into republican subjectivities. Sinn Féin *cumainn* and republican prisoners often wrote to their local newspapers. Critical engagement with activist publications and correspondence is vital to access contrasting perspectives within ostensibly unified republican organisations.

However, as Daniel Finn has recently argued, how these publications were framed, interpreted, and distributed requires consideration. Drawing upon the insights of former PIRA intelligence officer Kieran Conway, Finn questions the extent to which the Provisional movement's political ideas were discussed throughout the movement.[46] Such reservations are reasonable: in a republican tradition that understandably distrusted 'politicians', detailed debates concerning the finer points of a federalised united Ireland or of the praxis of international revolution were often regarded with suspicion. Equally, in a movement concerned in large part with prosecuting a guerrilla campaign, such discussions were impractical for republican volunteers on the run.

Evidence from historical activist publications must therefore be synthesised critically in an analysis that questions power dynamics within the movement. Additionally, alternative sources – especially oral histories and recent retrospectives – are crucial for considering contested memory of republicanism's configuration. In a political tradition that has witnessed mass mobilisation combined with

---

[46] Kieran Conway, *Southside Provisional: from freedom fighter to the Four Courts* (Blackrock: Orpen Press, 2014), p. 52; Finn, *One man's terrorist*, 85.

serial schisms, multi-layered memory embellishes discussions of the movement's historical and contemporary composition.

This book is by no means the first study of republicanism to engage oral histories: for decades, republican ex-combatants have granted scholars interviews. In *Provisional Irish republicans* (1993), Robert W. White highlighted the complicatedness, even contradictoriness, of individual politics.[47] Republicans' testimonies have historicised their struggle. PIRA ex-prisoners Laurence McKeown, Brian Campbell, and Felim O'Hagan edited *Nor meekly serve my time* (1994), featuring extensive republican testimony in a heroic narrative of solidarity among prisoners during the protests of the late 1970s and 1980s.[48] In 2015, Cavan, Fermanagh, and Monaghan ex-prisoners' group Fáilte Cluain Eois published an anthology of excerpts from life history interviews with republican ex-combatants and their families.[49]

Oral histories do not function here to 'check facts' (as if they could), or in a Rankean attempt to reconstruct republicanism 'as it really was'. Rather, these testimonies are apt to explore the processual and subjective qualities of republican experience. They link the individual with social milieux and problematise the individual's relationship within a wider movement. As Donatella della Porta has noted, wide-ranging life history interviews

> permit understanding not only of individual psychology, but also group phenomena; not only movement ideology, but also movement counterculture; not only organisational stories but also the dynamics of small networks. Where other techniques offer static images, life histories are better suited to describe processes.[50]

Interviews' inherent subjectivities offer insights into the 'cultural life' and 'networks' of groups within movements, elucidating subtle processes typically beyond the purview or purpose of historical documents.[51]

Analysing interviews through the prism of memory, this book considers how oral histories alternately collapse or complexify a republican group's internal

---

[47] White, *Provisional Irish republicans*.
[48] McKeown, Campbell, & O'Hagan (eds.), *Nor meekly serve my time*.
[49] Fáilte Cluain Eois, *Their prisons, our stories* (Castleblayney: Fáilte Cluain Eois, 2015).
[50] Donatella della Porta, 'Life histories in the analysis of social movement activists', in Mario Diani & Ron Eyerman (eds.), *Studying collective action* (London: Sage, 1992), p. 187.
[51] Donatella della Porta, 'In-depth interviews', in Donatella della Porta (ed.), *Methodological practices in social movement research* (Oxford: Oxford University Press, 2014), p. 255.

dynamics.[52] This approach follows Neil Ferguson and James W. McAuley, who suggested oral testimony's homogenising effects in their work with former loyalist paramilitaries in Northern Ireland: Ferguson and McAuley noted oral testimonies emphasising how collective identities formed and consolidated.[53] Assessing oral histories of deindustrialisation, Tim Strangleman argues present-day narratives negotiate the past 'as a source of pride and pain' and produce 'a selective reworking of the past in the present'.[54]

In recent years, oral histories of Irish republicanism have increasingly benefited from the participation of a heterogeneous range of participants beyond Sinn Féin. Marisa McGlinchey's 90 interviewees whose breaches with the Provisional movement ranged temporally from the 1980s to the early twenty-first century.[55] Dieter Reinisch's history of *Cumann na mBan*, for example, drew upon interviews with 25 female republicans. Reinisch's snowballing and gatekeeper techniques facilitated an extensive range of interviews, especially with members of Republican Sinn Féin (RSF).[56] With the possible exception of Robert W. White, no other scholar of republicanism has matched McGlinchey's and Reinisch's sample range. The Official republican movement, although receding from republican positions through the 1970s, has received just one book-length treatment,[57] while the only book dealing with the IRSP-INLA was published more than 25 years ago and is concerned primarily with its internal feuding from the late 1980s.[58]

While this book focuses on the period from 1969 to 1998, its relevance today derives from its concern with memory and commemoration practices in Irish republicanism. This book analyses the counterposing forces of attempts to build a unified, uniform republican movement, contrasted with dissonances,

52 For a detailed study of republican memory processes in oral testimonies, see Jack Hepworth, '"We're getting the victory we fought for", we were told': retrospective subjective analysis in oral histories of Irish republicanism', *Oral History*, 48 (2020), pp. 68–79.
53 Neil Ferguson & James W. McAuley, 'Ulster loyalist accounts of armed mobilisation, demobilisation, and decommissioning', in Bosi & de Fazio (eds.), *Troubles in Northern Ireland*, 111–128.
54 Tim Strangleman, 'Deindustrialisation and the historical sociological imagination: making sense of work and industrial change', *Sociology*, 51 (2017), p. 475.
55 McGlinchey, *Unfinished business*.
56 Dieter Reinisch, 'Women's agency and political violence: Irish republican women and the formation of the Provisional IRA, 1967–1970', *Irish Political Studies*, 34 (2019), pp. 420–443.
57 Brian Hanley & Scott Millar, *The lost revolution: the story of the Official IRA and the Workers' Party* (Dublin: Penguin Ireland, 2009).
58 Henry McDonald & Jack Holland, *INLA: deadly divisions* (Dublin: Poolbeg, 2010) [First edition Dublin: Torc Books, 1994].

dilemmas, and transformations through the strata of republican organisations. Throughout the conflict, hostile British government perspectives and Provisional leaders alike represented republicanism as a monoglot movement: the former to deny republican ideology, the latter to cohere and discipline their guerrilla movement. The history of the conflict in and about Northern Ireland is as much about struggles within political identities – the British political establishment, unionism-loyalism, and nationalism-republicanism – as between them.

Competing republican versions of the past variously challenge and consolidate established narratives of republican struggle. Power struggles within political traditions shape much of the turmoil and malaise in Irish (and British) politics today. Brexit has exposed the British political establishment's historical ignorance of, and indifference towards, its 'province'. Even after the Democratic Unionist Party became key to parliamentary arithmetic in 2017, the party was subject to growing criticism among grassroots unionists and loyalists. Escalating poverty and public health crises, and the devolved assembly's three-year hiatus from January 2017, further drove working-class alienation from the major political parties.

This book connects historical points of conflict in republicanism and ongoing intra-republican fragmentation today, amid the context of Brexit, Stormont's precarity, and ongoing judicial and political struggles surrounding the legacies of the past. Complexifying republican perspectives on the peace process, for example, enriches a growing discussion concerning the limitations of socioeconomic or cross-community change. Such debates are especially vital in a polity that retained 109 'peace walls' as recently as January 2019.[59]

Many of the primary sources consulted have either never, or only fleetingly, been used by other scholars. Of itself, this does not render such sources valuable or even remarkable. However, this extensive archival work has generated many snapshots and amplified voices across the strata of several republican organisations. Revisiting other studies' wide range of republican oral testimonies, combined with this study's original interviews and archival research, the words and writings of more than 250 republican activists feature directly in this book. The emphasis on the Provisional movement is justified, since that movement dominated republicanism politically and numerically from 1970. However, the book also considers republican trajectories in People's Democracy (PD), the Official movement in the early 1970s, the IRSP and INLA from their foundation in the mid-1970s, and other groups that appeared from the late 1980s, including Republican Sinn Féin (RSF) and the League of Communist Republicans (LCR).

---

[59] Ruairí Lennon, 'Housing in the six counties: the front line in the battle for class unity', *An Spréach*, 3 (January–March 2019).

This archival range is supplemented by 27 loosely structured one-to-one interviews, and two group interviews. Interviews explored how subjective experience and memory inform political allegiances and how individual identity plays out within a radical group. These interviews follow social movement theorists' emphasis upon layers of individual agency, networks, and allegiances within social structures and movement organisations.[60]

Of the 25 interviewees, ten had previously given interviews for comparable projects. Some participants demonstrated greater familiarity with the protocols and presented a more 'organised', or 'composed', narrative, than others. Rehearsed, curated versions of the self recall Graham Dawson's conception of 'composure' in oral testimonies. For Dawson, interviewees persistently attempted to forge a coherent version of the past.[61] Composure's epistemological quality flows from its complexities, and seeming contradictions.

Some 20 of the interviewees had been members of the Provisional republican movement. Of these 20, eight were no longer active members of Sinn Féin – although those eight spanned strident critics of the movement and others who had simply ceased activism for a variety of personal reasons. A further five had experience of the Official republican movement and/or the IRSP and INLA.

Chapter structure

Drawing upon activist publications, press reports, and oral testimony, this book's five chapters thematise republican variation sequentially. The opening chapter situates Irish republicanism in the global '68 and its aftermath, exploring how some republicans framed their struggle as one component of a global liberation zeitgeist while others looked to a more parochial and distinctly Irish historic tradition. Chapter 2 assesses shifting tactics and strategic transformation in Irish republicanism throughout these decades, especially concerning republican electoral interventions and peace initiatives in the 1980s and 1990s respectively. The third chapter analyses how left-wing politics permeated Irish republicanism after 1968, while Chapter 4 elucidates republican engagements with the politics of second-wave feminism and women's rights. The final chapter discusses diverse republican engagement with Catholicism temporally as a powerful political institution, and in salvific terms as an influential philosophical body of thought.

---

[60] David A. Snow, Louis A. Zurcher, Jr., & Sheldon Ekland-Olson, 'Social networks and social movements: a microstructural approach to differential recruitment', *American Sociological Review*, 45 (1980), pp. 787–801.

[61] Graham Dawson, *Soldier heroes: British adventure, empire and the imagining of masculinities* (London: Psychology Press, 1994), p. 23.

Each chapter is thematic in focus, and spans the three decades in question. Internally, each chapter is organised chronologically.

Note on terminology

Language surrounding the conflict is understandably loaded, with designations often taken to indicate particular understandings of agency, responsibility, causation, and justification. As social movement theorist Charles Tilly notes: 'The cultural milieu provides languages and symbols through which participants and observers make sense of their collective action.'[62] For instance, describing the republican campaign as, variously, 'armed struggle', 'political violence', 'subversive activity', or 'terrorism' confers contrasting degrees of legitimacy and moral probity.

This study generally uses 'the Troubles' as per ubiquitous public and media usage. 'Northern Ireland' and 'the north of Ireland' are used to describe, as accurately as possible, geographical spaces and not to signify any particular political position. The 'north of Ireland', for instance, is used here as helpful shorthand for a combination of Northern Ireland and border counties of the Republic of Ireland, rather than as a nationalist cipher for 'the six counties'. By the same token, 'Northern Ireland' is used to reflect legal and constitutional reality, rather than any subjective commitment to the union.

Geography aside, this book engages much of the language that is meaningful among republicans: for example, 'volunteer', 'activist', and 'ex-combatant' instead of 'paramilitary'. As republican veteran Séanna Walsh explained in interview, republicans generally disdain 'paramilitary'.[63] Also, in line with its own tradition, the 'republican socialist movement' here broadly signifies the IRSP, founded in December 1974, and its military wing, the INLA. Unless otherwise noted, all references to Sinn Féin from 1970 onwards refer to the Provisional movement's political organisation.

This book follows Paddy Hoey's useful contemporary distinction between 'dissident' and 'dissenting' republicans: 'dissidents' advocate armed struggle today, whereas 'dissenters' oppose violence but criticise the peace process.[64] In recognition of both labels' highly contentious quality within republicanism, 'dissidents' and 'dissenters' are used within quotation marks. Activist publications and oral testimonies are, of course, quoted faithful to the original.

[62] Tilly, *Contentious performances*, 8.
[63] Séanna Walsh interview with Jack Hepworth. Belfast, 12 August 2015.
[64] Paddy Hoey, 'Dissident and dissenting republicanism: from the Good Friday/Belfast Agreement to Brexit', *Capital & Class*, 43 (2018), p. 3.

1

The Global '68 and its Afterlives

In 1968, Northern Ireland's escalating civil rights protests gained widespread publicity. The ensuing loyalist reaction and state repression precipitated militant republicanism's re-emergence from 1969. Meanwhile, an international protest cycle was challenging the political order in Europe and beyond. In France, from May 1968, students and workers commenced a major strike. Across Europe, protesters launched solidarity movements against the Soviet Union's invasion of Czechoslovakia. Before and after Martin Luther King's assassination in April 1968, African-American civil rights dominated political discourse in the US. Meanwhile, demonstrations against the US campaign in Vietnam were a focal point for anti-imperialists and leftists worldwide.

George Katsiaficas's capacious formulation captures the essence of New Left politics: a global network of movements for democracy, personal autonomy, liberty, and international solidarity, spanning workers, students, and intellectuals, challenging fascism, capitalism, and imperialism.[1] The New Left rejected the 'bureaucratic' Old Left that had aligned with the Soviet Union. New Leftists typically sympathised with radical national liberation movements and transcended rigid Cold War binaries.

New Left positions on political violence evade straightforward explanation. Radicals in West Germany's Trotsky League and the USA's Students for a Democratic Society, for example, opposed violence that invited state repression. This Trotskyist critique posited that violence was an inadequate substitute for mass revolutionary consciousness.[2] Yet many activists who joined Italy's Brigate

---

[1] George Katsiaficas, 'The global imagination of 1968: the new left's unfulfilled promise', in Karen Dubinsky, Catherine Krull, Susan Lord, Sean Mills & Scott Rutherford (eds.), *New world coming: the sixties and the shaping of global consciousness* (Toronto: Between the Lines, 2009), p. 350.

[2] Belinda Davis, 'New leftists and West Germany: fascism, violence, and the public sphere, 1967–1974', in Philipp Gassert & Alan E. Steinweis (eds.), *Coping with the*

Rosse and West Germany's Rote Armee Fraktion were products of the New Left. For these militants, armed struggle was integral to attacking capitalist development and exposing the 'terrorist' state.[3]

In Ireland, the fiftieth anniversary of 1968 – as a metonym for international upheaval, and also as a threshold in the island's history – prompted widespread commemoration and critical reflection. The themes of the discussion in 2018 reflected those of previous decades: contesting 'ownership' of Northern Ireland's civil rights legacy and contrasting '68 with contemporary debates. Viewed decades later, '68 became a repository for celebration or commiseration depending on subjective perspectives. Situating Irish republicanism within transnational patterns of contentious politics tests assumptions within the historiography about republican ideology and strategy. Assessing how republicans by turns imitated, refracted, and repudiated New Left ideas illuminates the multiplicity of Irish republicanism in 'the '68 years'.[4]

Several leading scholars have examined how armed republicanism eclipsed a hitherto dominant, and ostensibly peaceful, civil rights movement in Northern Ireland. Jim Smyth compared the mobilising frames and collective identities driving civil rights and republican activists alike.[5] Focusing on Derry, Niall Ó Dochartaigh highlighted republicans appropriating the language and stated aims of the civil rights movement. For Ó Dochartaigh, republicanism tapped into the popular agitation and grassroots alienation of 1970 to launch its incipient armed campaign.[6] Lorenzo Bosi and Gianluca de Fazio have engaged social movement theory to examine mobilisation between civil rights protest and republican armed struggle in the late 1960s.[7]

Nazi past: West German debates on Nazism and generational conflict, 1955–1975 (New York: Berghahn, 2006), p. 226; Terry H. Anderson, The movement and the sixties: protest in America from Greensboro to Wounded Knee (New York: Oxford University Press, 1995), pp. 328–329.

[3] David Moss, The politics of left-wing violence in Italy, 1969–1985 (Basingstoke: Macmillan, 1989), pp. 35, 43, 68, 85; Sebastian Gehrig, 'Sympathising subcultures? The milieus of West German terrorism', in Martin Klimke, Jacco Pekelder, & Joachim Scharloth (eds.), Between Prague Spring and French May: opposition and revolt in Europe, 1960–1980 (New York: Berghahn, 2011), pp. 233, 235.

[4] Xavier Vigna, L'insubordination ouvrière dans les années 68: essai d'histoire politique des usines (Rennes: Rennes University Press, 2007).

[5] Jim Smyth, 'Moving the immovable: the civil rights movement in Northern Ireland', in Linda Connolly & Niamh Hourigan (eds.), Social movements and Ireland (Manchester: Manchester University Press, 2006), pp. 106–107.

[6] Niall Ó Dochartaigh, From civil rights to Armalites: Derry and the birth of the Irish troubles (Cork: Cork University Press, 1997), pp. 197, 310–311.

[7] Lorenzo Bosi & Gianluca de Fazio (eds.), The troubles in Northern Ireland and theories of social movements (Amsterdam: Amsterdam University Press, 2017).

Historians have often been reluctant to include Ireland in broader analyses of the global '68 and the emergent New Left. A notable exception, Brian Dooley's *Black and green* (1998), explicitly connected protest cycles and repertoires of contention among civil rights activists in the USA and Northern Ireland.[8] However, in general, the latter has been conspicuous by its absence from international assessments of 'the global '68'.[9] Consequently, physical-force republicanism has often appeared to be an aberrant, violent footnote in the wider historiography of '68 and its 'afterlives'.[10] Chris Reynolds has argued compellingly that Northern Ireland's conflict sat uneasily with scholarly analyses of 'progressive' legacies of '68.[11]

With the exception of Dooley's pioneering scholarship, historiographical treatment of Northern Ireland in the context of an international '68 has been a recent development. Especially after the fortieth anniversary of 1968, historians such as Simon Prince and Gregory Maney placed Northern Ireland's civil rights movement in the 'rising tide of radicalism' among Europe's '68ers struggling against 'imperialism, capitalism, and bureaucracy'.[12] This opening chapter chronologically extends that analysis, examining Irish republicanism's resurgence from 1969 into the early 1970s. It addresses differing republican interpretations of developments inside and outside Ireland.

The chapter begins by counterposing the acutely local character of republican reawakening in 1969 against the transnational memory of '68. This juxtaposition opens a discussion of how republican activists spatialised their struggle differently, especially in the context of the split in the

---

[8] Brian Dooley, *Black and green: the fight for civil rights in Northern Ireland and black America* (London: Pluto Press, 1998).

[9] Northern Ireland receives a chapter-length treatment in Martin Klimke and Joachim Scharloth's edited collection *1968 in Europe: a history of protest and activism, 1956–1977* (Basingstoke: Palgrave Macmillan, 2008), but is absent from other notable accounts of '68 and its aftermath. See, for example, Anna von der Goltz (ed.), *'Talkin' 'bout my generation': conflicts of generation building and Europe's '1968'* (Göttingen: Wallstein Verlag, 2011); Gerd Rainer-Horn & Padraic Kenney (eds.), *Transnational moments of change: 1945, 1968, 1989* (Lanham, Maryland: Rowman & Littlefield, 2004); Vladimir Tismaneanu (ed.), *Promises of 1968: crisis, illusion and utopia* (Budapest: Central European University Press, 2011).

[10] Kristin Ross, *May '68 and its afterlives* (Chicago: University of Chicago Press, 2002).

[11] Chris Reynolds, 'Beneath the troubles, the cobblestones: recovering the "buried" memory of Northern Ireland's 1968', *American Historical Review*, 123 (2018), pp. 744–748.

[12] Simon Prince, 'Mythologising a movement: Northern Ireland's '68', *History Ireland*, 16 (September–October 2008), p. 29; Gregory Maney, 'White negroes and the pink IRA: external mainstream media coverage and civil rights contention in Northern Ireland', in Bosi & de Fazio (eds.), *Troubles in Northern Ireland*, 71–90.

republican movement emerging from 1969 and 1970. The chapter explores how republican mobilisation in the early 1970s tapped into conceptions of localised memory and the politics of place. It also draws out localised variations in the relationship between civil rights and republicanism. The final section analyses how, a decade after 1968, republicans mobilised collective memory of civil rights.

Irish republicanism and the global '68

Prior to the split in the IRA and Sinn Féin, the republican movement's leadership resembled, to a large degree, a New Left milieu. In 1968, IRA Chief of Staff Cathal Goulding broadly endorsed New Left opposition to the Soviet invasion of Czechoslovakia and the USA's war in Vietnam.[13] Goulding's international outlook mirrored that of Belfast student radicals in PD and Northern Ireland's Young Socialist Movement.[14] His voluble support for the National Liberation Front in Vietnam would have been equally familiar to Trotskyists, Maoists, and anarchists in France's May '68, or to leftists in Britain's International Marxist Group.[15]

Sinn Féin's intellectual leaders in 1968, including C. Desmond Greaves, Anthony Coughlan, Roy Johnston, and Tomás Mac Giolla, were acutely concerned with global politics. Yet the degree to which international protest cycles could inform the Irish struggle was a point of debate. Sinn Féin's northern regional organiser, Seán Ó Cionnaith, framed the Irish context as unique. Addressing a party meeting in Letterkenny, County Donegal in November 1969, Ó Cionnaith insisted that while republicans could

> learn from the struggles of other oppressed peoples... we are not being dictated to or dominated by a philosophy designed for another country.[16]

---

[13] 'Irish bodies voice their indignation', *The Irish Press*, 23 August 1968; 'Sinn Fein re-organising meeting in Letterkenny', *Donegal News*, 22 November 1969.

[14] Michael Farrell, 'Introduction', in Michael Farrell (ed.), *Twenty years on* (Dingle: Brandon, 1988), p. 20.

[15] Subsequently, the International Marxist Group supported a Vietnam Solidarity Campaign in 1969 as a model for its later Irish Solidarity Campaign in 1971, giving 'unconditional support' for Irish republicans' war against 'British imperialism and its puppets'. John Callaghan, *The far left in British politics* (Oxford: Basil Blackwell, 1987), p. 132.

[16] 'Sinn Fein re-organising meeting in Letterkenny', *Donegal News*, 22 November 1969.

Implicitly rejecting any association with east or west, Ó Cionnaith employed plain egalitarian terms to describe republicans' crusade against 'the domination of Nation by Nation and of man by man'. In a coded rebuke to the USSR, he celebrated Irish forebears James Connolly and James Fintan Lalor, whose 'socialism' had 'nothing to do with Atheism or totalitarianism'.[17]

Although interested in international events, senior republicans on the left asserted the primacy of Irish revolutionaries par excellence, primarily James Connolly, when they addressed the movement's grassroots. Speaking at Sinn Féin's Connolly Week meeting in Dublin in May 1968, leading republican theorist Anthony Coughlan attacked job insecurity and the profit incentive. Coughlan preferred to cite Connolly's conception of the social emancipation of labour, rather than referring to the late Martin Luther King's contemporary 'Poor People's Campaign', for example.[18] Celebrating Connolly reinforced the sense of an Irish struggle *sui generis*: at a republican meeting in Sligo in January 1969, Coughlan declared Connolly's connection of national and social questions of supreme significance for Irish revolutionaries.[19] Connolly's labour movement credentials were vital for republicans following Goulding's directives to connect with trade unions in 1968: Dublin Sinn Féin invited two leading union organisers to commence their Connolly Week events with a lecture on workers' solidarity.[20]

After the republican movement split in 1969 and 1970, those who remained with the so-called Official wing – aligned with Goulding's leftist republican leadership of the 1960s – engaged especially with radical critiques of US imperialism and racial injustice. Seamus Ó Tuathail, editor of the Officials' *United Irishman* newspaper, read Black Panther leader Bobby Seale and compared the Panthers' urban activism to events in Belfast in 1971, where republicans were 'defending the ghettoes'.[21] Thomas 'Jonty' Johnson, a veteran of Northern Ireland's civil rights movement and confidant of Official IRA (OIRA) leader Billy McMillen, was involved with Belfast protests against the Vietnam War.[22]

Official leaders lambasted conservative Irish America and connected police repression in the US and Northern Ireland. Writing in August 1970, Ó Cionnaith compared Northern Ireland's Royal Ulster Constabulary (RUC) with right-wing Chicago Mayor Richard Daley – both had used tear gas 'against their own citizens'.[23] Daley's ignominious record on civil rights protests

---

17 'Sinn Fein re-organising meeting in Letterkenny', *Donegal News*, 22 November 1969.
18 'Ideal still unachieved', *The Irish Press*, 3 May 1968.
19 'New stirrings of radical thoughts', *The Sligo Champion*, 10 January 1969.
20 'Lecture on Connolly', *Evening Herald*, 1 May 1968.
21 Seamus Ó Tuathail, 'A day in the life of an internee', *Sunday Independent*, 10 October 1971.
22 'Thomas "Jonty" Johnson', *LookLeft*, Volume 2, Issue 2 (n.d. [2015]).
23 Seán Ó Cionnaith, 'Fianna Fail and CS gas', *Irish Independent*, 29 August 1970.

informed Official opposition to his proposed visit to Ireland in 1971. For Ó Cionnaith and Máirín de Burca, Daley emblematised 'American imperialism' and repression.[24] Official republican condemnation contrasted with the approach of the more moderate nationalist John Hume. In 1974, Hume met Daley in Chicago and invited wealthy Irish-American business executives to invest in Northern Ireland.[25]

Official republicans harnessed international politics at both strategic and theoretical levels, although seldom without reference to Irish precedent. Rejecting exclusively military means, the OIRA's New Year statement in 1972 invoked the failed republican 'border campaign' of the late 1950s and early 1960s:

> It has never been and is not now our intention to launch a purely military campaign... We do not... want a repetition of the fifties.[26]

Even before the split of the late 1960s, those who later formed the Official leadership cited the border campaign when they advocated a broad-based movement. Mindful that the republican leadership in 1962 had publicly abandoned the campaign for want of popular support, Officials *avant la lettre* backed a National Liberation Front comprising connections with the Gaelic Athletic Association, tenants' unions, trades unions, and cultural societies. Their repertoires of contention widened considerably in 1968: the Derry IRA, for example, helped residents fight eviction threats, building barricades and guarding homes.[27]

While Official leaders closely followed radical African-American activism, the founding Provisional leaders in the early 1970s were less inclined to situate Ireland among contemporary struggles worldwide. Until *An Phoblacht* and *Republican News* merged in 1979, the Provisionals' publicity scarcely referred to foreign conflicts. These lacunae reflected key strategic differences between the leadership of the two republican factions. PIRA Chief of Staff Seán Mac Stíofáin explained in the movement's newspaper in March 1970 that the Provisionals would not prioritise politicisation: 'You've got to have military victory and then politicise the people afterwards.'[28] Mac Stíofáin's belief that a short but

---

[24] 'Sinn Fein Claim Rejected', *The Munster Express*, 8 January 1971.

[25] 'Hume in U.S. trade mission', *Irish Examiner*, 17 April 1974.

[26] M. L. R. Smith, *Fighting for Ireland? The military strategy of the Irish republican movement* (London: Routledge, 1995), p. 88.

[27] Brian Hanley, '"Agitate, educate, organise": the IRA's *An tOglach*, 1965–1968', *Saothar*, 32 (2007), p. 55.

[28] Seán Mac Stíofáin quoted in 'Our aims and methods', *An Phoblacht*, March 1970, cited in Michael von Tangen Page & M. L. R. Smith, 'War by other means: the

devastating guerrilla campaign would swiftly prompt a British withdrawal relegated the need for a developed political programme.

The emphasis upon localised insurgency was prominent almost 30 years on for founding Provisional Billy McKee. Interviewed in 1997, McKee described 1970, a year in which the PIRA planted 153 bombs, many of which targeted Protestant businesses. As McKee put it: 'It was property we wanted to destroy and make them pay the penalty for what they were doing to our people and our houses.'[29] In contrast, OIRA leader Cathal Goulding told *New Left Review* that Ireland's revolution was integral to global leftism.[30]

To the extent that founding Provisionals alluded to international politics at all, these references were usually to heartening examples of victorious guerrilla anti-imperialism in Cyprus (1960) and Aden (1967). Invocations of British imperial decline were intended as general encouragement, and not as detailed reflections on revolutionary theory or strategy. Addressing a public meeting in Portlaoise in September 1971, editor of the Provisionals' *An Phoblacht*, Éamonn Mac Thomáis, confidently located Ireland in succession to Cyprus, Aden, and Malaya. Casting the Provisionals as the latest 'revolutionary' movement that the British 'gutter press' had condemned, Mac Thomáis implied that Ireland would be the next stage in an anti-imperial process.[31] At a press conference in Derry in June 1972, PIRA Chief of Staff Seán Mac Stíofáin cited Cyprus as evidence of British vulnerability. Anticipating ceasefire talks, Mac Stíofáin was unfazed by the prospect of an uncompromising stance from Secretary of State Willie Whitelaw: had not the British initially refused to negotiate with revolutionaries in Kenya and Cyprus?[32]

Until important recent studies by Marc Mulholland and Daniel Finn,[33] typologies of Irish republicanism routinely excluded PD, the leftist group that

problem of political control in Irish republican strategy', *Armed Forces & Society*, 27 (2000), p. 90.

29 Billy McKee interview with Peter Taylor, 1997. *Provos: The IRA and Sinn Fein – Episode 1: Born Again* (BBC1, broadcast 23 September 1997).

30 'The new strategy of the IRA', *New Left Review*, 64 (November–December 1970).

31 'Sinn Fein meeting in Portlaoise', *Leinster Express*, 1 October 1971.

32 'Invitation – and a warning – from the Provos', *Irish Independent*, 14 June 1972. Britain's withdrawal from India in 1947 was conspicuous by its absence from the Provisionals' potted history: their violent campaign differed sharply from Gandhi's movement. Challenged by a pacifist observer to justify the PIRA campaign in 1976, two members of the Provisionals *Ard Comhairle* said they had 'no admiration' for Gandhi's legacy. P. J. Kearney & Cathal Kelly, 'Open letter to IRA', *The Irish Press*, 20 December 1976.

33 Marc Mulholland, 'Northern Ireland and the far left, *c.*1965–1975', *Contemporary British History*, 32 (2018), pp. 542–563; Daniel Finn, 'The British radical left and Northern Ireland during the "troubles"', in Evan Smith & Matthew Worley (eds.),

began at Queen's University Belfast in 1968 as a radical fringe of the civil rights movement. Yet some PD activists in the late 1960s later participated in republican armed struggle. Furthermore, many of the group's leading ideologues, most prominently Bernadette Devlin and Michael Farrell, sympathised with the aspirations of left-leaning republicans, even if they criticised their methods and remained aloof from the armed campaign.

During the '68 years, PD activists emulated the New Left in ways which Provisional and Official republicans did not. From its origins at Queen's University, PD contained many of the coalitions and contradictions of the period. A former PD member who later graduated to Official republicanism, Brendan Holland remembered the group embracing 'all sorts of different kinds of Marxists, anarchists, and... republicans'.[34] Speaking in 1969, Michael Farrell differentiated the group from the wider civil rights umbrella. For Farrell, PD was 'a revolutionary organisation... considerably influenced by the Sorbonne Assembly' and 'concepts of libertarianism'.[35]

Those who identified explicitly as republicans in 1969 invoked a political identity entangled in an 'age-old struggle' for Irish unity and independence.[36] By contrast, PD activism originated in the more specific '68 contexts of the student movement and the civil rights campaign. Channelling the libertarian, anti-authority elements of Paris's May '68, PD radicals mobilised in 1969 and 1970 and criticised the tactics of the Northern Ireland Civil Rights Association (NICRA). Young firebrands such as Eamonn McCann, who organised a PD-aligned group in Derry, dismissed NICRA's reformism and constitutionalism: by 1969, McCann was infuriated that for two years NICRA had done 'nothing except issue press statements calling on the Unionist Government to be a bit more liberal'.[37] In October 1970, Belfast PD activist Kevin Boyle pronounced NICRA a 'sham... stifled by respectable politics'. For Boyle, NICRA placed 'excessive faith' in reform, campaigning

---

Waiting for the revolution: the British far left from 1956 (Manchester: Manchester University Press, 2017), pp. 201–217.

[34] Brendan Holland interview with Rogelio Alonso. Rogelio Alonso, *The IRA and armed struggle* (Abingdon: Routledge, 2007), pp. 35–36.

[35] 'People's Democracy: a discussion on strategy', *New Left Review*, 1:55 (May–June 1969).

[36] A Sinn Féin policy document published in 1974 situated the ongoing campaign in a historical lineage spanning centuries: 'the Irish people are on the verge of victory in the age-old struggle for national liberation'. Linen Hall Library Northern Ireland Political Collection (hereafter, LHL NIPC) P952: Sinn Féin, *Mining and energy: the Sinn Féin policy* (Dublin: Elo Press, 1974).

[37] 'People's Democracy: a discussion on strategy', *New Left Review*, 1:55 (May–June 1969).

for a universal bill of rights and forgetting that 'law is a ruling class instrument'.[38]

PD's affinity with student organisations among the French New Left pervaded the group's strategy from 1968. Activists connected with workers across Northern Ireland to raise public awareness on key civil rights issues, as well as more arcane matters of social and industrial policy. Raising funds in Belfast and Armagh, PD was the only political group in Northern Ireland to send money to striking workers at Cement Limited in Drogheda, County Louth. In 1969, PD launched its Plan to Inform the People campaign in Newry, Armagh, and Dungannon, defying repression to publicise factory closures. The group also railed against trade union bureaucracy and inadequate housing.[39]

PD's membership declined to approximately 100 late in 1969. Former National Union of Students vice-president Rory McShane reported that many students ceased activism in late 1969 and early 1970 since approximately 50 per cent of members lived at home in Belfast and were reluctant to engage in political activity after violence escalated.[40] Key tactical and strategic changes emerged from this numerical nadir. Having broken with NICRA, PD declared itself a revolutionary socialist organisation in October 1969 and imitated the continental New Left by establishing pirate radio stations in Belfast and Derry.[41] Activists who remained involved with PD transmuted the group's agenda towards a programme for Irish unity and socialist revolution. In contrast to November 1968's proposals for teach-ins, leafletting, and legal challenges,[42] by 1974, PD lionised rioters destabilising the 'sectarian state'.[43]

As PD activists stepped out of NICRA's shadows in the early 1970s, they identified closely with Provisional republicans. Belfast republicans embraced Michael Farrell, who shared an anti-EEC platform with leading Provisional Joe Cahill in 1972, and addressed Provisional anti-internment rallies.[44] While the Provisionals generally remained aloof from other organisations at this juncture, an exception was made for Farrell, celebrated in *Republican News* as 'a man of great personal courage' and a 'fearless opponent of the Unionist regime' – and

---

[38] Kevin Boyle quoted in 'NICRA campaign attacked', *The Times*, 17 October 1970.
[39] 'The PD & the cement strike', *Anarchy*, 6 (1970); J. Quinn, 'History of the early PD', *Anarchy*, 6 (1970).
[40] Conor O'Clery, *Fortnight*, 3 (23 October 1970).
[41] J. Quinn, 'History of the early PD', *Anarchy*, 6 (1970).
[42] Bob Purdie, *Politics in the streets: the origins of the civil rights movement in Northern Ireland* (Belfast: Blackstaff, 1990), p. 210.
[43] LHL NIPC PPO0483: People's Democracy, *Fight! Don't Vote!* (1974).
[44] 'Anti-E.E.C. rally in Manorhamilton', *Leitrim Observer*, 6 May 1972.

regarded as such by 'many members of the [Provisional] Republican Movement'.[45] In August 1973, when Farrell and his comrade Tony Canavan were on hunger strike for special-category status in Crumlin Road Jail, a west Belfast Sinn Féin *cumann* coordinated a public vigil to demonstrate 'our complete solidarity' with the two PD prisoners.[46]

Formal alignment between PD and the Provisionals was restricted to the short-lived Northern Resistance Movement in 1971 and 1972, but the ideological influence of PD's socialist republicanism was more enduring, as Marc Mulholland and Daniel Finn have adroitly demonstrated.[47] Activist networks overlapped: former PD member Peter Cosgrove remembered the group's newspaper *Unfree Citizen* selling well in republican areas of Armagh City and Belfast in the early 1970s. Cosgrove recalled Belfast PD activists lauding the Provisionals for defending Catholic communities.[48]

However, republican feuds irked PD activists. Intra-republican disputes were both a cause and a symptom of PD's distance from republican milieux. PD members did not discern the territorial and often personal dimensions of republican schisms. Instead, the Provisional-Official antagonism appeared a factional dispute frustrating unified socialist republicanism.

Although perhaps unattuned to the dynamics of allegiance within republicanism, Farrell appreciated the limitations of media representations of the split. Writing in PD's discussion journal in 1970, he insisted that while the Provisionals 'may consist mainly of right-wingers and traditionalists' they also included 'some genuine if confused radicals'.[49] Farrell attempted to cut through intra-republican arguments. In December 1971, he denounced 'dangerous' Provisional slurs portraying Officials as communist puppets of Moscow. A PD activist from Letterkenny, County Donegal, dismissed as 'superstitious slander' Provisional accusations that Officials were 'taking their orders from Moscow'. Farrell insisted that Marxist ideas were vital for 'genuine revolutionary socialists' and therefore relevant to grassroots PIRA volunteers who wanted 'to see Ireland ruled by her people, not by the bosses'.[50]

---

[45] 'Ex-Minister of Home Affairs sends Michael Farrell to jail', *Republican News*, 27 June 1973.

[46] 'Programme for internment week', *Patriot Bulletin* (n.d. [1973]).

[47] Mulholland, 'Northern Ireland and the far left', 559; Finn, 'The British radical left and Northern Ireland', 208.

[48] Peter Cosgrove, 'People's Democracy Member 1969: Part 3' (21 November 2014). Available at https://irishrepublicanmarxisthistoryproject.wordpress.com/2014/11/21/peoples-democracy-member-1969-part-3/ (accessed 15 February 2017).

[49] Mike Farrell, 'The split in Sinn Fein', *The Northern Star*, 1 (n.d. [1970]).

[50] Dara Vallely, 'New assailant in the Sinn Fein controversy', *Donegal Democrat*, 21 January 1972.

Precisely which Marxist ideas influenced PD members remains unclear. Contemporary descriptions of PD's 'hostility to theoretical work' with 'only the very slightest interest in political education' go some way towards explaining this lacuna.[51] Farrell was wary of the unstable implications of international sympathies. PD members were encouraged to be cautious when citing global influences, as Farrell explained in 1970. Due to its association with Stalin, 'communism' was a 'dirty word' in Northern Ireland; PD identified with Lenin but would 'avoid talking about Cuba and China' lest the movement become internally divided or stratified: as Farrell diplomatically put it, PD members' degrees of familiarity with political theory differed.[52]

PD activists' international interests were diverse. Kevin Boyle thought neither China nor the USSR were 'socialist at all', while Eamon O'Kane scorned US consumerism.[53] To avoid revolutionary sectarianism and invite broad sympathy among radicals and republicans in Ireland, Farrell and PD's propaganda preferred the more capacious language of 'anti-imperialism'.[54]

Perspectives on international protest grafted on to two broad responses to the repression of civil rights protests in Northern Ireland: those who considered violence legitimate for oppressed peoples' self-defence, and those who followed Mahatma Gandhi and Martin Luther King and advocated non-violent resistance or civil disobedience. For civil rights activists in Northern Ireland's 1968 who later graduated to constitutional nationalism – of which the Social Democratic and Labour Party (SDLP) was the chief institutional expression from 1970 – the memory of King and the Southern Christian Leadership Conference was most important. Ivan Cooper and Austin Currie, later leading SDLP figures, narrated mobilisation inspired by Gandhi and King in 1968.[55] By contrast, '68ers who moved towards physical-force republicanism remembered reformism and civil disobedience failing to address enduring rights-based grievances – and justifying an armed campaign.[56]

---

[51] Brian Trench, 'Misplaced hopes: People's Democracy in the Six Counties', *International Socialism*, 74 (January 1975), pp. 26–27.

[52] Barbara Bright, 'People's Democracy in Northern Ireland', *Institute of Current World Affairs* (31 August 1970).

[53] Barbara Bright, 'People's Democracy in Northern Ireland', *Institute of Current World Affairs* (31 August 1970).

[54] Michael Farrell, *Northern Ireland: the orange state* (London: Pluto Press, 1980), p. 12.

[55] Robert Gildea, James Mark, & Anette Warring (eds.), *Europe's 1968: voices of revolt* (Oxford: Oxford University Press, 2013), p. 262; Simon Prince, *Northern Ireland's '68: civil rights, global revolt and the origins of the troubles* (Dublin: Irish Academic Press, 2007), p. 119.

[56] Niall Ó Dochartaigh, 'What did the civil rights movement want? Changing goals and underlying continuities in the transition from protest to violence', in Bosi & de Fazio (eds.), *Troubles in Northern Ireland*, 33–52.

Until 1969, student radicals in PD aligned with more moderate civil rights activists in NICRA, but this coalition fragmented over tactical disagreements. PD's restlessness within NICRA developed through that year, especially after Bernadette Devlin controversially announced a march from Belfast to Stormont. Several members of NICRA's executive feared that the march would provoke Protestant reaction, spark violence, and alienate liberals. Fred Heatley, John McEnerney, Raymond Shearer, and Betty Sinclair resigned in protest at the young radicals' tactics.[57] In Dungannon, County Tyrone, PD's antagonistic approach to the unionist establishment aggrieved the local civil rights organisation.[58] These tactical disputes mirrored similar divisions among civil rights campaigners in the US, where the Congress of Racial Equality would not countenance self-defence for civil rights workers, whereas organisations inspired by Black Power ideology, such as the Deacons for Defense, promoted a more confrontational response to state violence.[59]

Today, memories of Northern Ireland's civil rights movement are inevitably intensified by hindsight's knowledge of the three decades of conflict that followed. Reviewing Daniel Finn's *One man's terrorist* (2019), former PD activist Henry Patterson was at pains to clarify his position regarding the controversial march between Belfast and Derry in January 1969. Patterson claimed 'the majority' of PD members recognised the 'inevitably polarising effect' of traversing unionist areas and opposed the march.[60] Patterson's memory partakes in a wider discourse which posits 1969 as a missed opportunity to reform Northern Ireland and avert subsequent trauma.

Yet tactics alone cannot explain fractures within NICRA; the politics of class and internationalism in 'the '68 years' also informed divisions in the movement. Moderate civil rights activists emphasised the uniqueness of Ireland's position, and interpreted radical international influences as malign interference. In February 1970, three members of NICRA's executive protested to the membership about elements inspired by 'International Revolutionary Socialism' attempting to 'manipulat[e]' the movement. Although Bríd Rodgers, John Donaghy, and Conn McCluskey did not mention PD explicitly, they condemned Farrell, its most prominent activist, for his liaisons with Black Panthers, which would alienate 'socially-conscious Protestants whom we must attract'. Young

---

[57] Hazel Morrissey, 'Betty Sinclair: a woman's fight for socialism, 1910–1981', *Saothar*, 9 (1983), p. 130.

[58] Conn McCluskey, *Up off their knees: a commentary on the civil rights movement in Northern Ireland* (Dungannon: Conn McCluskey & Associates, 1989), p. 137.

[59] Simon Wendt, 'The roots of black power? Armed resistance and the radicalisation of the civil rights movement', in Peniel E. Joseph (ed.), *The black power movement: rethinking the civil rights-black power era* (London: Routledge, 2006), p. 146.

[60] Henry Patterson, 'A lick of red paint', *Dublin Review of Books*, 188 (January 2020).

radicals were accused of hijacking NICRA magazine *The Citizen Press* to amplify their agenda.[61] McCluskey later remembered elections to NICRA's executive in 1970 as a communist-inspired Official republican takeover.[62]

Repudiating provocative tactics and revolutionary associations in the early 1970s, the remaining members of NICRA found media coverage eclipsed the civil rights causes that had ignited popular politics in the late 1960s. As republicans fought to sap Westminster's will to maintain the union, NICRA's demands remained integrationist. In 1972, executive member Fred Heatley implored the British government to extend the Race Relations Act of 1968 to Northern Ireland.[63] The upsurge in sectarian violence in 1975 dismayed civil rights activists, who again looked to the British government to implement a bill of rights for all Northern Ireland's citizens 'to end violence and defuse sectarianism'.[64]

Especially after the OIRA called a ceasefire in May 1972, Official republicanism moved ever closer to NICRA's integrationist, rights-based politics. With the guerrilla campaign suspended, the Officials prioritised civil rights legislation and class solidarity above the national question. In February 1972, leading Official theorist Roy Johnston summarised his movement's affinity with civil rights activists: both sought 'reform of Stormont by Westminster'.[65]

Officials' civil rights politics informed their growing perception of the Provisionals exacerbating community polarisation. Writing from Long Kesh in 1973, Belfast OIRA prisoner Brendan Mackin argued that the Provisionals' escalating campaign had 'alienated most of the Protestant people' from the 'mass' civil rights movement.[66] By this juncture, the Officials' Republican Clubs overlapped with NICRA in personnel as well as strategy: both organisations collaborated in anti-internment protests outside RUC and British Army barracks in 1974.[67] Former NICRA chair Ivan Barr was active in the Official movement in Strabane, County Tyrone, through much of the decade.[68]

---

[61] LHL NIPC P6534: *Communication to NICRA members from Bríd Rodgers, John Donaghy, and Conn McCluskey* (Published by the authors, 1970).

[62] Of 14 members elected to NICRA's executive in 1970, five belonged to the Officials' Republican Clubs, four others identified as republicans, and three more were communists. Sean Swan, *Official Irish republicanism, 1962–1972* (Belfast: Lulu Press, 2006), pp. 327–328.

[63] LHL NIPC P1060: Robert Heatley, *Direct Rule: Civil Rights NOT Civil War* (Belfast: NICRA, 1972).

[64] LHL NIPC PPO0492: NICRA, *A Bill of Rights Now* (1975).

[65] 'Letter from Roy Johnston', *Fortnight*, 34 (23 February 1972).

[66] Brendan Macklin [*sic*], 'Is the Protestant left marching towards socialism', *An Eochair: A Bulletin of the Irish Republican Movement, Long Kesh*, 2 (July–August 1973).

[67] 'More C.R.A. protests planned against Army tactics', *The Irish People/An Choismhuintir*, Volume 2, Number 35 (6 September 1974).

[68] 'Strabane bids final farewell to Ivan Barr', *An Phoblacht*, 15 May 2008.

Republicanism, place, and 'community', c.1968–c.1973

Analysing republicanism in 'the '68 years' necessitates attention to the split in the republican movement, which has been the subject of a wide-ranging historiography. As Matt Treacy's trailblazing study has demonstrated, discussions of 1960s republicanism are entangled in contested historical and contemporary questions of intra-republican legitimacy.[69] Dispelling the widespread scholarly view that republicanism before 1969 was moribund and unpopular at the grassroots, Brian Hanley went some way towards rehabilitating the movement's record in the 1960s.[70] Similarly, Liam Cullinane has highlighted the IRA's numerical strength and wide-ranging activism under Cathal Goulding's leadership in the late 1960s.[71]

Dissensions over strategy defined divisions within the IRA leadership by 1969. A faction including young militant Seamus Costello advocated escalating the crisis to render the north ungovernable. A separate network around Roy Johnston and Anthony Coughlan considered the provincial parliament at Stormont capable of reforming Northern Ireland and fashioning a non-sectarian polity, pending national reunification.

IRA Chief of Staff Cathal Goulding oversaw significant changes in the movement from 1964. Goulding introduced Marxist theory and encouraged a diverse programme of social agitation beyond the traditional emphasis on armed struggle. While Goulding's new departure caused friction within the movement throughout the decade, the split crystallised only in 1968 and 1969. The hierarchy disagreed over the appropriate republican response to the outbreak of violence that attended the repression of Northern Ireland's civil rights movement. When loyalists and state actors attacked civil rights protests and rioting ensued in Belfast in August 1969, Goulding opposed deploying IRA volunteers. Armed defence of nationalist communities, his argument ran, would constitute a sectarian action likely to alienate liberal Protestants who supported the civil rights campaign. For Goulding, defending northern Catholics was not the IRA's purpose. From August 1969, divisions cascaded through the republican middle-ranks and grassroots.

The politics of place were central to the foundational narrative of the Provisional movement that emerged 'out of the ashes' of west Belfast in August

---

[69] Matt Treacy, *The IRA, 1956–1969: rethinking the republic* (Manchester: Manchester University Press, 2011), p. 153.

[70] Brian Hanley, '"I ran away"? The IRA and 1969 – the evolution of a myth', *Irish Historical Studies*, 38 (2013), pp. 671–687.

[71] Liam Cullinane, '"A happy blend"? Irish republicanism, political violence and social agitation, 1962–1969', *Saothar*, 35 (2010), pp. 49, 60–61, 63.

1969.[72] Community defence underpinned the Provisionals' initial recruitment in the urban areas of Belfast and Derry where police repression and loyalist violence was most commonplace in late 1969. Accordingly, Provisional narratives of the split frequently cite the Goulding leadership's 'failure' to defend Catholics.[73] Addressing American visitors on a tour of west Belfast more than 25 years later, former PIRA prisoner Jim McVeigh evoked a defenceless nationalist community in 1969, when 'there really was no IRA'.[74]

The origins of 'Free Derry' lay in January 1969: local vigilante groups expelled the RUC and policed Bogside and Creggan. During a two-day confrontation in August 1969, the RUC deployed tear gas, more than 1,000 cartridges, and 161 grenades.[75] These seminal events immediately entered Derry Catholics' collective memory as the 'Battle of the Bogside': a moment of heroic resistance against police incursions. A photograph album produced 'in response to popular demand' later that year celebrated this 'victory for the ordinary people of Bogside'.[76] With its implicit class solidarity and explicit anti-state quality, the symbolism of the popular 'defender' quickly gained political capital in Derry and Belfast alike. The nascent Provisional movement immediately recognised its legend as the guardian of besieged nationalists: a Provisional publicity poster of 1970 invited the viewer to 'remember August '69... Bombay St. subject to organised attack... We are your insurance that it won't happen again.'[77]

Established community networks in Belfast and Derry shaped mobilisation in defence committees from August 1969. These committees – namely, Derry Citizens' Defence Association (DCDA) and, in Belfast, the Central Citizens' Defence Committee (CCDC) – were localised organisations built around pre-existing connections. Tommy McKearney has noted the initial cooperation between the early Provisionals and citizens' defence committees.[78] Naturally, these groups were concerned primarily with maintaining barricades and ensuring the supply of essential goods. To the extent that committee members linked their

---

[72] Shane Mac Thomáis, 'Out of the ashes arose the Provisionals', *An Phoblacht*, 6 January 2005.

[73] See, for example, Gerry Adams, 'A republican in the civil rights campaign', in Farrell (ed.), *Twenty years on*, 49–50.

[74] David McKittrick, 'And your guide for today's tour of Belfast', *The Independent on Sunday*, 29 August 2004.

[75] Marc Mulholland, *The longest war: Northern Ireland's troubled history* (Oxford: Oxford University Press, 2002), p. 71.

[76] LHL NIPC P872: *Battle of Bogside* (Derry: Bogside Republican Appeal Fund, 1969).

[77] Eileen Hickey Irish Republican History Museum, Belfast (hereafter, EHI): *So you think you are safe! A reminder lest you forget!* (1970).

[78] Tommy McKearney, *The Provisional IRA: from insurrection to parliament* (London: Pluto Press, 2011), pp. 58, 75.

work to broader political questions, there was a pronounced republican dynamic. DCDA chair Seán Keenan told a NICRA meeting in October 1969 that only Irish unity could guarantee justice.[79] Although the DCDA was heterogeneous – one member observed a 1,000-strong 'mixsome gathering' at a meeting in August 1969[80] – its leadership included several senior republicans, with some activists subsequently joining the PIRA.[81]

August 1969 into 1970 was the epoch of local defence committees, but by late 1970 Belfast's escalating crisis and the unfolding republican offensive separated the CCDC and PIRA, which had previously overlapped.[82] The CCDC upheld republicans' roles in protecting nationalists from 'the evils of Unionism' and RUC incursions, but considered Provisionals resorting to violence in 1970 'the enemies of justice'. While cognisant of 'the trauma of August, 1969 [which] swept some young men off their feet', CCDC leaders sought reform, not revolution. To this end, they coordinated youth schemes and cooperative projects, and rebuilt areas devastated by fires in 1969.[83] Defence committees were not insulated from the republican feud: leading Official Jim Sullivan chaired the CCDC, likely accelerating Provisionals' departure.[84]

Militant republicanism eclipsed the CCDC from late 1970, with the remainder of the defence committees left to meetings with police authorities and lobbying for reform of the RUC.[85] Relations between defence committees and republicans deteriorated from November 1970, when the Provisionals accused the CCDC of hedging the national question and undermining republican armed struggle.[86] By this juncture, the CCDC was no longer the republican-dominated

---

[79] Keenan had served 12 years in prison for republican activities. In April 1972, he represented the Provisional movement on a coast-to-coast tour of the USA, fundraising as a trustee of Irish Northern Aid. 'Paper reforms only say Sligo speakers', *Western People*, 18 October 1969; Kathleen Teltsch, 'In a Bronx storefront office, a campaign outpost for the I.R.A.', *The New York Times*, 30 July 1972.

[80] Neil Gillespie quoted in LHL NIPC P8279: Derry Citizens Defence Association, *Meeting of Derry Citizens Defence Association: Celtic Park, 10 August 1969.*

[81] Alongside Keenan, Tom Mellon, Barney McFadden, Tommy Carlin, and Liam McDaid later joined the Provisionals. Wichert, *Northern Ireland since 1945*, 134.

[82] During a public dispute between Belfast Provisionals and the CCDC in November 1970, the Provisionals referred to some among 'our members who are also members of the CCDC'. Ranagh Holohan, 'Republicans critical of C.C.D.C.', *The Irish Times*, 14 November 1970.

[83] LHL NIPC P4203: CCDC, *Stop! Stop! Stop!* (Belfast: CCDC, 1970).

[84] Heathwood Video Archive (hereafter, HVA) D01260 Tape 93: *Sullivan's Story* (UTV, 28 September 1989).

[85] LHL NIPC P1026: CCDC, *Northern Ireland: The Black Paper – The Story of the Police* (Belfast: CCDC, 1973).

[86] Ranagh Holohan, 'Republicans critical of C.C.D.C.', *The Irish Times*, 14 November 1970.

street movement that Brian Feeney has portrayed.[87] By 1972, pacifying elements close to the Church were foremost in the CCDC, whose chairman Tom Conaty coordinated a petition for peace in Belfast and served on a committee advising British Secretary of State Willie Whitelaw.[88] By 1973, the breach between republicans and the CCDC was final, when the Committee implored the Provisionals to call a ceasefire.[89]

The fraught circumstances of 1969 profoundly recast the social order in working-class areas of Belfast and Derry, with young activists in both cities repudiating Church authority amid the incipient emergency. Especially for a younger generation, 1969 represented what Walter Benjamin termed the historical 'rupture' that disrupts earlier modes of conformity and destabilises 'the previous unthematized foundations of social life'.[90] During riots on 12 July 1969, Catholic youths attacking Victoria Barracks pushed aside Father Mulvey of St Eugene's Cathedral in Derry.[91] Mulvey admitted that the Bogside was 'in revolt'.[92] Residents of Belfast's Ardoyne district branded Father Gillespie a 'cheek-turning fool' when he argued against armed community defence in August 1969.[93]

The chaotic '68 years further discredited formal constitutional politics in besieged areas. Within 24 hours of Brian Faulkner's government introducing internment in August 1971, activists on Derry's barricades, spanning DCDA, republicans, and Labour Party Young Socialists, commenced a rent and rates strike in Creggan and St Columb's Well. Organisers castigated the area's 'elected leadership' who had 'failed miserably' to gauge the public mood.[94] A few days

---

87 Brian Feeney, *Sinn Féin: a hundred turbulent years* (Madison, Wisconsin: University of Wisconsin Press, 2002), p. 260.

88 'The Past Two Weeks', *Fortnight*, 51 (30 November 1972); Robert Fisk, '40,000 Catholics sign Belfast petition condemning violence', *The Times*, 2 June 1972. Conaty later became a leading member of the Community of the Peace People (CPP), before he was expelled in February 1977. A devout Catholic, Conaty criticised CPP leaders who argued that the Church had failed to take a 'clear moral lead on the question of violence'. Martin Huckerby, 'Peace People drop official over attack on leaders', *The Times*, 9 February 1977.

89 Robert Fisk, 'IRA attack on airport failed to deter British pilots', *The Times*, 5 June 1973.

90 Walter Benjamin, *Illuminations: essays and reflections* (New York: Schocken Books, 1977), pp. 261–262.

91 Henry Patterson, *The politics of illusion: republicanism and socialism in modern Ireland* (London: Hutchinson Radius, 1989), p. 71.

92 Peter Waymark, 'Priest criticises Ulster police', *The Times*, 26 September 1969.

93 Patrick Bishop & Eamonn Mallie, *The Provisional IRA* (London: Heinemann, 1987), p. 88.

94 'No rent! No rates!', *Barricade Bulletin*, 10 August 1971.

later, local activists sought the city's parliamentary representative John Hume for advice. Unable to reach Hume, who was working in Belfast, Derry's barricade volunteers dispensed with the 'nonsense' and announced a newly autonomous movement.[95]

Some 50 years on, activists who remember August 1969 reinforce the crisis as a visceral historical threshold that was experienced profoundly locally. In a group interview, two veteran Belfast republicans instinctively narrated their republicanism from mid-August 1969, and could recall how events unfolded almost hour by hour, street by street.[96] A former Official republican internee from Belfast stressed the localism of defence committees, asserting the spontaneity of a community in revolt:

> The defence committees were just made up of each street, even if you weren't on the frontline. So every street had a defence committee elected. So that was young *and* old, it was a mentality. People wonder why a community rises, but the whole community had been kept down.[97]

Patrick Magee experienced the escalating crisis transnationally and locally. Living in East Anglia, Belfast-born Magee felt compelled to 'witness' events in his native city – to which he returned in 1971, aged 20. Subsequently, Magee's observations in north Belfast formed a profound realisation:

> It wasn't until internment happened in 1971 that I really felt a need to come back here [to Belfast] to be witness to it. I was an age then – as we all were then, it was a very politically astute generation – where we were interested in Vietnam, in the civil rights in the States, the events in Europe with the Prague Spring and the happenings in Paris and things like that. It's happening here, in a place I care about: I wanted to be a witness to it. I was also aware we weren't getting the full truth in the newspaper reports. I just tried to absorb as much as I could, walking around, usually in the aftermath of stuff. It actually took me a while to get a hold on it, you know, but eventually I wanted to be a part of it: I wanted to be a part of what I saw was happening in the districts I was in, and it was the people

---

[95] *Barricade Bulletin*, 13 August 1971.
[96] Kevin Hannaway and Francie McGuigan interview with Jack Hepworth. Belfast, 6 December 2017.
[97] Former Official republican internee interview with Jack Hepworth. Belfast, 31 March 2016.

of those areas defending themselves. These were very poor areas, very few resources. The British state had seemed to declare war on them. The area I was living in then was called Carrick Hill. It was called Unity Flats in those days. It was saturation point. There was an Army sangar and there was only three or four hundred residences in the whole of that estate. There was an Army sangar on top of the library, there was always two foot patrols, there were two Army barracks and a police barracks within half a mile, so there was a heavy presence. And during a particularly bad time in '72 the whole sectarian thing kicked off, with the loyalists... They were really intense times. As a witness to all that, I wanted to be part of the resistance.[98]

Similarly, Gerry MacLochlainn, a Derry native who had moved to south Wales, recalled 'the '68 years' in terms of international cycles of contestation combined with intense experiences on visits to his home city. MacLochlainn, whose father was a trade unionist, had

always been proud of the labour movement, but I think as the civil rights campaign was getting going, as the Vietnam situation was going, there was lots of big Vietnam protests, the black civil rights movement, we identified a lot of this as social justice, and South Africa – we'd heard about Sharpeville – was about equality and justice... The Prague Spring, the student unrest across Europe and the civil rights movement was beginning here, and the students were travelling.[99]

Derry, MacLochlainn, recalled, joined 'the tourist list for aspiring revolutionaries as they travelled around Europe'. In January 1969, MacLochlainn joined the civil rights march from Belfast to Derry at Claudy, County Derry, and recalled loyalists and the RUC ambushing the march as it approached Derry. He vividly recalls this experience that transformed his politics:

We made our way to the Bogside and sort of fought back, and it was very exhilarating, because you knew once you'd fought the police back, you couldn't put the genie back in the bottle. When you saw them running, it changed your way of thinking.[100]

---

[98] Patrick Magee interview with Jack Hepworth. Belfast, 13 August 2015.
[99] Gerry MacLochlainn interview with Jack Hepworth. Derry, 12 December 2017.
[100] Gerry MacLochlainn interview with Jack Hepworth. Derry, 12 December 2017.

Embattled communities in Belfast and Derry in August 1969 demanded armed defence against loyalists, the RUC, and, later, the British Army. As Gianluca de Fazio has argued, through 1970 and 1971, the Provisional republican movement successfully outbid its rivals, presenting as a distinctly militant faction.[101] Fidelity to a specifically Irish tradition, and imperviousness to foreign manipulation, underpinned the Provisionals' projected identity.

The memory of August 1969 as a foundational moment for the Provisional movement served, and continues to serve, primarily as an indictment of Goulding's pre-split IRA. Nevertheless, for two years after Provisional and Official factions crystallised in 1970, Official republicans were also involved in urban vigilantism, guarding barricades and convening checkpoints. In west Belfast's Lower Falls district, for example, the Officials retained numerical superiority into 1971 and 1972. As one leading Provisional later recalled, until violent inter-republican feuding complicated the situation, in the Lower Falls the Officials 'had the bulk of the weaponry and... the majority of the support'.[102]

Until the ceasefire of May 1972, Officials on the ground remained sworn to community defence. Interviewed by a visiting American journalist, the Officials' leader in Derry City, Tommy McCourt, clearly delineated the OIRA's role: 'Our job is defence and retaliation. We're here to defend our people.'[103] For their part, Official republicans reciprocated Provisionals' aspersions, portraying their rivals as ideologically underdeveloped and fixated with militarism. Just weeks before the OIRA declared its ceasefire in 1972, McCourt cast the PIRA as crazed mavericks: 'If a fellow says he just wants a gun, we tell him to go to the Provos. We're not bloody idiots.'[104]

The PIRA's military campaign quickly evolved in the early 1970s. Through 1970 and early 1971, the Provisionals described an essentially defensive campaign: a statement from a PIRA unit in Ballymurphy, west Belfast in 1970 echoed the Army Council's commitment 'to protect our people against attack from Crown

[101] Gianluca de Fazio, 'Intra-movement competition and political outbidding as mechanisms of radicalisation in Northern Ireland, 1968–1969', in Lorenzo Bosi, Chares Demetriou, & Stefan Malthaner (eds.), *Dynamics of political violence: a process-oriented perspective on radicalisation and the escalation of political conflict* (Farnham: Ashgate, 2014), pp. 115–136.

[102] Brendan Hughes, 'IRA volunteer Charlie Hughes and the courage of the brave', *The Blanket: A Journal of Protest and Dissent* (September 2002).

[103] Bernard Weinraub, '"Free Derry", I.R.A.-run is a state within a state', *The New York Times*, 27 April 1972.

[104] Bernard Weinraub, '"Free Derry", I.R.A.-run is a state within a state', *The New York Times*, 27 April 1972.

forces and sectarian bigots'.[105] However, at the Sinn Féin *ard fheis* of October 1971, the Army Council narrated the campaign's progression from a 'defensive role to retaliation' and subsequently 'an offensive campaign of resistance' over the previous 12 months.[106] Events and external conjuncture informed the PIRA's intensification. In October 1971, the Provisionals demanded Stormont's abolition as a prerequisite for talks with the British government.

When Stormont was prorogued on 24 March 1972, republican demands advanced: a PIRA statement stipulated that direct rule from Westminster was 'not acceptable'.[107] By this juncture, the Provisionals' strategy had developed strikingly beyond the movement's foundational defenderist image. As Derry PIRA leader Martin McGuinness baldly put it in April 1972:

> The job, as far as I'm concerned, is fighting the British Army. *Ours is an offensive role*. No one likes to kill. I don't. But we're at war. These people are invaders.[108]

There were local inflections to community defence in both Belfast and Derry. In Derry, 1,000 Christian signatories of a petition for peace in 1972 wanted the PIRA to remain as a defensive force in Bogside and Creggan; in Belfast, peace campaigners called for a Provisional ceasefire.[109] Further from the epicentres of violence, Catholics placed greater hope in clerics' capacity for moral leadership.[110] In Newtownabbey, nine miles from Belfast and scarcely touched by the violence of 1969, approximately 200 local people joined clergy to establish a peace committee.[111]

The Provisionals' immediate narrative – portraying its ranks as saviours of urban nationalists left vulnerable by toothless Officials – was not lost on the

---

[105] LHL NIPC P13526: *Freedom Struggle by the Provisional IRA* (Dublin: Irish Republican Publicity Bureau, 1973).

[106] LHL NIPC P13526: *Freedom Struggle by the Provisional IRA* (Dublin: Irish Republican Publicity Bureau, 1973).

[107] LHL NIPC P13526: *Freedom Struggle by the Provisional IRA* (Dublin: Irish Republican Publicity Bureau, 1973).

[108] Bernard Weinraub, "'Free Derry', I.R.A.-run is a state within a state', *The New York Times*, 27 April 1972. Italics added.

[109] Robert Fisk, '40,000 Catholics sign Belfast petition condemning violence', *The Times*, 2 June 1972.

[110] 'Moral leadership' here follows Antonio Gramsci's understanding of religious institutions among the 'hegemonic apparatuses' of civil society. Chantal Mouffe, 'Hegemony and ideology in Gramsci', in Chantal Mouffe (ed.), *Gramsci and Marxist theory* (London: Routledge & Kegan Paul, 1979), p. 187.

[111] LHL NIPC P769: John Darby, *Intimidation in Housing* (Belfast: Northern Ireland Community Relations Commission, 1974).

OIRA Chief of Staff. Interviewed by *New Left Review* in 1970, Cathal Goulding assessed the recent split and argued that his movement had simply misjudged the scale of the emergency in August 1969. Yet Goulding also recognised that the Officials' intentions the previous year had become a moot point: the Provisionals had secured the designation of true community defenders.[112]

Admitting the Provisionals had mobilised substantial sections of the Catholic population in Belfast and Derry, by the end of 1970 Official republicans faced a strategic dilemma. The rapid escalation of the northern crisis prompted political review. After debates in party *cumainn*, a Belfast branch of Official Sinn Féin (OSF) identified two distinct avenues for protest: either a straightforward nationalist demand for Irish unification, in line with the Provisionals' rhetoric, or agitation around 'radical social demands' for jobs, housing, and civil rights. Asserting that strategy must be sensitive to the vicissitudes of timing, the McKelvey Republican Club advocated reanimating civil rights claims. Demanding Irish unity immediately, the argument ran, had 'substantially less' potential to mobilise and unite militants across the north.[113]

At grassroots level in 1969 and 1970, contingent factors such as family, friendships, and territorial ties initially shaped allegiance between Provisionals and Officials. Albert Allen was 16 years old in 1970 and later became a longstanding PIRA volunteer. He recalled the split in Belfast:

> It depended on what area you were in, who was recruiting. I was in an area that was predominantly Official IRA, so I was in the Fianna, joined the IRA, the Official IRA. Hadn't got a clue. It was only as time goes by, and you realise.[114]

A former Official internee reflected similarly:

> If someone had come up the road in '69 with a van load of weapons and said, *you've to forget all about the Official IRA and join the Provisional IRA*, you'd have said, *yeah, okay* [...] Somebody said to me at the time – I argued with him: he had been a member [of the Officials]. And I said to him, *you know what you're doing* [joining the Provisionals] *is wrong*. And he says, *I agree with you entirely, but I live in Ardoyne* – in other words, surrounded by loyalists, and politics

---

[112] 'The new strategy of the IRA', *New Left Review*, 64 (November–December 1970).
[113] LHL NIPC P1461: McKelvey Republican Club, *Freedom manifesto for the seventies* (n.d. [1970]). Emphasis in original.
[114] Albert Allen interview with Jack Hepworth. Belfast, 13 December 2017.

didn't matter as much as survival... Sometimes it boiled down to whatever area you lived in.[115]

For Tommy McKearney in Moy, County Tyrone, allegiance in 1971

wasn't so much at that time quite an ideological decision. I didn't decide in terms of: are the Officials more or less left-wing? That didn't occur to me at all. It was in many ways a question of efficiency and effectiveness, and who was seen to be best striking back at that stage... in terms of removing the obstacle.[116]

Despite the element of contingent factors that shaped allegiances, subsequently organisational identities acquired potency. Enmity between Provisionals and Officials flared sporadically but fatally later in the decade, most notably in a series of killings from 1975 to 1977. These internecine feuds were concentrated in Belfast, and were lamented especially by one republican who had lent support to both groups. Noel Jenkinson was convicted of the OIRA bombing of the British Army barracks in Aldershot in 1972, in which six civilians and a military chaplain were killed. Writing from jail in September 1976, Jenkinson espoused support for the group he considered the most efficacious and best equipped. Calling for 'anti-imperialist unity' and 'All Volunteers, All Funds, All Equipment To The Provisionals', Jenkinson deplored infighting among republicans who, he argued, were engaged in futile arguments over 'who is the most revolutionary'.[117]

Long after the Provisional Army Council announced its new offensive in October 1971, collective memory of the Provisionals as an essentially defensive force remained deeply embedded in Belfast and Derry. In 1973, Provisional publicity hailed prominent Belfast republican Joe Cahill as the 'defender of the Falls'.[118] As late as 1980, former republican prisoner Maureen Gibson remembered young republican Gerald McAuley, who died on 15 August 1969 'while defending the area'.[119] A west Belfast republican's poem honouring the area's PIRA volunteers – celebrated locally as 'the dogs' – reflected the

---

[115] Former Official republican internee interview with Jack Hepworth. Belfast, 31 March 2016.

[116] Tommy McKearney interview with Jack Hepworth. Armagh, 15 September 2015.

[117] Noel Jenkinson, "'Stand by the Provos'", *The Irish People*, Volume 5, Number 36 (11 September 1976). Born into a Protestant family in County Meath, Jenkinson was living in London at the time of his arrest in 1972. Within a month of declaring his support for the Provisionals in September 1976, Jenkinson suffered a fatal heart attack.

[118] LHL NIPC PPO1241: *Release Joe Cahill* (1973).

[119] Margaretta D'Arcy, *Tell them everything* (London: Pluto Press, 1981), p. 66.

symbiotic relationship of localism and nationalism among the movement's supporters:

> From Falls Road to Cullingtree
> and Grosvenor to the Pound…
> The valiant fighting men…
> Through the length and breadth of
> Erin's Isle unequelled [*sic*] anywhere.[120]

The Provisionals' international sympathisers were similarly familiar with their defenderist reputation. In December 1971, sympathisers in Irish Northern Aid in the USA implored supporters to assist Provisional 'DEFENSE PATROLS'.[121]

Despite the rhetoric of an 'offensive' announced late in 1971, leading Provisionals continually invoked the movement's foundational legend to legitimise an ongoing campaign. Army Council member Dáithí Ó Conaill asserted in March 1972 that the PIRA did not seek conflict with unionists or the Orange Order, but republicans would 'defend the Catholic population against attack by elements of the Unionist Regime'.[122] In February 1972, even when announcing a renewed bombing campaign, Belfast PIRA adjutant Ivor Bell compared the organisation to the Jewish 'resistance' against the British after the Second World War.[123]

When internment was introduced in August 1971, Free Derry became a no-go area for the RUC and British Army. As a quasi-autonomous area, Free Derry became a site of particular importance for the Provisionals: a majority at a public meeting in April 1972 voted for the PIRA to exclude permanently British troops from the Bogside.[124] On 30 January 1972, members of the

---

120 'Tribute to the "dogs"', *Na Madraí: The Newssheet of the Seamus Burns/Charlie Hughes Sinn Fein Cumann, Lower Falls*, 27 November 1976.

121 Irish Northern Aid Committee Hartford Chapter, 'A dance to be held at the Irish American Home' (3 December 1971). Available at https://www.scribd.com/document/342197180/FBI001 (accessed 17 October 2017).

122 Timothy B. Brennan, Press Relations for Irish Republican Publicity Bureau, 27 March 1972. Available at https://www.scribd.com/document/342197180/FBI001 (accessed 17 October 2017).

123 'P. Michael O'Sullivan interview with Belfast Brigade IRA Adjutant Ivor Bell in Belfast, February 1972', Irish Republican Marxist History Project. Available at https://irishrepublicanmarxisthistoryproject.wordpress.com/2017/08/22/p-michael-osullivan-interview-with-belfast-brigade-ira-adjutant-iver-bell-in-belfast-february-1972/ (accessed 22 September 2017).

124 Timothy B. Brennan, Press Relations for Irish Republican Publicity Bureau, 18 April 1972. Available at https://www.scribd.com/document/342197180/FBI001 (accessed 17 October 2017).

Parachute Regiment shot 26 unarmed civilians after a civil rights march in Derry: 13 people died that day; a fourteenth, John Johnston, died of his injuries in June 1972. In the Bogside and beyond, the traumatic memory of Bloody Sunday reinforced the image of Provisional defenders in urban collective memory.[125]

In its urban heartlands, the Provisional movement quickly defined itself by its disdain for authority and refusal to compromise. Provisional denigration spared neither the Catholic Church, NICRA, Official republicans, nor more moderate nationalists who eschewed armed force. In 1973, *Republican News* listed NICRA and the Officials among 'defeatist and deluded collaborators with fascism and imperialism... [and] British and Orange force'.[126]

The relationship between civil rights politics and militant republicanism varied across time and space. In Belfast and Derry, the violent upheaval of 1969 immediately stimulated republican recruitment, displacing many political alternatives. By contrast, County Fermanagh had been relatively insulated from the most acute violence of 1969 but had a long history of discrimination and civil rights controversies. Here, the boundary between civil rights protests in the late 1960s and physical-force republicanism in the 1970s was especially porous.

Outside of Belfast and Derry, republican mobilisation was slower. Civil rights groups contained many activists who later became frustrated with the perceived failure of reform and advocated armed struggle. Liam Slevin from Belleek, County Fermanagh, had been involved with PD and NICRA in the late 1960s, but by late 1969 he was among Sinn Féin's founders. Slevin was later charged with PIRA membership.[127] Like many Fermanagh republicans, Tommy Maguire from Enniskillen first experienced political activism in the Fermanagh Civil Rights Association and later joined the PIRA, serving a prison sentence from 1977 to 1985.[128] In the mid-1980s, all three Sinn Féin representatives on Fermanagh District Council were former civil rights activists.[129]

Blurring between civil rights and republican activism in County Fermanagh meant civil rights organisations sympathised with the armed struggle where NICRA activists in Belfast or Derry did not. Fermanagh Civil Disobedience Committee echoed republican martyr Pádraig Pearse's oration at Jeremiah

[125] Graham Dawson, 'Trauma, place and the politics of memory: Bloody Sunday, Derry, 1972–2004', *History Workshop Journal*, 59 (2005), pp. 151–178.

[126] 'Sectarianism!', *Republican News*, 19 May 1973.

[127] 'Claimed he was "framed" by British undercover agents', *Donegal Democrat*, 11 October 1974.

[128] Fáilte Cluain Eois, *Their prisons, our stories* (Castleblayney: Fáilte Cluain Eois, 2015), pp. v, 219.

[129] 'Sinn Fein's 11 selections', *Fermanagh Herald*, 20 April 1985.

O'Donovan Rossa's funeral: 'Ireland unfree shall never be at peace.' In 1975, Fermanagh civil rights activists saluted the PIRA's 'unpaid volunteer soldiers'.[130] Veteran civil rights activist and independent nationalist MP Frank McManus addressed a meeting in March 1972, shortly after direct rule from Westminster was imposed. McManus analogised Stormont's prorogation as 'one point' won in the 'game', and urged supporters to persist for the ultimate victory: Irish unification.[131]

In the mid-1970s, the Provisionals' community organisation remained rudimentary, relying predominantly on PIRA activities as distinct from Sinn Féin campaigns. In May 1975, Sinn Féin's *cumann* in Clonard, its foundational west Belfast stronghold, comprised only 11 party activists. Beleaguered organiser Patricia Davidson complained that only four of those were active, distributing flyers and knocking on doors to energise crowds for demonstrations.[132]

When the Ulster Workers' Council, protesting against the Sunningdale Agreement, declared a strike in May 1974, the Provisional movement in Belfast expanded its community-oriented cooperativism and vigilantism. The PIRA's Second Battalion urged local people to remain 'calm and resolute' during the 'emergency' caused by the 'fascist strike'. Anticipating loyalist incursions into nationalist areas, Belfast Provisionals reprised their foundational role of 1969. This time, republicans coordinated cooperatives for foodstuffs and medical provisions, and increased vigilante presence on the streets near community interfaces.[133] The PIRA's Belfast Brigade reiterated its role as 'the people's army'. Deepening its engagement with grassroots communities in Belfast especially, the Provisional movement into the mid-1970s revamped its defenderist origins to prophesy an imminent breakthrough. As the public relations officer of a west Belfast Sinn Féin *cumann* boldly forecast in September 1974:

> The Irish Republican Movement has shown the necessary leadership and competence to defend the minority in the six counties and lead the whole Irish people to independence.[134]

---

[130] 'The men of today', *Concerned: Official Organ of the Fermanagh Civil Disobedience Committee*, 172 (8 February 1975).

[131] Timothy B. Brennan, Press Relations for Irish Republican Publicity Bureau, 27 March 1972. Available at https://www.scribd.com/document/342197180/FBI001 (accessed 17 October 2017).

[132] EHI: Sinn Féin Belfast Comhairle Ceantair monthly report (16 May 1975).

[133] EHI: 'Statement from 2nd Battalion, Oglaigh na h-Éireann', *Irish Prisoners of War*, 1 (n.d. [1974]).

[134] James Daly, P.R.O. Gerald McAuley Cumann, 'Republican movement will lead Irish people to independence', *Republican News*, 14 September 1974.

Republicanism and collective memory of '68 ten years on

Republicans and former civil rights activists contested the legacies of '68 on its tenth anniversary. These commemorations were no parochial dispute over Northern Ireland's past; rather, they had contemporary political resonance. From 1976, prisoners convicted for republican activity would no longer have special-category, or 'political', status. The British government's 'criminalisation' policy sought to delegitimise republican claims to political motivation.[135]

From 1976, the grassroots campaign against criminalisation complexified the republican offensive. Writing in 1974, NICRA organisers recognised that their movement had lost the momentum it had enjoyed in the late 1960s: republican armed struggle now dominated media coverage.[136] From 1978, republicans marched again. Campaigns supporting republican prisoners in this period renewed the language of rights so dominant in 1968 and 1969.

Republican protests and commemorations, braided through the anti-criminalisation campaign, were not confined to 1978. The mass campaign against criminalisation culminated in the hunger strikes of 1980 and 1981. For a new generation of republicans, the hunger strike of 1981 joined 1969 in collective memory's nodal points for renewed recruitment. Gathering data from 60 Sinn Féin activists in 1999, Cynthia Irvin found that some 65 per cent of her sample charted their pathways to mobilisation from civil rights or anti-criminalisation protests.[137]

While 1969 remained totemic for the Provisionals' foundational narrative, the PIRA leadership emphasised that its struggle and strategy had matured in the intervening decade. Interviewed in 1978, a senior member of the Provisional Army Council explained that the movement had refined its recruitment and re-organised volunteers into secretive cells. Contrasting the perceived naivety of the nascent Provisionals, the PIRA leader evoked a streamlined, enhanced movement in 1978:

> We don't have as many volunteers as we did five or six years ago and this is no bad thing. People were joining for all the wrong reasons, hundreds simply because they wanted a gun to defend their immediate area. Now we have a much more politicised volunteer corps.[138]

---

[135] The pre-eminent study of the anti-criminalisation movement is F. Stuart Ross, *Smashing H-block: the rise and fall of the popular campaign against criminalisation, 1976–1982* (Liverpool: Liverpool University Press, 2011).

[136] 'NICRA organisers' report for the April 1974 AGM' quoted in Maney, 'White negroes and the pink IRA', 84.

[137] Cynthia L. Irvin, *Militant nationalism: between movement and party in Ireland and the Basque country* (Minneapolis: University of Minnesota Press, 1999), p. 144.

[138] *Magill*, Volume 1, Number 11 (August 1978).

In 1978, the Provisional leadership contended that mass commemorations of '68 evidenced 'continued massive support for the armed struggle'. Yet the movement's hierarchy did not collapse historical time or inscribe core republican ideals on the original civil rights moment. Rather, the Provisional narrative of the previous decade charted an evolving campaign and context. The reformist civil rights campaign's strategic limitations, the argument ran, had proven the necessity of revolutionary armed struggle. Republicanism was configured as the logical and enlightened endpoint of hitherto moderate forms of opposition and agitation. A front-page editorial in *Republican News* proclaimed:

> The resistance movement now on the streets is different from the one which emerged ten years ago. Today we are more mature; we are conscious of what direction we are heading in... Ten years ago its [*sic*] was a spontaneous emotional upsurge... But most of us were ignorant about how to win the struggle... The aim of today's struggle is certainly different. The people now realise civil rights can not be obtained within the Orange statelet.[139]

A decade on, contemporary political debates profoundly shaped how activists remembered Northern Ireland's '68. In August 1978, ten years after the seminal NICRA march between Coalisland and Dungannon, County Tyrone's Relatives Action Committees – the primary organisational expression of anti-criminalisation protest – organised a march. The Tyrone representatives demanded political status for republican prisoners and British withdrawal. The rump of the NICRA organisation repudiated the 1978 march.

Civil rights activists who remained committed to non-violence portrayed the 1978 march as a violent perversion of its progressive, reformist antecedent. For Gerry Fitt, the repeat event was 'under completely different auspices' to the 1968 demonstrations for 'jobs, homes and votes'. According to Fitt, a decade of conflict in Northern Ireland had vindicated NICRA moderates' warnings in 1968:

> Had the people who are running this march listened to what we had to say in 1968 and took heed of our position on violence, there would not have been 10 tragic years in between and there would be no prisoners.[140]

---

139 'From civil rights to armed struggle', *Republican News*, 2 September 1978. Bold in original.
140 Jim Cusack, 'Ex-leaders shun march', *Belfast Telegraph*, 26 August 1978.

County Tyrone's NICRA branch acknowledged that 'discrimination, repression and blatant sectarianism' continued to dominate politics in Northern Ireland, but insisted that 'violence from whatever source is evil and terrible'. Tyrone Civil Rights Association pleaded with Westminster to 'grant Civil Rights' to undercut popular support for 'the men of violence'. A former civil rights activist in the county and, by 1978, a senior figure in the SDLP, Austin Currie dismissed the march as 'run by the IRA'.[141]

By contrast, republican supporters of the march stressed continuity between civil rights causes of the 1960s and enduring grievances in 1978. This intransigence was not the preserve of younger former PD leftists such as Bernadette Devlin, Michael Farrell, and Eamonn McCann; republican supporters of the 1978 march included civil rights veterans campaigning for British withdrawal, including Kevin Agnew, Frank Maguire, and Fermanagh's Frank McManus. In Derry, former Nationalist Party MP Eddie McAteer said he planned to march in October 1978 to confront 'the primary wrong – the British presence in Ireland'.[142] Devlin asserted a unifying thread through her politics since 1968:

> It seems strange to me that certain people can claim that today's march has nothing to do with that of 10 years ago. I was one of those people who walked then and whose head was filled with ideas of how we could achieve a better life. The very people who say today has nothing to do with ten years ago are the ones who started it all by sowing the seeds of these ideas in our heads... It is not true that the demands have changed and have nothing to do with our original requests for houses, jobs and votes... We are demanding the withdrawal of all British interference in Ireland because we have discovered where the root of the problem lies.[143]

Standing for election to the European parliament in 1979, Devlin invoked 1968 as an agitational zenith requiring urgent renewal. At a press conference launching her campaign, Devlin implored her supporters to fulfil the 'pledges' of civil rights in emerging struggles, primarily against criminalisation: 'eleven years ago the flag of Civil Rights was planted... Today we have little civil liberty left.'[144] In January 1979, at a commemorative event for the civil rights

---

[141] 'Tyrone CRA and "the struggle for democracy ten years on"', *Ulster Herald*, 2 September 1978.
[142] 'Counter march headache', *Belfast Telegraph*, 5 October 1978.
[143] 'On the road again from Coalisland to Dungannon', *Ulster Herald*, 2 September 1978.
[144] 'I'll take H-block case into Europe – McAliskey', *Belfast Telegraph*, 28 May 1979.

march ambushed at Burntollet Bridge a decade earlier, IRSP representative Terry George similarly lamented years of political impasse:

> Many of the young men in H-block now were perhaps only 8 or 9 years old when that historic march took place and yet today it falls to them despite their age to bear the full brutality of British repression.[145]

Bound by mutual support for republican prisoners on the blanket protest, marches in 1978 renewed connections between Provisionals and PD veterans. Marking the tenth anniversary of the civil rights march of 5 October 1968, Sinn Féin supporters in Derry wore blankets to highlight prisoners' plight, and heard speeches from local Relatives Action Committee activist Mary Nelis and prominent leftists Michael Farrell and Eamonn McCann.[146] The 3,000-strong crowd marching between Coalisland and Dungannon in August 1978 heard a statement from PIRA prisoners in Long Kesh. Unsurprisingly given the conditions in jail, prisoners in H-blocks 3, 4, and 5 were less concerned with anniversaries than with the more immediate ramifications of criminalisation. The prisoners invoked the '68 years only to portray an unbendingly repressive state that was now incarcerating a new generation: during the civil rights protests of ten years earlier, their statement noted, 'many of us were barely nine or ten years old'.[147]

Recapitulating a '68 civil rights zeitgeist during the campaign against criminalisation prompted the Provisional leadership to contemplate a multi-organisational alliance. After previous unsuccessful broad front initiatives, Provisional leaders initially demanded primacy in a new alliance. The results were rancorous. In 1979, on a point of principle, Provisionals boycotted an anniversary march between Belfast and Derry. Belfast Provisionals lambasted organisers after some participating groups notified police in advance. Not all Provisionals observed the boycott: Sinn Féin members in County Derry joined the march en route. But PD organisers excoriated republicans for their

> inflexibility... Sinn Fein have never been happy working with other organisations. Time and again they have withdrawn from united committees and united fronts.[148]

---

[145] 'Successful Burntollet commemoration', *The Starry Plough/An Camchéachta* (January 1979).

[146] '67 police injured in clashes with loyalists', *Belfast Telegraph*, 9 October 1978.

[147] Republican PoWs, H-Blocks 3, 4 and 5, Long Kesh, 'Our revolutionary resolve is still as strong as ever', *Republican News*, 2 September 1978.

[148] 'Burntollet: marching against repression', *Socialist Republic: Paper of Peoples' Democracy*, Volume 2, Number 1 (1979).

The IRSP was similarly critical of Provisional supremacy: the republican socialist movement's official history chronicles Provisionals demanding control of the National H-Block/Armagh Committee (NHBAC) in 1980.[149] To this day, former IRSP and INLA members recall Provisional republicans repeatedly presuming authority over other groups, not least during imprisonment. IRSP veteran Fra Halligan remembers

> there were some within the Provisional republican movement that to put it nicely would have loved the republican socialist movement to disappear, and over the years the republican socialist movement felt this dislike in many different ways, but continued nonetheless.[150]

Ex-INLA volunteer Gerry Foster:

> The Provos never respected any other organisation. They were the one true legitimate army of Ireland, and the only legitimate opposition to British rule: that was their elitism. There wouldn't have been respect.[151]

Former INLA prisoner Seamus McHenry remembered the prison protests of the late 1970s:

> You knew the Provisionals didn't like you. They tried to put their authority on you. If you'd have been weak, you'd have fell in with them, so you would've. They wanted to debrief me as being a member of their organisation, and it was only when you were willing to say, *fuck off, I'm nothing to do with yous; this is who I am.*[152]

Provisional republicans routinely use 'the republican movement' as shorthand specifically for their own organisation.[153]

The NHBAC constituted the most elaborate and enduring broad front among republicans and fellow travellers in the first two decades of the conflict. However, in committees marking the tenth anniversary of Northern Ireland's '68, and in

---

[149] IRSP, 'H-Block/Armagh Broad Front: an assessment' (1981). Available at http://www. hungerstrikes.org/racs/assessment.html (accessed 15 February 2017).

[150] Fra Halligan interview with Jack Hepworth. Belfast, 15 September 2015.

[151] Gerry Foster interview with Jack Hepworth. Belfast, 13 August 2015.

[152] Seamus McHenry interview with Jack Hepworth. Belfast, 7 December 2017.

[153] A former Provisional prisoner cast the INLA outside republicanism: 'The INLA... I just didn't have a lot of time for them... It's a pity they didn't apply themselves and join the republican movement.' Former Provisional republican activist interview with Jack Hepworth. County Donegal, April 2017.

the NHBAC, republicans accentuated organisational identity and independence. While ostensibly cooperating, Provisional republicans, IRSP-INLA members, and PD activists retained strong senses of being separate groups with particular histories. In September 1978, Sinn Féin's *Ard Comhairle* barred IRSP speakers from sharing Provisional platforms.[154]

By 1978, PD had undergone several shifts since its foundation at Queen's University Belfast nine years earlier. After declaring itself a revolutionary socialist movement for a 'workers' republic' in October 1969, the organisation comprised a couple of hundred militants. PD split in 1976 and many of those who remained helped to establish Relatives Action Committees to protest against criminalisation. Absorbing support from the Irish section of the Fourth International – the Movement for a Socialist Republic – PD looked not only to its civil rights past, but to an international revolutionary movement: by 1978, the group celebrated its 'co-operation with fraternal Marxist organisations in other countries through the Fourth International'.[155]

In tones reminiscent of their critical participation in the wider civil rights movement a decade earlier, the rump of PD activists upbraided Provisionals in the NHBAC for privileging the PIRA campaign and monopolising the broad front. For PD's strategists, harnessing the legacy of '68 required tactical malleability, even pragmatism, to mobilise a mass movement. In January 1978, when Provisional delegates proposed that support for the PIRA should be a precondition for participating in the NHBAC, PD members asserted that such a clause would alienate support. Over the following 18 months, PD won the argument, and the Provisionals acquiesced in the NHBAC as a single-issue campaign amplifying republican prisoners' five demands.[156]

Concerned that Provisional propaganda would appropriate the NHBAC's activities, PD's representatives on the joint committee remained vigilant. In June 1981, when PIRA prisoner Paddy Agnew won the Dáil seat for Louth, PD member Brian Hughes told an NHBAC conference that Agnew should resign the seat to allow a non-abstentionist alternative to bring the anti-criminalisation campaign into Leinster House.[157]

Remembering civil rights a decade after '68, PD activists criticised NICRA for neglecting class politics and the national question. A PD member writing in

[154] Henry McDonald & Jack Holland, *INLA: deadly divisions* (Dublin: Poolbeg, 2010) [First edition Dublin: Torc Books, 1994], p. 168.

[155] 'Long live Peoples Democracy', *Socialist Challenge*, 74 (30 November 1978).

[156] LHL NIPC P1001: PD, *Prisoners of Partition: H-Block/Armagh* (Belfast: PD, 1980).

[157] Public Record Office of Northern Ireland (hereafter, PRONI) Public Records CENT/1/10/62: A. K. Templeton, 'Northern Ireland Office: Protests and second hunger strike: Weekly Bulletin No. 28, 0900 Thursday 3 September – 0900 Thursday 10 September' (10 September 1981).

the group's newspaper in 1979 denounced NICRA for allowing 'right-wingers like John Hume' and Derry Citizens' Action Committee to divert activists from 'local defence committees' in 1969.[158] Another PD writer perceived past strategic errors as a guide for the present, claiming that NICRA had become an 'irrelevant talk-shop' since it did not demand British withdrawal: 'We don't want to make the same mistake with the H-Block Campaign.'[159]

Alongside the 'lessons' of Northern Ireland's '68, contemporary revolutions in Iran and Nicaragua also suffused PD's manifesto for the NHBAC as a vehicle for mass mobilisation against British rule in the late 1970s. As they had ten years earlier, republican leftists located Ireland in a sequence of popular anti-imperial revolutions. An editorial in PD newspaper *Socialist Republic* in 1979 celebrated the Iranian Revolution as a breakthrough for 'Mass Action', vindicating general strikes and large-scale demonstrations.[160] For PD activist Ciaran Mac Naimidhe, the Sandinistas' victory in Nicaragua in 1979, and the cohesion of the Farabundo Martí National Liberation Front, formed of five left-wing organisations in October 1980, demonstrated mass action's revolutionary potential.[161]

Conclusion

It is unsurprising that few scholars have located resurgent Irish republicanism among New Left politics in Europe and North America. Activists in Northern Ireland's civil rights movement graduated to diverse political trajectories. Those who proceeded to defence committees in Belfast and Derry in 1969, and subsequently to militant republicanism, sit uneasily among taxonomies of the international New Left. More broadly, Northern Ireland's trajectory into an enduring and bloody conflict from 1968 deviates considerably from prevailing typologies of New Left legacies. Anna von der Goltz's survey of '68ers' pathways reflected many activists' dismay at the 'terrorist' afterlives of '68 in Europe.[162]

Unease with political violence stemming from '68's global revolt is not restricted to academics. In their colossal oral history synthesis of the New

---

158 The lessons of August '69', *Socialist Republic: Paper of Peoples Democracy*, Volume 2, Number 1 (1979).

159 LHL NIPC P1008: PD, *H-Block Struggle: Irish Revolution on the March* (Belfast: PD, 1980).

160 'Iran: Mass action shows the way. Victory to the revolution!', *Socialist Republic: Paper of Peoples' Democracy*, Volume 2, Number 1 (1979).

161 Ciaran Mac Naimidhe, 'U.S. hands off El Salvador!', *Socialist Republic: Paper of Peoples' Democracy*, Volume 4, Number 2 (1981).

162 von der Goltz (ed.), *'Talkin' 'bout my generation'*, 33.

Left, Robert Gildea, James Mark, and Anette Warring found '68ers equally disinclined to accommodate 'terrorism' among their multivalent legacies:

> In their accounts of activism, former 1968 militants are torn between a number of competing models or scripts of resistance. The first is the heroic model of the idealised revolutionary, a second that of the non-violent guru or civil rights campaigner, and a third, favoured by some female activists, that of the leader of a mass movement. *One model to be avoided was that of the gun-toting terrorist. Activists who are drawn to the heroic model of the revolutionary need to avoid any association with terrorism by demonstrating that they inflicted no harm on innocent people.*[163]

Northern Ireland's variegated civil rights movement is more readily accommodated among the global New Left. Yet NICRA comprised diverse, embryonic ideas on the eve of sustained political upheaval: either side of its split in 1969, NICRA spanned liberal unionists, student radicals, Official republicans – who edged towards NICRA's leadership after the OIRA ceasefire in May 1972 – and enduringly militant Provisionals.[164]

In a global context, republicanism in the '68 years eludes straightforward categorisation. Before the republican movement split in 1969 and 1970, Sinn Féin's hostility towards the American and Soviet regimes reflected New Left positions: addressing the Sinn Féin *ard fheis* of 1968, party president Tomás Mac Giolla denounced the Soviet Union's 'imperialist' invasion of Czechoslovakia.[165] At least until 1973, Official republicans' international politics were marked by their fluidity. In the early 1970s, the Officials resembled an essentially Old Left tradition, to the extent that they grew closer to the Soviet Union. In October 1973, Mac Giolla, accompanied by OSF's Education Officer Des O'Hagan and National Organiser Seán Garland (an erstwhile critic of the USSR), attended the World Congress of Peace Forces in Moscow. Party propaganda celebrated this 'clear statement that the Soviet Union had embraced' the Officials.[166] The pro-Soviet stance crystallised through the movement's subsequent evolution.[167]

---

163 Gildea, Mark & Warring (eds.), *Europe's 1968*, 279. Italics added.

164 By February 1972, Officials occupied ten of the 14 places on the NICRA executive. Vincent Browne, 'SF Officials controls CRA', *The Irish Press*, 17 February 1972.

165 *Reflections on centenaries and anniversaries: discussion i – 'The republican movement divides: December 1969–January 1970'* (Newtownabbey: Island Publications/The Fellowship of Messines Association, 2020), p. 11.

166 LHL NIPC P1418: OSF, *The I.R.A. Speaks* (Dublin: OSF, 1973).

167 Comprising the remnants of the Official republican movement, The Workers' Party established fraternal relations with the Communist Party of the Soviet Union in

While foreign affairs largely defined European New Left politics, they were a distantly secondary concern for Sinn Féin leaders in the 1970s. More generally, republicans were broadly aloof from the libertarian and anarchist currents that suffused sections of the New Left. Memory further complicates these distinctions: many republicans now reconfigure their mobilisation as a transnational process, or as part of a global anti-establishment crusade, in ways they did not five decades ago.

Republicans and leftists in Ireland's '68 years differed in the extent to which they borrowed concepts from international developments. Official republicans and PD cadres situated their own struggle in an international context. Absorbing revolutionary theory and critical coverage of protests worldwide, leftist republicans perceived interconnected cycles of protest that were meaningful in Ireland as well as in Europe or the USA. Through 1968 and 1969, PD consciously imitated the Sorbonne Assembly, convening a loose organisation and 'faceless committee' to discuss strategy. France's student activism reverberated in PD students' alliances with workers and trade unions.

Official leaders in 1970 situated Ireland in a global anti-imperialist, socialist revolution. By contrast, Provisionals in the early 1970s were generally less engaged with foreign politics, orienting themselves towards the local and the national. While Provisionals were not oblivious to international developments in the '68 years, they saw struggles elsewhere more abstractly. Any foreign resemblance to their own situation was perceived more as coincidental than didactic. Accentuating the particular Irish heritage of their campaign, Provisionals framed their struggle as unique and broadly disconnected from events outside Ireland. Conversely, civil rights activists involved with PD, or who later joined the SDLP, looked more closely to various strands of the African-American civil rights movement for tactical inspiration.

The legitimising precedents of Ireland's revolutionary past underpinned Provisionals' distinctly national frames in the early 1970s. Early Provisionals were shrewd and pragmatic interpreters of embattled northern nationalist communities. They positioned themselves in succession to the rebels of the early twentieth century while also asserting their acute relevance to the emergency of 1969. Provisional leaders cast their Officials rivals in a very different light. The 'sticks', the polemics claimed, were lofty intellectuals, militarily ineffective in the crisis, and more interested in Budapest than Ballymurphy.

The period from 1968 to 1973 witnessed violent insurgency and significant changes in how republicans related to the New Left. In urban Belfast and Derry, the fledgling Provisional movement succeeded localised defence committees

1983. John Mulqueen, 'The red and the green', *Dublin Review of Books*, 2 December 2013.

and swiftly organised across large areas of the north. As Graham Spencer and Richard English have argued, the Provisionals cultivated their enduring image as defenders of the Catholic population beyond Northern Ireland's two major cities.[168]

From 1969 in Belfast and Derry, dormant republican networks reactivated. Provisional republicanism's social transformation stressed locality and rejected compromise, denigrating pillars of nationalist society such as the Catholic Church and NICRA. While the Provisionals' early emphasis on community defence and confronting police brutality echoed Black Panther rhetoric, the similarities were coincidental; only leftist revolutionaries such as Bernadette Devlin and Eamonn McCann more explicitly cited the Panthers as inspiration.

Local inflections were prominent and particular. In Counties Fermanagh and Tyrone, for instance, civil rights activism and republican politics interacted and overlapped far more than in Derry and Belfast. In Derry City in 1973, civil rights activists hoped 'moderate opinion' would emerge in Creggan if the British Army ceased harassing residents.[169] Similarly, North Derry Civil Rights Association remained prepared to normalise British rule in 1971, regarding republicanism as a temporary expression of 'disillusionment with the British forces'.[170] In Derry and Belfast, republican mobilisation in 1969 and 1970 amid a severe emergency drew sharp contrasts between civil rights and republicanism. Further from the epicentres of violent upheaval, protest networks were more blurred and movement between civil rights and republican movements more commonplace.

Activist trajectories in particular republican organisations were especially important in shaping how republicans remembered '68 and narrated their struggle. Perspectives on the limitations of the civil rights campaign were integral to republican subjectivities in the late 1970s. Leftist republicans such as Bernadette Devlin and IRSP representative Terry George claimed the past political impasse necessitated revolutionary renewal. Former '68ers who graduated to constitutional nationalism repudiated republican commemorations in 1978 as perversions of a pacific, progressive civil rights legacy.

Yet while republicans instrumentalised the supposed shortcomings of 1960s reform to justify their ongoing struggle, recapitulations of their own past were not uncritical. Leading Provisionals insisted that the PIRA had jettisoned

---

[168] Graham Spencer, *From armed struggle to political struggle: republican tradition and transformation in Northern Ireland* (London: Bloomsbury, 2015), p. 46; Richard English, *Does terrorism work? A history* (Oxford: Oxford University Press, 2016), p. 100.

[169] '"Undeclared martial law" – CRA', *Derry Journal*, 17 August 1973.

[170] LHL NIPC P1071: North Derry Civil Rights Association, *Northern Ireland: There is Only One Way!* (Belfast: North Derry Civil Rights Association, 1971).

naïve hopes of instant victory and now constituted a newly politicised guerrilla army, prepared for a 'long war'. Invoking collective memory of '68 stirred a new mass movement, this time in support of republican prisoners. Although the broad-based campaign against criminalisation facilitated interactions between republican organisations, these alliances were often fraught: PD activists charged the Provisionals with monopolising the NHBAC.

Reflecting on the decade following 1968, it is tempting simply to remark upon seemingly quantum leaps in individual pathways through these tumultuous years, between civil rights and militant republicanism. Perhaps a more illuminating response is to understand such trajectories as evidence of the striking spectrum of NICRA in the late 1960s. Northern Ireland's variegated civil rights movement bequeathed similarly diverse republican responses to the escalating crisis throughout the 1970s.

2

Shifting Strategies

Think of all the lives that could have been saved had we accepted the 1975 truce. That alone would have justified acceptance. We fought on and for what? What we rejected in 1975.

Former Belfast PIRA commander Brendan Hughes (1948–2008), in conversation with ex-PIRA prisoner Anthony McIntyre in 2000[1]

By 2000, former Belfast PIRA leader Brendan Hughes was profoundly disillusioned with the Provisional republican movement. Between the Good Friday Agreement of 1998 and his death a decade later, Hughes became one of Sinn Féin's most prominent critics. Debates concerning the Provisional movement's historical trajectory remain potent today. Many so-called 'dissenting' and 'dissident' republicans denounce Sinn Féin as 'sell-outs' acquiescing in British rule. Formed in September 2016, Saoradh, which describes itself as a 'revolutionary socialist-republican party', constitutes the latest republican challenge to Sinn Féin. In 2017, a Saoradh spokesperson in Derry denounced Sinn Féin for abandoning 'principle and ideology' and 'assimilat[ing] into British imperialist structures'.[2]

By contrast, Sinn Féin representatives advocate a constitutional pathway to a united Ireland, and routinely condemn 'dissident' violence. As Deputy First Minister of Northern Ireland in May 2012, Martin McGuinness denounced 'dissident' groups such as the Real IRA and Continuity IRA as 'deluded' and 'pathetic' opponents of progress.[3]

---

[1] 'A dark view of the process', *Fourthwrite: Journal of the Irish Republican Writers' Group* (March 2000).

[2] 'Saoradh: Sinn Fein has capitulated. It is guilty of unparalleled treachery', *Derry Journal*, 10 November 2017.

[3] Henry McDonald, 'Martin McGuinness accuses dissident republicans of being enemies of Ireland', *The Guardian*, 26 May 2012.

This chapter analyses republican responses to changes in tactics and strategy between the prison protests of the late 1970s and the Good Friday Agreement of 1998. During this period, the Provisional movement engaged two broad processes: from the early 1980s, electoralism; from the late 1980s, peace initiatives. The first section interrogates the Provisionals' electoral turn in the 1980s. The second section examines Sinn Féin's role in the peace process of the 1990s, between the Downing Street Declaration (1993) and the Good Friday Agreement (1998).

Republicanism and electoralism, c.1979–c.1989

Since the Good Friday Agreement of 1998, republicans opposed to Sinn Féin's constitutional strategy have often located in the Provisionals' 1980s electoral experimentation the first steps towards compromise and 'sell-out'. Writing in 2005, Liam O'Ruairc, then aligned with the IRSP, narrated the Provisionals' transition from 'principled revolutionary organisation to opportunist, reformist, constitutional, nationalist party'. O'Ruairc's account began with Sinn Féin's electoral interventions in 1981.[4] The chronology of Anthony McIntyre's critique in 2008 extended further still. A former PIRA volunteer who spent 18 years in Long Kesh, McIntyre remembered the PIRA ceasefire of 1975 and 1976. He lamented how the 'post-truce leadership' had 'insisted on fighting to an inglorious conclusion'.[5] These retrospectives call attention to the gradualism and contingency of the Provisionals' tactical and strategic changes during the 1980s and 1990s. Electoralism entered Provisional repertoires of contention in piecemeal, stuttering fashion over many years.

Even among Provisional leaders, electoral interventions sharply divided opinion in 1981. Today, Sands's extraordinary election campaign is routinely considered a threshold moment for the rising northern leadership milieu around Gerry Adams. Yet the origins of Sands's campaign are contested. Joe O'Neill, a founding Provisional from Bundoran, County Donegal, claimed in 2006 that Dáithí Ó Conaill, an ardent abstentionist, had initially suggested Sands's candidacy, while Gerry Adams and his supporters were reluctant. Having left the Provisionals in protest at Sinn Féin's 1986 *ard fheis*, O'Neill had longstanding differences with Adams, and his testimony should not be uncritically accepted. However, his anecdote suggests the ad hoc experimentality of Sinn Féin's

---

[4] Liam O'Ruairc, 'Going respectable', *The Plough*, Volume 2, Number 36 (22 May 2005).
[5] Anthony McIntyre, *Good Friday: the death of Irish republicanism* (New York: Ausubo Press, 2008), p. 8.

electoral tactics that year.[6] Mitchel McLaughlin, later an elected Sinn Féin representative in Derry, initially refused to assist Sands's election campaign: 'I was a committed abstentionist and I was actually anti-electoralism.'[7]

Republican electoral successes in 1981 – not least during the hunger strike, when seven PIRA prisoners won 64,985 votes and gained three seats across the island – prompted prominent Provisionals to advocate further electoral challenges. Danny Morrison became an especially vocal proponent of tactical electoralism. Writing under a pseudonym in *An Phoblacht/Republican News* immediately after Northern Ireland's local elections of May 1981, Morrison criticised the party's constitution for preventing Sinn Féin candidacies. Considering the 'clear militant shift in nationalist opinion', Morrison argued it had been a 'miscalculation' for Sinn Féin not to contest council elections: 25 IRSP, Irish Independence Party, and PD representatives were elected.[8] More than 30 years on, Morrison admitted that he and his senior comrade Jimmy Drumm repudiated electoralism until they observed polling results in 1981:

> We started to see the propaganda advantages of participating in elections and were confident that there was a vote to be won on that.[9]

Yet the momentous events of 1981 did not convert all republicans to electoral opportunists. Oral histories reveal the complexity of historic misgivings about 'politics'. Patrick Magee favoured

> being politically on the ground at community level – yes, I completely bought that. But I was a late convert to the notion that through electoral politics – [...] It was such a learning curve through the hunger strike.[10]

Histories of negotiation and compromise in 1921 and 1975 loomed large in republican collective memory, and 1981 did not eliminate these concerns. 'Politics' was the business of those who sold short military sacrifice. Conor

---

6 'Facts wrong on hunger strike – Joe O'Neill', *Donegal Democrat*, 18 May 2006.
7 Mitchel McLaughlin interview with Robert W. White, 1990. Robert W. White, *Provisional Irish republicans: an oral and interpretive history* (Westport, Connecticut: Greenwood Press, 1993), p. 142.
8 Peter Arnlis, 'H-Blocks rocks middle ground', *An Phoblacht/Republican News*, 30 May 1981.
9 Danny Morrison interview with Graham Spencer. Graham Spencer, *From armed struggle to political struggle: republican tradition and transformation in Northern Ireland* (London: Bloomsbury, 2015), p. 114.
10 Patrick Magee interview with Jack Hepworth. Belfast, 13 August 2015.

Murphy, who subsequently became a Sinn Féin councillor in 1989 before being elected as a Member of the Legislative Assembly (MLA) and as an MP, recalls:

> There always was a sense, when you got down to the theory of revolution – Irish revolutions had failed in the past in that the military people had fought to whatever the negotiations, a small number of people done the negotiations, then a political class came in and took over the solution.[11]

Such misgivings were apparent in April 1985, weeks before local government elections, when four Belfast PIRA volunteers were expelled for allegedly opposing funding for Sinn Féin's council campaigns.[12]

The particular circumstances surrounding each electoral campaign determined Sinn Féin's approach from 1981 to 1985. Danny Morrison and Owen Carron, senior party figures at the forefront of the electoral experiments of 1981, did not propose Sinn Féin intervention in the elections of October 1982. Morrison and Carron met PD and SDLP representatives in Carrickmore, County Tyrone, five months before polling day for the Assembly, seeking a unified boycott. Sinn Féin only decided to stand candidates when it emerged that the SDLP was doing so.[13]

Even those Provisionals who advocated electoralism in October 1982 did not necessarily envisage future interventions. Rather, the immediate objective was solely to invalidate British Secretary of State James Prior's new Assembly. Mindful that the SDLP had refused to boycott the Assembly elections, seven County Tyrone prisoners in Magilligan considered Sinn Féin candidates' abstentionist campaigns vital to 'boycott this farcical British Assembly'. The republican women in Armagh Jail implored the 'Nationalist community' to vote Sinn Féin to stymy Prior's attempt to 'reinstate the Unionist regime of old'.[14] Brian Feeney's argument that the Provisional leadership championed a 'twin-track' strategy of military and electoral campaigns simply to 'keep the IRA on board while seeking a move into the political mainstream' does not ring true for this position in the mid-1980s.[15] Even after council elections in 1985, future electoral interventions remained a discussion point. The party

---

[11] Conor Murphy interview with Jack Hepworth. Newry, 16 September 2015.

[12] M. L. R. Smith, *Fighting for Ireland? The military strategy of the Irish republican movement* (London: Routledge, 1995), p. 169.

[13] 'Sinn Féin and the Assembly elections', *Iris*, 4 (November 1982).

[14] 'Prisoners support Sinn Fein', *Ulster Herald*, 16 October 1982.

[15] Brian Feeney, *Sinn Féin: a hundred turbulent years* (Madison, Wisconsin: University of Wisconsin Press, 2002), pp. 14–15.

leadership hosted community forums to discuss strategy, mindful of the seemingly 'irreconcilable contradictions' involved when a 'revolutionary' party employed electoralism as a tactic.[16]

Oral histories also attest the range of views within the Provisional movement regarding electoral experiments in the early 1980s, even among activists unified by support for the initiative then and now. Raymond McCartney, a PIRA prisoner from 1977 to 1994, remembered how each election in the early 1980s was judged on its own merits, with debate developing subsequently:

> With Bobby's success in 1981 and the election of the two TDs, they were seen as successes... I remember the first Assembly election in 1982: the story was Sinn Féin... People then ask other questions, because what's the success for? Why get elected? You get elected to represent people. The discussion around the politics of it then came.[17]

By contrast, veteran ex-prisoner Séanna Walsh described the movement's tactics in the early 1980s in more straightforwardly destructive terms: 'Whatever the Brits put up, we'd knock it down.'[18] Testimonies also highlight how individual perspectives shifted with developments through the mid-1980s. By 1986, McCartney was open to abandoning the movement's historic abstentionist policy in the Dublin parliament, Leinster House: 'My view was that abstentionism doesn't work in a state where the majority of people recognise that parliament.'[19]

For republicans who have left the Provisional movement, reflections on electoralism through the 1980s reinforce dichotomies between republican militancy and 'politics' that featured in discussions of the republican split of 1969 and 1970. Kevin Hannaway

> never came into the republican movement to be a politician; it was about Irish freedom, which is a God-given right, and no country has the right to be in another man's country... As far as I was concerned, it was black and white to me, it wasn't the political thing, it was to get them out and sort the country out after that.[20]

---

[16] 'Forums', *Iris*, 10 (July 1985).
[17] Raymond McCartney interview with Jack Hepworth. Derry, 18 September 2015.
[18] Séanna Walsh interview with Jack Hepworth. Belfast, 12 August 2015.
[19] Raymond McCartney interview with Jack Hepworth. Derry, 18 September 2015.
[20] Kevin Hannaway interview with Jack Hepworth. Belfast, 6 December 2017.

Albert Allen, a former PIRA veteran, asserts that he never joined the movement's political wing: 'I never would have liked to become a Sinn Féin councillor, which I had every opportunity to do.'[21]

Even the leading architects of Provisional electoralism maintained throughout the 1980s that the PIRA's armed struggle remained republicanism's 'cutting edge'. Election campaigns offered potential propaganda coups and encouraged the movement to develop its grassroots connections. A Provisional statement published in September 1981 insisted that the party would not participate in 'constitutional politics' until a united Ireland had been achieved. The statement's authors either forgot or discounted Sinn Féin councillors serving in the Republic since 1974.[22] Anticipating the Assembly elections of October 1982, Morrison reassured readers of the movement's weekly newspaper that the Provisionals were not abandoning the armed struggle – or, as Morrison had it, alluding to the OIRA's ceasefire of May 1972, 'going Sticky'. There could be no 'parliamentary road' to a united socialist republic, nor could any number of electoral successes displace the 'primacy' of the armed struggle.[23]

Sinn Féin's internal education programme repudiated the 'reformist' notion that the electoral process could 'democratise' Northern Ireland.[24] The party's activism would neither undermine nor detract from the PIRA's armed campaign. Rather, Sinn Féin would play a secondary, supporting role. 'Whether Sinn Féin increases its vote, or decreases its vote', constitutional politics would 'not deliver' a British withdrawal, said Gerry Adams in 1984.[25] When Sinn Féin won 59 council seats in May 1985, Martin McGuinness told reporters that 'winning any amount of votes' would not 'bring freedom to Ireland'; only 'the cutting edge of the IRA' could 'bring freedom'. Supporters in Derry's Guild Hall chanted 'I-R-A' and 'Up the 'RA' as they held victorious Sinn Féin candidates aloft, suggesting that they shared McGuinness's insistence on the salience of armed struggle.[26]

[21] Albert Allen interview with Jack Hepworth. Belfast, 13 December 2017.

[22] 'IRA attitude on elections', *An Phoblacht/Republican News*, 5 September 1981. For example, despite his militaristic reputation, Jim Lynagh of Monaghan was among Sinn Féin's councillors in the Republic. Elected to Monaghan Urban District Council on his release from jail in 1979, Lynagh railed against the Broadcasting Act that prevented Sinn Féin representatives from appearing on Raidió Teilifís Éireann. 'No support for Sinn Fein motion', *Drogheda Argus and Leinster Journal*, 4 January 1980.

[23] Peter Arnlis, 'The war will go on', *An Phoblacht/Republican News*, 16 September 1982.

[24] LHL NIPC P2009: Sinn Féin Education Department, *Election Interventions – Historical & Contemporary* (Dublin: Sinn Féin, 1983).

[25] HVA D00770 Tape 63: *Brasstacks: The Armalite and the Ballot Paper* (BBC, Broadcast 17 July 1984).

[26] HVA D00860 Tape 70: *Real Lives: At the Edge of the Union* (BBC, Broadcast 16 October 1985).

McGuinness's reassurances were popular among the Provisional membership at large: a majority at the *ard fheis* of 1982 stipulated that all election candidates must 'be unambivalent in support of the armed struggle'.[27] Primers for new members of Sinn Féin emphasised the historical legitimacy and efficacy of 'electoral intervention': in 1983, the Education Department briefed members on historical precedents for 'electoral interventions'. Party literature asserted the efficacy of Kieran Doherty's and Paddy Agnew's more recent election to the Dáil, which had 'destabilised the Free State government and forced an early general election in 1982'.[28]

PIRA prisoners were an important source of support for electoral interventions in the early and mid-1980s. Prisoners welcomed these campaigns as an additional strand of struggle apt for demonstrating mass republican sympathies and delegitimising British rule in Ireland. Especially in Long Kesh, hunger strike elections were remembered as moments of profound, if temporary, elation. Sands's election had sparked jubilation in the H-blocks in April 1981. PIRA prisoner Tony O'Hara – brother of INLA volunteer Patsy, who joined the hunger strike on 22 March – recorded in a comm dated 10 April:

> I find words hard to describe the jubilation felt here this evening. With the result of the election there is a feeling here tonight which has not been here in a very long time... and the screws are visibly shattered – it's just great![29]

Observing the mass mobilisation of 1981, prisoners in H6 argued that Sinn Féin should contest elections to local councils in Northern Ireland and to the Dáil alongside 'other left-wing and anti-imperialist groupings'.[30]

Especially for prisoners who had experienced anti-criminalisation protests in the late 1970s and early 1980s, electoral campaigns had enormous potential to publicise republican grievances. Sinn Féin's successes in 1982 reinforced these memories of the previous year. Writing on behalf of the PIRA men in Long Kesh in May 1983, the prisoners' public relations officer argued that the Assembly elections had vindicated Morrison's 'ballot box and armalite' strategy. This 'principled abstention' policy had its part to play in undermining normalisation

---

[27] LHL NIPC Tom Hartley Collection PH504: Sinn Féin, *Ard Fheis 1982: Clár agus Rúin* (Dublin: Sinn Féin, 1982).

[28] LHL NIPC P2009: Sinn Féin Education Department, *Election Interventions – Historical & Contemporary* (Dublin: Sinn Féin, 1983).

[29] Aidan Hegarty, *Kevin Lynch and the Irish hunger strike* (Belfast: Camlane Press, 2006), p. 50.

[30] LHL NIPC PA0144: H6 resolutions for the Sinn Féin *Ard-Fheis*, 8 October 1981 (1981).

and ending British rule: Sinn Féin received 64,191 votes, yielding five candidates elected, in October 1982.[31] Writing from Leicester Prison in December 1982, Brian Keenan applauded Sinn Féin's electoral victories as propaganda successes representing 'who speaks for the oppressed'. For Keenan, even the most ardent PIRA militarists recognised that the 'savage war of peace' awaited a victorious republican movement: republican elected representatives would form 'an embryo of our future government'.[32]

Republican prisoners regarded electoral campaigns as opportunities to garner international publicity. Exhorting support for Danny Morrison's EEC election campaign in June 1984, Fermanagh PIRA prisoners celebrated the opportunity for Irish nationalists to 'expose repression… on an international platform'.[33] Conor Murphy, imprisoned from 1981 to 1984, remembered that jailed republicans

> would have considered the political struggle, involved in the elections, trying to get as many votes as to demonstrate support for our prisoners, as an important – maybe not as important – but certainly an important new direction to try and generate, you know. It was part of the same struggle as far as we were concerned. So there was quite a degree of overlap between who was involved in the military struggle and who was involved in trying to start to build the political struggle.[34]

For Patrick Magee, popular support for Sinn Féin in the mid-1980s constituted a 'new field' enabling Provisionals 'to demonstrate our power'.[35]

Electoral interventions broadened Sinn Féin representatives' grassroots commitments, chiefly through the party's advice centres. Party workers lobbied the Housing Executive, offered advice on welfare and social security, and compiled evidence of security force 'harassment'. By June 1983, Sinn Féin had opened full-time advice centres in all of the constituencies it had contested in

---

[31] LHL NIPC PA0147: H-block prison comm from PRO for the 1983 hunger strike commemoration (1983).

[32] National Archives of Ireland (hereafter, NAI) DFA/2012/59/1662: Brian Keenan, 'Letters from Irish POWs incarcerated in prisons in England', *P.O.W.: Bulletin of the Irish Political Prisoners in Britain* (December 1982).

[33] Liam Ferguson, Kevin Lynch, Gerry Mulligan, Marcus Murray, Eamon McElroy, James Tierney, Eugene Cosgrove, Republican POW's, H-Block, 'Vote Sinn Fein say prisoners', *Fermanagh Herald*, 9 June 1984.

[34] Conor Murphy interview with Jack Hepworth. Newry, 16 September 2015.

[35] Patrick Magee interview with Jack Hepworth. Belfast, 13 August 2015.

the Assembly elections eight months earlier.[36] A Sinn Féin candidate elected to Belfast City Council in March 1984, Sean McKnight implored constituents to direct 'any problem' to the party's full-time advice centres.[37]

A focal point for civil rights politics with powerful historical connotations for the north's minority community, housing was especially important in Provisional activism. After five candidates were elected to the Assembly in October 1982, Belfast Sinn Féin instituted a Housing Department to engage with the Housing Executive. In each of the ten party branches in west Belfast, at least one member was assigned as a dedicated housing activist.[38] Sinn Féin representatives campaigned for the unpopular Divis and Moyard flats to be demolished, public housing to be allocated fairly, and deficiencies such as subsidence and poor sanitation to be remedied. In 1985, Lagan Valley Sinn Féin representatives Lucy Murray and Damien Gibney were noted for having 'fought and won cases with the local Housing Executive'.[39]

Through the late 1980s and early 1990s, Provisional representatives across the north strengthened their ties with embattled working-class communities. Support for the underprivileged dovetailed with wider anti-authority sentiment. In 1987, as chair of the local Sinn Féin *cumann*, P. J. Branley of Ballyshannon, County Donegal attacked councillors who advocated disconnecting water supplies: these 'anti-working class' practices deprived 'already hard-pressed residents'.[40] Several years later, the PIRA in Derry City went further, threatening Northern Ireland Electricity's management after Bogside defaulters' supplies were cut. The movement's distaste for 'arrogant and insensitive' businesspeople combined with solidarity with 'people living in nationalist areas who are already the victims of economic and social deprivation'.[41]

Sinn Féin's electoral experimentation from the early 1980s attracted critical support from what remained of PD. PD activists' habitually criticised the Provisionals for prioritising an 'elitist' armed campaign above building a revolutionary workers' programme. Yet Sinn Féin's successes in the Assembly elections of October 1982 encouraged several PD cadres to advocate cautious support for Sinn Féin candidates in the following year's general election. Provisional representatives' growing grassroots activism appealed to PD

---

[36] EHI: 'Sinn Fein: the voice of principled leadership' (Dungannon: Sinn Féin Election Headquarters, 1983).

[37] EHI: Sean McKnight, Belfast City Council Election (22 March 1984). Election flyer: *For an uncompromising stand on the national question.*

[38] Sean Delaney, 'Sinn Féin and Housing in Belfast: Building community confidence', *Iris*, 9 (December 1984).

[39] EHI: *Lagan Valley Bulletin*, 3 (April 1985).

[40] 'Question to Councillor on service charges', *Donegal Democrat*, 20 November 1987.

[41] 'Mayor lashes "gangsterism"', *Derry Journal*, 17 February 1993.

members' conceptions of mass agitation. In November 1984, assessing changes in Provisional tactics, leading PD theoretician James Gallagher welcomed the Provisionals' 'turn to the left'.[42]

PD's qualified support for the Provisionals in the mid-1980s reflected an essentially pragmatic position. In June 1984, the editorial board on PD's newspaper admitted that a 'small party of revolutionary marxists' lacked the 'means' to stand candidates in elections. Accentuating Provisionals' community activism and leftist rhetoric, PD's leaders determined to support Sinn Féin election candidates, pointing to republican militants' 'potential' to build a revolutionary movement.[43] PD's National Committee exhorted Provisionals to 'turn their campaign outwards along the lines of the H-Block movement to gain the attention of the mass of organised workers'.[44]

However, PD's orientation towards the Provisionals remained uneasy. Radicals suspected that the Provisionals' socialism was superficial. Prioritising the PIRA's campaign, the argument ran, would continue to marginalise political development in a putative mass movement. In 1983, PD's official position pressed Provisionals to 'go beyond the rhetoric about a Socialist Republic', mobilise through trades unions, and 'state clearly their strategy'.[45] A book reviewer in *An Reabhloid* in 1984 lauded Sinn Féin's electoral successes, but argued that the Provisionals must prioritise broadening their base.[46]

Present-day oral histories illuminate how republicans interpreted electoralism, and the enduring contentiousness of this tactical innovation. As Michael Frisch argued, oral histories chart the complex interaction between experience and memory: in retrospect, individual recollection negotiates its social context and

---

[42] Irish Left Archive (hereafter, ILA): James Gallagher, *Our Orientation to the Republican Movement* (10 November 1984).

[43] That the editorial anticipated 'political sectarians in the socialist movement' insisting that Sinn Féin was 'not a workers [*sic*] party' suggests internal dissent against this support for the Provisionals. For some of PD's former '68ers, the affinity with the Provisionals in the mid-1980s caused alarm. Writing in 1991, former PD member Clara Connolly rued erstwhile comrades moving 'into line (some uneasily) behind the "men of war"'. 'Fighting Back: The P.D. View', *An Reabhloid: Journal of Peoples Democracy*, Volume 1, Number 1 (June 1984); Clara Connolly, 'Communalism: obstacle to social change', *Women: A Cultural Review*, 2 (1991), p. 217.

[44] 'EEC elections', *Socialist Republic: Paper of Peoples' Democracy*, Volume 7, Number 2 (April 1984).

[45] 'Why socialists should vote Sinn Fein', *Socialist Republic: Paper of Peoples' Democracy*, Volume 6, Number 3 (June 1983).

[46] 'Book Reviews', *An Reabhloid: Journal of Peoples Democracy*, Volume 1, Number 1 (June 1984). Belfast PD councillor John McAnulty, a senior member of the organisation, edited book reviews in *An Reabhloid*.

inevitably partakes in present-day discourse.[47] 'Dissident' republicans trace to the early 1980s processes they repudiate in Sinn Féin today. Released from prison in 1982, Nuala Perry worked in Sinn Féin's new Housing Department. A founding member of socialist-republican party Saoradh and a staunch critic of Sinn Féin, Perry reflected in 2016 on an 'election stunt to get the people on our side' in advance of the general election of 1983, when Gerry Adams won West Belfast.

> People were coming in[to the Department] with their problems – I mean, I was still a member of the IRA – but people were coming in and talking to you about problems with their housing. We were saying, *yes, we'll do this, we'll do that.* But to me it was being filed under, *let's pretend,* and *we don't want anything to do with that.* And I found that a very difficult thing to do.[48]

Francie McGuigan recalled an authoritarian tendency in the Provisional leadership's tactical innovation at the Sinn Féin *ard fheis* of 1986: 'Most of the people in Belfast, and I assume in other parts, were ordered which way to vote.'[49] Similarly, Gerry McKerr, formerly a senior Provisional in Lurgan, County Armagh, recalled being denied delegate status to the *ard fheis.* He scorned the suggestion that prisoners genuinely supported the Adams's leadership's motion: McKerr claimed that jailed volunteers had been told that early releases awaited if they supported dropping abstentionism.[50] Interviewed during the peace process, veteran Belfast republican Billy McKee – who had argued for retaining abstentionism a decade earlier – remembered the 1986 vote as a dismal milestone in the Provisionals' decline:

> The political group were taking over the IRA. And it was quite obvious – when an army is at war, if it starts talking peace, the one side that starts talking peace – it's not in good straits.[51]

By contrast, Conor Murphy, a former prisoner who became a Sinn Féin councillor in 1989 and remains an elected representative today, narrates electoral

[47] Michael Frisch, 'Oral history and *Hard Times*: a review essay', *Oral History Review,* 7 (1979), pp. 70–79.
[48] Nuala Perry interview with Jack Hepworth. Belfast, 30 March 2016.
[49] Francie McGuigan interview with Jack Hepworth. Belfast, 6 December 2017.
[50] Gerry McKerr interview with Marisa McGlinchey. Marisa McGlinchey, *Unfinished business: the politics of 'dissident' Irish republicanism* (Manchester: Manchester University Press, 2019), p. 196.
[51] Billy McKee interview with Peter Taylor, 1997. *Provos: The IRA and Sinn Féin – Episode 3: Secret War* (BBC1, broadcast 7 October 1997).

experimentation from the early 1980s as an ongoing opportunity for mass mobilisation, flourishing from the grassroots:

> Quite a lot of people, apart from the thinkers at the top of the movement, quite a lot of ordinary volunteers when they hadn't been through the prison system where there was a sort of form of internal education, hadn't probably delved [into politics] too much, it was more an instinctive, you know, nationalist reaction rather than a thought-through political: *we want to change the nature of the state and here's what we want to put in its place.* But as the political started to develop, probably around the time of the hunger strikes, and a realisation that you could mobilise people, and you could mobilise that as part, as a parallel, if you like, to the armed struggle, then the thinking started a lot: *if we do mobilise people, if we can create political change, what sort of society do we want?*[52]

By the mid-1980s, Provisional republicans overwhelmingly identified the movement's leadership, especially Danny Morrison, as the pioneers of electoralism. Adams and his allies enjoyed considerable support and authority, especially among northern republicans. The *ard fheis* of 1985 passed motions congratulating the *Ard Comhairle* (party executive) for the tactic, after Morrison spoke extensively on 'electoral intervention and the armed struggle'. Sinn Féin's executive was appointed to determine future approaches to elections.[53]

Debates about tactics and their implications for overall strategy became more fractious through 1985 and 1986, during debates about Sinn Féin's abstentionist policy regarding Leinster House. PIRA prisoners were among the most prominent advocates for tactical innovation. Volunteers in English jails, who had been arrested operating outside Ireland, were perhaps less inclined to orthodoxies, and were especially vocal in 1985 and 1986. Incarcerated on the Isle of Wight, John Hayes differed from the anti-abstentionist majority among republican prisoners in English jails. In a letter to a rival republican party in 1987, Hayes denounced the Provisionals' decision as 'a lie and a betrayal', reducing the PIRA to a 'phantom army'.[54]

Several PIRA prisoners had written from English jails in 1985, exhorting the *ard fheis* to consider abstentionism a dispensable tactic.[55] The following year, high-profile republicans in Leicester Prison including Patrick Magee

---

[52] Conor Murphy interview with Jack Hepworth. Newry, 16 September 2015.
[53] 'IRA man at 'secret' session', *The Irish Press*, 4 November 1985.
[54] 'Truly revolutionary', *Republican Bulletin: Iris Na Poblachta*, 5 (April 1987).
[55] 'Electoral strategy', *An Phoblacht/Republican News*, 7 November 1985.

and Brian Keenan urged the Provisionals to end Dáil abstentionism and build support in the Republic 'through the ballot box'.[56] Brendan Dowd, described in 1976 as the PIRA's chief organiser in Britain, wrote from Frankland Prison to congratulate the movement for the 'courageous' decision to end abstentionism in 1986.[57] Additionally, PIRA prisoners from County Kerry including Martin Ferris and Michael Browne, arrested for transatlantic gun-running, immediately stated their support for the *ard fheis* decision.[58]

Group solidarity and the importance of collective identity in a large prison community likely discouraged PIRA prisoners in Long Kesh from overtly identifying with another organisation, even if privately sceptical about Provisional policy. Few prisoners publicly switched allegiance to Ruairí Ó Brádaigh's pro-abstentionist RSF. In January 1987, just three Long Kesh prisoners identified with RSF on 'principles', and admitted they would 'not identify totally with your politics'.[59] By October 1987, only 11 republican prisoners sent greetings to Ó Brádaigh's organisation.[60] However, tense undercurrents permeated Long Kesh after the vote, as Don Browne recalls:

> 1986, I was in the H-blocks, and the IRA started to split, with Republican Sinn Féin, and that started to come into the jail, because the IRA were running the jail, and I remember others objecting to it. **Objecting to dropping abstentionism?** Oh aye. Serious stuff. So by 1990, '91, '92, it was physical fights. Most people don't like to talk about it. But then, if I didn't like you, I would sabotage your cell.[61]

Activist trajectories and opinions of the leadership informed individuals' positions. Pat Doherty from County Donegal, an ally of the Adams leadership who served as Sinn Féin vice-president from 1989, noted Sinn Féin's electoral success in local elections in Northern Ireland in 1985. Doherty's *ard fheis* speech in 1986 lauded Adams and McGuinness, who had 'started to pick up the pieces' after 'the disastrous 1975 truce'. Doherty rebuked republicans 'engaging in public abuse and personalised attacks on the leadership'.[62] South Armagh Sinn Féin

[56] Richard Ford, 'Jailed IRA men back Provos' drive for Dail', *The Times*, 1 September 1986.

[57] Brendan Dowd, 'A message from Frankland', *Kerryman*, 5 December 1986.

[58] Stephen O'Brien, 'Brothers on opposing sides as Provos split', *Kerryman*, 28 November 1986.

[59] 'Long Kesh support', *Republican Bulletin: Iris Na Poblachta*, 3 (January–February 1987).

[60] 'Faoi ghlas ag gallaibh', *Saoirse*, 6 (October 1987).

[61] Don Browne interview with Jack Hepworth. Derry, 12 December 2017.

[62] LHL NIPC P2275: *The Politics of Revolution: The Main Speeches and Debates from the*

councillor Jim McAllister was another prominent *Ard Comhairle* advocate for dropping abstentionism.[63]

Republicans distant from Adams's presidency, including those former leaders displaced by the Adamsites' ascendancy, interpreted abstentionism as immutable. For these abstentionists who might be termed 'orthodox' – guided principally by ideas of historical legitimacy – entering Leinster House betrayed republican catechism. At the *ard fheis* of 1985, former Sinn Féin president Ruairí Ó Brádaigh's proposed that Sinn Féin unilaterally declare an all-Ireland assembly modelled on the 1921 Dáil. Several *Ard Comhairle* members, including Morrison, spoke against the 'impracticable' and 'unworkable' motion, and it was defeated.[64]

Historical precedent was paramount among resolute anti-abstentionists. Tom Maguire, the last survivor of the 1921 Dáil and a veteran of the War of Independence, rebuked the Provisionals in November 1986 for accepting 'the Leinster House partition parliament'.[65] At the RSF *ard fheis* of 1989, the *cumann* from Ballyshannon, County Donegal branded proposals for a federal Ireland a retreat from reconvening the Second Dáil of 1921.[66] For Dáithí Ó Conaill, formerly PIRA Chief of Staff, the Provisionals' 'naïve belief in the power of parliamentary politics' violated 'fundamental principles'. Ó Conaill ascribed a series of miscalculations to the Provisional leadership that had superseded himself and Ó Brádaigh: the 'long war' strategists around Adams were charged with lacking 'single-mindedness'.[67]

1986 Sinn Fein Ard-Fheis, *Including the Presidential Address of Gerry Adams* (Belfast & Dublin: Republican Publications, 1986).

[63] 'Abstentionism: an historic decision', *An Phoblacht/Republican News*, 6 November 1986.

[64] NAI TSCH/2015/89/61: Declan O'Donovan & Peter McIvor, 'Sinn Fein *ard fheis*, 2–3 November 1985' (12 November 1985). Marisa McGlinchey has highlighted how contested perceptions of republican legitimacy divided networks. McGlinchey's recent interview with Danny Morrison sharply summarises the argument, with an intergenerational inflection: 'Even on his death bed Ruairí [Ó Brádaigh] still believed that the Continuity IRA was the Government of Ireland, which is ridiculous... I don't believe that my authority to fight the Brits came from some seventy-nine-year-old man who was the last surviving member of the Second Dáil... I mean it's just nonsense. To me our mandate was the sense of oppression, physically, that we lived under, the conditions that we lived under and they and they alone justified armed struggle and that was our position. Not this other theological position which a lot of the older people were burdened with.' Marisa McGlinchey interview with Danny Morrison. McGlinchey, *Unfinished business*, 129.

[65] 'Sinn Fein split causing rifts', *Offaly Independent*, 21 November 1986.

[66] 'Éire Nua', *Saoirse*, 31 (November 1989).

[67] 'Limerick remembers Seán Sabhat', *Republican Bulletin: Iris Na Poblachta*, 4 (March 1987).

Sinn Féin's *ard fheis* of 1985 demonstrated how place and milieu informed intra-republican perspectives. Party branches from disparate areas of the Republic, unconnected to the Adams leadership, implored the conference to maintain abstentionism, and in some cases even to abandon electoralism altogether.[68] The debate did not produce clear-cut binaries: even veterans who accentuated military primacy could countenance taking seats in Leinster House if doing so meant 'winning the peace' in a future united Ireland. Joe Cahill, a leading Belfast republican since the 1930s, supported dropping abstentionism in 1986, 'confident' that by the next election, 'the freedom fighters of the IRA will have forced the Brits to the conference table'.[69] A close confidante of Monaghan PIRA commander Jim Lynagh recalled being surprised when Lynagh greeted him at the 1986 *ard fheis* declaring the need to 'move with the times' and drop abstentionism.[70]

Abstentionism did not crystallise straightforward geographical patterns of allegiance: commitment to abstentionism was not the preserve of southern republicans. As Robert W. White has noted, republican veterans of the 1940s close to Gerry Adams's leadership, including Joe Cahill and J. B. O'Hagan, supported the *ard fheis* decision.[71] Networks around tactical innovators in Sinn Féin's highest ranks perceived abstentionism obstructing efforts to broaden the base. Sinn Féin national organiser Caoimhghín Ó Caoláin from County Monaghan and vice-president John Joe McGirl from County Leitrim highlighted the party's poor electoral performance (no seats, and just 46,931 first-preference votes – 3.3 per cent of those cast) in the Republic's local elections in June 1985. For Ó Caoláin and McGirl, deficient organisation in the Republic was hampering Sinn Féin's vote. Offering local representation in the south could attract support, especially among young people who might sympathise with the party's social and economic policies, if not the armed struggle.[72]

In the Provisionals' middle ranks, opposing the *ard fheis* vote in 1986 did not automatically mean rupture with the movement. In County Donegal, for example, four Sinn Féin branches and three party delegates voted to retain

---

[68] LHL NIPC P1656A: Sinn Féin, *Ard Fheis '85: Clár agus Rúin* (Dublin: Sinn Féin, 1985).

[69] LHL NIPC P2275: *The Politics of Revolution: The Main Speeches and Debates from the 1986 Sinn Fein Ard-Fheis, Including the Presidential Address of Gerry Adams* (Belfast & Dublin: Republican Publications, 1986).

[70] 'Jim Lynagh Part 2: Loughgall Martyrs 20th Anniversary' (2008). Available at https://www.youtube.com/watch?v=NbXqC8Vm8x0 (accessed 14 March 2018).

[71] Robert W. White, *Out of the ashes: an oral history of the Provisional Irish republican movement* (Newbridge: Merrion, 2017), p. 222.

[72] 'Standing ovation for McGirl at Sinn Fein *ard fheis*', *Leitrim Observer*, 8 November 1986.

abstentionism. When the vote was lost, all three remained active party members.[73] Sinn Féin councillor Lughaidh Mac Giolla Bhrighde, an abstentionist from south Derry, told the *ard fheis* there should be no split: 'No-one is any more or less a republican according to their position on Leinster House.'[74]

Nuala Perry candidly highlights a less tangible, but nevertheless significant, dimension of debates concerning abstentionism:

> You see, most of us, ordinary volunteers on the streets, we couldn't have told you, we didn't care less about what was going on at the *ard fheis* in '86. We weren't really interested about what Ruairí Ó Brádaigh was saying or what Ruairí Ó Brádaigh wasn't saying. When I look back on it, it was profound.[75]

For many activists amid a guerrilla war, Sinn Féin's strategic introspection seemed distant, as Conor Murphy recalls:

> When you're outside, involved in the movement like that, you tend to be doing what you're doing and your part without – there's not – there's no away days, think-ins, or very little opportunity for them. It's just too dangerous. It wasn't hierarchical in that there was a chief and they just decided what to do; there was a structure where people got dialogues and strategies in terms of tactics. But you probably had less time to do that [outside prison] because you were evading the law and living hand to mouth, and, you know, less time for socialising with people than you would have had in jail where you had more time for sit-down dialogue and discussion. So the jail acted almost as the think-tank for the movement on the outside. Quite a lot of the ideas and thinking and discussions would have come back out from there. It was like a ready-made source for a think-tank.[76]

For republicans whose organisational allegiances have since changed, hindsight confers amplified importance on seminal moments. Reflections convey the impression that today's constitutionalism originated by stealth decades ago:

---

[73] 'Split in Donegal Sinn Féin after *ard fheis* decision', *Donegal Democrat*, 7 November 1986; 'Abstentionist Sinn Fein group to organise here', *Derry People & Donegal News*, 8 November 1986.

[74] 'Abstentionism: an historic decision', *An Phoblacht/Republican News*, 6 November 1986.

[75] Nuala Perry interview with Jack Hepworth. Belfast, 6 December 2017.

[76] Conor Murphy interview with Jack Hepworth. Newry, 16 September 2015.

I felt then [1986] that the ones who walked were wrong. I thought, *they're splitting the republican movement, we should be trying to revamp and regain momentum and we have split.* Now I know the people who split, split for all the right reasons! But at that time… you had people who were saying, *Well, the people who fought the war are still fighting the war, and still on board.* But we were too naïve to see that what was being played out at that point was basically a game of very bad brinkmanship. The people who walked had their eye on the ball. They knew where it was all going. It was a strange, strange time.[77]

Ceasefires and peace negotiations, *c.*1992–*c.*1998

In the belief that the Provisionals constituted the driving force in a campaign that was broadening and nearing a successful conclusion, PIRA prisoners were among the most prominent advocates for peace initiatives in the 1990s. In the early 1980s, PIRA prisoners supported electoral interventions to destroy the British initiatives of Ulsterisation and normalisation. By contrast, in the early 1990s, prisoners understood Sinn Féin's electoralism as a constructive step towards political dialogue facilitating a peaceful, united Ireland. Anticipating the general election of April 1992, County Tyrone PIRA prisoner Patrick Grimes lauded Sinn Féin as a 'party for change'.[78] In May 1993, ahead of local elections, three County Fermanagh Provisionals wrote from prison urging support for the party's 'new radical constructive initiative… A vote for Sinn Fein is a vote for peace with justice, equality and democracy'.[79] Pragmatists perceived the ceasefire as a step towards victory – and, if this did not succeed, the PIRA could return to war.

Sinn Féin leaders shaped peace initiatives in the 1990s, but prisoners were included in internal discussions. Through December 1993 and January 1994, volunteers jailed in Long Kesh debated the Downing Street Declaration, before reporting to their commanding officers in February 1994. Although many prisoners considered the Provisionals in a commanding position to attain Irish unity at the climax of their 'long war', they were highly suspicious of John Major's government. The failure of talks in 1972 and 1976 informed widespread republican suspicion of the British government. Writing from H3 in February

---

[77] Nuala Perry interview with Jack Hepworth. Belfast, 30 March 2016.
[78] Patrick Grimes, H4 Long Kesh, 'Peace is central to SF manifesto and how to achieve it', *The Irish Press*, 9 April 1992.
[79] Seán Lynch, Barry Murray, & Gerard Maguire, 'Republican prisoners urge vote for local SF candidates', *Fermanagh Herald*, 8 May 1993.

1994 to explain why he and his comrades had rejected the Declaration's 'masterpiece of ambiguity', Morrison also recalled British 'deception' during the hunger strike of 1980.[80]

Speaking from his cell in Long Kesh, PIRA Officer Commanding (OC) Seán Lynch unequivocally rejected the Declaration: 'Exactly what do they mean, the British government mean: *two acts of self-determination*? It's not acceptable.'[81] Morrison combined scepticism about the Declaration with enduring optimism about the struggle more broadly. Interviewed by Peter Taylor, Morrison rejected the suggestion that republicans could not win:

> I do not draw that conclusion from it. The conclusion I draw is it's going to go on longer... but at the end of it, Britain can go home proudly, saying we settled that honourably, or Britain can go home with its tail between its legs.[82]

Believing that the movement's military prowess was at an all-time zenith, a majority of PIRA prisoners were prepared at least to explore the peace initiative. Writing in 1994, Belfast Provisional Gerard Hodgins argued that a peaceful united Ireland was 'attainable' and unionist domination would 'never be imposed upon us again', provided the British ceased their 'intransigence' and cooperated with republican initiatives.[83] By December 1993, John Pickering from Belfast had spent 17 years in prison. Addressing a public meeting during Christmas parole, Pickering said of the Downing Street Declaration:

> Times change, people change. You can't just have war, war, war. The document looks like nothing, but it would be foolish to turn away.[84]

As a corollary of their considerable confidence, prisoners argued that Sinn Féin should repudiate the Declaration since the Provisionals could levy further pressure and receive a 'better opportunity' in future.[85] The prisoners insisted that

---

[80] 'Morrison: Why we haven't said "Yes"', *The Irish Press*, 25 February 1994.

[81] Seán Lynch quoted in *Provos: The IRA and Sinn Fein – Episode 4: Endgame* (BBC1, broadcast 14 October 1997).

[82] Danny Morrison quoted in *Provos: The IRA and Sinn Fein – Episode 4: Endgame* (BBC1, broadcast 14 October 1997).

[83] Gerard Hodgins, 'Past wrongs and healing truths', *The Captive Voice/An Glór Gafa*, Volume 6, Number 1 (Summer 1994).

[84] Carl Shoettler, 'Parolees from IRA talk peace', *Baltimore Sun*, 1 January 1994.

[85] Republican POWs, H-Blocks, 'Prisoners' address to Sinn Féin *ard fheis*', *The Captive Voice/An Glór Gafa*, Volume 6, Number 1 (Summer 1994).

the position was no 'golden opportunity' or 'last chance' for peace.[86] Ignacio Sànchez-Cuenca has argued retrospectively that the PIRA could no longer sustain its guerrilla campaign by the turn of the 1990s, but crucially, this did not define prisoners' outlook in 1994.[87]

In their statement to the *ard fheis* of February 1994, PIRA prisoners remained unconvinced by the Declaration's claim that Westminster would facilitate Irish unity if a majority within Northern Ireland voted for it. However, the prisoners interpreted their own leadership as the proactive authors of these initiatives for 'peace and unity'. It was incumbent upon Major's government to stop attempting to 'thwart' the progression towards a united Ireland, and instead 'join the ranks of the peace-makers' and 'persuade unionists to consider visualising an accommodation with the rest of the people of Ireland'.[88] In Portlaoise Prison in May 1994, senior republican Martin Ferris similarly framed the peace process as a republican initiative, downstream of Sinn Féin's 1986 *ard fheis*, policy document *Scenario for Peace* (1987), and talks with the SDLP (1988).[89]

Prisoners' responses to the PIRA ceasefire of 31 August 1994 reflected strong support for a leadership they considered the architects of the peace process. Discussing the ceasefire late in 1994, Long Kesh Provisionals praised the PIRA leadership's 'courageous initiative' and regarded British withdrawal as 'inevitable': the British government would help persuade the unionist community to accept all-Ireland self-determination.[90] Martin Ferris, released just weeks after the ceasefire, reported from his contacts with republicans in jails across Britain and Ireland that they were 'totally behind the ceasefire' and anticipating decommissioning in a united Ireland.[91]

Having spent three years as PIRA OC in Portlaoise, Ferris was a high-profile supporter of the Adams leadership, and his claims should be treated with caution accordingly. However, his testimony reveals that such conversations were happening in jails, prompted by highly regarded conduits. Republican optimism

---

[86] 'H-Block submission to Sinn Féin peace commission', *The Captive Voice/An Glór Gafa*, Volume 6, Number 1 (Summer 1994).

[87] Ignacio Sànchez-Cuenca, 'The dynamics of nationalist terrorism: ETA and the IRA', *Terrorism and Political Violence*, 19 (2007), p. 297.

[88] 'H-Block Submission to Sinn Féin Peace Commission', *The Captive Voice/An Glór Gafa*, Volume 6, Number 1 (Summer 1994).

[89] ILA: PRO Republican POWs, Portlaoise Prison, *Volunteer Jim Lynagh Lecture 1994: Peace strategy debated in Portlaoise*.

[90] Statement issued by prisoners in Sinn Féin's H-Block *cumann* (9 December 1994). Copy in author's possession.

[91] Conor Keane, 'Surrender of IRA arms a matter for talks says Marita Ann gunrunner', *Kerryman*, 16 September 1994.

was evident in west Belfast, too, where republican motorcades and tricolours greeted the ceasefire. The mothers of two PIRA prisoners joined crowds on the Andersonstown Road and looked forward to their relatives' early release from Long Kesh: 'I thought I'd never see the day. We've won and we'll go down in history.'[92]

As the Provisionals debated the Downing Street Declaration, INLA Chief of Staff Hugh Torney admitted that his organisation's future was uncertain. The future of the INLA campaign, Torney said, depended on 'the prevailing conditions' whenever the Provisionals announced their position on the Declaration. In view of the uncertainty, the INLA leader proposed to build 'a disciplined armed force which will always be available to strike at the opportune moment'.[93] Yet the strategic dilemmas inherent in this holding position were increasingly apparent after the PIRA ceasefire of August 1994. Interviewed in December 1995, Gino Gallagher, the IRSP's prisons spokesman said the INLA 'remain to be convinced of benefits of the peace process… in fact the climate today is much worse today than in September 1994'.[94]

Today, retrospectives outside the Provisional movement doubt the sincerity of the Provisionals' internal consultation. Don Browne, a former INLA prisoner subject to the PIRA's command structure from the late 1980s

> noticed, at the end of every conversation, it was, *we'll send this stuff forward, to the IRA, and ultimately the IRA will make a decision based on these thoughts*. But there was nobody ever seeing the votes.[95]

Prominent County Kerry republican Richard Behal had left the Provisionals to form RSF in 1986. Behal later alleged that a senior PIRA commander told him that the ceasefire of 1994 had been agreed on the condition that the British would withdraw within six months.[96]

Outside prison, senior Provisionals reassured veterans in 1994 that the movement was approaching a historic breakthrough. The PIRA's reputed Chief of Staff at this juncture, County Tyrone-born Kevin McKenna, crucially gave the ceasefire his blessing.[97] Longstanding comradeship between members of a guerrilla movement underwrote difficult conversations. Albert Allen reflects 'no

---

[92] 'Ceasefire', *Andersonstown News*, 3 September 1994.

[93] 'The INLA agenda…', *Belfast Telegraph*, 8 June 1994.

[94] Brendan Anderson, 'IRSP back in running with "distinct" brand of politics', *The Irish News*, 18 December 1995.

[95] Don Browne interview with Jack Hepworth. Derry, 12 December 2017.

[96] McGlinchey, *Unfinished business*, 71.

[97] Connla Young, 'One of the IRA's most influential leaders during the Troubles has died', *The Irish News*, 26 June 2019.

doubt about it, I trusted these people'.[98] Francie McGuigan remembers being told that the cessation was

> an opportunity for peace, that was the way you were supposed to look at it. *We're getting the victory we fought for* – that's what we were told.[99]

It is no coincidence that the PIRA prisoners who were mostly overtly hostile to the Sinn Féin leadership's moves in the mid-1990s were a small group of volunteers incarcerated away from larger republican networks, power structures, and celebrations in the north. In a statement to Sinn Féin's special conference on the peace process in September 1995, republican prisoners in the high-security unit at Belmarsh in south-east London criticised Adams and McGuinness for treating the British government as an 'honest broker' and 'accepting' its 'bona fides'. Detached from the cautious optimism of most republican inmates in Ireland, the Belmarsh republicans regarded the previous year's ceasefire as a major misstep:

> In retrospect, it is clear that the leadership should have sought clear guarantees from Britain before agreeing to a ceasefire.[100]

A generational dimension influenced subjectivities in 1994, too. Especially for a younger generation of republican prisoners, born in the 1970s and unburdened with memories of unsuccessful ceasefires in 1972 and 1975, 1994 seemed a relief from the conflict that had dominated their youth. Francie McGoldrick, a PIRA prisoner born in 1973 in Lisnaskea, County Fermanagh, remembered that in August 1994 he and his fiancée were 'overjoyed at the IRA initiative to push forward the political situation… neither of us had witnessed peace in our young lives'.[101]

South Africa's contemporary peace process was a major influence for both Gerry Adams, as Kevin Bean has argued,[102] and Seán Lynch, PIRA OC in Long Kesh from 1993. Writing in *An Phoblacht/Republican News* in June 1995, Adams hoped to emulate the African National Congress (ANC):

---

[98] Albert Allen interview with Jack Hepworth. Belfast, 13 December 2017.
[99] Francie McGuigan interview with Jack Hepworth. Belfast, 6 December 2017.
[100] 'Weapons in the "peace process"', *Living Marxism*, 89 (April 1996).
[101] Francie McGoldrick quoted in *Journal of Prisoners on Prisons*, 7 (1996–1997), p. 11.
[102] Kevin Bean, *The new politics of Sinn Féin* (Liverpool: Liverpool University Press, 2007), p. 148.

> While there are obvious difficulties between Ireland and South Africa, there are also similarities. I hope to have the opportunity to learn from their experience of developing a peace process and to translate their efforts into the Irish peace process.[103]

Lynch, from County Fermanagh, was the first OC since Bobby Sands to enjoy access to all republican prison wings.[104] Identifying the Provisionals' struggle with the ANC's long campaign against the apartheid regime, Lynch supported the Sinn Féin leadership's initiatives before and after the ceasefires of 1994 and 1997. Early in his tenure as OC, Lynch lauded Adams as a 'real peace-maker' for engaging with SDLP leader John Hume.[105] After reading Mandela's autobiography, Lynch saw the Provisionals following 'lessons' from ANC strategy, declaring a ceasefire in 'good faith'. Lynch noted that the ANC had deployed a 'mass action strategy' in its community bases while securing F. W. de Klerk's agreement in February 1992 for political prisoners to be released and liberation groups to be de-proscribed. Excited by the South African precedent, Lynch could envisage in negotiations a 'giant step forward'.[106]

Lynch derived confidence from the South African situation, considering the 'universal experience of people imprisoned for their political beliefs' and anticipating Long Kesh becoming, like Robben Island, a museum.[107] Lynch's international outlook and confidence in this new tactical flexibility reflected Adams's portrayal of Provisional strategy. Shortly after the ceasefire of August 1994, the Sinn Féin president said that since the mid-1980s he had identified the

---

[103] Quoted in Michael Cox, 'Bringing in the "international": the IRA ceasefire and the end of the Cold War', *International Affairs*, 73 (1997), p. 678.

[104] Peter Foster, 'Inside story of the Maze, a jail like no other', *Daily Telegraph*, 28 July 2000.

[105] Sean Lynch, H-Block 5 (A Wing), Long Kesh, 'Prisoners' support for Adams/Hume talks', *Fermanagh Herald*, 11 December 1993.

[106] Seán Lynch, 'Lessons of a peace process', *The Captive Voice/An Glór Gafa*, Volume 8, Number 1 (Winter 1996).

[107] Seán Lynch, 'Jail Struggle – a universal experience', *The Captive Voice/An Glór Gafa*, Volume 8, Number 2 (Spring 1997). Lynch's hopes for Long Kesh proved prophetic. HMP Maze closed in 2000, and Maze Long Kesh Development Corporation reported that 450,000 people visited the site for events and tours from 2012 to 2018: 'A site once associated with conflict has the potential to become a transformational project of international significance.' In May 2013, the Corporation envisaged the site becoming a 'landmark development of local, regional and international significance'. See http://mazelongkesh.com/ (accessed 10 April 2018).

international dimension as a very important one. The experience of South Africa, the Palestinian situation and Central America is that when there is a stalemate, an outside element can in fact move the situation on.[108]

For Adams, Irish-America and the European Union provided the external impetus. For Lynch, South Africa provided the inspiration.

However, during the 18-month ceasefire from August 1994 to February 1996, many PIRA prisoners became increasingly frustrated with the British government's response. Writing to *An Phoblacht/Republican News* after the PIRA ceasefire ended with the Docklands bomb on 9 February 1996, prisoner Tarlac Ó Conghalaigh from Armagh attempted to rally his comrades, who had 'come down' after the initial excitement of the ceasefire.[109]

Republicans who understood Sinn Féin as the instigators of the peace process identified Major's government as spoilers and stallers, and reminded their comrades that the ceasefire was not sacrosanct: armed struggle remained viable. In Maghaberry, one year after the cessation, PIRA OC Rosaleen McCorley asked: 'What have we gained?' Ailish Carroll doubted Major's 'sincerity' and argued the British government remained committed to 'breaking forever the republican movement'.[110] By July 1995, the government's prevarication had angered County Tyrone PIRA prisoners, who reiterated that their struggle would 'never be over until the Brits leave Irish soil for good'. Unless Major showed greater 'imagination', the military campaign would resume.[111]

After the ceasefire of August 1994, prison amnesties were unsurprisingly of interest to those PIRA prisoners across Northern Ireland who studied global conflict transformations. In April 1995, PIRA prisoners from south Armagh looked to Palestine and South Africa, where prisoner releases had been 'essential' to peace processes, and lamented republicans' 'unresolved' position. Calling for Major's government to respond positively to the 'courageous' ceasefire, 18 PIRA

---

[108] '"Sooner rather than later": Gerry Adams speaks out', *Andersonstown News*, 24 September 1994.

[109] Letter from Tarlac Ó Conghalaigh, IRA prisoner, H5, to *An Phoblacht/Republican News*, 28 March 1996.

[110] Rosaleen McCorley interview with Philomena Gallagher and Ailish Carroll interview with Philomena Gallagher. Maghaberry, 1995. Philomena Gallagher, 'An oral history of the imprisoned female Irish Republican Army', MPhil (Trinity College Dublin, 1995), p. 48.

[111] Tyrone P.O.W.'s Long Kesh, *Martin Hurson* (13 July 1995). Copy in author's possession.

prisoners from Belfast issued a statement proposing that immediate releases should be a precondition of the peace process.[112]

Established in December 1994, Sinn Féin's ginger group Saoirse campaigned on prisoners' behalf. Noting that the ANC had negotiated early releases for its prisoners, Saoirse organised local groups, harnessing prisoners' relatives and recently released PIRA volunteers. Saoirse's attempts at mass mobilisation beyond the republican core recalled the umbrella NHBAC during the anti-criminalisation campaigns of the late 1970s and early 1980s. Newry PIRA prisoner Sean Mathers hoped Saoirse could imitate the mass mobilisation of the hunger strike campaigns. Mathers implored clergy, community groups, trades unions, and students to publicise prisoners' 'plight' and engage 'world-wide attention'.[113]

Sinn Féin's new departure triggered greater unease among PIRA prisoners after the party leadership accepted the Mitchell Principles in May 1996. Named after United States Senator George Mitchell, the Principles stipulated rules for all political parties engaging in peace talks. Parties were compelled to disband paramilitary organisations and engage solely in democratic politics. In May 1996, one month before all-party talks, Sinn Féin's leadership announced that it would cooperate.[114] Some prisoners in Long Kesh tolerated this position as necessary pragmatism to ensure a seat at the negotiating table. Others worried that Sinn Féin was 'deliberately distancing itself' from the armed struggle.[115]

Yet even rumours of expedited releases did not render all prisoners uncritical advocates of the peace process. Shortly after being released from Maghaberry, Mary Ellen Campbell addressed Sinn Féin *ard fheis* of March 1996. When the party's County Leitrim executive proposed to make a prison amnesty the priority of the peace process, Campbell opposed the motion. The women in Maghaberry, Campbell argued, understood that their circumstances were only one component in a broader process.[116] Even Liam Ó Duibhir, a PIRA prisoner serving a 30-year sentence in Belmarsh in a Special Security Unit, isolated for

---

[112] 'Statement from the S. Armagh/Newry Republican POW's, Long Kesh' (1995); 'Statement from the S/Strand, Markets & L/Ormeau Rd Republican Prisoners' (1995). Copies in author's possession.

[113] Sean Mathers, H4B Long Kesh, *Saoirse* (1995). Copy in author's possession.

[114] David McKittrick, 'Sinn Fein ready to accept Mitchell principles', *The Independent*, 20 May 1996.

[115] *Mitchell Principles* (1996). 'The following report, compiled from a series of discussions among the membership of the H-Block Sinn Féin Cumann (June 1996), outlines our position in relation to the announcement by the Sinn Féin leadership in regard to the Mitchell Principles'. Copy in author's possession.

[116] Mairtín Óg Meehan, 'Sinn Féin's 90th *ard fheis*: A POW delegate's view', *The Captive Voice/An Glór Gafa*, Volume 8, Number 2 (Summer 1996).

16 hours per day, recognised an amnesty as 'trivial… compared to the broader political questions which will form the basis of all-party talks'.[117]

Most prisoners, including ardent opponents of the Principles, chiefly insisted that the movement must not split. Reminiscent of prison debates on the Downing Street Declaration in 1993, Sinn Féin's H-Block *cumann* discussed the Mitchell Principles in 1996. Representatives reported that although there was consternation among the prison population, the majority remained optimistic, provided the movement stayed unified and continued internal consultation on the peace process:

> There is a general feeling that pragmatism has served us well. We have advanced enough politically to understand that a pragmatic approach to the difficulties that confront us is a sound one and is not a dilution of our principles.[118]

County Tyrone prisoners scorned the Principles in May 1996, asserting that the PIRA would 'reserve the right to take up arms' until British jurisdiction in Ireland ceased. Yet they backed the leadership's strategy and urged the public to support Sinn Féin candidates on 30 May.[119] In April 1997, County Fermanagh prisoners railed against the Principles as Major's attempt to extract concessions from republicans, or even to exclude republicans from talks altogether. Nevertheless, they held that popular support for Sinn Féin candidates in May 1997's general election would advance the peace process.[120]

Despite misgivings, the majority continued to endorse the Provisional leadership early in 1996. At Sinn Féin's *ard fheis* of March 1996, the H-Block *cumann* pledged support for Adams and McGuinness.[121] Probably encouraged by prison releases – the Dublin government released 12 PIRA prisoners from Portlaoise in July 1995, and the British government restored 50 per cent remission in November 1995 – some 18 prisoners who had opposed the PIRA's cessation in August 1994 lamented the end of the ceasefire in February 1996.[122]

---

[117] 'Weapons in the "peace process"', *Living Marxism*, 89 (April 1996).

[118] *Mitchell Principles* (1996).

[119] Tyrone POWs statement (1996). Copy in author's possession.

[120] '"Give us a voice" says McHugh', *Fermanagh Herald*, 30 April 1997.

[121] Mairtín Óg Meehan, 'Sinn Féin's 90th *ard fheis*: A POW delegate's view', *The Captive Voice/An Glór Gafa*, Volume 8, Number 2 (Summer 1996).

[122] Eddie Cassidy, 'Republican prisoners seek a restoration of ceasefire', *The Cork Examiner*, 25 March 1996; Alan Murdoch, 'Dublin frees IRA prisoners to bolster peace', *The Independent*, 29 July 1995; 'North paramilitaries freed', *Evening Herald*, 17 November 1995.

The Provisionals' ceasefire in 1994 and position on the Mitchell Principles in 1996 were more unpopular among the active PIRA and Sinn Féin organisers in border areas than among prisoners. PIRA volunteers in north Monaghan defied the ceasefire of 1994 by continuing to test mortar bombs along the border throughout 1995.[123] When the PIRA held a convention in County Donegal to discuss the Mitchell Principles in October 1997, a majority of senior volunteers granted Sinn Féin leaders 'special dispensation' to endorse pragmatically the Principles to advance negotiations.[124] However, 35 leading PIRA volunteers reportedly resigned in protest, including the majority of the South Armagh Brigade's First Battalion. In bordering County Louth, four members of the party's *Comhairle Ceantair* resigned in November 1996, reporting declining confidence in party strategy and repudiating the Principles.[125]

In contrast to PIRA prisoners' experiences of discussions, aggrieved Sinn Féin members in County Louth resigned in November 1997 citing a lack of intra-party consultation. In Dundalk, former Sinn Féin candidate Owen Hanratty and the party's assistant secretary, Rory Duggan, were among more than 12 who resigned in November 1997. Hanratty complained 'we never got a chance within the party to debate the Mitchell Principles or whether we should accept them or not'.[126]

In the IRSP and INLA, opinions of the PIRA ceasefires of 1994 and 1996 were mixed. Some INLA volunteers straightforwardly repudiated the cessation as a cipher for surrender. The PIRA ceasefire in 1994 disillusioned Gerry Foster, a Belfast INLA volunteer released from prison that year:

> I came out in 1994 and walked away from it all, because all the talk was about the ceasefires. I thought it was wrong: I thought we should be increasing the level of violence, that we could still win this militarily. I took a very dim view of it. I just thought: it's over, and the good guys lost.[127]

As late as 1997, IRSP spokesperson Willie Gallagher argued that the majority of INLA prisoners in Long Kesh favoured escalating attacks and repudiated military cessations.[128] INLA leaders, by contrast, were open-minded about peace

---

[123] 'Two who attempted to kill security force members among nine IRA men to be freed', *The Irish Times*, 18 December 1997.

[124] Suzanne Breen, '35 said to have quit IRA in south Armagh', *The Irish Times*, 12 November 1997.

[125] 'Journalists first to know about SF resignations', *An Phoblacht*, 13 November 1997.

[126] 'More defections from SF feared', *Evening Herald*, 7 November 1997.

[127] Gerry Foster interview with Jack Hepworth. Belfast, 13 August 2015.

[128] 'British Army cuts back on security patrols in Belfast', *Irish Examiner*, 29 July 1997.

talks, but eager to prevent Provisionals from dominating negotiations. In April 1995, the INLA leadership declared it had observed an unannounced ceasefire since July 1994. It now advocated 'a new non-violent approach' and the IRSP prepared a delegation to the Forum for Peace and Reconciliation.[129]

Through 1995 and 1996, perceived preferential treatment for PIRA prisoners sharpened organisational identity and considerably worsened pre-existing inter-republican tensions in jails. Former INLA prisoner Eddie McGarrigle from Strabane, County Tyrone, remembered that in Long Kesh in the mid-1990s, PIRA

> camp staff were controlled directly by Adams and McGuinness and the rest of the IRA Army Council outside... They controlled the prisoners and controlled their thought and no dissent was allowed in the jail. The last thing they wanted was an INLA volunteer standing his ground.

INLA prisoners' relationships with senior PIRA figures were

> poor enough. [PIRA] camp staff didn't want INLA volunteers on the wing. We were coming into this process and we had a different viewpoint on the Downing Street Declaration, for example, and we voiced it.[130]

McGarrigle recalled PIRA staff incensing INLA volunteers by branding them 'civilians', and thought the 'majority' of PIRA prisoners only acquiesced in the nascent peace process as they

> would have done anything to get out of jail... [the] level of political awareness was pretty low. I think they would have swapped their freedom for their principles.[131]

In August 1995, four INLA prisoners in English jails began a blanket protest after Conservative Home Secretary Michael Howard refused to repatriate the men to Ireland or reduce security during visits.[132] The same year, three INLA

---

[129] 'INLA started ceasefire last July, court told', *Irish Examiner*, 26 April 1995.

[130] Eddie McGarrigle interview with Prisons Memory Archive. Long Kesh, 2007. Available at http://prisonsmemoryarchive.com/portfolio_entries/full/page/2/ (accessed 28 January 2019).

[131] Eddie McGarrigle interview with Prisons Memory Archive. Long Kesh, 2007. Available at http://prisonsmemoryarchive.com/portfolio_entries/full/page/2/ (accessed 28 January 2019).

[132] Republican Socialist P.O.W.s H-6, Long Kesh, 'Blanket Protest', *Strabane Chronicle*, 5 August 1995.

volunteers in Portlaoise commenced hunger strike for parity with PIRA prisoners on early releases and compassionate parole.[133] In December 1996, INLA prisoners in Portlaoise protested when their PIRA counterparts enjoyed two extra days of temporary leave at Christmas.[134] Yet outside prisons, splits once again damaged the INLA: in internal feuds in 1996, six INLA volunteers and nine-year-old Barbara McAlorum were killed, while others were injured.[135]

Through 1997 and 1998, INLA prisoners and IRSP leaders jointly criticised the Sinn Féin hierarchy's organisational supremacy in a peace process republican socialists increasingly dismissed. In 1997, fearing the Provisionals would imminently settle for 'a revamped Northern state', the IRSP *Ard Comhairle* declared 'opposition' to the peace process and demanded immediate dialogue with Sinn Féin.[136] No such talks were forthcoming, and after the Good Friday Agreement of April 1998, the IRSP *Ard Comhairle* condemned Sinn Féin's 'arrogant' leadership for its 'capitulation to reactionary unionism' in a settlement that would 'copper-fasten partition'. The IRSP executive decried Sinn Féin for 'despicable attempts to neutralise and marginalise... the republican ideal' and courting Irish-America's 'imperialist capitalism'. In contrast, republican socialists advocated

> an Ireland for the ordinary people, not for big multi-national business, not for the Americans... [nor] for the capitalist pan-nationalist front.

The IRSP exhorted rank-and-file Provisionals to oppose 'the Adams leadership'.[137] Similarly, INLA prisoners in Long Kesh lambasted Sinn Féin's 'compromise' leadership for the 'sell-out of the Republican Struggle' and 'marginalising' republican socialism. Critiquing the Good Friday Agreement, INLA prisoners reiterated their support for the 'leadership of the Republican Socialist Movement'.[138]

From May to August 1998, two momentous events left the IRSP-INLA especially isolated and triggered abrupt changes. In May, the referendum on the Good Friday Agreement passed with a 71.1 per cent majority. In August, a Real IRA bomb in Omagh, County Tyrone, killed 29 civilians, causing widespread

---

[133] 'INLA end fast without gains', *Irish Independent*, 1 September 1995.

[134] Eamon Timmins, 'Prisoner protest looms over IRA Christmas parole', *Irish Examiner*, 24 December 1996.

[135] Jim Cusack, 'Torney's death ends present INLA feud', *The Irish Times*, 4 September 1996.

[136] IRSP, *The Republican Forum* (1997).

[137] 'Easter Message from the Leadership of the Republican Socialist Movement 1998'. Copy in author's possession.

[138] 'Easter Statement from R.S. P.O.W.s, Long Kesh' (1998). Copy in author's possession.

outrage, especially towards the 'dissidents' who maintained armed struggle. The IRSP had campaigned for a 'No' vote in the referendum, and at the party's *ard fheis* in December 1997 a 109–11 majority had defeated a motion calling for an INLA ceasefire. A motion for the INLA to continue its policy of 'defence and retaliation', which had been in place since March 1995, was unanimously approved.[139] Days after the Omagh bombing, the IRSP *Ard Comhairle* reversed the position of the *ard fheis* eight months earlier and implored the INLA to declare a ceasefire since there was 'now no basis for continuation of armed struggle by Irish republicans'. The *Ard Comhairle* acknowledged that INLA prisoners were divided on the issue.[140]

Through the late 1990s, a smaller section of republicans who disagreed with the Provisionals' ceasefires did not join opposing factions, but quietly demobilised. Lacking the media attention that schisms and 'dissident' declarations achieved, these narratives are largely hidden from history, but they merit mention nonetheless. For example, John Noonan, a Dublin-born republican who joined the PIRA after Bloody Sunday, thought the leadership missed several prime opportunities for insurrectionary escalation in the 1990s. Bemused by the strategic reorientation, Noonan left the movement that had defined his adult life:

> When the first ceasefire came into play [1994]... I didn't agree with it. My view was that it was the wrong time – but other people who were involved in the leadership had a bigger picture than me and accepted it. When that ceasefire broke down I thought it was the right thing for us to get stuck in and build up again because of the oncoming British election. But when that didn't happen I decided there was another way for me to go, another life for me to have.[141]

By the time Sinn Féin convened for its *ard fheis* in Dublin in May 1998, the leadership faced negligible internal opposition to its major dual proposal. The *Ard Comhairle* called for the party to endorse 'yes' votes in referenda on the Good Friday Agreement in Ireland north and south the following month. Furthermore, the party executive moved the conference to amend its constitution to allow successful candidates to take seats in the prospective assembly. Both resolutions passed by an overwhelming majority of 331 against 19.[142]

---

[139] Peter Urban, 'IRSP *ard fheis*' (23 December 1997). Available at http://www.hartford-hwp.com/archives/61/276.html (accessed 31 October 2018).

[140] 'INLA set to call ceasefire, says its political wing', *Irish Examiner*, 18 August 1998.

[141] John Noonan interview with Jason O'Toole, 2007. Jason O'Toole, 'Inside the IRA', *Hot Press*, 1 February 2007.

[142] 'An historic step for Sinn Fein', *Dundalk Democrat*, 23 May 1998.

Conclusion

The distinction between 'tactics' and 'strategies' underpins this chapter. Social movement theorists such as Charles Tilly and Lee A. Smithey distinguish sharply between tactics – the actions and sub-mechanisms publicly deployed to advance strategic aims – and strategies – the overarching pathway towards the movement's objectives.[143] However, from the early 1980s, the Adams leadership repeatedly blurred these categories. Adamsites framed new departures – for example, standing abstentionist Sinn Féin candidates for elections in 1981, or recapitulating the language of civil rights in council chambers from 1985 – as expedient 'tactical' changes. As the debate over abstentionism at Sinn Féin's *ard fheis* in 1985 demonstrated, 'tactics' were temporary and dispensable, and did not commit the movement to any more profound changes to its fundamental 'strategy': a military-led campaign to force the British government to withdraw from Northern Ireland.

Ultimately, these purportedly 'tactical' shifts through the 1980s developed into more profound 'strategic' changes, culminating in the Provisionals' commitment to 'exclusively democratic means' by 2005. The armed struggle was no more. How, when, and why tactical adaptation bled into strategic change is paramount in republican fragmentation and controversy today.

This chapter has analysed the internal dynamics of the Provisional republican movement through tactical and strategic innovation in the 1980s and 1990s. The movement had a history of entrusting such decisions to its leaders. The party *ard fheis* of 1977 took no final decision on whether to contest European elections. Instead, Gerry Adams's successful amendment left the *Ard Comhairle* to decide 'how best to combat the EEC'.[144] Through electoralism and peace strategies alike, Sinn Féin leaders initiated piecemeal tactical experimentation, securing support among middle ranks and ostensibly consulting, and often influencing, the grassroots.

Despite generating adverse publicity, breakaways from the Provisional movement in 1986, 1996, and 1997 did not entirely destabilise the organisation. Of course, many activists who drifted from the movement quietly for various reasons are hidden from history. Yet the bulk of the Provisional movement remained intact. Relative to its size, defections from the Provisional movement through the 1980s and 1990s were minor. In 1985, four senior PIRA volunteers in Belfast were expelled, while in 1986 approximately 130 people formed

---

[143] Charles Tilly, *Popular contention in Great Britain, 1758–1834* (Cambridge, Massachusetts: Harvard University Press, 1995), p. 41; Lee A. Smithey, 'Social movement strategy, tactics, and collective identity', *Sociology Compass*, 3 (2009), p. 660.

[144] 'Ard-Fheis dodges Euro-vote', *Irish Examiner*, 24 October 1977.

RSF after the Provisionals ended Dublin abstentionism.[145] The LCR publicity admitted its membership was small and restricted almost entirely to Long Kesh.[146] Defence analysts suggested the Real IRA, founded in 1997 by opponents of the PIRA ceasefire, had from 70 to 170 members.[147]

Tactical change avoided catastrophic splits thanks to two central factors: influential individuals in Sinn Féin and the PIRA vocally supported new departures; and the rank-and-file were broadly confident in their leaders and the struggle's overall prospects. Differentiating strategic thought in this period, we can distinguish between what might be termed 'pragmatic' and 'orthodox' Provisionals. Positive that British withdrawal was either imminent, or inevitable in the longer term, the majority of Provisionals considered electoral interventions, ceasefires, and peace negotiations welcome additions to their 'repertoires of contention'. Tactical pragmatists embraced variations in what Doug McAdam terms 'the structure of political opportunities'.[148] Often, factions formed around the extent to which individuals and their milieux identified with the Adams leadership that emblematised these changes. Personal connections and spatial affinity with Northern Ireland shaped these dynamics. 'Pragmatists' were not necessarily any less committed to republican aspirations or particular methods, such as armed struggle, than 'orthodox'. Rather, a greater tendency to perceive shifts in political opportunities and to innovate tactically set pragmatists apart.

By contrast, republican 'principles' and historical precedent were orthodox lodestars. Orthodox republicans repudiated pragmatists' new departures. For example, Frank McCarry, an Antrim councillor who transferred his allegiance from Sinn Féin to the pro-abstentionist faction RSF in March 1987, proclaimed his 'allegiance to the 32-County Irish Republic as proclaimed in 1916'.[149] Tactical innovators did not alter the fundamental 'master frames' of their struggle, invoking instead timeless ideas of republican history. In November 1985, in a rare *ard fheis* appearance, a member of the Provisional Army Council told delegates that the PIRA campaign would 'not end until every British soldier has been driven from our shore', recalling the movement's chiliastic rhetoric of the early 1970s.[150]

---

[145] Robert W. White, *Ruairí Ó Brádaigh: the life and politics of an Irish revolutionary* (Bloomington, Indiana: Indiana University Press, 2006), pp. 307–308.

[146] LHL NIPC P3600: League of Communist Republicans, *From Long Kesh to a Socialist Ireland* (Shannon: League of Communist Republicans, 1988).

[147] 'How the Real IRA was born', *The Guardian*, 5 March 2001.

[148] Doug McAdam, *Political process and the development of black insurgency, 1930–1970* (Chicago: University of Chicago Press, 1982), pp. 41–42.

[149] 'Antrim councillor pledges allegiance', *Republican Bulletin: Iris Na Poblachta*, 5 (April 1987).

[150] Gerry Adams, Martin McGuinness, and Danny Morrison abstained from the vote, but advocated the 'tactic' lobby. The other five members of the *Ard Comhairle* voted

Yet not all of the Provisionals' critics upheld republican orthodoxy. In the late 1980s, erstwhile Provisionals in the LCR in Long Kesh critiqued particular aspects of Sinn Féin's electoral strategy, rather than all electoral strategy per se. The LCR diagnosed in Provisional electoralism a drift from revolutionary socialism to populism. LCR prisoners looked to an alternative 'tradition', drawing upon the Republican Congress, founded by anti-Treaty republican socialists in 1934. In October 1987, James Tierney, an LCR member in Long Kesh, explained that his comrades sought 'the re-founding of the Republican Congress... the basic skeleton for a popular front must be constructed'.[151]

Tactical innovation in the Provisional movement originated at its apex, but entailed consulting, informing, and influencing the middle-ranks and grassroots. Pragmatists recognised both the political capital of the republican past, and the need for tactical change to appear gradual and reversible. In 1983, to appeal to republican orthodoxists, Sinn Féin Education Department published a booklet charting past republican electoral successes such as Philip Clarke and Tom Mitchell, IRA prisoners who won Westminster polls in May 1955.[152]

After the fact, critiques of Sinn Féin portray the peace process as a series of events that happened *to* the Provisionals. For Timothy Shanahan, the Provisionals 'capitulated' to British initiatives.[153] However, debating the ceasefire in 1994 and negotiations in subsequent years, Provisional pragmatists perceived themselves driving the process. They configured Major's government as the obdurate party which would eventually be overwhelmed by a multifaceted republican campaign. Prisoners from County Fermanagh reflected this combination of frustration and determination as they observed the Drumcree standoff in July 1996. As disputes flared over Orange marches traversing Catholic areas of Portadown, County Armagh, Fermanagh prisoners denounced Catholics' ongoing suffering – 'nothing has changed over the past 28 years' – but reaffirmed that 'the days of Nationalists lying down are over'.[154]

---

four to one in favour of 'tactic' over 'principle'. 'IRA man at 'secret' session', *The Irish Press*, 4 November 1985.

[151] James Tierney quoted in LHL NIPC P3080A: *Armed Struggle: The Communist Party's Open Letter to the Provisional IRA and the Complete and Unedited Contributions to the Debate that Appeared in the Party's Press* Irish Socialist *and* Unity (Dublin: Communist Party of Ireland, 1988).

[152] LHL NIPC P2009: Sinn Féin Education Department, *Election Interventions – Historical & Contemporary* (Dublin: Sinn Féin, 1983).

[153] Timothy Shanahan, *The Provisional Irish Republican Army and the morality of terrorism* (Edinburgh: Edinburgh University Press, 2009), p. 2.

[154] "U'-Turn at Drumcree no surprise – Fermanagh Republican Prisoners', *Fermanagh Herald*, 31 July 1996.

Broadly speaking, Sinn Féin leaders successfully navigated their own movement's heterogeneity during peace talks and negotiations, to the extent that they appeared to consult their base and move gradually, without committing to swingeing compromises. From the Downing Street Declaration of December 1993, PIRA prisoners were determined to maintain input in the movement's tactics. In Portlaoise Prison in May 1994, 'numerous' PIRA volunteers reiterated the need for prisoners to contribute to these debates.[155]

David A. Snow and David A. Benford argue that 'anchoring master frames… constrain' movement tactics,[156] but the Provisionals' master frame – of British rule as the central problem – was sufficiently broad to accommodate considerable tactical change. As Gordon Clubb has argued, the PIRA's 'disengagement frame… maintained narrative fidelity with the mobilising frame that underpinned the PIRA in the 1960s'.[157] The peace strategy's advocates handled internal dissent by privately framing tactical changes as pragmatic means towards Irish unity. Bernadette Sands, who co-founded the 32 County Sovereignty Committee in December 1997, remembered challenging Sinn Féin over its compromises in the peace process. Sands recalled a Sinn Féin strategist's typical response: 'It's only a bit of paper, it means nothing. We're still going to achieve our objectives.'[158]

After 1998, the Provisional leadership refuted its internal critics more publicly and forcefully. Paddy Fox from Dungannon, County Tyrone, was a PIRA prisoner from 1991 to 1996, but after criticising the peace process, local Provisionals threatened him with violence:

> When people asked me what I thought of the [Good Friday A]greement, I would voice my opinion. I tell them I don't think the struggle was worth that. Is that what men were fighting and dying for? Is that why we went to jail?[159]

---

[155] ILA: PRO Republican POWs, Portlaoise Prison, *Volunteer Jim Lynagh Lecture 1994: Peace strategy debated in Portlaoise*.

[156] David A. Snow & David A. Benford, 'Master frames and cycles of protest', in Aldon C. Morris & Carol McClurg Mueller (eds.), *Frontiers in social movement theory* (New Haven, Connecticut: Yale University Press, 1992), p. 146.

[157] Gordon Clubb, 'Selling the end of terrorism: a framing approach to the IRA's disengagement from armed violence', *Small Wars & Insurgencies*, 27 (2016), p. 614.

[158] 'Interviews with Dissident Republicans Bernadette Sands and Rory Duggan'. Available at https://www.youtube.com/watch?v=mvuI3c4nsBo (accessed 23 October 2018).

[159] Henry McDonald, 'I spoke against peace so now they want to kill me', *The Observer*, 31 January 1999.

Provisional discussions of peace initiatives in the 1990s drew heavily upon international politics, whereas conversations about electoral interventions in the 1980s had not. In the 1980s, Sinn Féin's electoralists asserted local credentials in republican communities across the north; from the mid-1990s, the leadership looked further afield, finding diplomatic potential in South Africa's peace process and Irish-America. Mark Ryan situated the Provisionals' new departures in a global context spanning the USSR's collapse and conflict transformations in Palestine and South Africa.[160] Yet until conversations about prisoner releases from 1995, the PIRA rank-and-file seldom spoke of emulating conflict resolutions elsewhere. Sinn Féin representatives across Ireland celebrated Nelson Mandela's release from prison in February 1990, but this was hardly the preserve of republican radicals.[161]

The transnational component of republicans' strategic thinking regarding electoralism and peace initiatives was most concentrated among Gerry Adams, Seán Lynch, and Danny Morrison. Imprisoned in the early 1990s, Morrison read ANC activist Albie Sachs's *The soft vengeance of a freedom fighter* (1990). In a letter to Gerry Adams in October 1991, Morrison quoted Sachs on the need to 'confront hard decisions' and

> accept major but incomplete breakthroughs now, transforming the terrain of struggle in a way which is advantageous to the achievement of our ultimate goals.[162]

Oral histories illustrate the polyvocality of subjective positions on debates concerning electoralism and abstentionism. Individuals formed and negotiated positions in various ways. First, there was the interpersonal level. Social movement theorists David A. Snow, Louis A. Zurcher, and Sheldon Ekland-Olson found that personal networks were pivotal in determining initial mobilisation.[163] In the Provisional republican movement, these connections remained vital *after* mobilisation. Kinship and friendship ties were important, especially during schisms within the movement. Writing in March 1983, shortly before Seamus Kerr became Sinn Féin's first

---

[160] Mark Ryan, *War and peace in Ireland: Britain and the IRA in the new world order* (London: Pluto Press, 1994), pp. 7, 9.

[161] Within five months of Mandela's release, Fianna Fáil Taoiseach Charles Haughey hosted Mandela in a state reception in Dublin, where he received the freedom of the city. 'What A man!', *Western People*, 11 July 1990.

[162] Danny Morrison interview with Graham Spencer. Spencer, *From armed struggle*, 144.

[163] David A. Snow, Louis A. Zurcher, & Sheldon Ekland-Olson, 'Social networks and social movements: a microstructural approach to differential recruitment', *American Sociological Review*, 45 (1980), pp. 787–801.

councillor in Northern Ireland, PIRA prisoner John Tracey hoped his friend Kerr would win to 'reinforce' Sinn Féin's demand for a British withdrawal. Tracey trusted Kerr as a kindred spirit outside jail.[164] Seán MacManus, who chaired Sinn Féin's *ard fheis* in 1986, reflected that the anti-abstentionist position profited greatly from having 'people of the calibre' of veterans John Joe McGirl, Fergie Albert McGovern, and Joe Cahill. 'Certainly hundreds of delegates who would have seen them as inspirational figures [were] to some degree swayed', MacManus argued.[165]

Second, the complexity revealed in oral testimony showed a conjunctural dimension. Views were subject to ad hoc, contingent considerations in particular times and places. Friendships influenced republicans' experience through internal divisions and disagreements. Clonard republican Nuala Perry, whose local friends Eddie Carmichael and Dan McCann were expelled from the PIRA in 1985 for criticising electoralism, remembered how Carmichael drifted from the Provisionals whereas McCann rejoined and was later killed in Gibraltar in 1988. For both men

> I think it was basically a fish out of water feeling. A lot of people weren't talking to Dan on the road, the same with Eddie. They were completely ostracised by so many people. I think Eddie was sort of of the opinion, *we've been betrayed here.* I think Dan was of the opinion, *well the war is still going on and maybe it can work out.*[166]

Third, there was a cognitive dimension. Very few activists immutably maintained a conservative position on tactics. At pivotal moments, some republicans moderated or even jettisoned their support for tactical innovation. Peter Albert McGovern, from Swanlinbar, County Cavan, whose republican activities dated back to the late 1950s, initially sided with the Provisionals at the split in 1986, but later joined RSF.[167] Despite being elected as Sinn Féin's first councillor in Northern Ireland in 1983, Seamus Kerr had misgivings about extending the party's electoral involvement, and in 1986 he favoured retaining abstentionism from Leinster House.[168] Similarly,

---

[164] John Tracey, H-Block 3, Long Kesh, 'Sinn Fein's message', *Ulster Herald*, 19 March 1983.

[165] Seán MacManus interview with John Morrison, 29 May 2008. John Morrison, 'Why do people become dissident Irish republicans?', in P. M. Currie & Max Taylor (eds.), *Dissident Irish republicanism* (New York: Continuum, 2011), p. 28.

[166] Nuala Perry interview with Jack Hepworth. Belfast, 30 March 2016.

[167] 'Obituaries', *Fermanagh Herald*, 25 May 2005.

[168] 'Interview: Seamus Kerr', *Frontline*. Available at https://www.pbs.org/wgbh/pages/frontline/shows/ira/inside/kerr.html (accessed 19 April 2018).

RSF's Belfast organiser, Bob Murray, had endorsed Provisional electoralism until the mid-1980s. But by 1986, Murray – a veteran of the 1950s border campaign, and Gerry Adams's driver in the 1980s – baulked at the prospect of 'recognising a partition parliament', and became a founding member of RSF. Interviewed the following year, Murray pinpointed his breach with Sinn Féin to the abstentionism position:

> I had been fighting it for three years. I saw it coming. Don't get me wrong, I have no problem with the dual strategy, but recognising a partition parliament is wrong... When Sinn Féin began to fight elections in 1981, I supported it. I have no problems with that. It was necessary to bring along popular political support for the armed struggle. But this electoral thing, I fear now, will take over, and the military campaign will suffer and be wound down and stopped.[169]

As the Provisional leadership transformed and reoriented in the 1980s and 1990s, a combination of interpersonal, conjunctural, and cognitive dynamics informed republican subjectivities. Amid republican fragmentation today, stark contrasts exist between memories emanating from 'dissenting' or 'dissident' republicans on the one hand, and 'new Sinn Féin' activists on the other.[170] These tendencies in memory exaggerate and reduce the messiness of the historical processes in question. This chapter has demonstrated the importance of intra-republican networks, allegiances, and generational cohorts during tactical and strategic debate within the movement. It has also testified the salience of trust and optimism at crucial moments in the movement's history. The fissiparous potential of theoretical and cognitive debates repeatedly collided with the imperative of maintaining movement unity.

---

[169] 'The two camps in Sinn Féin', *The Irish Press*, 20 March 1987.
[170] Agnès Maillot, *New Sinn Féin: Irish republicanism in the twenty-first century* (Abingdon: Routledge, 2004).

3

The Revolutionary Left

Irish republicans generally repudiated leftist 'terrorist' splinters of the New Left in West Germany, Italy, and France during the 1970s and 1980s. In an interview approved and distributed by the movement's hierarchy in 1989, an anonymous volunteer declared unequivocally that the Provisionals had 'no connection... nor indeed any sympathy' with Western European militants in the Rote Armee Fraktion, Brigate Rosse, or Action Directe.[1] Furthermore, those groups' strategies and composition differed markedly from Irish republicanism. West German and Italian left-wing 'terrorists' spanned radical students and intellectuals, trade union militants, and socialist subcultures. Designed to stir the masses and trigger state repression, their armed actions included attacks on business leaders and far-right activists.[2]

For the revolutionary left, the period from 1968 to 1994 spanned the international afterlives of '68 and the Soviet Union's disintegration.[3]

---

[1] 'Inside the IRA: Two men tell us why they're at war with Britain', *Living Marxism*, 10 (August 1989).

[2] Sebastian Gehrig, 'Sympathising subcultures? The milieus of West German terrorism', in Martin Klimke, Jacco Pekelder, & Joachim Scharloth (eds.), *Between Prague Spring and French May: opposition and revolt in Europe, 1960–1980* (New York: Berghahn, 2011), p. 235; Dorothea Hauser, 'Terrorism', in Martin Klimke & Joachim Scharloth (eds.), *1968 in Europe: a history of protest and activism, 1956–1977* (Basingstoke: Palgrave Macmillan, 2008), pp. 269, 271–272; Guido Panvini, 'Neo-fascism, the extraparliamentary left wing, and the birth of Italian terrorism', in Karen Dubinsky, Catherine Krull, Susan Lord, Sean Mills, & Scott Rutherford (eds.), *New world coming: the sixties and the shaping of global consciousness* (Toronto: Between the Lines, 2009), pp. 87–96; David Moss, *The politics of left-wing violence in Italy, 1969–1985* (Basingstoke: Macmillan, 1989), pp. 2, 36, 43, 49.

[3] This chapter follows John Molyneux's definition of the 'revolutionary left' whose 'central task is to transform the elemental working class struggle within capitalism into a political struggle to overthrow capitalism. This is essentially

Throughout these years, republicans engaged critically with the international left in different ways. In so doing, they negotiated tensions between national developments and international politics, and between nationalism and socialism more broadly.

Among academics, there is near consensus that the Provisional movement's socialism was ambiguous. For Kevin Bean, the Provisionals 'were not Marxist in either the orthodox Soviet or Trotskyist sense', instead synthesising guerrilla 'anti-imperialism and radical nationalism'.[4] Eoin Ó Broin similarly described Provisional socialism as 'rhetorical and declaratory rather than based on a serious critique of Irish, European or global capitalism'. Ó Broin's critique characterised Sinn Féin's relationship with socialism as 'ambiguous, underdeveloped and at times contradictory'.[5] Surveying Sinn Féin's foreign policy, Martyn Frampton noted 'innate pragmatism and flexibility' in a movement that simultaneously espoused sympathy with the world's oppressed while courting neoconservatives in Irish-America.[6]

Mark Ryan and Tommy McKearney have located the Provisionals' tactical malleability in the 1980s as both a cause and consequence of republican disinterest in the global left. Writing in 1994, Ryan argued that Sinn Féin's pan-nationalist alliance in the late 1980s indicated that the movement had become 'a traditional social-democratic party'.[7] A left-wing activist and former Provisional, McKearney denounced the movement's lack of a 'clear socialist programme'.[8] The Provisionals modified and marginalised theory as their repertoires of contention changed.

Such entangled debates have both dispelled and generated much polemic. Daniel Finn's assertion that context was pivotal in republican pronouncements on leftism is well made. For example, Gerry Adams's oft-quoted disowning of Marxism in an interview with *Hibernia* magazine in 1979 reflected his

a struggle for state power, which requires the revolutionary to ally fidelity to Marxist principles with close contact with the mass workers' movement.' John Molyneux, 'What do we mean by ultra-leftism?', *Socialist Worker Review*, 80 (October 1985).

[4] Kevin Bean, *The new politics of Sinn Féin* (Liverpool: Liverpool University Press, 2007), pp. 74, 147.

[5] Eoin Ó Broin, *Sinn Féin and the politics of left republicanism* (London: Pluto Press, 2009), pp. 297, 308.

[6] Martyn Frampton, '"Squaring the circle": the foreign policy of Sinn Féin, 1983–1989', *Irish Political Studies*, 19 (2004), pp. 43–63.

[7] Mark Ryan, *War and peace in Ireland: Britain and the IRA in the new world order* (London: Pluto Press, 1994), pp. 71, 75.

[8] Tommy McKearney, *The Provisional IRA: from insurrection to parliament* (London: Pluto Press, 2011), pp. x, 107, 135.

pragmatism: the Belfast Provisional tactfully prevented republicanism becoming subject to a 'red scare'.[9]

Recently, Richard English asserted that socialism constituted a 'significant secondary goal' for the Provisional movement.[10] Delineating diverse positions on republicanism among Ireland's fragmented revolutionary left, Marc Mulholland has analysed the 'uneasy' dialogue between republicanism and radicalism.[11] These inquiries call attention to how socialism pervaded republican politics. This chapter explores how republicans negotiated left-wing ideas within an enduring master frame that primarily opposed the British presence, rather than international capitalism per se.

The nexus of republicanism and socialism is inextricably linked to historical and theoretical disputes concerning the relationship between Marxism, nationalism, and guerrilla warfare. Leon Trotsky considered 'terrorism... very striking in its outward forms... but absolutely harmless' to the 'social system'.[12] By contrast, Mao Tse-tung's and Che Guevara's theories of guerrilla war regarded armed actions as vital revolutionary tactics.[13]

This chapter grounds uneasy interactions between Irish republicanism and radical politics in those terms that are especially controversial today. Kevin Bean's assessment of a 'porous' republican tradition's 'susceptibility to the ideological pull of external forces' foregrounded many disillusioned republicans' critiques.[14] For these dissenters, Gerry Adams and his supporters superficially invoked socialist rhetoric to bolster revolutionary credentials before 'selling out' to the British establishment. Now a leading critic of Provisional strategy, former PIRA volunteer Richard O'Rawe has acidly evoked how Provisional leaders treated socialism in the late 1970s and early 1980s:

> In many ways the language of socialism which was used was very wispy and airy-fairy. It was as if we were going to take over the whole country, not just the North, and have a thirty-two county

[9] Daniel Finn, *One man's terrorist: a political history of the IRA* (London: Verso, 2019), p. 139.

[10] Richard English, *Does terrorism work? A history* (Oxford: Oxford University Press, 2016), pp. 109–110, 129.

[11] Marc Mulholland, 'Northern Ireland and the far left, c.1965–1975', *Contemporary British History*, 32 (2018), pp. 542–563.

[12] Leon Trotsky, 'Why Marxists oppose individual terrorism' (1911), in *Marxism and terrorism* (New York: Pathfinder Press, 1995), pp. 5–11.

[13] Mao Tse-tung, *On guerrilla warfare* (transl. Samuel B. Griffith II) (Champaign, Illinois: University of Illinois Press, 2000 [1937]); Che Guevara, *Guerrilla warfare: a method* (Beijing: Foreign Languages Press, 1964).

[14] Bean, *New politics*, 74.

socialist republic. We were not concerned about democracy because that was about the dreaded proletariat.[15]

Now a prominent member of socialist-republican party Saoradh, Nuala Perry scorns the 'trendy left-wing thing' that 'really, really took off' in the Provisional movement in the late 1970s. 'These people who talked all the socialist talk in the prison, when they came out, were anything but.' Perry remembers supporters of Gerry Adams in the late 1970s and early 1980s calling for the movement to expel one of its legendary founders, Billy McKee, on the supposition that McKee was a 'Catholic conservative'.[16]

Similarly, INLA testimonies discuss the turmoil that theoretical debates about socialism triggered in their own movement's complex history. In September 1984, the IRSP formally adopted the teachings of Marx, Engels, and Lenin, but the party's membership was not uniform. Former INLA volunteer Gerry Foster said his politics as a young prisoner in the early 1980s were

> quite simple: we're right, they're wrong. They're using violence to maintain the state, and I can use violence to try and break it... I didn't even know what the IRSP stood for! I didn't even know it existed. That's how uninterested I was. So I had no great left-wing ideology.[17]

Subjective representations of socialism as an article of faith undergird diverse organisational identities. For former Official republican and IRSP activist Tommy McCourt from Derry, the contrast between the Provisional movement's origins and its later claims smacked of duplicity:

> The Provisional Movement from its inception had never a clear class or socialist policy. It adopted strategies and policies as and when it suited them. I remember way back when the Provos were first coming on the ground they were writing on the wall in the Brandywell – Better dead than red. Then they become suddenly – we are a revolutionary organisation.[18]

---

15 Richard O'Rawe interview with Graham Spencer. Graham Spencer, *From armed struggle to political struggle: republican tradition and transformation in Northern Ireland* (London: Bloomsbury, 2015), p. 61.

16 Nuala Perry interview with Jack Hepworth. Belfast, 12 December 2017.

17 Gerry Foster interview with Jack Hepworth. Belfast, 13 August 2015.

18 Tommy McCourt interview with Marisa McGlinchey. Marisa McGlinchey, *Unfinished business: the politics of 'dissident' Irish republicanism* (Manchester: Manchester University Press, 2019), p. 49.

This chapter comprises two sections. The first analyses republican interpretations of the Soviet Union and the 'Third World' from 1968 to the early 1980s, when Gerry Adams and his supporters won the Provisional leadership.[19] It also discusses Éire Nua, Sinn Féin's socioeconomic programme from 1971 to 1982. Éire Nua is noteworthy both as a site of contestation within the Provisional movement, and for encapsulating the nuanced redistributive economics of the founding Provisional leadership.

The chapter's second section examines leftist republicanism between the hunger strike of 1981 and the PIRA ceasefire of 1994. This period witnessed significant political and strategic disjunctions within the IRSP and INLA. Simultaneously, left-wing critics organised within the Provisional movement. This section also interrogates republican responses to the Soviet Union's disintegration and the 'new world order' into the 1990s. The question of republicanism's porosity to external influence and conjuncture is prominent throughout.

Republicanism, the Cold War, and the 'Third World', c.1968–c.1982

In the early 1970s, the founders of the Provisional republican movement rejected 'imperialist' Cold War blocs as absolutely as they opposed British rule. Unlike comparable liberation movements, such as Algeria's Front de libération nationale, the Provisionals did not engage formally with the Non-Aligned Movement's 'insurgent neutralism'.[20] Nevertheless, Provisional leaders celebrated non-aligned nations' neutrality in a global context.

For Sinn Féin president Ruairí Ó Brádaigh and Belfast PIRA leader Joe Cahill, 'communism' connoted foreign dictatorship. Ó Brádaigh's founding manifesto for the Provisionals held that 'Eastern Soviet state capitalism... with its denial of freedom and human rights' was incompatible with the Easter Proclamation of 1916.[21] Speaking in 1972, Cahill represented 'communism' as inherently undemocratic: 'This is a democratic country', Cahill explained: 'we are not communists'. Cahill insisted the Provisionals would not accept aid from communist states.[22] By contrast, Official republican leaders Tomás Mac Giolla,

---

[19] 'Third World' is now a largely defunct category, but is employed here to reflect historical usage.

[20] Jeffrey James Byrne, 'Beyond continents, colours, and the Cold War: Yugoslavia, Algeria, and the struggle for non-alignment', *International History Review*, 37 (2015), pp. 913, 920.

[21] Ruairí Ó Brádaigh, 'Restore the means of production to the people', *The Irish Press*, 3 December 1970.

[22] Christopher Macy, 'Sinn Fein and the IRA's: 1', *Humanist*, Volume 87, Number 1, Ulster Special Issue (January 1972).

Seán Garland, and Des O'Hagan attended the World Congress of Peace Forces in Moscow in October 1973. The following month, OSF's *ard fheis* approved ties with the USSR.[23]

Early Provisional republicanism's economic nationalism and national neutrality borrowed from the Easter Proclamation's conceptions of public ownership of national wealth and natural resources. For Eoin Ó Broin, these were the politics of *Christian* socialism;[24] the categories of 'Irish' or 'nativist' – fixated with national precedent and ideas of authenticity – could equally apply.[25]

Early Provisionals invoked Officials' Soviet sympathies to portray an Official movement under the aegis of an oppressive 'foreign' power. Provisionals disdained Officials' theoretical, internationally oriented perspectives. More immediately, in 1969 and its aftermath, they considered Official tactics a betrayal of northern nationalists. Both local and global dimensions underpin Provisional justifications of the split of 1969 and 1970, and remain prominent in Provisional republican memory today. Remembering the emergency in west Belfast in August 1969, Belfast Provisional argued 'the Goulding leadership was a communist leadership no matter how you look at it'. Yet Hannaway's criticism of the 'reds' hinged upon the argument that Gouldingites deliberately demilitarised the republican movement, diverting it from its historic course late in 1969:

> They demilitarised the IRA on the pretence they were going to upgrade weapons, which didn't happen... [They] aggravated, and interfered with, civil rights programmes.[26]

Officials' perceived failure in August 1969 became an essential theme for Provisionals' foundational legend.[27]

For republicans immediately associated with the Provisionals from late 1969, oral testimonies recall the events and split of that year as a zero-sum contest between two loaded positions: 'politics' and 'republicanism'. The former implies

---

[23] *1975: In Memoriam, 2015: The Struggle Continues* (Belfast: National Commemoration Committee of the Workers' Party, 2015), p. 7. Copy in author's possession.

[24] Ó Broin, *Sinn Féin*, 233.

[25] For comparable analysis of 'nativism' in the Zimbabwean context, see Sabelo J. Ndlovu-Gatsheni, 'Making sense of Mugabeism in local and global politics: "So Blair, keep your England and let me keep my Zimbabwe"', *Third World Quarterly*, 30 (2009), pp. 1139–1158.

[26] Kevin Hannaway interview with Jack Hepworth. Belfast, 6 December 2017.

[27] On August 1969 and the Provisionals' foundational myths, see Stephen Hopkins, *The politics of memoir and the Northern Ireland conflict* (Liverpool: Liverpool University Press, 2013), p. 28; Brian Hanley, '"I ran away"? The IRA and 1969 – the evolution of a myth', *Irish Historical Studies*, 38 (2013), pp. 671–687.

demilitarisation, while the latter signifies the movement's 'true' trajectory. Francie McGuigan remembered Cathal Goulding's leadership

> downgrading the military side of the IRA... trying to turn it into a purely political organisation... The result is, the older generation sort of moved away, the likes of [Billy] McKee and a lot of people like that... Anybody who disagreed with this Marxism attitude within the republican movement were being ostracised or pushed to the side.[28]

McGuigan recalled Belfast republican Jimmy Steele's famed oration at a commemoration event in Mullingar, County Westmeath in July 1969 as an epochal moment exposing the dichotomy between 'politics' and 'republicanism'. The veteran Steele had publicly castigated the Goulding leadership and was swiftly suspended from the movement. Within weeks, he was among the PIRA's founders. McGuigan quoted Steele, who 'lacerated' Goulding's talk of political theory and 'isms' with a telling retort: *As far as I'm concerned, there's only one ism, and that's republicanism.*[29]

Portraying Official republicans under 'undemocratic' Soviet control was an important feature of early Provisional rhetoric. Yet the acrimony has often obscured from posterity the complexity of Provisional leaders' politics. The PIRA's founding Chief of Staff, Seán Mac Stíofáin, argued that capitalism could not deliver 'a fair, square deal and rights for everybody'.[30] Belfast Provisional Joe Cahill declared himself a 'great admirer' of 'Russia': 'the only workable system... which really benefits the working man'. Cahill's quarrel with Official republicanism was more nuanced than a Cold War binary: he implied that Officials would impose diktats on an unwilling population, whereas Cahill's own movement would unify the island and 'leave the path to socialism to the people'.[31]

During the Provisional–Official feud of 1975, Ruairí Ó Brádaigh invoked the Officials' 'totalitarianism' and desired 'Marxist socialist republic' to justify PIRA attacks on 'the Sticks'.[32] Provisional publicity eschewed the label of 'anti-Marxist', but accused Officials of employing 'undemocratic' methods to

---

[28] Francie McGuigan interview with Jack Hepworth. Belfast, 6 December 2017.
[29] Francie McGuigan interview with Jack Hepworth. Belfast, 6 December 2017.
[30] Seán Mac Stíofáin interview with Robert W. White, 1990. Robert W. White, *Out of the ashes: an oral history of the Provisional Irish republican movement* (Newbridge: Merrion, 2017), pp. 45–46.
[31] Christopher Macy, 'Sinn Fein and the IRA's: 1', *Humanist*, Volume 87, Number 1, Ulster Special Issue (January 1972).
[32] *1975: In Memoriam, 2015: The Struggle Continues* (Belfast: National Commemoration Committee of the Workers' Party, 2015), p. 16. Copy in author's possession.

'alter' the republican movement's 'historic course'.[33] Today, Provisional veteran Raymond McCartney candidly suggests the language surrounding the split fortified a specious dichotomy between armed struggle and politicisation:

> The split away from the Officials, who were the reformists, was the right thing to do, but was perhaps done in the wrong way… It became, *are you opposed to politics, or are you opposed to the armed struggle?*[34]

Through the 1970s, Provisional spokespersons stressed that socialism was a secondary concern for a movement that repeatedly forecast imminent victory. Short-term militaristic thinking accommodated economic nationalism as a statement of intent, but usually rendered socialism peripheral. An editorial in *Republican News* in October 1972 stressed that socialism would become important in the 'new Ireland', but until then 'the prime consideration must be the war of National Liberation'.[35]

The degree to which Ruairí Ó Brádaigh studied international politics was somewhat exceptional among the early Provisional leadership. Ó Brádaigh located Ireland among the world's 'small nations', such as Bretons and Catalans: 'struggling peoples with a legacy of colonial oppression'. Resistance to imperialism and superpowers in Washington and Moscow unified these suppressed communities.[36] After independence, the new Ireland would trade with non-aligned Third World nations, rejecting east and west alike in the Cold War, and imitating Israel, Denmark, and Yugoslavia by curtailing foreign investment.[37]

Despite protestations to the contrary from both factions, the distinction between founding Provisionals and Officials was no straightforward disagreement over socialism. Rather, two questions were paramount for both groups' leaders: how to understand the events in Belfast and Derry in July and August 1969; and how to configure international politics when explaining Ireland's experience.

---

[33] *An Phoblacht* (21 February 1975) quoted in Ian Geldard & Keith Craig, *IRA, INLA: foreign support and international connections* (London: Institute for the Study of Terrorism, 1988), p. 84.

[34] Raymond McCartney interview with Jack Hepworth. Derry, 18 September 2015.

[35] 'Socialism without national liberation is a farce', *Republican News*, 13 October 1972.

[36] Ó Brádaigh's international worldview was strikingly consistent. In 1990, four years after leaving the Provisional movement, Ó Brádaigh led the RSF *Ard Comhairle* that echoed his position of two decades earlier, calling for Ireland to support and emulate 'neutral and unaligned' national communities of Eastern Europe. LHL NIPC P6125: RSF, *Ard Fheis 1990: Clár agus Rúin* (Dublin: RSF, 1990).

[37] Ruairí Ó Brádaigh, 'Restore the means of production to the people', *The Irish Press*, 3 December 1970; LHL NIPC P2872: Sinn Féin, *Presidential Address of Ruairí Ó Brádaigh to 76th Ard-Fheis* (Dublin: Sinn Féin, 1980).

Official theoreticians located Ireland firmly in 'world revolution', whereas Provisionals tended to think in more sectoral terms.

A former Official republican internee evoked how Officials perceived themselves in the vanguard of a global socialist movement when the republican movement split:

> You see, people like me and younger people then, we thought then – this was the end of the sixties – we believed we were on the verge of world revolution, and that in ten or fifteen years' time the world would be socialist, and that the rebellion, if you like, that we were part of would be at the forefront.[38]

Officials' admiration for national liberation movements worldwide inspired maverick thinking:

> I remember some of our members got released and they came out and said it was up to us to move up to the Gaeltacht areas in Donegal to liberate them.[39]

Leading PD activists Michael Farrell and Dara Vallely straddled the republican divide. While they did not share Officials' enthusiasm for the USSR, Farrell and Vallely also railed against Provisional polemic that dismissed Marxism. Buoyed by the global '68 and PD's endurance, albeit as a small revolutionary group, in March 1971 Farrell optimistically prophesised that socialism's prospects in Northern Ireland were 'much better than they have been at any time in the last ten years'.[40] While distancing PD's socialism from Khrushchev's Soviet Union, Vallely suggested that republicans should be more concerned about 'allied British and American imperialism' than

> the vague spectre of distant Siberia… If Russia has its Hungary and Czechoslovakia, then American has its far worse list of interventions in Latin America and South East Asia.[41]

---

[38] Former Official republican internee interview with Jack Hepworth. Belfast, 31 March 2016.

[39] Former Official republican internee interview with Jack Hepworth. Belfast, 31 March 2016.

[40] 'Socialist's view on the north', *The Irish Press*, 16 March 1971.

[41] Dara Vallely, 'New assailant in the Sinn Fein controversy', *Donegal Democrat*, 21 January 1972.

The Third World was the chief source of inspiration for Official republicans in the 1970s. Triumphant liberation movements worldwide constituted revolutionary models and augured excitingly for a new post-imperial order. At the OSF *ard fheis* of December 1972, the party *Ard Comhairle* paid tribute to the Vietnamese whose 'heroic' stand against 'American imperialism' had 'shown the world how to fight'.[42] Addressing the International Conference on the Rights of Peoples in 1976, OSF president Tomás Mac Giolla insisted Ireland was a Third World country 'in every meaning of the term' and 'the potential Cuba of western Europe'.[43]

While Provisionals attacked the UK, USA, and USSR as oppressive imperial powers, Officials highlighted imperialism's particularly capitalist impulse. Connecting imperialism and financial exploitation in the Third World, in 1978 Sinn Féin The Workers' Party councillor Donnchada Mac Raghnaill of County Louth explained his party's hostility to 'multi-nationals and their roles from Chile to Angola'.[44] Provisional republicans, somewhat distantly, championed diverse anti-imperialist movements during the 1970s. By contrast, Official republicans, from OSF president Tomás Mac Giolla to younger OIRA internees in Long Kesh, identified specifically with *leftist* revolutionaries. From 1973 to 1976, Officials studied and supported the Mozambique Liberation Front (FRELIMO) in Mozambique, Chile's embattled Socialist Party, and the Viet Cong.[45]

In the late 1970s, Ruairí Ó Brádaigh celebrated independent Third World nations as small states maintaining relative autonomy during the Cold War. Aloof from the far left, Ó Brádaigh formulated his position not in response, for example, to the vicissitudes of the Sino-Soviet split, but in the implicit belief that Ireland's struggle and culture were unique. As Marie-Violaine Louvet has noted, Ó Brádaigh was also committed to stateless nations in Europe, such as Bretons and Basques, who he regarded as Celtic allies.[46]

Independent Third World nations represented ideal types for a Provisional leadership that saluted self-supporting, culturally 'authentic' Celtic nations. In 1979 and 1980, Ó Brádaigh's and Mac Stíofáin's eclectic international sympathies

---

[42] 'Stop sectarianism, urges Mac Giolla', *Irish Examiner*, 18 December 1972.

[43] Tomás Mac Giolla quoted in 'Third world and Ireland', *United Irishman: Monthly Newspaper of Sinn Féin* (August 1976).

[44] Donnchada Mac Raghnaill, 'Innocent people have died in these tragedies', *Drogheda Independent*, 15 December 1978.

[45] 'The Chilean conflict… The atrocities continue', *United Irishman* (June 1972); 'Mac Giolla welcomes delegates', *United Irishman: Monthly Newspaper of Sinn Féin* (August 1976).

[46] Marie-Violaine Louvet, *Civil society, post-colonialism and transnational solidarity: the Irish and the Middle East conflict* (Basingstoke: Palgrave Macmillan, 2016), pp. 125–126.

included solidarity greetings to Nicaragua, Zimbabwe, and Poland, where the global standing of the USA, UK, and USSR respectively had declined. In 1980, Mac Stíofáin described his timeless affinity with 'the oppressed against the oppressor', and hailed Robert Mugabe as 'one of the greatest political leaders to come out of the struggle in Southern Africa'. Mac Stíofáin fondly listed independence movements in Algeria, Cuba, Angola, Mozambique, Guinea-Bissau, and Aden.[47] In his presidential address to the Sinn Féin *ard fheis* of November 1980, Ó Brádaigh excoriated the foreign policies of Washington and Moscow and celebrated the Patriotic Front's breakthrough in Zimbabwe as 'another dent... in the armour of the Iron Lady!'[48]

Drafted by Ruairí Ó Brádaigh and PIRA director of publicity Dáithí Ó Conaill in 1971, policy document Éire Nua (New Ireland) expressed the leadership's socioeconomic blueprint. Throughout the decade, Éire Nua was revised and contested within the movement. The Provisional Army Council accepted the proposals in 1972 and republican prisoners discussed them in Long Kesh: PIRA public relations officer Seamus Loughran told readers of a republican bulletin that the proposals were 'worth reading' and 'worth discussing, perhaps even as much as we [prisoners] have'.[49] Through the mid-1970s, Sinn Féin *cumainn* issued flyers and newsletters explaining the programme, and convened discussion groups.[50] An ally of Ó Brádaigh and Ó Conaill, Christene Ní Elias, revised and re-publicised Eire Nua in four *Republican News* articles in 1977.[51]

Éire Nua combined economic nationalism with plans for a federalised Ireland. As Kevin Bean and Mark Hayes have argued, the proposals fused 'cooperative socialist' ideas with a vision for decentralised governance to 'assuage' unionist fears of a united Ireland.[52] Ireland's four historic provinces would be units of

---

[47] 'Interview with Seán Mac Stíofáin', *Fight Racism! Fight Imperialism!*, 3 (March–April 1980).

[48] LHL NIPC P2872: Sinn Féin, *Presidential Address of Ruairí Ó Brádaigh to 76th Ard-Fheis* (Dublin: Sinn Féin, 1980).

[49] EHI: Seamus Loughran, Camp P.R.O., 'Letter from Long Kesh', *An Guth: Bulletin of the Terry McDermott Sinn Féin Cumann (Gransha)*, Number 11 (n.d. [1972]).

[50] 'Eire Nua is local democracy', *An Troid: The Turf's Own Republican Newssheet*, 8 (19 July 1975).

[51] 'Know your Eire Nua: Power in the New Ireland', *Republican News*, 4 June 1977; 'Know your Eire Nua: "Regionalisation"', *Republican News*, 18 June 1977; 'Know your Eire Nua: Principles of "Regionalisation"', *Republican News*, 9 July 1977; 'Know your Eire Nua: An Chomhairle Cheantair (The District Council)', *Republican News*, 13 August 1977.

[52] Kevin Bean & Mark Hayes, 'Sinn Féin and the new republicanism in Ireland: electoral progress, political stasis, and ideological failure', *Radical History Review*, 104 (2009), p. 133.

regional government. Ó Brádaigh and Ó Conaill took their inspiration not from international socialism, but from ideas of historical legitimacy and Irish uniqueness: the programme's architects billed its communalism, localism, and economic nationalism as hallmarks of 1916 and distinctive national practice. Addressing a Sinn Féin meeting in Monaghan in August 1975, Ó Brádaigh cited the medieval Brehon Laws and the Irish tradition of neighbourly cooperation, *Comhar na gComharsan*, as he explained that Éire Nua sought 'maximum benefit for Ireland's people from Ireland's natural resources'. Farms and mines would be brought under state control. Economic nationalism would 'break the grip of the multi-national combines and exploiters on the wealth of the country' so the 'ordinary people of Ireland could benefit'.[53] In his memoir, published in 1975, PIRA Chief of Staff Seán Mac Stíofáin was on similar lines when he advocated 'the democratic socialism that was preached and practised by the men of 1916'.[54]

Within the imagined, quintessentially Irish 'socialist-federal republic', there was detailed sensitivity to provincial distinction. Sinn Féin posters projected 'self-governing communities'. A clause held that the new Ireland's four tiers of government would reflect the 'socio-economic patterns and the varying traditions of a given area'[55] – especially apt for the industrialised, divided society in Ulster. The emphasis on localised democracy also had an international resonance: decentralised governance would counteract the tendency towards a monolithic state dictatorship that Ó Brádaigh and Ó Conaill abhorred in the Soviet Union. As Martyn Frampton has posited, Ó Brádaigh's leadership looked less to 'a global anti-imperialist continuum' than 'a context that was both historical and specifically Irish'.[56]

In the late 1970s, contestation over Éire Nua intensified within the Provisional movement.[57] For Adrian Guelke, Sinn Féin vice-president Gerry Adams and his supporters campaigned to remove Éire Nua from the party's manifesto since they considered it 'an obstacle to socialist planning'.[58]

---

[53] 'O'Bradaigh on "Immorality of Internment"', *The Anglo-Celt*, 15 August 1975.

[54] Seán Mac Stíofáin quoted in Richard Davis, 'The convergence of orange and green socialism: the Marxist quagmire', in Alan O'Day (ed.), *Terrorism's laboratory: the case of Northern Ireland* (Aldershot: Dartmouth Publishing, 1995), p. 178.

[55] LHL NIPC PPO0306: Sinn Féin Belfast Executive, *Éire Nua* (1979).

[56] Frampton, 'Squaring the circle', 48.

[57] In November 1979, Gerry Adams revealed that revisions were afoot after 18 months of internal debates. Ó Broin, *Sinn Féin*, 235.

[58] Adrian Guelke, 'Loyalist and republican perceptions of the Northern Ireland conflict: the UDA and Provisional IRA', in Peter H. Merkl (ed.), *Political violence and terror: motifs and motivations* (Berkeley, California: University of California Press, 1986), p. 108.

However, Guelke's assessment elides several modifications to Éire Nua through the late 1970s and draws a false left–right dichotomy between the future Provisional leadership under Adams, and earlier leaders Ó Brádaigh and Ó Conaill.

In the late 1970s and early 1980s, Éire Nua's revisions, and eventual rejection, reflected key geographical differences throughout Sinn Féin. Mobilising against Éire Nua, Adamsites drew support chiefly from northern republicans. Many were concerned by the (southern) Provisional leadership's efforts through the 1970s to accommodate Northern Ireland's loyalists, as Brian Feeney has noted.[59] Ó Brádaigh had advocated talks with loyalist paramilitaries in 1974, and the PIRA instructed its volunteers to cease targeting off-duty members of the Ulster Defence Regiment.[60] Ó Conaill optimistically perceived embryonic separatist tendencies in Ulster loyalism, and made overtures to the paramilitary Ulster Defence Association to this effect.[61]

Adams's supporters in the north feared that Éire Nua would fortify loyalist dominance in a nine-county Ulster. In October 1978, Dáithí Ó Conaill moved the Sinn Féin *ard fheis* to welcome discussions with loyalists. Although the motion passed, it elicited considerable northern opposition. Adams's ally Tom Hartley, a Belfast Sinn Féin representative, was among several northern dissenters. There could, Hartley argued, be no question of accommodation with loyalism, which 'divides our people, stands for emigration, bad housing, no education, and the gerrymander'.[62]

Not all northern republicans were so suspicious of Éire Nua. A Sinn Féin *cumann* in west Belfast interpreted Éire Nua as a vital accommodation with recalcitrant loyalists: 'A Federal Solution, whereby Ireland is under 4 Provinces... is the only REAL solution.'[63] Confidently anticipating imminent British withdrawal in 1975, Sinn Féin's *Comhairle Ceantair* in County Donegal pitched federalism as an invitation to unionists. In this

---

[59] Brian Feeney, *Sinn Féin: a hundred turbulent years* (Madison, Wisconsin: University of Wisconsin Press, 2002), p. 321.

[60] Henry Patterson, '1974 – year of liberty'? The Provisional IRA and Sunningdale', in David McCann & Cillian McGrattan (eds.), *Sunningdale, the Ulster Workers' Council strike and the struggle for democracy in Northern Ireland* (Manchester: Manchester University Press, 2017), p. 147.

[61] Marc Mulholland argues that Desmond Fennell, who wrote for *An Phoblacht* under a pseudonym, was 'an important non-republican resource' for the Provisional leadership's federalist thought. Mulholland, 'Northern Ireland and the far left', 554–555.

[62] 'Sinn Fein ready to talk with Loyalists on North aims', *Irish Independent*, 23 October 1978.

[63] 'U.D.I. or an Irish republic...', *Na Madraí: The Newssheet of the Seamus Burns/Charlie Hughes Sinn Fein Cumann, Lower Falls*, 20 November 1976.

border county of the Republic, Adamsites' fears of a loyalist-dominated Ulster provincial assembly gained little apparent traction. On the contrary, the Donegal Provisionals were at pains to envisage Éire Nua undergirding a 'pluralist society' of 'self-governing communities':

> To the Unionist-minded people we say that an Ulster Parliament for the nine counties will guarantee the rights of all.[64]

Adamsites' opposition to Éire Nua did not constitute leftist rebellion. On the contrary, left-leaning Provisionals worked with, not against, the proposals, modifying Éire Nua in 1979 to 1980 to promote an extensive 'economic resistance' programme. Amendments passed at Sinn Féin's *ard fheis* of 1980 stipulated that firms in 'the new Ireland' could only remain private if they demonstrated 'reasonable efforts' to develop the nation's economy. An updated edition, *Éire Nua: The Social Dimension*, proposed nationalisation for finance, insurance, and key industries, with limits on individual landholding.[65] By 1980, Éire Nua's economic nationalism and redistributive communalism particularly emphasised Pádraig Pearse's assertion that 'all rights to private property must be subordinate to the public right and welfare'.[66]

Debates about Éire Nua resurfaced at the Sinn Féin *ard fheis* of November 1981, highlighting stark differences between how Ó Brádaigh's and Adams's supporters formulated political ideas. This was a struggle between generations and geographies. While Ó Brádaigh situated Éire Nua as 'decentralised socialism' in a future independent Ireland, Adamsites addressed ongoing power struggles within Northern Ireland, and within the Provisional movement.[67] At the 1981 *ard fheis*, in tones reminiscent of his hostility to the 'dictatorial' USSR a decade earlier, Ó Brádaigh defended Éire Nua as a plan for a self-supporting united Ireland that would not fall prey to 'evil' centralisation or Cold War partisanship. By contrast, Fermanagh republican and Adams supporter Owen Carron dismissed Éire Nua's 'compromise' with loyalism.[68]

---

[64] 'The only basis for permanent peace', *Derry People & Donegal News*, 11 October 1975.

[65] LHL NIPC Oversize P8801: Sinn Féin, *Sinn Féin Explained* (Belfast: Sinn Féin, 1979); 'Adams: "Guns no solution"', *The Cork Examiner*, 21 January 1980.

[66] 'Plan for economic resistance launched', *The Irish Press*, 21 January 1980; 'Eire Nua: The social dimension', *An Phoblacht/Republican News*, 26 January 1980.

[67] Dominick Bruno & Matthew Costello (eds.), *Éire Nua: a new beginning* (Belfast: Cumann Na Saoirse Náisiúnta, 2012), p. 17.

[68] 'Large Fermanagh Sinn Fein delegation at *ard fheis*', *Fermanagh Herald*, 6 November 1982.

Oral testimonies illustrate the complexity of perspectives on Éire Nua, mapping entangled views of the republican movement's historical trajectory. Memory of this elaborate political programme has complexified since Eamonn McCann dismissed the 'harebrained' Éire Nua plan in 1974.[69] For republicans who today disagree with Sinn Féin's direction, Éire Nua's final defeat at the party's 1982 *ard fheis* marks the threshold moment when Adams and his supporters secured the Provisional leadership. However, for northern Provisionals who supported Adams's leadership, Éire Nua was at best impracticable, and at worst plainly irrelevant to republican struggle. Speaking in 2000, former Belfast Sinn Féin councillor Bobby Lavery claimed:

> No-one understood what Éire Nua was for. No-one I knew had ever read what it was about. It didn't mean anything to us.[70]

Localised nuances suffuse memories of Éire Nua. Former PIRA prisoner Eamonn MacDermott, from Derry City, where 'unionism was just a sideshow', echoed Adams's evocation of federalism: 'dumped because it was a sop to unionism'.[71]

Yet oral history's capacity to bring the past into the present is especially evident when subjective positions mutate over time. Identifying the peace process with Adams's leadership, some dissenting republicans who have broken with Sinn Féin since 1982 now rehabilitate Éire Nua. Members of RSF, who broke with Adams's movement in 1986, retain Éire Nua in their programme today. Similarly, Belfast republican Francie McGuigan, who left the Provisionals in the 1990s, recalls being a 'great believer' in Éire Nua. Casting federalism as a missed opportunity, McGuigan imagined what might have been, recounting how the proposals received moderate approval from Desmond Boal, a barrister close to unionist leader Ian Paisley.[72]

Connecting Éire Nua's demise with Adams's rise to power, commentary on the proposals has carried wide-ranging dissent. Former Belfast PIRA volunteer Tommy Gorman linked Éire Nua's abandonment with broader processes he lamented in Provisional republicanism, chiefly socialism's decline and the ascendancy of 'right wing... dog soldiers [who] follow the leader no matter what the leader says'.[73]

---

[69] Eamonn McCann, *War and an Irish town* (London: Pluto Press, 1993) [First edition Harmondsworth: Penguin, 1974], p. 311.

[70] Bobby Lavery interview with Jonathan Tonge, 28 June 2000. Jonathan Tonge, 'Sinn Féin and "new republicanism" in Belfast', *Space & Polity*, 10 (2006), p. 139.

[71] Eamonn MacDermott interview with Jack Hepworth. Derry, 17 September 2015.

[72] Francie McGuigan interview with Jack Hepworth. Belfast, 6 December 2017.

[73] Tommy Gorman interview with Jonathan Stevenson. Jonathan Stevenson, *"We wrecked the place": contemplating an end to the Northern Irish troubles* (New York: Free Press, 1996), p. 118.

Socialist republican Tommy McKearney, who left the Provisionals in the late 1980s, reflects on contestation over Éire Nua as a factional clash within the movement:

> Those who set out to rubbish the Éire Nua programme were striving to take the organisation over, and did so, and by rubbishing the Éire Nua programme they effectively side-lined the older, southern-based leadership of Dáithí Ó Conaill, Ruairí Ó Brádaigh, whatever other people were there... It was politically expedient [to expunge Éire Nua] in order to side-line opponents as part of a power struggle.[74]

Retrospective subjectivities around Éire Nua subtly reflect how the proposals are remembered in association with the Ó Brádaigh leadership deposed in the early 1980s. Remaining a committed activist today, Gerry MacLochlainn assesses the proposals as thoughtful, if 'unrealistic':

> Éire Nua was an, I think, good attempt to reach out to Protestants, to say, *you're nervous about a united Ireland, do you think we're going to do to you what you done to us? We're not. Here's the structures we would have, it would be a nine-county Ulster.* They couldn't have been ignored. We also believed in power being devolved down. None of those are bad ideas. I think the problem with Éire Nua was that it wasn't realistic. It didn't attract Protestants at all. They didn't see anything in it at all. Far better just to stay with Britain. There was nothing there to move them on. It was one of those idealistic things where people sit down in a backroom, but it was a genuine attempt to reach out to the Protestant community. We only really started to understand how we were going to reach out to the Protestant community well into the peace process.[75]

MacLochlainn's praise for the Éire Nua's originality and creativity foregrounds the Adams leadership's later innovation in the peace process of the 1990s, in which MacLochlainn participated.[76]

Debates around Éire Nua attest the enduring importance of networks and alliances shaping subjectivities during intra-republican discussion. In the early

---

[74] Tommy McKearney interview with Jack Hepworth. Moy, 8 December 2017.

[75] Gerry MacLochlainn interview.

[76] As Sinn Féin's representative in London, MacLochlainn was among a party delegation that met Labour's junior Northern Ireland spokesperson, Paul Murphy, in December 1994. 'British Labour Party confirms having had talks with Sinn Fein', *The Irish Times*, 30 December 1994.

1980s, rejection of Éire Nua heralded a new, northern Provisional leadership around Gerry Adams, Martin McGuinness, Danny Morrison, and their supporters. Just two days after the Sinn Féin *ard fheis* debated federalism in 1981, former PIRA Chief of Staff Seán Mac Stíofáin resigned from the party's *Ard Comhairle*, protesting how the debate had been conducted.[77] Mac Stíofáin complained that party chairman Phil Flynn had allowed 'certain delegates' to aim 'low' insults towards the architects of the federal programme.[78] When all references to Éire Nua were removed from the party constitution in 1982, several long-serving allies of Ó Brádaigh, including Richard Behal, Joe O'Neill, and Tom Sullivan, left the *Ard Comhairle*.[79]

Differences on the interaction of political theory and practice, and disagreements on Ireland's place in the world, were not exclusive to the Provisional movement. Debates about socialism and its implications for revolutionary strategy were pertinent throughout republicanism, especially as leftist republicans became increasingly organised through the 1980s.

Republican socialism and the 'new world order', c.1981–c.1994

In 1979, Provisional theoreticians espoused solidarity with mass anti-imperialist movements such as Nicaragua's Sandinistas and Zimbabwe's Patriotic Front, but smaller leftist sects such as West Germany's Rote Armee Fraktion and Revolutionäre Zellen were beyond the pale. In contrast, members of the IRSP and INLA in the early 1980s identified specifically with leftist revolutionaries worldwide.

The IRSP-INLA's eclectic international sympathies included left-wing 'terrorist' groups that, for the Official movement from which they had broken, confirmed their rivals as an 'opportunist... lunatic left' faction.[80] During a tour of Europe in May 1975, IRSP *Ard Comhairle* representative Peter Pringle from Killybegs, County Donegal, encapsulated the party's radical international outlook: Pringle remarked upon the 'essential unity of the world wide anti-imperialist struggle'.[81] The spike in left-wing terrorism in West Germany in the late 1970s inspired INLA hunger striker Patsy O'Hara to profess 'the greatest respect and admiration' for the Rote Armee Fraktion's 'struggle against

---

[77] 'Resigned', *Drogheda Independent*, 4 December 1981.
[78] Michael Devine, 'MacStiofain leaves Sinn Fein', *Belfast Telegraph*, 25 November 1981.
[79] White, *Out of the ashes*, 201.
[80] Technological University Dublin Library Services: OSF, *Ard Fheis 1976 reports*. Available at https://arrow.tudublin.ie/ (accessed 28 May 2018).
[81] LHL NIPC IRSP Boxes: Speech by Peter Pringle for European tour, May 1975.

imperialism and national capital'.[82] In 1985, IRSP general secretary Jim Lane said his party and the West German militants shared a 'common enemy' and a 'common aim'.[83]

The INLA's attempts to transpose its radical solidarities into guerrilla action constituted a few sporadic incidents. In 1980, while the British & Irish Lions rugby union team toured South Africa, INLA volunteers firebombed a County Wicklow rugby club in a demonstration of support for the 'South African forces of liberation'. A statement released after the bombing warned the game's governing body in Ireland and South African residents of the Republic: 'Wealthy South African businessmen will not be allowed to enjoy their ill-gotten gains in the safety of Irish country houses.'[84] The IRSP reasserted its support for the Irish Anti-Apartheid Movement's campaign to prevent a South African tour in 1981.[85]

Several years later, Dunnes Stores supermarket employees waged a prolonged strike, refusing to handle goods imported from South Africa. Some nine months into the industrial action, the INLA bombed a Dunnes Stores branch in Dublin. The mainstream Irish Anti-Apartheid Movement and the South African Council of Churches, led by Desmond Tutu, condemned the bombing. The strikers lambasted the INLA's action for undermining the strike: 'They have destroyed nine months' work in one morning.'[86]

In the early 1980s, the Provisionals' support for the South African liberation movement took the more direct form of training Umkhonto we Sizwe guerrillas. Published in 2011, the memoirs of prominent ANC activist Kader Asmal revealed that PIRA volunteers helped to plan the bomb attack on Sasol's oil refinery near Johannesburg in June 1980.[87] In an authorised interview later that year, PIRA representatives pledged operational assistance and 'total support' for the ANC.[88]

In contrast to the INLA's rare and dramatic interventions, Provisionals looked to sympathisers of numerical and financial import. Some of the movement's most prominent American backers held ambivalent, if not conservative, positions on African-American civil rights struggles. A leading representative of the Provisionals' American supporters in Irish Northern Aid, Michael Flannery

82 Geldard & Craig, *IRA, INLA*, 24–26.
83 Geldard & Craig, *IRA, INLA*, 24–26.
84 'Bombers declare war on I.R.F.U.', *Irish Independent*, 30 June 1980.
85 'Rugby racists to tour?', *The Starry Plough/An Camchéachta* (February 1981).
86 'Tanaiste condemns Dunnes Stores bomb', *The Irish Press*, 22 April 1985.
87 Mark Moloney, 'IRA key to anti-apartheid "spectacular" by ANC bombers', *An Phoblacht*, September 2011.
88 'Interview with Provisional IRA', *Fight Racism! Fight Imperialism!*, 7 (November–December 1980).

sympathised 'to a limited extent' with black protest in the United States, but repudiated African-American activism 'above the law of the land' and asserted that

> there is freedom in America: laws can be changed and abuses corrected by the elected representatives of the people. The situation is entirely different in Ireland.[89]

In contrast, a specific commitment to emancipatory radicalism defined the IRSP's international solidarities. In 1982, the IRSP hosted Omali Yeshitela, chair of the African People's Socialist Party. The republican socialist movement announced it would accept no financial donations from Irish-American organisations that did not espouse 'Black Liberation and National Liberation and Socialism in Ireland, and Africa'.[90]

However, in the early 1980s, journalistic commentary increasingly claimed international factionalism was emerging within the IRSP and INLA. In 1982, a member of the INLA's General Headquarters gave a rare interview. The movement's 'staff' member asserted that the INLA would not resist internal education or centralised discipline in the movement:

> After intensive discussions and serious political analysis any divisions which did exist in the INLA have now been sorted out... The INLA realises that military action without political awareness is as useless as a gun with damp ammunition... We fully support the IRSP.[91]

Yet such clarity of purpose was unevenly distributed throughout the IRSP and its military wing. On the party's tenth anniversary in 1984, chair Jim Lane censured the membership for inactivity in local branches and declared: 'There is little to be satisfied with... We have failed to define our socialism.'[92] Spearheaded by Lane, the *Ard Comhairle* attempted to codify its politics and assert primacy over the INLA. The INLA's leading proponent for political elaboration was prisoner Ta Power, who wrote extensively during his incarceration. At Easter 1985, the INLA leadership ostensibly supported internationalist Marxism. After

---

[89] Frank McDonald, 'The American Provisionals', *The Irish Press*, 16 March 1972.

[90] 'Irish Republican Socialist Party statement on African-Irish unity', *Burning Spear: Official Organ of the African People's Socialist Party* (27 October 2015). Available at http://www.theburningspear.com/2015/10/Irish-Republican-Socialist-Party-IRSP-statement-on-African-Irish-unity (accessed 18 October 2017).

[91] 'INLA interview', *The Starry Plough/An Camchéachta* (July–August 1982).

[92] ILA: 'Address by IRSP national chairperson Jim Lane to Ard-Fheis' (8 September 1984).

the IRSP *ard fheis* formally adopted the writings of Marx, Engels, and Connolly, the INLA's Easter statement projected confidently towards a

> victorious conclusion of the Irish National Liberation struggle which will then provide an inspiration for freedom fighters throughout Western Europe.[93]

Yet within the INLA, disputes over the relationship between political theory and tactics continued. A group around Gerard Steenson, a prisoner from Belfast, interpreted political codification as an attempt to relegate the INLA's armed struggle. Writing in May 1985, Steenson argued that the INLA had become 'associated with trendy leftism' and was 'irredeemable'.[94] Just two years later, Steenson led one of the two factions in an internal feud in which 11 republican socialists died. Supergrass trials compounded the movement's fragmentation: 27 people were convicted of INLA activity on renegade volunteer Harry Kirkpatrick's evidence in December 1985.

Ardent militarists were not alone within the republican socialist movement in regarding political elaboration with suspicion. Writing in 1983, an IRSP member from Derry City feared that debating socialist theory would mire republican socialists in dogmatic irrelevance. Pat Doherty implored the movement to reject the contested categories of Marxism-Leninism, Maoism, and Stalinism:

> I always thought that the IRSP was not locked into the argument between stalinism [and its critics]… We can learn from the total history of marxist thought and working class struggles.[95]

Jim Lane's attempts to enunciate republican socialism contributed to a proselytising mission within republicanism more widely. Lane and the IRSP's general secretary regarded the Provisional movement's electoral experimentation in the early 1980s as a pathway to 'clientelism and all its attendant evils'. Accordingly, they contacted Sinn Féin's *Ard Comhairle*, but received no reply.[96] While Lane distinguished the IRSP's 'Marxist-Leninist' position from Sinn Féin's milder 'social democracy', he nevertheless believed the Provisional

---

[93] EHI: 'Fighting on: Easter message from the Irish National Liberation Army', *Saoirse: Newspaper of the Irish Republican Socialist Party* (n.d. [1985]).

[94] Henry McDonald & Jack Holland, *INLA: deadly divisions* (Dublin: Poolbeg, 2010) [First edition Dublin: Torc Books, 1994], p. 271.

[95] Pat Doherty, 'Marxist-Leninist', *The Starry Plough/An Camchéachta* (September 1983).

[96] ILA: 'Address by IRSP national chairperson Jim Lane to Ard-Fheis' (8 September 1984).

movement contained 'a good number of revolutionary socialists' deterred from finding a home in the IRSP only for 'historic reasons' of inter-organisational enmity.[97]

Generational differences, correlating to divergent experiences, underpinned disagreements in the IRSP and INLA. The INLA's older volunteers were typically from Official republican backgrounds, and had become conversant with political theory during internment in the early 1970s. Describing life in Long Kesh in 1974, OIRA prisoner Gerry Heatley emphasised how 'a lot of our spare time is taken up with political discussion and education'. The pedagogical culture was a source of pride for Officials: Heatley described 'a university for revolution from which will graduate a stronger and more determined Republican Movement'.[98]

By the early 1980s, the INLA also included younger volunteers whose mobilisation was distinctly local, and whose education developed later, usually in prison. Gerry Foster was uninitiated in revolutionary theory when he was imprisoned in Long Kesh in 1983. Ex-Officials who had

> either been interned or in the cages of Long Kesh had been released and so from their experience they knew... instead of giving you Karl Marx to read – I mean, we'd Catholic upbringing and schooling, where communist Russia was to be detested and hated, so they knew there was no sense getting you Mao's little red book or something, or *Das Kapital* or stuff like that. They knew you were too far removed from that. So they brought you in through Irish nationalism, to British left-wing thinking, to internationalising the conflict and conflicts around the world.[99]

Mirroring the IRSP *Ard Comhairle*'s efforts from 1984, the INLA's prison education introduced young recruits to a distinctly Irish republican socialist canon, before internationalising discussions of the revolutionary left:

> It was in prison that the politics came to me... It's frightening how naïve you can be at that age. There was no sense talking to me about Marxism and communism: they knew that you were more militaristic than political. So the way they would set about getting you into the left-wing politics would have been to give you books on left-wing Irish

---

[97] 'Interview with Jim Lane', *The Starry Plough/An Camchéachta* (September 1983).
[98] Gerry Heatley, 'Letter from Long Kesh', *The Plough: South Down/South Armagh's Own Republican Paper*, Volume 1, Number 3 (n.d. [1974]).
[99] Gerry Foster interview with Jack Hepworth. Belfast, 13 August 2015.

rebels. They were trying to broaden it, take it away from Ireland, take it away from just purely Irish militaristic nationalism, bring it into social issues concerning Ireland. They were trying to show that the British working class can actually be your allies and not your enemy. It was a hard hurdle to get over because whether I like it or not, it was purely Irish nationalist militaristic attitudes I had... [We] were encouraged to read books by left-wing political thinkers as well, not just in relation to Ireland but in general. They were obviously trying to point out that Britain could be an ally as well.[100]

Peadar Lagan, who joined the INLA in rural south Derry in the early 1990s, attributed his allegiance to friends and networks in his schooldays:

I knew a few Provisionals in our area and some of them would have been left-leaning, but not as much as the INLA. But you ran with whoever you were friendly with. That's basically what it was down to, a lot of it. I was fairly clued up, but it was because I was friendly with this guy, swung me to the INLA at that particular time.[101]

Lagan's interest in Connolly

came from school, there was a teacher at school when I was fourteen... He would have explained Burntollet, Bloody Sunday, the whole modern history, then we went back to Connolly, Larkin, the lock-out, then back to the penal law times. That particularly struck me: fighting for the ordinary man in the street. Taking away that both Protestants and Catholics joined together in the Belfast shipyards. There was a unified approach they all took during the great lock-out in 1913, and I actually found that intriguing.[102]

In the mid-1980s, adopting the teachings of Marx, Engels, and Connolly elicited profound misgivings in the INLA. In December 1984, a GHQ representative acknowledged that 'many within our ranks who have a more traditional republican viewpoint' were uneasy with the IRSP *ard fheis* decision.[103] Even after the feud that decimated the INLA in 1987, sections of the republican socialist movement remained indifferent, or even hostile, to politicisation and

---

[100] Gerry Foster interview with Jack Hepworth. Belfast, 13 August 2015.
[101] Peadar Lagan interview with Jack Hepworth. Bellaghy, 11 December 2017.
[102] Peadar Lagan interview with Jack Hepworth. Bellaghy, 11 December 2017.
[103] LHL NIPC IRSP Boxes: *'Quietly confident': INLA speaks* (1984).

democratic centralism. As late as 1989, IRSP spokespersons sought to reassure comrades that they would not attempt to 'build a party of clones'.[104]

For a core group within the IRSP, Marxist theory remained paramount for programmatic authority and rectitude. Doctrinaire sections of the republican socialist movement examined the perceived deficiencies of the wider radical left in Ireland. Writing in 1989, IRSP member Seamus Morgan excoriated, inter alia, the Communist Party of Ireland and Socialist Workers Movement for refusing to support the republican armed struggle. In a detailed analysis far removed from the IRSP's and INLA's internal strife, Morgan adumbrated Marx's and Lenin's pronouncements on the use of force and positioned himself as an 'internationalist'.[105]

However, theoreticians were just one component of the republican socialist movement. Into the 1990s, the gulf between IRSP thinkers and other factions endured. Writing from Long Kesh after the feud, INLA prisoner Eamonn McCallion denounced 'political bankrupts' undermining 'comrades who were undertaking a genuine attempt to assert the supremacy of politics'.[106] Imprisoned from 1993, INLA volunteer Peadar Lagan remembered some comrades embracing the movement's education programme while others were disinterested:

> Education was the key factor. You were encouraged to read up on your history, remember who you are and who you represented... Some of them had got immersed in topics inside, got degrees, and some of them just went with the flow and were more interested in planning escapes.[107]

Politicised elements in the republican socialist movement connected with the British left. Hosting delegates from the Communist Party of Great Britain in June 1987, the IRSP leadership attributed internal schisms to its failure to become a disciplined 'communist' vanguard.[108] The INLA also drew support from Red Action, a small group mainly comprising former members of the Socialist Workers Party expelled for physical anti-fascism or 'squaddism'. Liam Heffernan from Manchester, who participated in Red Action's militant

[104] Francis Glenn, 'IRSP reply to criticism', *The Starry Plough*, 6 (n.d. [1989]).
[105] Seamus Morgan, 'Marxism, violence and internationalism', *The Starry Plough*, 6 (n.d. [1989]).
[106] Eamonn McCallion, 'Ireland's agenda', *The Leninist*, 58 (21 January 1988).
[107] Peadar Lagan interview with Jack Hepworth. Bellaghy, 11 December 2017.
[108] Alan Merrik, 'The Irish crisis', *The Leninist*, 52 (17 July 1987).

anti-fascist activism in the late 1980s, received a 23-year prison sentence for INLA bombings in 1993.[109]

Today, IRSP veterans who have stayed with the republican socialist movement lament past feuds as catastrophic attacks on the organisation's foremost visionaries. Former INLA prisoner Seamus McHenry recalled before 1987 'a very enlightened movement' with 'enlightened leaders':

> If you think about the assassination of some of our members, your Ronnie Buntings, your Ta Powers, your Gino Gallaghers – that was where I seen we were a progressive movement, we had people like that willing to engage themselves.[110]

For long-standing Belfast IRSP activist Fra Halligan, Ta Power's assassination in 1987 signalled dissenters' attempts to 'close this organisation down... they had to kill the strategist'.[111] Attempts to articulate theoretical positions on the revolutionary left were profoundly divisive in the IRSP and INLA, and the resulting feuds cast a long shadow.

Left-wing politics also stimulated considerable debate and disagreement in the Provisional movement in the 1980s. While socialism was broadly compatible with the Provisionals' overarching aspiration to Irish unity, the movement's leaders were wary of programmatic leftism as a potential threat to internal cohesion. To manage the growing socialist influence in the movement, senior Provisionals sought to coax leftists towards commemorating specifically Irish radical precedents.

In 1981, Sinn Féin's Education Department warned that shifting to the left would spark 'confusion and uncertainty within the Movement' and alienate conservative sections of the support base. In one of several primers circulated to Sinn Féin *cumainn* nationwide for internal party education, the Department grounded the Provisionals' economic policies firmly in Irish revolutionary precedent. The introductory booklet stressed the Easter Proclamation's redistributive credentials and cited Pádraig Pearse's *The sovereign people* on public ownership of land and finance.[112] Speaking in 1983, Sinn Féin's National Organiser, Paddy Bolger, warned colleagues against leftist rhetoric and jargon. Bolger insisted that 'sloganizing about socialism'

[109] Matt Seaton, 'Charge of the new Red Brigade', *The Independent on Sunday*, 29 January 1995.
[110] Seamus McHenry interview with Jack Hepworth. Belfast, 7 December 2017.
[111] Fra Halligan interview with Jack Hepworth. Belfast, 15 September 2015.
[112] LHL NIPC P938: Sinn Féin Education Department, *Nationalism and Socialism* (Dublin: Sinn Féin, 1981).

as a 'magic formula' would be unhelpful. Rather, the struggle must be rooted in localised 'agitational politics'.[113]

The Provisional Education Department kept Irish nationalist historiography integral to its revised programme in the early 1980s. A reading list commended to new members of the movement included texts covering conflicts in Algeria and the Middle East, but accounts of Marxian revolutions were limited to John Reed's *Ten days that shook the world* and Che Guevara's *Guerrilla warfare*. While radical anti-colonial texts such as Frantz Fanon's *The wretched of the earth* and Robert Taber's *The war of the flea* were deemed 'suitable literature', a distinctly Irish republican canon dominated the reading list. Just four revolutionaries of the early twentieth century (Dan Breen, James Connolly, Ernie O'Malley, and Pádraig Pearse) accounted for 16 of the 50 recommended texts.[114]

For left-leaning former prisoner Gerry MacLochlainn, republicans were habitually hazy about their socialism. Writing to the newspaper of the Communist Party of Great Britain, MacLochlainn hoped that the miners' strike would precipitate '*mass* socialist politics in Britain'. He asserted that Irish republicans had

> always seen our struggle as part of a world struggle against imperialism, although we may not have always seen it as clearly as that and been able to articulate it that way.[115]

Through the 1980s, pedagogy became an increasingly crucial, and contested, component of jail experience for many PIRA prisoners. In Long Kesh, radical former hunger striker Tommy McKearney coordinated education early in the decade. Although the leadership outside soon removed McKearney from this role, he maintained in jail a network that would organise separately as the LCR from 1986:

> There was, among the rank-and-file, a possibility of intellectual laziness, where: *we're an army, we just do what we're told, follow the line, don't need to think too much*. This wouldn't have facilitated the move into electoral politics if people thought in that black-and-white fashion, so word was coming in from the outside to get some political education. I was put in charge of political education, but of course right away I opted for a different line... Of course, whether it was

---

[113] 'New departures for Sinn Féin?', *Gralton* (August–September 1983).
[114] LHL NIPC Tom Hartley Collection PH1571: Sinn Féin Education Department, *New Members Course: Notes for Sinn Féin Education Officers* (Belfast: Sinn Féin, 1981).
[115] '"We've had similar struggles"', *The Leninist*, 15 (December 1984).

politically wise of me or not, what I said we should take was a very simple, hard-line Marxist-Leninist position, which did not receive approval. My rationale was, to me, the idea of the professional revolutionary, the transformation of society, where the working class are in charge of the means of production, distribution – you know the jargon. That's what we're talking about if we're going to make an appeal south of the border... I said that Marxism-Leninism was a clear position they could understand, and it was a position – well I was there anyway! But as I say, my run, or my period, as the education officer for the prison came to an end, when word was: *no, that's a bridge too far.* So that happened probably reasonably early '82, '83. I can't remember. But I still had a circle, because there was discussions within the prison.[116]

Prison became a focal point for education, with many long-serving inmates studying for degrees. Yet debates about socialism and tactical innovation were not limited to jail. Before 1983, when Sinn Féin president Ruairí Ó Brádaigh occasionally denounced the USSR and the USA, Provisionals were generally unified, to the extent that they engaged at all. However, through the 1980s, international interests among the Provisional grassroots diversified, sometimes in unorthodox directions: a motion proposing Sinn Féin align with Cuba, North Korea, Vietnam, Kampuchea, Afghanistan, Mongolia, and Laos was withdrawn only on the eve of the *ard fheis* of 1986.[117]

Wide-ranging Provisional engagements with international politics dovetailed with emergent discussions on the extent to which leftism should define the movement's agenda. Addressing a Troops Out Movement meeting in Brighton in 1986, Derry Sinn Féin representative Daisy Mules admitted that the movement lacked 'a clear social and economic strategy', but insisted vaguely that there was a 'commitment to socialism'. Mules inadvertently highlighted confusion on the movement's aspirations when she presented Éire Nua as party policy, even though the proposals had been dropped four years earlier.[118] In a frank contribution to a Provisional discussion journal in 1990, Sinn Féin's Education Officer in Derry, Tony Doherty, explained that over the previous five years he had

---

[116] Tommy McKearney interview with Jack Hepworth. Moy, 8 December 2017.
[117] Alan Merrik, 'Ireland's fight! Our fight!', *The Leninist*, 44 (4 December 1986).
[118] LHL NIPC P2028: Brighton Troops Out Movement, *Sinn Fein Speaks in Brighton: Text of a Speech by Daisy Mules, S.F. Trade Union Department* (Brighton: Brighton Troops Out Movement, 1986).

discovered that far from being an ideologically united party (movement) we encompassed many strains some who don't even think about politics.[119]

Doherty perceived heterogeneous international perspectives among his comrades, ranging from Soviet sympathisers, through Trotskyism and labourism, to 'even more vague social democratic mish mash'.[120]

A sense that the Provisional movement was moving towards electoral opportunism informed the decision of approximately 25 PIRA prisoners to establish the LCR in Long Kesh in 1986. Through their education programmes and reading habits, left-leaning prisoners had been recognised as an in-group in the jail for several years. LCR founder Tommy McKearney recalled how 'the bulk of the leftism' in the PIRA was 'contained and confined' in Long Kesh.[121] Belfast PIRA volunteer Micky McMullan declared himself a Connollyite socialist and remembered that 'incredibly' his comrades in Long Kesh ostracised him for being 'communistic'.[122] Veteran PIRA prisoner Albert Allen recognised the commitment of his leftist comrades in jail, but thought their politics had 'started going haywire' in the 1980s. Of one prominent radical who later left the Provisionals, Allen said:

> Don't get me wrong, he was a good man... one hundred percent republican, smashing fella like, but it wasn't republicanism. They lost the plot.[123]

With prisoners' journal *Iris Bheag* reflecting debates among committed republicans, a degree of acrimony pervaded discussions. In October 1987, Sinn Féin director of publicity Danny Morrison rebuked PIRA prisoners who used 'Marxist Esperanto'. Responding, the prisoners of C Wing in H5, Long Kesh, revealed left-wing Provisionals' exasperation with the 'conservative lot, slow to embrace change, too slow some would say'.

The row exposed differences even among senior Provisionals. In a private letter to a friend in the Communist Party of Great Britain, veteran prisoner Brian Keenan excoriated 'the "Marxist Esperanto" prat' Morrison's 'nasty letter'.

---

[119] Tony Doherty, 'The end and the means', *Iris Bheag*, 27 (September 1990).
[120] Tony Doherty, 'The end and the means', *Iris Bheag*, 27 (September 1990).
[121] Tommy McKearney interview with Richard English, 20 September 2000. Richard English, *Armed struggle: the history of the IRA* (London: Pan Books, 2012) [First edition London: Macmillan, 2003], p. 233.
[122] Micky McMullan interview with Rogelio Alonso. Rogelio Alonso, *The IRA and armed struggle* (Abingdon: Routledge, 2007), p. 88.
[123] Albert Allen interview with Jack Hepworth. Belfast, 13 December 2017.

Keenan admitted being 'rash' in his response to Morrison, suggesting wider tensions between Provisional leftists and Sinn Féin leaders.[124] Meanwhile, the PIRA leadership was hostile to the LCR's foundation, detailing senior Belfast republican Brendan Hughes to discredit the 'counter-revolutionary' breakaway. Hughes later became a prominent dissenter against the leadership of his former comrade Gerry Adams: remembering the LCR episode 15 years later, Hughes chastised himself for being 'so naïve'.[125]

The LCR's complex critique of the Provisionals' direction in the late 1980s was complex and rooted both in theoretical positions and tactical changes. Leftist prisoners asserted that a vanguard republican movement must organise the Irish working class. LCR members criticised Provisional electoralism and perceived reliance on an increasingly aimless armed campaign. In a rare moment of concord with the Sinn Féin leadership in the late 1980s, Anthony McIntyre supported Gerry Adams's call to the PIRA 'to be careful and careful again' after several operations resulted in civilian casualties.[126] For Tommy McKearney, the decision of the Sinn Féin *ard fheis* of November 1986 to drop abstentionism in the Dublin parliament consigned the Provisionals to reformism and irrelevance: Sinn Féin could not 'claim to be revolutionary in either the Fenian or the socialist mould'.[127] Meanwhile, the INLA feud of 1987 fuelled McKearney's concerns that the IRSP-INLA was not sufficiently committed to the primacy of politics.[128]

Debates among LCR members in Long Kesh featured in 14 issues of the group's *Congress '86* journal from 1987 to 1991. Activists studied international politics to sharpen their interpretations of the conjuncture facing socialist republicans. Rejecting the dogmatic stringency of many leftist groups, the LCR coupled theoretical principles with a degree of tactical flexibility. Writing in 1988, two LCR theoreticians found in the revolutions in Nicaragua and South Africa the necessity of a revolutionary vanguard and guerrilla campaign allied with mass movement. Revolutionary breakthroughs abroad pinpointed the Provisionals' errors. The Sandinistas' 'concrete analysis' and socialist programme contrasted with the 'Irish anti-imperialist movement...

---

[124] 'Bad language', *Iris Bheag*, 5 (December 1987); Brian Keenan to Jack Conrad, 29 January 1988; Brian Keenan to Jack Conrad, 28 February 1988, quoted in 'Prisoner B26380's dilemma', *WeeklyWorker*, 732 (20 July 2008).

[125] Brendan Hughes interview with Liam O'Ruairc, 7 September 2001. Liam O'Ruairc, *The League of Communist Republicans, 1986–1991* (Published by the author, 2001), p. 5 n. 9.

[126] A. McIntyre, 'Letter from a Republican prisoner', *Workers Press: Weekly Paper of the Workers Revolutionary Party*, 156 (11 March 1989).

[127] 'Letter from Long Kesh', *Republican Bulletin: Iris Na Poblachta*, 4 (March 1987).

[128] Tommy McKearney, 'Irish message', *The Leninist*, 58 (21 January 1988).

in a shambles'.[129] The South African Communist Party, meanwhile, taught Irish activists the importance of mobilising a 'brave, politicised trade union leadership'.[130]

Conversely, reverses for revolutionaries in Palestine and Burma in the late 1980s corroborated LCR assessments of Provisionals' tactical errors. In June 1988, Sinn Féin's general secretary Tom Hartley urged an internal party conference to support an alliance with the SDLP. Several months later, drawing upon events in Burma, the LCR renounced the pan-nationalist pact: the 'ill-defined nationalism of a pro-independence [sic] grouping' portended 'isolationism'.[131] The Palestinian liberation movement also demonstrated the dangers of flawed alliances and reformism. The Palestine Liberation Organization's dependence on the USSR and 'various Arab states' had 'broken down' and the Camp David Agreement had provoked internal unrest:

> Revolutionaries must never let a thirst for political power or the mirage of sympathetic constitutional support side-track them from the back-breaking work of sowing revolution.[132]

The contrasting fortunes of revolutionary movements worldwide emboldened the LCR's programme for a 'workers' and small farmers' republic' and substantiated their criticisms of an Irish anti-imperialist movement they perceived in turmoil. Tommy McKearney recalls highlighting the ANC's mass mobilisation as a critique of Provisional military elitism:

> I think at the time we talked about South Africa. We said, *look, the ANC did not focus its entire weight on the armed campaign, the ANC has a political, electoral dimension, also on the streets, but we have no position on the streets, we have ignored the streets, we have ignored the trade union, we haven't impacted on unionised labour.* From my point of view, these weren't just opportunist avenues. I said, *if we're talking about socialist, or a workers' republic, we don't have a significant presence in organised labour, nor do we have a programme that will prevent us*

---

[129] 'Nicaragua must survive', *Congress '86*, 5 (Winter 1988).
[130] 'South Africa in struggle: Lessons for Ireland', *Congress '86: Quarterly Journal of Communist Republican Prisoners and their Associates*, 4 (n.d. [1988]).
[131] 'Reaction in Rangoon', *Congress '86: Journal of Communist Republican Prisoners*, 6 (Spring 1989).
[132] 'Palestinians struggle against Zionism and Imperialism', *Congress '86: Quarterly Journal of Communist Republican Prisoners and their Associates*, Volume 1, Number 3 (n.d. [1987]).

falling down over the cliff of reformism, and eventually your reliance on the armed wing to save us is going to be ended.[133]

Left-wing republican critique extended beyond the LCR. In correspondence with the newspaper of Britain's Workers Revolutionary Party in 1989, radical republican Anthony McIntyre expressed his misgivings with Provisional tactics. A long-serving PIRA prisoner, McIntyre counted himself among 'Marxist Republicans... trying to raise socialism to the agenda at all times'. Sinn Féin had become preoccupied with appealing to conservative Fianna Fáil voters in the Republic of Ireland, McIntyre argued. His conclusions had existential implications for the Provisional campaign:

> Throughout its history the Republican movement has shown little inclination to view working-class potential in the manner that Marxists do ... perhaps, then, the Republican strategy is hopeless.[134]

Adrian Guelke has argued convincingly that the end of the Cold War had less impact on the Irish war than for conflict transformations in Israel-Palestine and South Africa.[135] However, divergent republican responses to revolutions in Eastern Europe from 1989 to 1991 highlighted salient differences in how republicans understood their struggle and engaged with international class politics. For many Provisional republicans, and their erstwhile comrades who now constituted RSF, *glasnost*, *perestroika*, and German reunification constituted revolutionary moments for national communities. Conversely, while radicals in the IRSP, PD, and Provisional left initially celebrated the demise of 'Stalinism' in Europe in 1989 and 1990, they soon became more cautious about the longer-term prospects for left-wing anti-imperialism. By 1991, radical republicans feared that reformism, compromise, and reinvigorated capitalism would displace revolutionary politics worldwide.

When the Berlin Wall fell in November 1989, Provisional leaders and publicists, and former Provisionals in RSF, were jubilant. Propagandists optimistically portrayed troop withdrawals from the Rhine a 'major climb-down for British imperialism'.[136] For Gerry Adams, addressing Sinn Féin's *ard fheis* of 1990, events in Eastern Europe boded well for 'lasting democracy and self-determination' throughout Europe.[137] RSF

---

[133] Tommy McKearney interview with Jack Hepworth. Moy, 8 December 2017.

[134] A. McIntyre, 'Letter from a Republican prisoner', *Workers Press: Weekly Paper of the Workers Revolutionary Party*, 156 (11 March 1989).

[135] Adrian Guelke, 'The peace process in South Africa, Israel and Northern Ireland: a farewell to arms?', *Irish Studies in International Affairs*, 5 (1994), p. 106.

[136] 'Berlin's border destroyed', *An Phoblacht/Republican News*, 16 November 1989.

[137] LHL NIPC P4181: Sinn Féin, *Ard Fheis 1990* (Dublin: Sinn Féin, 1990).

president Ruairí Ó Brádaigh and his party's *Ard Comhairle* similarly relished the 'flame of liberty rekindled' and suggested that Eastern Europe's emergent nationalisms would galvanise Irish aspirations to unification.[138]

Initially, in 1989 and 1990, most leftist republicans responded positively to the 'autumn of nations'.[139] Writing from Long Kesh, PIRA prisoner Martin Livingstone considered the demise of Romania's Ceausescu regime 'progress' for 'democratic socialism'.[140] LCR writers lauded the 'regeneration of Marxism' and forecast that class struggle internationally would 'intensify': freed from unwanted connotations of dictatorship and bureaucracy, socialism could become 'a genuinely attractive alternative' in the new world order. *Glasnost* and *perestroika* would facilitate 'flourishing socialist democracy'.[141]

Hopes of renewal in global socialism redoubled leftist disillusionment with Provisionals' pan-nationalism. For LCR prisoners Tommy McKearney and Tom McFeely, Sinn Féin's negotiations with the SDLP and Fianna Fáil erased critiques of capitalism.[142] LCR associates James Tierney and Eugene Byrne suggested that 'pan-nationalism' was 'too sweeping' to possess a meaningful political programme. For Tierney and Byrne, Sinn Féin's insufficiently discerning approach would attract 'just about anyone capable of humming "The Rising of the Moon"'.[143] Writing in April 1989, an IRSP member in Strabane, County

---

[138] Motion 79 at the RSF *ard fheis* of October 1990 'welcomes the emergence of democracy and national communities within Europe as a positive way forward towards peace'. LHL NIPC P6126: *Presidential Address of Ruairí Ó Brádaigh to the 86th Ard-Fheis of Sinn Féin in the Spa Hotel, Lucan, County Dublin, 27–28 October 1990* (Dublin: RSF, 1990).

[139] At this juncture, Adams's former ally Brian Keenan, imprisoned in Britain, was unusual among PIRA ranks in his scepticism concerning Gorbachev's policy. From 1987 to 1989, Keenan corresponded regularly with Jack Conrad of the Communist Party of Great Britain. Conrad later recalled their letters: 'Brian wanted to get to grips with our ideas. His central concerns surface time and again. How is the struggle for communism to be taken forward? What role could Sinn Féin play? What is going on in the Soviet Union?' In a letter to Conrad in November 1987, Keenan expressed his fears that the Soviet Union would disintegrate under *glasnost* and *perestroika* and cause 'compromise with imperialism' worldwide. Brian Keenan to Jack Conrad, 19 November 1987, quoted in 'Prisoner B26380's dilemma', *WeeklyWorker*, 732 (20 July 2008).

[140] Martin Livingstone, 'Eastern Europe: Socialism or Barbarism?', *The Captive Voice/An Glór Gafa*, Volume 2, Number 2 (Summer 1990).

[141] 'Socialism is alive and well' and 'Restructuring in the U.S.S.R.: Contents, targets & main tendencies', *Congress*, 8 (Spring 1990).

[142] Tommy McKearney & Tom McFeely, 'Reject pan-nationalist drift', *Congress '86: Special Supplement* (n.d. [1987]).

[143] James Tierney & Eugene Byrne, 'We call for a congress', *Congress '86: Special Supplement* (n.d. [1987]).

Tyrone asserted that Sinn Féin's 'Broad Front type talks' with the SDLP would 'offer nothing to the working class'.[144]

Opposition to the 'broad front' connected to internal Provisional perceptions of a seeming drift from leftism. For one anonymous Provisional, the failure of Sinn Féin's *ard fheis* of November 1989 to discuss German reunification confirmed that Sinn Féin was not 'a socialist party'. Tellingly, the Provisional correspondent imagined party colleagues insisting 'that the *ard fheis* is not the forum for a debate such as this'.[145] Similarly, an editorial in PD's journal that cheerfully proclaimed 'the Prague Spring has begun again' also berated republicans who considered their struggle 'in isolation':

> We must ensure that the Irish question becomes part of that debate…
> by direct contact with the new national liberation movements.[146]

By 1990 and 1991, republican leftists were generally uncertain about the implications of Europe's revolutions for Ireland's war. For the most part, radicals remained hopeful that a reinvigorated international left could still inspire the Provisional movement. When the Soviet Union finally unravelled late in 1991, Tommy McKearney insisted that 'Socialism will never fade while Capitalism exists': 'class struggle' remained 'crucial' for revolutionaries worldwide.[147] By contrast, in an open letter to comrades in the Socialist Workers Movement in 1990, PD leaders were strikingly clear-sighted in their revulsion at a burgeoning 'capitalist offensive' in Eastern Europe.[148]

By the time capitalist development and ethnonational conflict pervaded Eastern Europe in the early 1990s, few Provisionals addressed these tumultuous aftermaths of 1989. Provisional leftist Matt Treacy was among the few who openly lamented the precise configuration of this 'new world order'. Writing from Portlaoise in 1992, Dublin PIRA volunteer Treacy regretted the resurgence of monetarism and far-right politics in Eastern European republics. Without mentioning Provisional leaders by name, Treacy lambasted those who had been 'naïve enough' to imagine that the

---

[144] P. McColgan, Irish Republican Socialist Party, Strabane, 'I.R.S.P. aims', *Strabane Chronicle*, 8 April 1989.

[145] Eric, '*ard fheis* Bordom [*sic*]', *Iris Bheag*, 25 (April 1990).

[146] 'Editorial', *An Reabhloid: Journal of Peoples Democracy*, Volume 4, Number 2 (December 1989–February 1990).

[147] 'Where the socialist cause now stands', *Congress*, 14 (Winter 1991), quoted in O'Ruairc, *League of Communist Republicans*, 18.

[148] 'East equals west?', *An Reabhloid: Journal of Peoples Democracy*, Volume 5, Number 1 (n.d. [1990]).

USSR's disintegration portended world peace and the rise of nationalisms worldwide.[149]

In the three intervening decades, historical interpretations of the events of Europe's 1989 have evolved profoundly, as a leftist who remained in the republican movement attests. Gerry MacLochlainn remembers republicans celebrating German reunification and championing reform in the USSR. Yet more extensive hindsight frames the autumn of nations as a period of decline for the global left:

> The Berlin Wall's an interesting one, because I don't know any republicans who didn't welcome the reunification of Germany, because we believe in countries being independent and united, so we liked that. An awful lot of us would have understood the significance of the Soviet Union, and irrespective of the problems with the Soviet Union, the Soviet Union stood as a bulwark against America – maybe against is taking it too far, but they stood as an alternative. And, you know, it's not been good. The Americans being the sole dominant power in this world has not been good… A lot of us understood the significance of the Soviet bloc. It's a better world when there's two powers up there. That said, the Soviet Union needed a lot of cleaning up and sorting out.[150]

Retrospectives negotiate entangled historical subjectivities in the context of present-day positions. Raymond McCartney was the PIRA's OC in Long Kesh from 1989 to 1991, and later served as a Sinn Féin MLA from 2004 to 2020. Having endorsed popular participation in politics, McCartney remembers the autumn of nations dispelling utopian ideologies:

> My experience of imprisonment was you looked at socialism in other places around the world with rose-tinted glasses. The fall of the Soviet Union and East Germany undermined absolutism: you have to make politics relevant to people, and they're not going to get caught up in the mantras of an ideology. You have to make it real.[151]

The implication of McCartney's testimony is that pragmatic accommodation was crucial after 1989. By contrast, in 2005, former Dublin Sinn Féin activist Philip

---

[149] Maitiú O Treasaigh, 'What price European unification now?', *The Captive Voice/An Glór Gafa*, Volume 4, Number 2 (Summer 1992).

[150] Gerry MacLochlainn interview.

[151] Raymond McCartney interview with Jack Hepworth. Derry, 18 September 2015.

Ferguson castigated the Provisional leadership for assuming that the revolutions of 1989 would benefit Irish republicanism.[152] Ferguson had remained a member of Sinn Féin until 1994, but his later representation of the past connected historical moments of transformation in international politics and republicanism alike.

Conclusion

It is hardly surprising that many republicans considered socialism secondary to the historical telos of a united Ireland. Especially in the early 1970s – when an almost millenarian belief in imminent victory was most influential – the practical demands of fighting a guerrilla campaign marginalised detailed theoretical consideration. Outside prisons, the practical demands of fighting a guerrilla campaign, especially when that campaign was infused with an almost millenarian belief in imminent victory in the 1970s, marginalised detailed theoretical considerations. A former PIRA volunteer in Derry City, Eamonn MacDermott recalled how

> socialism was always there in theory, but there'd have been no real thought given to what it meant. We were very much short-term in thinking, as we actually believed we were going to get the Brits out... The socialist aspect was certainly secondary.[153]

Analysing changes in Provisional republican strategy through the 1980s and 1990s, Mark Ryan argued that 'Irish republicanism has always been deeply influenced by the changes taking place in world politics'.[154] Ryan's verdict rings true for some sections of the Provisional movement. While socialism was an important influence, a powerful tradition in Irish republicanism persistently stressed the primacy of the national struggle, even to the point of exceptionalism. As one PIRA prisoner noted in the early 1990s, republican attempts to classify Ireland's place in a global arena had never achieved consensus.[155]

During the 1970s, Provisional leaders stressed particularly Irish precedents for their socioeconomic programme, Éire Nua. Irish neutrality in a Cold

---

152 Philip Ferguson, 'Behind the betrayal', *The Plough*, Volume 2, Number 36 (22 May 2005).

153 Eamonn MacDermott interview with Jack Hepworth. Derry, 17 September 2015.

154 Mark Ryan, 'From the centre to the margins: the slow death of Irish republicanism', in Chris Gilligan & Jon Tonge (eds.), *Peace or war? Understanding the peace process in Northern Ireland* (Aldershot: Ashgate, 1997), p. 73.

155 Basil Hardy, 'Is Ireland a third world country?', *The Captive Voice/An Glór Gafa*, Volume 4, Number 2 (Summer 1992).

War context was sacrosanct: the movement aligned with the world's small and non-aligned nations. When leading Provisionals declared an 'economic resistance' campaign, they directed republicans to agitate on grassroots issues such as housing and unemployment, not to theorise as to the rectitude of the Soviet, Chinese, or Cuban revolutionary models. In Clonard, west Belfast, for example, from 1977, Sinn Féin's advice centre invited local people to log complaints about sub-standard housing. Activists promised to intercede with the Housing Executive on residents' behalf.[156]

By contrast, Official republicans in the early 1970s identified explicitly with left-wing national liberation movements, often aligned with Moscow – beyond the pale for Provisional interpretations of an oppressive, imperialist USSR. Disagreements over socialism were not, of course, the only factors shaping allegiance in the Provisional–Official rivalry: conflicting interpretations of republican agencies in Belfast and Derry in 1969 were paramount.

Senior Provisionals lauded revolutionary movements detrimental to the global standing of the USSR, USA, or UK, but eschewed deeper strategic debate, preferring straightforward exchanges of solidarity greetings with Poland, Nicaragua, Zimbabwe, or Honduras, among others. Left-leaning Provisionals, often at lower ranks, and those who established the LCR in the late 1980s, studied revolutionary movements in greater detail, refining their socialist theory to examine critically the republican movement's shifting tactics.

Especially through the 1980s, for the Provisional movement and the IRSP-INLA alike, negotiating the relationships between socialism and nationalism, and between party and army, occasioned power struggles. Early in the decade, the Provisional executive pinpointed 'sloganising about socialism' as a threat to the movement's unity. Conversely, radical Provisionals accused the leadership of dogmatic militarism and inordinate tactical malleability. The republican socialist movement experienced similar strife when the IRSP *Ard Comhairle* asserted control of the INLA and announced a politicisation programme. Militarist opposition emerged and the movement fractured.

Codifying socialist ideas caused controversy among republicans in the 1980s, reflecting fundamental differences in how individuals and their support networks interpreted 'legitimacy' and political priorities. For Ó Brádaigh, Adams, and their supporters, socialism was influential but never a defining priority. Instead, redistributive economics were best framed in the pliable historical context of 1916. Writing in *Hibernia* in October 1979, Adams defined republicanism by

---

[156] EHI: '"Pool" housing crisis!!' (1977). Published by Sinn Féin Clonard Martyrs cumann, 1977.

the 1916 declaration which in itself is a radical document. It talks about the wealth of Ireland belonging to the people of Ireland. Also as radical was the democratic programme of the first Dáil. If we are to be true republicans we have to adhere to what it says in those documents.[157]

In a discussion at the West Belfast Festival in August 1989, Belfast Provisional and noted Adams supporter Jim Gibney rooted republicanism in everyday struggles as

a liberating philosophy... a creative marxism, not one that is dogmatic... over whether Lenin said this, or Trotsky said that, or Stalin said the other.[158]

Republicans of several political hues shared Gibney's resistance to doctrinaire leftism. The fissiparousness often associated with the revolutionary left exasperated many republican volunteers concerned primarily with executing a guerrilla campaign. Left-wing PIRA prisoner Anthony McIntyre articulated republican irritation with the 'seemingly incessant' factionalism of the British left in 1989:

Republicans look at their own experience, sacrifices and achievements, no matter how minor the latter may be, and they cannot be faulted for thinking that, in spite of their theoretical inadequacies, they have posed a greater challenge to the British state over the past 20 years than the entire British left for all its theoretical clarity and revolutionary wisdom.[159]

Today, republicans who continue to support Sinn Féin can espouse socialist aspirations while maintaining that the unity of a broad mass movement is paramount. Interpreting republicanism's prospects positively, Gerry MacLochlainn credits Adams with galvanising the republican base by avoiding potentially divisive international political theory and 'ideology':

---

[157] Paul Bew & Henry Patterson, *The British state and the Ulster crisis: from Wilson to Thatcher* (London: Verso, 1985), pp. 118–119.

[158] 'A liberating philosophy...', *An Reabhloid: Journal of Peoples Democracy*, Volume 4, Number 2 (December 1989–February 1990).

[159] A. McIntyre, 'Letter from a Republican prisoner', *Workers Press: Weekly Paper of the Workers Revolutionary Party*, 156 (11 March 1989).

Adams's work, from Long Kesh when he was interned, writing the Brownie columns, there was the struggle to politicise – or as he put it, republicanise – our base. The phase we're in now, Adams's groundwork in politicising our base means we can handle it more, the setbacks… The communist movements would talk about studying Marxism, Leninism, historical materialism. But the equivalent in the republican struggle wasn't reading those books; it was basically internalising republicanism, internalising your independence.[160]

IRSP-INLA theorists such as Jim Lane and Ta Power repudiated what they considered republican nostalgia and instead found inspiration specifically in programmatic socialism. In 1984, the IRSP leadership distanced itself from the Provisionals' 'veneer of left-wing rhetoric' and denounced 'parliamentary means', 'left-republicanism', and 'Hibernianised socialism'. The IRSP approached republican past after 1798 critically, situating its 'roots… in bourgeois democracy'.[161]

Kevin Bean has argued that the 'eclecticism' of the Provisionals' global solidarities from the late 1970s signified the 'porous nature of the Republican theoretical tradition and its susceptibility to the ideological pull of external forces'.[162] Although Bean's assessment applies to the Provisional left, the leadership generally resisted outside influences during the Cold War. During the 1980s, senior Provisionals engaged with developments outside Ireland to the extent that doing so could yield funding and military materiel, or forge solidarities to embarrass British diplomats. In 1986, for example, Gerry Adams and Joe Cahill, chair of Sinn Féin's North American Committee, encouraged the Provisionals' supporters in the USA to combine fundraising with lobbying public representatives and humanitarian organisations.[163]

Even at crucial moments in the Cold War, the Provisionals studiously remained aloof. Writing in 1985, Sinn Féin director of publicity Danny Morrison admitted that 'Sinn Féin has never really voted on a policy toward Eastern Europe'.[164] Internal criticisms of Sinn Féin's Foreign Affairs Bureau in 1990 reflected the leadership's sense of detachment from major developments worldwide: even amid these seismic months in European history, the Bureau's

---

[160] Gerry MacLochlainn interview.
[161] ILA: 'A historic step forward' (IRSP press release, 20 September 1984).
[162] Kevin Bean, *New politics*, 74.
[163] Andrew Wilson, 'The conflict between Noraid and the Friends of Irish Freedom', *Irish Review*, 15 (1994), p. 43.
[164] *Ireland after Britain* (1985) quoted in Geldard & Craig, *IRA, INLA*, 84.

resources were at an all-time low, according to its leader, Ted Howell.[165] Howell was not the first occupant of this office to lament its meagre resources: addressing Sinn Féin's *ard fheis* of 1985, director of foreign affairs Síle Darragh complained the Bureau was 'nowhere near operating at optimum level'.[166]

When the Soviet Union disintegrated, many Provisionals, the leadership included, hailed a pan-European nationalist upsurge. Through 1990 and 1991, most grassroots republican leftists remained sanguine, bullishly forecasting socialist renewal. However, as the implications of conflict transformations worldwide played out through the 1990s, leftists' hopes faded. By 1994, PIRA prisoner Matt Treacy's assessment of South Africa, even with Nelson Mandela elected president, was profoundly negative. For Treacy, Joe Slovo and the South African Communist Party had 'abandoned the goal of leading a socialist revolution'. Treacy lamented the '"new world order"... in which socialism no longer seems to provide a ready-made alternative economic system.'[167] As the world transformed through the late twentieth century, republicans envisaged the new Ireland in vastly different ways.

---

[165] LHL NIPC P4181: Sinn Féin, *Ard Fheis 1990* (Dublin: Sinn Féin, 1990).

[166] 'Neutrality stance confirmed', *An Phoblacht/Republican News*, 7 November 1985.

[167] Maitiú O Treasaigh, 'Whither South Africa?', *The Captive Voice/An Glór Gafa*, Volume 6, Number 2 (Winter 1994).

4

Feminism and Women's Activism

> I think [Cumann na mBan]1 still had this Irish colleen
> view of young Irish women: do your chapel, do this, do
> that. I think they lost sight of that young women were
> getting caught up in all this for the first time, and all sorts
> of boundaries were getting broken. Women didn't want to
> hear that anymore. Some did, others didn't. So when I was
> just turned eighteen [in 1975], I left Cumann na mBan and
> was sworn into the ranks of the IRA
>
> Former PIRA prisoner Nuala Perry interviewed by Jack
> Hepworth (Belfast, 30 March 2016)[2]

The quote above highlights tensions between constructed gender norms and lived experiences of women's activism in the Northern Ireland conflict. This chapter assesses interactions between Irish republicanism, feminism, and women's republican activism. Throughout this period, some republicans emphasised feminist ideas and invoked women's experiences in Ireland and beyond. These differentiated dynamics connected to broader intra-republican debates about revolutionary theory and tactics, and illuminate how authority was distributed and contested within republicanism.

The complex nexus between women's experiences and feminism in republicanism also contributes to wider theoretical debates regarding the interaction

---

[1] Dieter Reinisch has charted *Cumann na mBan*'s curious history. Women could join the PIRA from its foundation in 1970, but *Cumann na mBan* continued as a semi-separate organisation. Until 1986, *Cumann na mBan* members were active in the PIRA campaign, but when the movement split at the *ard fheis* of 1986, *Cumann na mBan* swore allegiance to RSF and the Continuity Army Council. Dieter Reinisch, '*Cumann na mBan* and women in Irish republican paramilitary organisations, 1969–1986', *Estudios Irlandeses*, 11 (2016), pp. 149–162.

[2] Nuala Perry interview with Jack Hepworth. Belfast, 30 March 2016.

between feminisms and nationalisms in contentious politics. For Anne McClintock and Joane Nagel, for example, nationalist organisations' fixation with the legitimating stamp of tradition lends profoundly patriarchal characteristics.[3] By contrast, Kumari Jayawardena argues that involvement in revolutionary groups can offer new and unanticipated outlets for women's political agency and stimulate radical feminist discourses.[4]

A more particular discussion of how the Provisional republican movement approached feminism has been the subject of critical perspectives among scholars, left-wing analysts, and dissenting republicans alike. According to these commentators, the Provisional high command marginalised feminist thought, perpetuated internal patriarchy, acquiesced in social conservatism, and stymied progressive positions on reproductive rights.[5] In the early 2010s, revelations regarding historical abuse within the Provisional movement prompted further sombre reflection on women's experiences in republicanism.[6]

Sinn Féin representative Eoin Ó Broin and Niall Gilmartin have complexified historiographical interpretations of feminism being muted and frustrated in republicanism. Ó Broin has noted 'radically socialist-feminist' currents in Sinn Féin addressing 'economic discrimination, physical and sexual violence against

[3] Anne McClintock, 'Family feuds: gender, nationalism and the family', *Feminist Review*, 44 (1993), pp. 61–80; Joane Nagel, 'Masculinity and nationalism: gender and sexuality in the making of nations', *Ethnic and Racial Studies*, 21 (1998), p. 254.

[4] Kumari Jayawardena, *Feminism and nationalism in the third world* (London: Zed Books, 1986).

[5] Monica McWilliams, 'Women in Northern Ireland: an overview', in Eamonn Hughes (ed.), *Culture and politics in Northern Ireland, 1960–1990* (Milton Keynes: Open University Press, 1991), pp. 91, 99; Carol Coulter, 'Feminism and nationalism in Ireland', in David Miller (ed.), *Rethinking Northern Ireland* (London: Longman, 1998), pp. 162, 164; Begoña Aretxaga, *Shattering silence: women, nationalism and political subjectivity in Northern Ireland* (Princeton, New Jersey: Princeton University Press, 1997), p. 151; Geoffrey Bell, *The British in Ireland: a suitable case for withdrawal* (London: Pluto Press, 1984), p. 48; Mark Ryan, *War and peace in Ireland: Britain and the IRA in the new world order* (London: Pluto Press, 1994), p. 75; Liam O'Ruairc, 'Going respectable', *The Plough*, Volume 2, Number 36 (22 May 2005).

[6] In October 2013, former Provisional Liam Adams was convicted of raping and sexually assaulting his daughter in the late 1970s and early 1980s. In October 2014, Maria Cahill told the media that a Provisional had raped her when she was 16 years old. Cahill remembered the PIRA 'interrogating' her about the allegations in the late 1990s. Cahill's great-uncle, Joe Cahill, who died in 2004, had been among the Provisionals' founders in 1969. 'Liam Adams – brother of Sinn Féin's Gerry Adams – found guilty of raping his daughter', *Belfast Telegraph*, 1 October 2013; Henry McDonald, 'IRA accused of trying to cover up rape claim', *The Guardian*, 14 October 2014.

women, the right to contraception, divorce and childcare' in the 1980s.[7] Drawing upon 25 oral history interviews, Gilmartin argued that grassroots Provisional women's activism heightened feminist consciousness. Volunteers forged their ideas independent of their organisational affiliation, the argument ran, and their radicalism frequently outflanked the movement's position on women's rights.[8]

Coining 'second-wave feminism' in her description of the National Organization for Women in 1968, American writer Martha Weinman Lear heralded a new epoch of women's activism. Campaigns addressed domestic violence and lobbied for employment opportunities, reproductive rights, and divorce legislation.[9] In Ireland, a diverse women's movement emerged in the early 1970s. To the extent that its followers engaged with the emerging conflict in the north, the national question was acutely divisive: as Clara Connolly has noted, republicans comprised just one of many strands in Irish feminism.[10] Irish feminists' divergent engagements with the conflict have been richly documented in contemporary accounts and historical analyses.[11] This spectrum of opinion lies largely beyond the purview of this chapter, which is concerned primarily with specifically republican subjectivities and comprises three chronological sections.

This chapter opens by examining republican interpretations of 'women's liberation' in the 1970s, drawing upon grassroots republican publications and underutilised interviews with the Provisional movement's founding leadership. The second section analyses Sinn Féin's Women's Department, founded in 1979, amid Provisionals' efforts to broaden their appeal in Ireland and enhance their international connections in the early 1980s. Finally, we assess radical feminist

---

[7] Eoin Ó Broin, *Sinn Féin and the politics of left republicanism* (London: Pluto Press, 2009), p. 251.

[8] Niall Gilmartin, 'Negotiating new roles: Irish republican women and the politics of conflict transformation', *International Feminist Journal of Politics*, 17 (2015), pp. 61, 68.

[9] Martha Weinman Lear, 'The second feminist wave', *The New York Times*, 10 March 1968.

[10] Clara Connolly, 'Communalism: obstacle to social change', *Women: A Cultural Review*, 2 (1991), p. 218.

[11] See, for example, Margaret Ward (ed.), *A difficult dangerous honesty: ten years of feminism in Northern Ireland* (Belfast: Women's Book Collective, 1986); Christina Loughran, 'Writing our own history: organising against the odds – 10 years of feminism in Northern Ireland', *Trouble & Strife*, 11 (Summer 1987); Carmel Roulston, 'Women on the margin: the women's movement in Northern Ireland, 1972–1988', *Science & Society*, 53 (1989), pp. 219–236; Margaret Ward, '"Ulster was different"? Women, feminism and nationalism in the north of Ireland', in Yvonne Galligan, Eilís Ward, & Rick Wilford (eds.), *Contesting politics: women in Ireland, north and south* (Boulder, Colorado: Westview Press, 1999), pp. 219–239.

politics emerging within the Provisional movement in the late 1980s, especially among PIRA prisoners in Long Kesh and Maghaberry.

Republicanism and 'women's liberation', 1968–c.1979

Today, radical republicans often criticise women's historical experiences and the representation of women in republicanism. Feminist grievances that historically were marginalised or self-censored within the movement now constitute an important strand of critique of Provisional republicanism. This motif is especially pronounced among women who have left the movement.

Surveying the past conflict, critics charge Provisional leaders with failing to incorporate feminist politics. In 2007, during debates about Sinn Féin's abortion policy, a former leader of the party's Women's Department rebuked herself for 'publicly supporting' the Provisionals' opposition to abortion during the 1980s:

> Many of us have tried, through having motions passed at *ard fheiseanna*, to have the abortion issue comprehensively discussed throughout the party, throughout Ireland, as we did in Derry in the late 1980s. So far, this hasn't happened. When are we going to stop being influenced by particular political 'climates' (while women continue to have 'secret' abortions) and stand up for the rights of women? Until we accept that women have the right to determine/ make choices about their own fertility, we do not support equality for Irish women.[12]

At the end of the 1960s, women's liberation was at the forefront for New Leftists in West Germany's student movement and the multitude of consciousness-raising groups in New York, Chicago, and San Francisco.[13] At that extraordinary conjuncture in Northern Ireland, feminism received little dedicated attention among republicans or leftists. Former PD radical Margaret Ward remembered the politics of women's liberation being notably absent from the group's discussions.[14]

Broadly speaking, Provisional leaders' radicalism in the early 1970s did not take into account women's rights as a substantive issue, especially regarding marriage and reproduction. The PIRA's founding Chief of Staff, Seán Mac

---

[12] Daisy Mules, 'Assembly motion on abortion', *An Phoblacht*, 1 November 2007.
[13] Barbara L. Tischler, 'The refiner's fire: anti-war activism and emerging feminism in the late 1960s', in DeGroot (ed.), *Student protest*, 190, 193.
[14] Margaret Ward, 'From civil rights to women's rights', in Michael Farrell (ed.), *Twenty years on* (Dingle: Brandon, 1988), pp. 127, 129, 132.

Stíofáin, opposed abortion and argued that divorce should be subject to the state's aegis,[15] while Ruairí Ó Brádaigh argued that doctors should have 'tight control' of contraception.[16] Prioritising an escalating guerrilla campaign, early Provisionals regarded these social policies as largely irrelevant to their struggle. In 1971, when Irish Women's Liberation Movement activists invaded Leinster House, protesting the Seanad's failure to consider a bill pertaining to contraception, the demonstrations scarcely registered with republicans.[17]

Traditional gender norms could exist untroubled in the early Provisional movement, as a leader article in *Republican News* implied in September 1972. A profile of Matilda Witherington, Theobald Wolfe Tone's wife, hoped its subject would prompt Irish women to aspire to 'match the bravest man'. Witherington was said to embody 'the qualities that are distinctive of the woman... gentleness, sensibility, sympathy and tenderness'.[18]

Social conservatism was not the preserve of the Provisional leadership. In 1974, a Dublin Sinn Féin member framed the republican struggle as a moral crusade against British social mores flooding Ireland with 'excesses of drugs, drink and sexuality': liberalising access to contraceptives would undermine the 'happiness of married life'. Although *Republican News* presented the opinion piece as one activist's 'personal views', the editorial commendation of the article meriting 'serious thought' anticipated considerable sympathy within the movement.[19] In 1980, a correspondent to *An Phoblacht/Republican News* defended divorce laws and described female divorcees as 'pathetic'.[20]

Despite women's mobilisation in republicanism, many Provisional publicists and grassroots activists continued to locate women in distinctly domestic settings. The absence of an advanced feminist lobby in the movement recalled the experience of Algeria's *Front de libération nationale* in the 1960s: many of its estimated 11,000 female activists swiftly returned to unpaid work in the home after national independence was achieved.[21] Similarly, radical women in France and West Germany after 1968 criticised male comrades' chauvinism.[22]

---

[15] Seán Mac Stíofáin quoted in Robert W. White, *Out of the ashes: an oral history of the Provisional Irish republican movement* (Newbridge: Merrion, 2017), pp. 45–46.

[16] John Rooks, 'Sinn Féin president talks to unionists', *Belfast Telegraph*, 28 July 1972.

[17] Áine Mannion, 'Women leading the way', *LookLeft*, Volume 2, Issue 21 [2015].

[18] 'Irish womanhood', *Republican News*, 16 September 1972.

[19] 'Contraceptive bill', *Republican News*, 9 February 1974.

[20] Aisling Ni Bhiorthagra, 'Women's rights', *An Phoblacht/Republican News*, 31 May 1980.

[21] Nagel, 'Masculinity and nationalism', 254.

[22] Kristina Schulz, 'The women's movement', in Martin Klimke & Joachim Scharloth (eds.), *1968 in Europe: a history of protest and activism, 1956–1977* (Basingstoke: Palgrave Macmillan, 2008), p. 288.

Especially in the conflict's early stages, Provisional publicity underscored women as particularly vulnerable under British rule. Ill-treatment of women was represented as the obscenest indictment of the security forces. In 1973, a Sinn Féin bulletin in Andersonstown framed 'the internment of young girls' as the British Army's utmost barbarism: the 'struggle for self determination' would not cease 'while girls are being interned by British gangsters'. Imprisoning women was positioned as a wanton incursion upon traditional family life. The implication was that women were somehow politically unthreatening, mere 'pawns in the cruel game of repression being played from Headquarters in Warminster'.[23]

The conception of women's imprisonment as particularly deplorable also gained currency among PIRA men. In September 1973, republican men from Armagh regarded women's incarceration as 'an attack on the sanctity of family life'.[24] The following year, the publicity officer of a west Belfast Sinn Féin *cumann* described the internment of 'women and girls' as a cause célèbre and invited support for 'these brave girls'.[25]

In sharp contrast, PD's newspaper highlighted women's republican activism as evidence of revolutionary consciousness. In 1973, *Unfree Citizen* editorialised against republican portrayals of women as 'weaklings or fods whose spirits will easily be broken'. On the contrary, republican women were

> liberated in the true sense of the word… even though they are behind prison bars – they are the people who are truly emancipated and free.[26]

Throughout the 1970s, in campaigns against internment, security forces, and criminalisation, republican women in Belfast and Derry often embraced the language and imagery of maternity. After the British Army killed two teenage boys in Belfast's Turf Lodge district in 1975 and 1976, local residents established a Mothers Action Committee to rattle bin lids when Army patrols approached.[27] In 1977, a 'Blanket Mother' from Divis Flats wrote to the nationalist *Andersonstown News* publicising republican prisoners' strife.[28]

---

23 'The girls', *The Volunteer* (n.d. [1973]). Published by Sinn Féin's Cathal Brugha *cumann*, Andersonstown.

24 K. Trainor, P.R.O., Armagh Republican Prisoners, S.F. Cumann, Long Kesh to *Unfree Citizen: Newspaper of the People's Democracy*, Number 2, Volume 51 (17 September 1973).

25 'Liz McKee', *Republican News*, 9 February 1974.

26 'The women inside', *Unfree Citizen: Newspaper of the People's Democracy*, Number 2, Volume 51 (17 September 1973).

27 Joan Lally, 'Three Irish women talk about their sons' deaths', *Spare Rib*, 62 (September 1977).

28 'Picture Ireland 1978: Prisoner's Mother's View', *Andersonstown News*, 6 May 1978.

When the Provisionals commenced a campaign for political status for their prisoners from 1976, PIRA volunteers' female relatives led the movement's ambitious European campaign. In September 1977, five women from Belfast and Derry visited Paris to address press conferences on the plight of their sons enduring the blanket protest in Long Kesh.[29] The Provisional movement's propagandists reinforced the perception of women as volunteers' stoical, suffering relatives, forced to survive house raids and raise families in a war zone. In 1978, a representative of Sinn Féin's Foreign Affairs Bureau declared that 'Ireland's H Block mothers... never forget the suffering of their sons'.[30]

Class dynamics figured strongly in the nexus between republicanism and feminism. Many working-class women in urban republican communities became embroiled in contentious politics through community defence in the early 1970s, and subsequently in campaigns for political status. Republican activism defined everyday life, whereas 'feminism' and 'women's lib' connoted a distinctly middle-class politics far removed from the Irish war. Working-class republicans such as Anne Marie Loughran associated 'Womens [sic] Groups' with 'purely women's issues – contraception, abortion, nurseries – in middle class areas and mostly from middle class backgrounds'. A member of the Relatives Action Committees campaigning against criminalisation, and a prominent activist in the republican-feminist alliance Women Against Imperialism in the late 1970s, Loughran regarded her comrades as 'ordinary working class women' whose political consciousness stemmed from the lived realities of conflict.[31]

Early Provisionals considered mainstream feminists' concerns with family and sexuality as suspiciously 'middle class' and irrelevant to an escalating war situation. Recalling the consciousness-raising groups associated with women's liberation movements in Britain and the USA, a female ex-prisoner highlights republican perceptions of second-wave feminism in the 1970s:

> I don't think there was discussions [of women's politics within republicanism]. I think it was made very clear because I remember going to a woman's conference one time in Dublin, not long after I got out of prison, and it was very clear that, you know, the feminists didn't want the republicans making a contribution, but more importantly the republicans didn't want republicans making a feminist contribution! So, you know, it was an awful place to be, it was a difficult place to be stuck in because there was lots of stuff happening to women and, you know, women's issues were starting to get raised in the general

[29] 'Irish mothers bring protest to France', *Republican News*, 1 October 1977.
[30] Eldrida, 'The women of May Place', *Republican News*, 2 September 1978.
[31] 'Ireland: women at war', *Women's Voice*, 33 (1979).

media anyway... Feminism at the time, it was seen as something that middle-class women did. Working-class women didn't do feminism because it was all about poverty and the ghettos and, you know, feminism was something – It was like something you could aspire to be, but you'd to sort out all this other stuff first.[32]

Class-based hostility to the global image of middle-class feminism gained currency across multiple republican organisations. An OSF bulletin in west Belfast pledged support for 'working women' and their 'genuine' demands for equal rights, pay, and opportunity. The editorial voice emphasising material conditions and economic pressures facing working-class women castigated

the more publicity-conscious but less serious, ultra-left 'Women's Libbers' group... who believe that the whole question of women's liberation can be solved by burning bras.[33]

In the late 1970s, the small yet influential feminist-republican group Women Against Imperialism confronted republican suspicion of 'women's liberation'. As well as coordinating Reclaim the Night marches in Belfast, Women Against Imperialism pressed the Provisional movement to take feminism seriously as a core republican demand:

In the struggle for national liberation, women's liberation is not secondary. Women's liberation is part and parcel of the overall struggle of our people against the injustices under British Imperialism.[34]

Although Sinn Féin instituted its Women's Department in 1980, international feminism or socialist critique of patriarchy did not feature in this discussion. Gerry Adams's analysis of women's political grievances was acutely national, rather than international: repeatedly stressing women's contribution to the republican struggle, past and present, Adams particularly accentuated how British rule in the north, and Catholic theocracy in the south, oppressed Irish women.[35] In 1985, Adams admitted Sinn Féin had 'failed to become involved'

---

[32] Former Armagh republican prisoner interview with Jack Hepworth. County Armagh, 2017.

[33] 'Women's rights', *Ballymurphy News* (n.d. [c.1975]).

[34] 'Violence against women', *Beansaor/Free Woman: Journal of Women Against Imperialism*, 4 (September 1979).

[35] Especially through the 1980s, republican feminists critically examined the political agency of the Catholic Church. Chapter 5 addresses these issues in a discussion of republican engagement with religious authority.

in the Republic of Ireland's abortion referendum two years earlier. Yet the Sinn Féin president warned republicans against the 'benign imperialism' of British feminists from 'different cultures'. Adams cast international feminism as a potential distraction from a republican agenda that would presumably transform the lives of all Irish citizens.[36]

For republicans on the left who engaged more extensively with international political theory throughout the 1970s, including Officials and members of the IRSP and PD, women's emancipation was at the core of global revolution. Leftist republicans' broadsides against Irish socio-political conservatism drew upon universal ideas about freedom. The Official republican movement published 13 demands for women's rights as an essential component of their 'Republican Socialism'.[37] In 1975, delegates from OSF National Women's Committee addressed the World Congress on Women.[38]

Socialist feminism pervaded the Official movement more broadly: OIRA prisoners codifying their politics in Long Kesh in 1973 located women's oppression in male-dominated 'capitalist society' and scorned so-called republicans who derided women's liberation. The incarcerated volunteers rebutted conservative shibboleths around marriage – which left 'no room for human emotions and the healthy sexual appetite of any young woman' – and education – that 'conditioned' women

> to believe that they are inferior to men and that from the cradle to the grave their main purpose in life is to serve, love, honour and obey the male.[39]

Predating the Provisionals' Women's Department by several years, OSF's National Women's Committee attacked the moralism and economic structures that underpinned women's subjugation in the Republic. The Committee's key figure, Máirín de Burca, repeatedly repudiated state and Church interference in private life. In 1976, when a Dublin court awarded £14,000 to a man who claimed that his wife had 'been enticed' from him, de Burca attacked the ruling that treated women as 'chattels', and demanded the state recognise women's autonomy as 'human persons, not inanimate lumps of protoplasm, to be the subject of monetary haggling between superior males'.[40]

---

[36] 'Brilliant, biting and mediocre', *Sunday Independent*, 7 July 1985.
[37] LHL NIPC P1341: OSF, *Ard Fheis Report 1973* (Dublin: OSF, 1973).
[38] 'World congress on women', *Irish Examiner*, 25 October 1975.
[39] 'Women's lib a fight for justice', *An Eochair: A Bulletin of the Irish Republican Movement, Long Kesh*, 2 (July–August 1973).
[40] 'Act that "makes women chattels"', *The Irish Press*, 10 February 1976.

'The Age-Old Struggle'

Emerging from a split in the Official movement in the mid-1970s, the Irish Republican Socialist Party (IRSP) similarly identified capitalism and its nuclear family as the root causes of women's oppression. On its foundation, the IRSP immediately campaigned during 1975, International Women's Year, for equal pay and a 'wider choice of jobs' for women.[41] For Derry IRSP secretary Fionnbarra O'Dochartaigh, women's liberation was unattainable in a capitalist society that rooted women within the home:

> Under capitalism women have become social-engineers. They have thus become 'privatized' within the home and nuclear family.[42]

Officials and IRSP activists sustained their radical feminist convictions independent of the mainstream Irish feminist movement: in 1973, Dublin's Women's Liberation Movement rejected OSF election literature that espoused 'Women's Liberation' in a 'socialist united Ireland'.[43] The founding IRSP *Ard Comhairle* claimed mainstream Irish feminists 'ignored the need for mass social change' and 'a new socialist consciousness'.[44] An editorial in the party newspaper in 1976 implored Irish feminists to 'recognise that the main enemy is capitalism' and realise 'the necessity of the national liberation struggle'.[45]

Negotiating women's agency in the Provisional movement, *c*.1980–*c*.1986

In the Republic of Ireland in September 1983, a referendum was held on the proposed Eighth Amendment to the constitution. The putative amendment held that

> the state acknowledges the right to life of the unborn and, with due regard to the equal right to life of the mother, guarantees in its laws to respect, and, as far as practicable, by its laws to defend and vindicate that right.[46]

---

[41] 'International women's year', *The Starry Plough/An Camchéachta*, Volume 1, Number 1 (April 1975).

[42] LHL NIPC P16410: Fionnbarra O'Dochartaigh, *A Woman's Place? Pairtí Poblachtacht Soisalach na hÉireann, Doire colmcille Discussion Document* (Derry: IRSP, 1984).

[43] 'The election', *The Irish Press*, 28 February 1973.

[44] 'The repression of women', *The Starry Plough/An Camchéachta*, Volume 1, Number 7 (October 1975).

[45] 'Women: slaves of slaves', *The Starry Plough/An Camchéachta*, Volume 1, Number 13 (April 1976).

[46] Jennifer E. Spreng, *Abortion and divorce law in Ireland* (Jefferson, North Carolina:

After months of combative debate, the 'yes' campaign won the referendum with 66.9 per cent of the vote, and from October 1983 the Republic of Ireland constitution stipulated that abortion would be inaccessible in the vast majority of instances.

Within a month of the amendment's confirmation in the Dáil, Gerry Adams was elected president of Sinn Féin, displacing Ruairí Ó Brádaigh. The following year, the Women's Department was the largest in the party.[47] Prompted by the Department's growing activism, Adams and his comrades embroidered issues affecting Irish women into a broader set of criticisms of state provision and legislation. Adams portrayed women's activism as a subsidiary component of a widening republican struggle. Feminist demands were an adjunct to injustices under British rule and the Republic's 'neo-colonial' elite.

Unlike the IRSP's *Ard Comhairle*, Adams did not internationalise women's liberation. Rather, he accentuated specifically the experiences of republican women. The Women's Department's activism reflected this emphasis, especially in its campaigns against the strip-searching that female prisoners faced in Armagh Jail. On International Women's Day in 1984, Sinn Féin coordinated pickets at Armagh highlighting 'the obscene treatment of the republican women prisoners'.[48]

Through the early 1980s, Sinn Féin presidents Ó Brádaigh and Adams alike addressed the gender pay gap, sexism, and domestic violence. Adams repeatedly narrated women's 'forgotten' republican activism, and highlighted the conditions in Armagh Jail. In his presidential address at the Sinn Féin *ard fheis* of 1984, Adams criticised the movement for neglecting its female activists: 'Even in a movement like ours the women are usually eclipsed by the men.'[49]

Neither Ó Brádaigh nor Adams addressed sexuality and reproductive rights, or situated critiques of paternalism in socialist analyses. Rather, both party presidents sought to mitigate societal disapproval of abortion and divorce. Interviewed in April 1981, Ó Brádaigh claimed that the policy document *Women in the New Ireland* was confronting sexism and stereo-typing and dealing with equal pay for equal work, violence against women, family law, attitudes to contraception, abortion, illegitimacy, marriage law and child care.[50]

Yet the movement's policy on abortion was ambiguously constructed, lamenting Irish social mores while acquiescing in them. It was an

---

McFarland & Company, 2004), p. 88.

[47] Jane Plunkett, 'Focus on women's oppression', *An Phoblacht/Republican News*, 8 November 1984.

[48] Jane Plunkett, 'Women in action', *An Phoblacht/Republican News*, 15 March 1984.

[49] '"We have the right to be free"', *An Phoblacht/Republican News*, 8 November 1984.

[50] 'Ag labhairt leis an Uachtaran: Ruairi O Bradaigh', *Iris*, Volume 1, Number 1 (April 1981).

indictment of society that so many women should feel the need to avail of abortion… We are opposed to the attitudes and forces in society which impel women to have abortions.[51]

Even, or perhaps especially, at moments of heated debate regarding women's rights, Sinn Féin's leadership showed little inclination to address controversial social policy. Abortion debates dominated the Sinn Féin *ard fheis* of 1985, yet Gerry Adams made no reference to women's rights in his presidential address.[52] Even in 1989, with female and male PIRA prisoners debating abortion extensively in the movement's discussion journals, Sinn Féin's EEC manifesto's statement on 'women's rights' failed to address abortion.[53]

The founding leader of Sinn Féin's Women's Department in 1979 was Rita O'Hare, a Belfast republican recently released from Limerick Prison. Ó Brádaigh and Adams alike worked closely with O'Hare to concentrate the fledgling department's energies on women's experiences and opportunities *within* the movement, lest it drift from republican priorities. In 1984, O'Hare reflected on the five years since the department's foundation:

> When the department was first set up, it was viewed with a certain amount of suspicion by some Sinn Fein women. There was the fear that an autonomous group of women within Sinn Fein would become separate from the main body of the organisation, and that their activities would not reflect or promote a republican viewpoint.[54]

Such wariness percolated the Provisional movement for years to come: in 1984, Sinn Féin's Education Department exhorted republicans to 'advance the cause of women's liberation', but only in feminist organisations that fully endorsed the Provisionals' objectives.[55]

The party leadership's emphasis on *republican* women's subjugation contrasted with the universal rights and internationalist commitments that PIRA women espoused in Armagh Jail. Prisoners protesting for political status in Armagh in 1979 framed their struggle among human rights campaigns worldwide, declaring solidarity with the oppressed in Iran at the time of the conservative revolution:

---

[51] 'Women in the New Ireland', *An Phoblacht/Republican News*, 8 November 1980.
[52] 'Presidential address', *An Phoblacht/Republican News*, 7 November 1985.
[53] 'Vote Sinn Féin', *An Phoblacht/Republican News*, 1 June 1989.
[54] 'Women and the republican struggle', *Iris: The Republican Magazine*, 8 (August 1984).
[55] LHL NIPC P3887: Sinn Féin Education Department, *Economic Resistance* (Dublin: Sinn Féin, 1984).

> We were outraged lately by the Ayatollah Khomeini order that all women in Iran must wear the heavy black dress which covers them from neck to ankles, but were delighted to read that the women protested in the streets and refused to wear it.[56]

Similarly, when Sinn Féin protested strip-searching in Armagh in 1984, the PIRA prisoners regarded the policy not merely as a sinister security tactic in Ireland's ongoing war, but more profoundly as an 'attack on our sexuality'.[57]

At the grassroots, the Republic's referendum on the Eighth Amendment in 1983 prompted the Women's Department to grow. New branches were established in the Republic border towns of Monaghan and Dundalk.[58] At Sinn Féin's 1984 *ard fheis*, several party *cumainn* from the Republic successfully lobbied the movement to commit to a liberal position on any future referendum on divorce.[59] The same year, the women's committee on Donegal Sinn Féin's *Comhairle Ceantair* organised autonomously against sexual violence, lambasting the Republic judiciary's 'total discrimination [against] women involved in recent rape cases'.[60]

Provisional feminists in the Republic became increasingly prominent in the movement through the mid-1980s. Their backgrounds spanned a wide range of social circles and activist networks. Anne Rynne from County Clare was involved with anti-nuclear protests in the Republic before she joined Sinn Féin in 1985.[61] Mary McGing, who became Sinn Féin's representative for Mayo and Galway on the party *Ard Comhairle* in 1983, was a civil engineering graduate whose voluntary work in the 'Third World' informed her revolutionary politics. Reflecting on her experiences in Africa, McGing concluded that Western initiatives, 'however well-intentioned', were 'paving the way for increased exploitations by multinationals'. McGing transposed her observations to Ireland, where she advocated 'a revolutionary struggle of people' against 'evils and shortcomings in their society'.[62] In 1990, Pamela Kane received a ten-year sentence for a PIRA bank robbery, but her own background was unorthodox: Kane had known no republicans in

---

[56] Protesting P.O.W.'s, B Wing, Armagh Gaol, '"We have nothing to lose but our chains"', *Beansaor/Free Woman: Journal of Women Against Imperialism*, 4 (September 1979).

[57] Jane Plunkett, 'Women in action', *An Phoblacht/Republican News*, 15 March 1984.

[58] 'Women and the republican struggle', *Iris: The Republican Magazine*, 8 (August 1984).

[59] Jane Plunkett, 'Focus on women's oppression', *An Phoblacht/Republican News*, 8 November 1984.

[60] 'Sinn Fein sponsored walk', *Derry People & Donegal News*, 13 October 1984.

[61] 'Women's Department – Clare', *Iris Bheag*, 13 (September 1988).

[62] Mary McGing, '"No justice without removing the causes"', *Iris: The Republican Magazine*, 8 (August 1984).

her upbringing in the north Dublin suburbs.[63] In jail, Kane authored several blistering critiques of the Republic's institutions and politics.[64]

Provisional feminists lambasted the Republic's history and constitution as the hallmarks of a theocratic backwater. Their assaults on the state were not confined to issues affecting republicans. Provisional writer Siobhan O'Malley called for 'radical social change' to overcome the Republic's 'endemic' sexism: for O'Malley, 'women in the home, supposedly revered, protected and supported by the Free State Constitution' were the 'most discriminated against of all'.[65]

The emphasis on universal feminist conceptions of freedom led Provisional feminists to forge international connections. As Sinn Féin's director of foreign affairs in the 1980s, former PIRA prisoner Síle Darragh was among the most senior women in the Provisional movement. Under Darragh's leadership, the Foreign Affairs Bureau established relationships with national minorities and liberation movements, encouraging senior Provisionals to internationalise their politics. In 1984 and 1985, Foreign Affairs Bureau delegations attended meetings with humanitarian groups in Paris and conferences in Italy for 'Minorities in Europe' and the International League for the Rights of Peoples.[66] At home, the Bureau hosted American-Indians and Nicaraguan Sandinista Rosario Antúnez.[67]

International solidarities were a cornerstone of Sinn Féin's Women's Department's more radical commitments. Connections with women's groups in Cuba, Central America, and South Africa informed republican women's proposals for Provisional strategy. Reflecting on conversations with the Federation of Cuban Women in 1984, Rita O'Hare implored Provisionals to advance a feminist healthcare and education programme.[68] Reading women's resistance poetry from Central America and Cuba in 1989, PIRA prisoner Mary McArdle celebrated 'forceful confrontations of machismo'. McArdle exhorted republican women to challenge male comrades on contradictions between their 'macho attitudes' and supposedly 'revolutionary ideologies'.[69] Máiréad Keane

---

[63] Sorcha Berry, 'Pamela Kane: The fighting spirit of Tyrone and Dublin', *An Phoblacht*, 1 October 2010.

[64] Pamela Kane, 'Fighting back!', *Women in Struggle/Mna I Streachilt*, Volume 4 (n.d. [1993]).

[65] Siobhan O'Malley & Jane Plunkett, 'International Women's Day: Radical change not empty reforms', *An Phoblacht/Republican News*, 8 March 1984.

[66] 'Neutrality stance confirmed', *An Phoblacht/Republican News*, 7 November 1985.

[67] 'Jane Plunkett, 'Defending the revolution: Interview with a Sandinista representative', *An Phoblacht/Republican News*, 25 October 1984.

[68] Rita O'Hare, 'One part of the whole struggle', *An Phoblacht/Republican News*, 8 March 1984.

[69] Mary McArdle's review of Amanda Hopkinson's edited volume *Lovers and comrades*,

led the Women's Department when it hosted Nonkluleko Woko of the ANC Women's Section in 1991. Keane concluded that republicans with 'blinkers' must take seriously the struggle for women's rights.[70]

Provisional feminists also pioneered many of Sinn Féin's overtures to the British left from the mid-1980s. Accentuating their common opposition to Thatcherism, Provisional women shared platforms with British radicals and Labour activists. Women's experiences of the judicial system and imprisonment were foremost among the republican grievances that drew support from across the Irish Sea. On International Women's Day in 1984, Sinn Féin's Women's Department received solidarity greetings from diverse British radicals including Labour leftists, diaspora organisations, ecological campaigners, and ethnic-minority and feminist groups.[71] Especially after high-profile PIRA prisoners Martina Anderson and Ella O'Dwyer were transferred to Durham Jail in the late 1980s, feminist solidarities beyond the confines of republicanism underpinned campaigns against strip-searching. Regular protests in the north-east often attracted diverse crowds more than 1,000 strong, spanning republican groups, prisoners' relatives, Labour Women for Ireland, miners' wives, and students.[72] Prominent Provisional Mairéad Farrell also typified these eclectic socio-political engagements: in 1987, a year after being released from prison, Farrell joined Queen's University Belfast as a mature student. After her death as part of a PIRA unit in Gibraltar in March 1988, Farrell was mourned among the university's Women's Group, of which she had been an 'active' and 'respected' member.[73]

Inviting support from British leftists in the late 1980s, Women's Department leader Máiréad Keane portrayed government policy in Northern Ireland as an exercise in state repression that would, if unchallenged, be replicated against the left in Britain more generally. In discussion with radical Labour councillor Martha Osamor and representatives from Women Against Pit Closures in February 1989, Keane argued:

---

in 'Book Reviews', *The Captive Voice/An Glór Gafa*, Volume 1, Number 2 (Winter 1989).

[70] Máiréad Keane, 'Republican Women's Conference', *Women in Struggle/Mna I Streachilt*, Volume 1 (n.d. [1991]).

[71] These groups included the Labour Committee on Ireland Women's Group, Brixton Black Women's Group, the Asian Women's Resource Centre in Brent, *Spare Rib*, London Irish Women's Centre, and Greenham Common protesters. Jane Plunkett, 'Women in action', *An Phoblacht/Republican News*, 15 March 1984.

[72] Jane Olive, 'Strip march hits Durham', *Palatinate*, 18 June 1987.

[73] 'Women's Group lose a member', *Press Release: Newspaper of Queen's University Students Union, Belfast*, Volume 5, Number 5 (n.d. [1988]).

> Real socialists in Britain should be active campaigners against British imperialism in Ireland. They should be active not just because it is the correct anti-imperialist position but also because techniques of repression which are used in the laboratory which is the North of Ireland will be used against working class people in Britain. Riot police and criminalisation have been used already against the miners and Black people... It is in the interest of working class people to campaign actively to force the British government to adopt a policy of withdrawal.[74]

The influence of Sinn Féin's Women's Department was a considerable factor in encouraging sections of the Labour Party to engage more actively with Northern Ireland. Addressing the National Conference of British Labour Women in 1984, Belfast Women's Department representative Chrissie McAuley directed Labour feminists to oppose strip-searching in jails and 'supergrass' trials. McAuley pressed Labour to discard its traditional bilateralism and overtly advocate British withdrawal.[75] Later that year, Labour's spokesperson on women's affairs, Jo Richardson, visited Northern Ireland to further investigate strip-searching. After spending three hours with PIRA prisoners in Armagh, the Labour delegation attended a press conference in west Belfast. Highlighting 'growing concern in the Labour movement, indeed among the general public, about Armagh', Richardson vowed to lobby parliamentary colleagues to end 'sexist, humiliating and degrading' strip-searching.[76]

Labour policy on Ireland shifted incrementally in the mid-1980s. The party's left wing was especially sympathetic to republicans' grievances and aspirations, if not their methods. At the Labour Party conference of 1984, 75 per cent of delegates supported six resolutions from party women's sections and councils condemning no-jury courts and 'supergrass' trials in Northern Ireland. In a coded reference to Labour's former Northern Ireland minister Roy Mason's criminalisation policy of the late 1970s, these resolutions 'repudiate[d]' Labour's 'past collusion': the next Labour government would end strip-searching and 'repeal all such inequitable and repressive measures'.[77]

Through the late 1980s and early 1990s, protests against state repression and human rights infringements underpinned the Women's Department's continued connections with British and Irish diaspora feminists, the Troops Out Movement, and the Labour left. Prison conditions remained an important theme at this political intersection. In March 1989, for the third consecutive annual

---

[74] 'Women for socialism', *An Phoblacht/Republican News*, 2 March 1989.
[75] 'Northern focus at women's conference', *An Phoblacht/Republican News*, 17 May 1984.
[76] 'Labour visit to Armagh', *An Phoblacht/Republican News*, 15 November 1984.
[77] 'Northern focus at women's conference', *An Phoblacht/Republican News*, 17 May 1984.

International Women's Day, diaspora groups, human rights organisations, and British feminists joined republicans campaigning against conditions in Durham Jail and strip-searching in Britain and Ireland.[78] The Troops Out Movement and London Women in Ireland sent delegates to Sinn Féin's Women's Conference in 1991, and International Women's Day events in 1992 and 1993. Meetings addressed community sector concerns such as women's groups' public funding shortfalls, and more specifically prisoners' experiences in Maghaberry.[79] In 1992, Sinn Féin brought 42 English feminists to Maghaberry to hear a statement from women prisoners condemning the 'ongoing censorship' of 'democratically elected' Sinn Féin representatives.[80]

While the Women's Department connected with the British left in the 1980s, PIRA women in Armagh pressured their own movement to overturn the patriarchy that had survived Ireland's past revolutions. Provisional feminists opposed the Irish left's tendency to insist that women's emancipation must 'wait' for socialist revolution. In a statement on International Women's Day in 1982, the PIRA public relations officer in Armagh warned the movement's leadership against relegating women's liberation:

> We cannot allow the same situation to evolve as in the past where women played a comparatively strong role in the Rising and Civil War but afterwards disappeared into oblivion, gaining little or nothing for the rights of women.[81]

Similarly, in 1989, Maghaberry prisoners asserted that feminist struggle would not end with British withdrawal:

> Some injustices will not just disappear when the British have been forced out. The education process must be extended to communities in every way possible.[82]

---

[78] These groups included the United Campaign Against Strip-Searching, Irish in Britain Representation Group, Troops Out Movement and local women's groups in north-east England. 'Women's Day protest at Durham "hell-hole"', *An Phoblacht/ Republican News*, 16 March 1989.

[79] Irene Sherry, 'Report on SF Women's Conference', *The Captive Voice/An Glór Gafa*, Volume 3, Number 3 (Winter 1991).

[80] Clare Connor, 'International Women's Day delegation to Belfast, 4–7 March 1993', *Women in Struggle/Mná I Streachilt*, Volume 4 (n.d. [1993]).

[81] LHL NIPC P881B: *Notes for Revolutionaries* (Belfast: Republican Publications, 1983).

[82] Women POWs, 'Women and the national struggle', *The Captive Voice/An Glór Gafa*, Volume 1, Number 1 (Autumn 1989).

'The Age-Old Struggle'

Experiences of incarceration embedded radical feminism among PIRA prisoners in Armagh and Maghaberry. Prisoners increasingly broadened their politics to struggle for personal autonomy, self-determination, and socialism. In 1984, PIRA women in Armagh Jail extended solidarity to

> our sisters in Palestine, Nicaragua, Honduras, Chile, to the women of SWAPO, and indeed to all women striving, either military or politically, to bring social change and the freedom of the world's oppressed peoples.[83]

Writing in 1991, PIRA prisoner Ailish Carroll looked to leftist national liberation movements for inspiration and instruction. To achieve Marx's and Connolly's 'proletarian internationalism', Carroll argued, republican feminists needed 'to reinforce our links with other groups and countries' and 'examine conflicts on an international scale'. Carroll cited Grenadian socialist revolutionary Maurice Bishop's emphasis on removing 'artificial barriers of colonialism', and implored her comrades to recognise 'struggling races across the world' before 'establishing a socialist Ireland'.[84]

For female PIRA prisoners in the late 1980s, the British presence was no longer to be regarded as the sole oppressor of women. Writing in 1989, PIRA women in Maghaberry charted the dynamics of prison politics:

> Previously, we viewed the armed struggle as the one and only struggle... time and experience have taught us that more than British imperialism needs to be changed. Few [took] any part in the women's movement or seriously devoted much time to the struggle for women's rights [before imprisonment. However, in prison] discussion and debate... develop[ed] and raise[ed] our own consciousness. Through discussion and debate, we have each contributed to each other's education and helped to broaden our political horizons... on a range of issues.[85]

These conversations concluded that

---

[83] Jane Plunkett, 'Women in action', *An Phoblacht/Republican News*, 15 March 1984.
[84] Ailish Carroll, 'One people, one struggle, one destiny', *The Captive Voice/An Glór Gafa*, Volume 3, Number 1 (Spring 1991).
[85] Women POWs, 'Women and the national struggle', *The Captive Voice/An Glór Gafa*, Volume 1, Number 1 (Autumn 1989).

women's oppression is universal and that the source is the unequal balance of power between men and women... In a socialist Ireland, this imbalance of power must be rectified.[86]

Radical republican feminism, *c*.1986–*c*.1994

From the late 1980s, many Provisional republican feminists criticised their own movement's shifting strategies, as well as its perceived failure to commit to a feminist programme. The complex trajectory of socialist republican Bernadette Devlin highlights dynamic tensions across republicanism and feminism. Devlin was affiliated, by turns, with PD, the IRSP, the Independent Socialist Party, and the NHBAC. Although Devlin never joined the Provisional movement, she considered it a powerful, if imperfect, vehicle for contentious politics in Ireland. Devlin's analyses since the late 1960s provide vital insights into strategic questions facing republicans committed to advancing socialism and feminism in Ireland.

Interviewed in 1983, Devlin argued that Ireland's 'best feminists' had graduated from 'fighting against repression' as republican activists. For Devlin, feminist ideas proliferated among Provisionals, even though the movement, 'given its historical development and the level of consciousness', found it 'very difficult' to prioritise women's politics.[87] By the early 1990s, Devlin's confidence in the Provisionals' capacity to mobilise radical feminists had waned. Although Sinn Féin represented 'the leadership of progressive forces in this country', she doubted its fidelity to the stated goal of a pluralistic, socialist society.[88] Finally, in 1992, Devlin proposed that republican feminists should organise outside the Provisional movement. Gerry Adams supported the initiative.[89]

Sections of Sinn Féin's Education Department and Women's Department championed the radical positions to which Devlin alluded. In the 1980s, Provisional feminists addressed abortion, sexuality, capitalist patriarchy, and male republicans' attitudes. In a programme for new members of Sinn Féin in 1981, the Education Department promoted a socialist feminist position,

---

[86] Women POWs, 'Women and the national struggle', *The Captive Voice/An Glór Gafa*, Volume 1, Number 1 (Autumn 1989).

[87] LHL NIPC P17590: *Women Speak Out: British Counterinsurgency, Armed Struggle and the Mass Movement – Interview with Bernadette Devlin McAliskey and Martha McClelland* (1983).

[88] 'Bernadette McAliskey interviewed', *Women in Struggle/Mna I Streachilt*, Volume 1 (n.d. [1991]).

[89] 'Irish republican women call for change', *An Phoblacht/Republican News*, 12 November 1992.

declaring that 'capitalist society... discriminated against' women.[90] The same year, the Women's Department criticised the movement's 'total opposition' to abortion: 'Abortion *is an issue in Ireland* and will not end with a solitary sentence in a policy document.'[91] Party education programmes issued in 1984 held that many 'smug' republicans failed to engage with women's oppression. Comrades were charged with acknowledging women's contribution to the struggle but 'ignor[ing] the reality of male attitudes towards women'.[92]

PD's envisioned revolution was an inherently international assault on imperialism, capitalism, and patriarchy. The organisation was aligned with the Fourth International, whose world congress of 1979 branded the nuclear family an 'alien class institution' and prescribed intermeshing socialist, feminist, and anti-imperialist struggle.[93] PD's pamphlet literature duly celebrated female anti-imperialists worldwide, not least among Sandinista revolutionaries in Nicaragua.[94]

Through the 1980s, PD cadres implored the Provisional leadership to elaborate its feminism. PD activists located women's oppression globally in imperialist capitalism, and nationally in theocracy. Writing in 1981, PD activist Rose O'Mahony urged republican feminists to advance beyond reactive protests about conditions in Armagh Jail. For O'Mahony, it was imperative for the Provisionals to attack the 'Church's veto on state policy' and promote abortion and divorce rights.[95] Before the referendum on abortion rights in the Republic of Ireland in 1983, PD activist Pat Donnelly exhorted Sinn Féin to campaign against the amendment that would constitutionally ban abortion.[96]

Despite dissent from several *cumainn* at successive Sinn Féin *ard fheiseanna* in 1981 and 1982, the party's stance – voted by a majority at the conference of 1980 – stipulated 'total opposition' to abortion. Nevertheless, before the referendum

---

90 LHL NIPC Tom Hartley Collection PH1571: Sinn Féin Education Department, *New Members Course: Notes for Sinn Féin Education Officers* (Belfast: Sinn Féin, 1981).

91 LHL NIPC Tom Hartley Collection PH1640: Sinn Féin Department of Women's Affairs, *Abortion Ireland* (Dublin: Sinn Féin Department of Women's Affairs, 1981). Italics in original.

92 Sinn Féin Education Department, *Women in Ireland* (Republican Lecture Series No. 8, 1984).

93 In its 1979 resolution 'Socialist Revolution and the Struggle for Women's Liberation', the Fourth International aspired to lead the struggle for women's liberation, but noted that since working-class and feminist struggles were not identical, women must lead their struggle before and after socialist revolution. John Callaghan, *The far left in British politics* (Oxford: Basil Blackwell, 1987), p. 144.

94 LHL NIPC P367: PD, *A Woman's Place is on the Barricades* (Belfast: PD, 1984).

95 Rose O'Mahony, 'Women's movement: Which way forward', *Socialist Republic: Paper of Peoples' Democracy*, Volume 4, Number 2 (1981).

96 Pat Donnelly, 'A chance to reorganise', *Socialist Republic: Paper of Peoples' Democracy*, Volume 6, Number 2 (1983).

on the Eighth Amendment in September 1983, Sinn Féin resolved formally to abstain from the debate. Disappointed with the Provisionals' quiescence, the following year James Gallagher pressed Sinn Féin for 'greater programmatic clarity on the women's liberation movement'.[97] PD theorists recognised the Provisionals' unease on social issues: in 1987, PD policy document *Women in Struggle* pronounced Sinn Féin *ard fheis* debates on contraception and abortion clinics 'disappointing' for radicals who wanted 'an active feminist presence in the anti-imperialist movement'.[98]

For some senior Provisionals, the 'personal politics' of women's rights appeared divisive, or even distracting. In 1981, Sinn Féin director of publicity, Danny Morrison, acknowledged that abortion was 'a difficult question' with which the Provisionals had 'not come to terms'.[99] Writing in 1983, Dublin Sinn Féin organiser and party *Ard Comhairle* representative Paddy Bolger went further, arguing that republicans should avoid debating feminism and abortion: 'Can anyone seriously argue that [women's rights] have any real potential?'[100] After abortion was debated at consecutive Sinn Féin *ard fheiseanna* in the mid-1980s, a regular contributor to a Provisional discussion journal called for a moratorium: 'Sinn Fein policy should not evolve through bitter public conflict... Policy must evolve through consensus.'[101]

Abortion was the subject of heated contestation in the Provisional movement through the 1980s, and Sinn Féin's official position shifted on several occasions. The 'total opposition' to abortion in policy document *Women in the New Ireland* (1980) was amended incrementally in 1984: abortion was now opposed 'as a means of birth control'. The following year, by a vote of 77 to 73, Sinn Féin's *ard fheis* declared outright support for a 'woman's right to choose'.[102] This pro-choice position caused ructions, not least because it had been adopted in a debate at the end of the conference, by which point many delegates had left the Mansion House.

The tenor of the abortion debate at Sinn Féin's *ard fheis* in 1986 was especially vociferous: according to Belfast delegate Máire Ward, the 'disgraceful' policy adopted in 1985 was 'counter-republican' and 'counter-revolutionary', giving 'support for the murder of future members of the republican movement'.[103] In an

---

97 ILA: James Gallagher, *Our Orientation to the Republican Movement* (10 November 1984).
98 LHL NIPC P6570: PD, *Women in Struggle* (Dublin: PD, 1987).
99 Bob Rowthorn, 'Ireland's intractable crisis: interviews with the UDA and the Provisional IRA', *Marxism Today* (December 1981).
100 Paddy Bolger, 'Which way forward in the Free State?', *Iris*, 7 (November 1983).
101 Tonto, 'Policy making – abortion: "Let's be principled"', *Iris Bheag*, 13 (September 1988).
102 'Women's issues hotly debated', *An Phoblacht/Republican News*, 7 November 1985.
103 Fergal Keane, 'Sinn Fein takes anti-abortion line in stormy debate', *Sunday Tribune*,

attempt to unify the movement after the previous year's recriminations, Gerry Adams and the *Ard Comhairle* successfully advocated a more convoluted clause:

> We are opposed to the attitudes and forces in society which compel women to have an abortion. We are opposed to abortion as a means of birth control but we accept the need for abortion where the woman's life is at risk or in grave danger, for example ectopic pregnancy and all forms of cancer.[104]

An older generation of republican women were particularly uneasy about the movement's discussions of abortion. In his remarks at a meeting between the Sinn Féin leadership and Women's Department in June 1988, Gerry Adams identified a generational divide. Many female veterans already considered themselves 'liberated', Adams suggested. They were inclined to think 'all this talk about women's liberation to be just that – talk'.[105]

For several years, feminists outside the republican movement had recognised the Sinn Féin leadership's lukewarm approach to women's liberation. Reflecting on the party's aloofness from the Republic's referendum on the Eighth Amendment in 1983, feminist academic Margaret Ward argued that 'male socialists and republicans find it difficult to accept women as political equals'.[106]

By the late 1980s, Provisional feminists similarly associated the movement's limited feminist engagement with Adams's leadership. Radicals in the Women's Department in Derry and Belfast, and PIRA women in Maghaberry alike, criticised Adams and the movement's propagandists and educators. Derry Women's Department activists complained that 'the man at the top' was 'making the decisions, managing, defining, articulating the policies'. Demanding the leadership demonstrate 'commitment to the long-term objective [of] dismantling and destroying patriarchy', Derry Provisionals also denounced the absence of 'patriarchy' and 'patriarchal structures' from the party's education programme.[107]

When Sinn Féin representatives granted *Playboy* an interview in 1989, a PIRA prisoner in Maghaberry expressed outrage in republican discussion journal *Iris Bheag*. It was 'wrong' to deal with 'those pornographers... We must never align ourselves by prostituting the Republican Movement in their pages'.

---

2 November 1986.

[104] LHL NIPC P2275: *The Politics of Revolution: The Main Speeches and Debates from the 1986 Sinn Fein* Ard-Fheis, *Including the Presidential Address of Gerry Adams* (Belfast & Dublin: Republican Publications, 1986).

[105] 'The role of women in Sinn Fein', *Iris Bheag*, 11 (June 1988).

[106] Margaret Ward, 'We are all part of the same struggle', *Iris*, 7 (November 1983).

[107] 'The role of women in Sinn Fein', *Iris Bheag*, 11 (June 1988).

The demands made by 'An Deirfiur' ('The Sister') suggested more widespread disconcert among republican feminists: 'women will seriously question their place in the Republican Movement', the writer forecast, unless comrades reflected 'seriously' on their 'attitudes to women'.[108]

Many male PIRA prisoners in Long Kesh studied feminist politics, discussing issues including abortion in prison journals, especially *Iris Bheag*. More than 100 PIRA men undertook Women's Studies courses in jail in the late 1980s.[109] Rooting women's oppression in capitalist exploitation, class structures, and Catholic theocracy, many of these republican men were on the left of the Provisional movement, and proselytised among their male comrades. Writing in 1987, Portlaoise PIRA prisoner Sean Hick put it plainly: 'republicanism is associated with many things in the public eye and unfortunately feminism is not one of them'. Hick warned republicans that British withdrawal would not necessarily end 'class and gender divisions' that originated in capitalism and the many 'repressive manifestations of colonialism'.[110]

Writing from Long Kesh, Tommy Brogan from Strabane, County Tyrone, also criticised republicans' tendency to relegate social issues. Some male volunteers 'added to the oppression of their female comrades'. There could be 'no equality under the yoke [of] Capitalism', Brogan warned; only socialism, with its 'foundation stones equality and justice... can bring about equality'. For Brogan, the onus was on PIRA volunteers to engage with feminist 'educational politicisation' and 'consciousness raising'.[111]

Addressing women's economic and bodily autonomy, PIRA prisoners' feminist discussions entailed considerable self-criticism at individual and organisational levels. A prisoner in H3 summarised debates among PIRA men in Long Kesh in 1989:

> Much of women's oppression takes place in private, in personal relationships... Each man in the movement has a responsibility to eliminate his own sexist attitudes... Our Movement cannot be said to be revolutionary if it reproduces the relationships of power dominant in capitalism.[112]

In a reflective article in 1990, Derry PIRA prisoner Peter Whelan, who identified as a pro-choice feminist, maintained that everyone in the movement must

---

[108] An Deirfiur, 'Playboy interview', *Iris Bheag*, 18 (February 1989).
[109] Laurence McKeown, *Out of time: Irish republican prisoners in Long Kesh, 1972–2000* (Belfast: Beyond the Pale Publications, 2001), p. 145.
[110] Sean Hick, 'Women's affairs', *Iris Bheag*, 4 (November 1987).
[111] Tommy Brogan, 'Women's struggle', *Iris Bheag*, 20 (May 1989).
[112] H3, 'Men debate feminism', *Iris Bheag*, 19 (March 1989).

'challenge our own sexism and the ideas and structures which give us privilege'.[113] Editors of republican prison journal *The Captive Voice*, Brian Campbell and Leonard Ferrin, detected 'in men's everyday behaviour... a patronising, sexist (if non-violent) attitude which is degrading and demoralising'.[114]

Prisoners associated with the LCR, who had left the Provisional movement from 1986, were similarly committed to socialist feminist positions. Writing in 1988, an anonymous LCR member argued that historical materialism and 'the origins of class society', culminating in 'capitalism and imperialism', had trapped working-class women as 'domestic slave and dirt cheap labour'.[115] For LCR founder Tommy McKearney, Sinn Féin's position was typically equivocal. In a letter to the Communist Party of Ireland in January 1988, McKearney warned against perceiving the Provisional membership as uniformly progressive, pointing to the '60% (leadership included) who vote against [abortion]'.[116]

For some prisoners in Long Kesh, feminist politics threatened to destabilise the movement's internal unity: summaries of prisoners' discussions alluded to residual misgivings and 'fear of liberation for women'.[117] Nevertheless, by the late 1980s, several male PIRA prisoners publicly advocated a woman's right to abortion. Advocating 'legalising abortion on demand', Tommy Brogan criticised the 'hypocrisy' of 'conservative right wing elements within our society'.[118] In *Iris Bheag*'s written discussions, two Dublin prisoners endorsed Brogan's position, interpreting the Republic of Ireland's constitution through a lens of patriarchal power and 'control'. For these activists, legalising abortion represented 'the very essence of... our revolution – freedom'.[119]

At the turn of the decade, Maghaberry prisoners remained consistently outspoken on abortion. In 1988, in the belief that Sinn Féin's *ard fheis* had not 'condemned' a court ruling in the Republic preventing health centres providing information about abortion clinics, the Maghaberry prisoners accused the

113 Peter Whelan, 'Men & male power', *The Captive Voice/An Glór Gafa*, Volume 2, Number 2 (Summer 1990).

114 Editorial, *The Captive Voice/An Glór Gafa*, Volume 2, Number 2 (Summer 1990).

115 'Women: The slaves of slaves', *Congress '86: Quarterly Journal of Communist Republican Prisoners and their Associates*, Volume 1, Number 3 (n.d. [1988]).

116 Tommy McKearney quoted in LHL NIPC P3080A: *Armed Struggle: The Communist Party's Open Letter to the Provisional IRA and the Complete and Unedited Contributions to the Debate that Appeared in the Party's Press* Irish Socialist *and* Unity (Dublin: Communist Party of Ireland, 1988).

117 H3, 'Men debate feminism', *Iris Bheag*, 19 (March 1989).

118 Tommy Brogan, 'The abortion issue', *Iris Bheag*, 19 (March 1989).

119 Chucky, 'Womens' [sic] right to choose', *Iris Bheag*, 21 (July 1989); Jim Dunne, 'Abortion again', *Iris Bheag*, 21 (July 1989).

Provisional leadership of hypocrisy. The incarcerated volunteers disputed Sinn Féin's claims to be a

> non-sexist progressive party... Members of a movement who are constantly challenging and tackling oppression... should be upholding those rights – not helping to deny them.[120]

Mary McArdle demanded that the Provisionals adopt a more progressive position: 'Women must be allowed control of their own bodies and reproductive rights.'[121] An anonymous prisoner implored the movement to advocate a more comprehensive legal codification of rape that confronted 'the continuity of male dominance' in society.[122]

Among senior Sinn Féin representatives through the late 1980s and early 1990s, there were few indications of the socialist feminist positions advanced in Maghaberry and Long Kesh. Leading Provisionals' allusions to women in the movement were usually limited to lamenting the putative under-appreciation of women's contribution. The straightforward antidote to such diagnoses – highlighting and promoting women's advancement in Sinn Féin – configured women's rights as a matter for internal party scrutiny. At the *ard fheis* of November 1985, Women's Department representatives Rita O'Hare and Jacinta Duignan successfully advocated positive discrimination for women aspiring to elected and appointed roles in the party.[123] O'Hare later served as Sinn Féin's general secretary and succeeded Danny Morrison as director of publicity in 1990.[124]

For some members of the Women's Department, promoting women within the movement was mere tokenism. In an internal Provisional discussion in 1988, Belfast Women's Department accused the leadership of 'exploiting the election of some few women to influential posts to keep other women in boring and stereotyped roles'. The party's Education Department did not sufficiently address 'women's oppression' or 'challenge the sexist views of some members of the organnisation [*sic*]'. The Belfast branch demanded permanent Women's Department representation on the *Ard Comhairle* and Education Department, and a liberalised position on abortion:

> We believe that this organisation must resist any attempts to select policies on the basis of their popularity or respectability alone, and

---

[120] Women Republican POWs Maghaberry Gaol, 'Defend the clinics campaign', *Iris Bheag*, 7 (February 1988).

[121] 'Book reviews', *The Captive Voice/An Glór Gafa*, Volume 3, Number 3 (Winter 1991).

[122] P.O.W. Maghaberry Gaol, 'Rape', *Iris Bheag*, 17 (January 1989).

[123] 'Women's issues hotly debated', *An Phoblacht/Republican News*, 7 November 1985.

[124] Seth Linder, 'Sinn Fein's sisterhood', *The Independent on Sunday*, 19 February 1995.

that we must campaign to bring some issues which are currently frowned upon into the mainstream of Irish Politics. We believe that whatever one's personal views, the issue of abortion will not go away, if it is ignored. Such issues and the conflicts around them within the organisation can only be resolved through open discussion and debate, and not by attempting to shelve them, sweep them under the carpet, or minimise the support for them.[125]

While the Sinn Féin leadership framed and fixed women's rights as an issue to be addressed within the organisation, and occasionally at national level, PIRA prisoners studied classic feminist texts as well as more recondite international critiques. In a series of articles on 'women and culture' in April 1988, the anonymous editor of *Iris Bheag* demonstrated familiarity with Kate Millet's *Sexual politics* (1969) on women's economic agency and Simone de Beauvoir's work on consciousness-raising and new 'ways of seeing'. The editor also reviewed Stephanie Unduny's writing on women in Mozambique and Ann Carily's analysis of consumerism shackling women in domestic settings.[126] A Women's Department representative visiting County Tyrone prisoner Pauline Quinn in Maghaberry in 1988 noted Quinn's preoccupation with republican solidarities with revolutionaries in Nicaragua and South Africa.[127]

In contrast to the movement's official, and distinctly national, interpretation of women's oppression as a consequence of the British presence in Ireland, Provisional feminists harnessed international leftist influences and female voices from contemporary liberation struggles. In 1992, Sinn Féin Women's Department's journal coupled James Connolly's polemic on the 'suffering sisters of the wage earning class' with testimonies from women in Fatah and the Palestine Liberation Organization who had experienced sexism in their own organisations. Other quotations signalled activists' admiration for socialist feminism, including Bolshevik Alexandra Kollantai's critique of marriage and wives' 'chattel' status, and Mozambican FRELIMO leader Samora Machel's mantra that only 'working-class led revolution' could emancipate women.[128] In a poem published in 1992, Maghaberry prisoners counted among their 'teachers' not only Irish revolutionaries Tone, Pearse, and Connolly, but also Karl Marx.[129]

Yet the degree to which PIRA prisoners' feminism diverged from the

---

[125] 'The role of women in Sinn Fein', *Iris Bheag*, 11 (June 1988).
[126] 'Women and culture: part 2', *Iris Bheag*, 9 (April 1988).
[127] 'A visit to Maghaberry Prison', *A Woman's Voice*, 2 (September 1988).
[128] 'Women', *Women in Struggle/Mna I Streachilt*, Volume 2 (n.d. [1992]).
[129] See poem 'Volunteers' in 'Poetry', *Women in Struggle/Mna I Streachilt*, Volume 1 (n.d. [1991]).

movement's central authority in the 1990s requires some qualification. Critical debates about women's agency in the movement were most commonplace, and most practicable, in jail. Fundamentally, the PIRA women in Maghaberry maintained the Provisional movement's master narrative of the conflict: the 'main source of our oppression is the British occupation and domination of our country'.[130]

But by the early 1990s, Maghaberry prisoners' criticisms of the Provisional movement were increasingly frequent. Charging the leadership with inaction on discrimination in the movement, these damning critiques connected to wider reservations about the direction of the struggle. Observations of normalised sexism and paternalism in the movement accompanied profound misgivings about Sinn Féin's strategic reorientation. Often relating personal experiences, PIRA women destabilised republican narratives' habitual heroism. In 1993, Mary McArdle and Ailish Carroll argued that the movement 'continually judged' republican women whose husbands were imprisoned. These women's social lives were 'restrict[ed] even by those within the Republican Movement'. McArdle and Carroll insisted the movement

> should take the lead and discourage the more judgemental elements…
> [and] strive to offer more practical and emotional support to prisoners'
> partners.[131]

Imprisoned in Durham, Martina Anderson and Ella O'Dwyer attacked 'machismo' in republican communities. Although they acknowledged the initiatives of 'male feminist POWs… in Long Kesh', they argued that 'beyond the prison gates' many republicans did not 'recognise and acknowledge' women's activism.[132] Shortly after her release from Maghaberry in July 1991, Nancy McCullough argued that the movement 'discriminated' against women in its ranks by ignoring its female prisoners and promoting PIRA men to positions of influence instead.[133] A Sinn Féin councillor in Derry City since 1985, Dodie McGuinness reflected on her experiences of sexism in the movement: 'Some fellow republicans… dismiss me as "just a woman". Not in words so much as

---

[130] Quoted in a statement by the 17 PIRA prisoners in Maghaberry. Women POWs, Maghaberry, 'Women and struggle', *The Captive Voice/An Glór Gafa*, Volume 2, Number 2 (Summer 1990).

[131] Mary McArdle & Ailish Carroll, 'How free are prisoners' partners?', *The Captive Voice/An Glór Gafa*, Volume 5, Number 2 (Summer 1993).

[132] Martina Anderson & Ella O'Dwyer, 'Let's talk', *The Captive Voice/An Glór Gafa*, Volume 5, Number 1 (Spring 1993).

[133] Irene Sherry, 'Report on SF Women's Conference', *The Captive Voice/An Glór Gafa*, Volume 3, Number 3 (Winter 1991).

by deeds.' McGuinness recalled being excluded from discussions, and advocated internal education 'to combat sexism'. Men who espoused 'good anti-sexist politics in theory' were 'failing in day-to-day, unconscious actions and practices'.[134]

The radicalism of an anti-imperialist guerrilla movement engaging post-'68 leftist ideologies inevitably pervaded many republicans' networks. The '68 zeitgeist disrupted a long tradition in the north, where, in the absence of nationalist coordination at Stormont, many lay Catholics had looked to the clergy for representation.[135] Furthermore, as Dieter Reinisch has noted, many republicans were raised around conservative influences inside and outside the home.[136] An undercurrent of social reaction persisted in some sections of the Provisional movement. For example, in its proposals to Sinn Féin's *ard fheis* of 1982, the Donegal *Comhairle Ceantair* typified the perception that the social liberalism of the Provisional majority was at best a distraction from republicanism. The Donegal executive criticised

> the tendency of the [Provisional] Movement to support the Gay Movement... [W]hilst respecting the rights of everyone to their own way of life it is a disservice to the Liberation struggle.[137]

Tensions between these contrasting zeitgeists on gender and sexuality formed one element of the complex relationship between republicanism and feminism throughout the conflict.

Conclusion

Writing in 1983, Suzanne Buckley and Pamela Lonergan argued that republican organisations had excluded women from influential positions during the 1970s.[138] This chapter largely supports Buckley's and Lonergan's conclusions for the first decade of the conflict. Many Provisional men, the leadership included, portrayed women as particularly vulnerable in the escalating war. In these formulations,

---

[134] Martha McClelland, 'Dodie McGuinness: Republican and public representative', *Women in Struggle/Mna I Streachilt*, Volume 3 (n.d. [1992]).

[135] Marianne Elliott, *The Catholics of Ulster: a history* (London: Allen Lane – Penguin Press, 2000), p. 457.

[136] Reinisch, '*Cumann na mBan*', 160.

[137] Tom Hartley Collection PH504: Sinn Féin, *Ard Fheis 1982: Clár agus Rúin* (Dublin: Sinn Féin, 1982).

[138] Suzanne Buckley & Pamela Lonergan, 'Women and the troubles, 1969–1980', in Yonah Alexander & Alan O'Day (eds.), *Terrorism in Ireland* (London: Croom Helm, 1983), pp. 75–87.

women were considered less as an integral part of republican struggle, and more as a support network occasionally subjected to wanton state repression.

Provisional women, meanwhile, were as aloof from liberal feminism's 'middle-class' agenda as they were from radical feminists championing women's autonomous organisation. On the contrary, female Provisionals participating in Sinn Féin's campaigns and the PIRA's armed struggle regarded themselves as a core constituency of the republican movement. They had neither the opportunity nor inclination to advance single-issue causes outside core republican demands. Feminists' struggles in continental Europe concerning abortion, for example – legalised in France and Italy in 1975 and 1978 respectively – were far removed from republican women's activities in the 1970s. More broadly, the PIRA campaign at this juncture did not integrate the radical social policies of, for instance, Basque nationalists, who targeted prominent anti-abortion lobbyists from the late 1970s.[139]

Instead, until the early 1990s, many of those Provisionals who identified as feminists worked alongside men in a broad anti-imperialist movement, in which feminist politics were often marginalised or diluted. Under Gerry Adams's leadership from 1983, Sinn Féin frequently lauded women's roles in republican struggle. Yet the movement generally ignored radical or socialist interpretations of women's subjugation worldwide. By October 1992, when Sinn Féin Women's Department leader Máiréad Keane convened a conference inviting 'women of all political persuasions' to discuss women's oppression and the national question, Adams assented to the move for a separate women's movement outside Sinn Féin.[140]

How successive Sinn Féin leaders Ruairí Ó Brádaigh and Gerry Adams and their supporters interacted with feminist politics reflected different ways of historicising and spatialising Irish republicanism. Ó Brádaigh and Adams looked to a distinctly Irish past to legitimise political positions in the present. The historical record provided examples of women active in republican insurgencies in 1798 and 1916, so both men readily endorsed continuing women's activity in the Provisional movement.

Like his predecessor, Adams addressed women's politics within narrow confines. Adams repeatedly asserted republican women's 'neglected' activism, but avoided overtly advocating bodily autonomy. Exclusively highlighting *Provisional* women's experiences, Adams eschewed broader international or leftist critique of women's oppression. To the extent that Ó Brádaigh and Adams addressed it, women's oppression was chiefly a product of British rule. Feminism was

---

[139] Carrie Hamilton, *Women and ETA: the gender politics of radical Basque nationalism* (Manchester: Manchester University Press, 2007), p. 155.

[140] Máiréad Keane, 'Women's Conference', *An Phoblacht/Republican News*, 29 October 1992.

not deemed suitable for extensive republican debate. Second-wave feminism internationally, especially in the USA, Britain, and Europe, appeared irrelevant, or even divisive.

For republicans on the revolutionary left in the 1970s, including members of the Official movement, IRSP, and PD, ideas of Irish republican historical legitimacy were important, but not to the exclusion of global leftist thought. Inspired by international anti-imperialism, these republicans located women's liberation as a central aspect of a projected socialist revolution overthrowing capitalism and patriarchy.

In 1987, Irish feminist Christina Loughran castigated feminists in the Provisional movement for 'giv[ing] up their autonomy' for incremental advances in Sinn Féin's policy on women's rights.[141] However, Loughran's criticisms predated the crystallisation of feminist politics in the Provisional movement: albeit subtly in the first instance, through the 1980s the politics of women's rights gradually permeated Provisional republicanism. After the Republic's referendum on abortion in 1983, diverse activists campaigned around Sinn Féin's Women's Department, especially across Belfast, Derry, and the Republic's border areas.

The Women's Department occupied a curious space in the movement, simultaneously close to the leadership and its strategy while occasionally diversifying the party's pronouncements on issues facing women in Ireland and beyond. From the mid-1980s, the Women's Department forged international connections with feminist anti-imperialists and the British left.

In the late 1980s, socialist feminist currents in the PIRA echoed the second-wave feminisms that had pervaded Britain, Europe, and the USA in the early 1970s. Harnessing the radical potential of pedagogy and debate in jail, left-wing prisoners in Long Kesh and Maghaberry criticised the movement's perceived lack of commitment to feminism. They also questioned strategic reorientation. Internationalising women's struggles furnished Provisional feminists with stinging rebukes for the theocratic aspects of Northern Ireland and the 'neo-colonial' Republic. Their analyses closely resembled those of British socialists whose feminism contributed to overarching anti-capitalist struggle.

There were specific local inflections to the feminist-republican dynamic. For example, Provisionals in Derry City consistently espoused pro-choice positions during Sinn Féin's abortion debates from the mid-1980s. Derry feminists frequently defied the *Ard Comhairle* and anti-abortion delegate motions at the movement's annual conferences. At the *ard fheis* of 1985, Daisy Mules argued against the party executive and moved the party to 'recognise that women have the right to choose' and 'every person should be free to follow their

---

[141] Christina Loughran, 'Writing our own history: organising against the odds – 10 years of feminism in Northern Ireland', *Trouble & Strife*, 11 (Summer 1987).

own personal beliefs and values'. Mules's fellow Derry delegate Paddy Logue similarly considered abortion 'a matter of civil liberties and rights – men cannot take that right away from women'.[142] The following year, when five northern Sinn Féin *cumainn* proposed the party should revert to its earlier policy of 'total opposition' to abortion, only Derry City's branch and *Comhairle Ceantair* dissented, demanding the right to abortion and 'non-directive pregnancy counselling embodying all choices' in a 'secular state'.[143]

Continuing their semi-autonomous activities in the early 1990s, Provisional feminists in Derry connected with international comrades and collaborated with women's groups beyond republicanism. On International Women's Day in 1991, Derry Sinn Féin collaborated with the city's Women's Aid group to unveil street art depicting local republican women and feminists alongside Nicaraguan workers. Local Sinn Féin representative said the mural celebrated 'sisterhood and anti-imperialist struggle throughout the world'.[144] The following year, Provisionals joined feminists to form a new women's drama group in the city, *Guth na mBan* (Women's Voice). Activists performed short plays in Derry's public spaces. Linking women's experiences inside and outside republicanism, topics included domestic violence and strip-searching in Maghaberry Prison and Castlereagh interrogation centre.[145] Derry witnessed overlaps between traditional republican activism and wide-ranging grassroots feminism. These links captured in microcosm the broadening heterogeneity of republican engagements with women's politics throughout the conflict.

---

[142] 'Women's issues hotly debated', *An Phoblacht/Republican News*, 7 November 1985.

[143] LHL NIPC P2303: Sinn Féin, *Ard-Fheis '86: Clár agus Rúin* (Dublin: Sinn Féin, 1986).

[144] Martha McClelland, 'Against the wall', *Women in Struggle/Mna I Streachilt*, Volume 1 (n.d. [1991]).

[145] Martha McClelland, 'A voice for the voiceless', *Women in Struggle/Mna I Streachilt*, Volume 3 (n.d. [1992]).

5

Catholicism

> I don't intend on this platform to attack any of the Catholic
> clergy. I'm a Catholic mother myself in Catholic Ireland, and
> I'm proud of it... I only say to them here and now tonight,
> Father Gallagher and your bishop, you're out of touch with
> things. Go and see the ordinary priests in the north.
>
> Sinn Féin *Ard Comhairle* representative Máire Nic Giolla
> Mhore addressing a meeting of the party's North-West
> Executive in Letterkenny, County Donegal, 3 January 1972[1]

The vast majority of Irish republicans active after 1968 were born and raised
in Catholic families and experienced aspects of a Catholic upbringing.[2] Some
republicans, but by no means all, have described themselves as practising
believers during their pathways to and through their mobilisation. For others,
being 'a Catholic' is an ethnic signifier rather than a descriptor of philosophy
or spirituality. As the quote above indicates, even for those republicans who
continually identified as faithful Catholics, interactions between republicanism
and the Church as a spiritual and political institution were often complicated.

The importance of religion in collective life has been heavily theorised. Emile
Durkheim connected subjective experiences of religion with evolving identities
and political allegiances: religion helped to define experiences and conceptions
of community and morality.[3] Paul Siegel's analysis of religion highlighted its
capaciousness and malleability: state authorities could appropriate religion as a
repressive force, yet progressive and even radical activists could find in religion

---

[1] 'Republicans challenge bishop to public debate', *Donegal Democrat*, 7 January 1972.
[2] Throughout this chapter, 'Catholic communities' refers broadly to 'ethnic' Catholics
in Northern Ireland and the Republic of Ireland's border counties, irrespective of
individual beliefs and practices.
[3] Bryan S. Turner, *Religion and social theory* (London: Sage, 1991), pp. xi–xii, 76, 80.

revolutionary ideology. For Siegel, the Marxian formulation of the 'opium' of religion could 'stimulate as well as stupefy'.[4]

The subjective dynamics of religion and politics are concomitantly complex in practice. Distinguishing between Irish republican perceptions of a supposedly ill-informed hierarchy and more sympathetic, community-oriented local clergy, Graham Spencer and Margaret M. Scull have illuminated the complexity of Irish republicans' attitudes towards the Church.[5]

Many academic discussions of religious identities and republican politics have focused on the specific question of whether sectarianism pervaded the Provisional republican movement. The original protagonists in this debate were Robert W. White, Steve Bruce, and Henry Patterson. White argued against perceiving the Provisional movement as sectarian,[6] while Bruce and Patterson disagreed.[7] The debate continued recently, when Rachel Kowalski argued that the Provisionals were 'for the most part, blind to religious diversity'.[8] Contending that republicans did not systematically attempt ethnic cleansing or genocide of the Protestant population, Matthew Lewis and Shaun McDaid coined 'functional sectarianism': for Lewis and McDaid, the PIRA campaign had 'sectarian implications' and was perceived as such among Protestant civilians.[9] This instructive nuance echoed Richard English's point that certain PIRA operations had a 'sectarianising impact'.[10]

Such debates are not, of course, confined to academic discourse. Contemporary political discussion continually characterises the republican past. Claim and counter-claim are heavily laden with difficult memory. Speaking in 2014,

---

[4] Paul N. Siegel, *The meek and the militant: religion and power across the world* (Chicago, Illinois: Haymarket Books, 2005), p. 44.

[5] Graham Spencer, *From armed struggle to political struggle: republican tradition and transformation in Northern Ireland* (London: Bloomsbury, 2015) pp. 65–66; Margaret M. Scull, 'The Catholic church and the hunger strikes of Terence MacSwiney and Bobby Sands', *Irish Political Studies*, 31 (2016), p. 283.

[6] Robert W. White, 'The Irish Republican Army: an assessment of sectarianism', *Terrorism and Political Violence*, 9 (1997), pp. 20–55.

[7] Steve Bruce, 'Victim selection in ethnic conflict: motives and attitudes in Irish republicanism', *Terrorism and Political Violence*, 9 (1997), pp. 56–71; Henry Patterson, 'Sectarianism revisited: the Provisional IRA campaign in a border region of Northern Ireland', *Terrorism and Political Violence*, 22 (2010), pp. 337–356.

[8] Rachel Caroline Kowalski, 'The role of sectarianism in the Provisional IRA campaign, 1969–1997', *Terrorism and Political Violence*, 28 (2016), pp. 658–683.

[9] Matthew Lewis & Shaun McDaid, 'Bosnia on the border? Republican violence in Northern Ireland during the 1920s and 1970s', *Terrorism and Political Violence*, 29 (2017), pp. 635–655.

[10] Richard English, *Does terrorism work? A history* (Oxford: Oxford University Press, 2016), p. 130.

then-First Minister of Northern Ireland, Peter Robinson, argued that the PIRA's 'sectarian' campaign in border areas of County Fermanagh had constituted 'ethnic cleansing' and 'genocide'.[11] In January 2018, Sinn Féin MP for West Tyrone, Barry McElduff, resigned after he was accused of mocking the victims of the Kingsmill massacre of 1976, in which ten Protestant workers were murdered in south Armagh. McElduff denied that he had intended to refer to the 'terrible atrocity of Kingsmill'.[12]

Interactions between religion and politics are particularly contested and potent across the north of Ireland. For Marianne Elliott, northern Catholicism since the partition of Ireland in 1921 has revolved around 'a largely passive sense on grievance'. Its collective identity has reinforced 'well-established traditions of the downtrodden and dispossessed Gael'.[13] Across Ireland, religious institutions' moral, political, and practical dominance in health care, welfare, and social politics has been partially dismantled. Yet even amid general secularisation and declining church attendance, religious affiliations can endure as ethnonational identifiers. In the north, three decades of conflict accentuated the importance of, and problematised, Catholic identity.[14] Steve Bruce has cautioned against commonplace misunderstandings: the Northern Ireland conflict was not *about* religion' but was 'heavily informed by religion' as an 'ethnic identity'.[15]

This chapter scrutinises divergent republican interactions with Catholicism – as both a spiritual philosophy and a politically engaged institution. Since 1968, the contentious politics of Irish republicanism have challenged and reshaped the Catholic Church's social roles. As Margaret M. Scull's salient recent work has demonstrated, the Church lacked internal consensus on republicanism: disagreement among clergy emerged gradually throughout the conflict.[16] Some clergy ardently opposed the republican movement, while others tried to understand republican grievances and espoused moderate nationalist positions. In unusually partisan instances, a small number of priests exhibited

---

[11] 'Peter Robinson: IRA carried out "genocide" in Fermanagh', *Impartial Reporter*, 6 February 2014.

[12] Henry McDonald, 'Sinn Féin MP Barry McElduff resigns after Kingsmill row', *The Guardian*, 15 January 2018.

[13] Marianne Elliott, *When God took sides: religion and identity in Ireland – unfinished history* (Oxford: Oxford University Press, 2009), pp. 155, 242.

[14] Callum G. Brown, 'A revisionist approach to religious change', in Steve Bruce (ed.), *Religion and modernization: sociologists and historians debate the secularization thesis* (Oxford: Clarendon, 1992), pp. 39, 50–52.

[15] Steve Bruce, *Religion in modern Britain* (Oxford: Oxford University Press, 1995), pp. 23, 128–129.

[16] Margaret M. Scull, *The Catholic church and the Northern Ireland troubles* (Oxford: Oxford University Press, 2019).

overt republican sympathies. Conversely, republicans were not passive in the face of clerical criticism. Their relationship with organised religion was neither entirely acrimonious nor entirely harmonious. Both individually and collectively, republican engagements with, and experiences of, religion varied markedly.

How republicans negotiated religion and politics has implications for how social environments and networks informed political ideas, and for how individual republicans interpreted their struggle across time and place. This chapter begins by discussing republican relationships with the Church in 'the '68 years', either side of the republican movement's split in 1969 and 1970. The second section considers how prison protests from 1976, and hunger strikes in 1980 and 1981, recast republican engagements with the Church. Finally, the chapter shifts focus to the radical republican minority among clergy, examining their connections to republican politics. This section also scrutinises how clergy and prisoners alike engaged liberation theology from the 1980s.

Republicans and the Catholic Church in 'the '68 years', c.1968–1973

From the beginning of the Northern Ireland conflict, the northern Catholic hierarchy understood the dispute revolving around 'their' flock being persistently denied civil rights. In 1969 and 1970, senior clergy such as Cardinal Conway, Archbishop of Armagh and Primate of all-Ireland, established fragile alliances with defence committees in Catholic areas of Belfast. Conway's principal fear was that violence would undermine the civil rights movement he supported. When rioting broke out in Belfast in August 1969, Conway exhorted Catholics to avoid becoming 'swept away by emotion – however natural and understandable such emotion may be'.[17]

On 23 August, a week after Belfast's disturbances began, six bishops insisted that north and west Belfast's embattled Catholic populace was the victim, not the instigator, of 'armed insurrection'. Implicitly, the bishops argued that a nationalist uprising would be morally unjustifiable and politically damaging. In their joint statement, Conway and the bishops of Clogher, Derry, Down and Connor, Dromore, and Kilmore, implored the Catholic community to honour their 'Christian duty' and remain calm.[18] Conway persistently attempted to marshal the Catholic community towards non-violent protest: in 1970 he publicised a new organisation styling itself the Movement for Peace in Ireland.[19]

---

[17] 'Keep cool, Cardinal advises Catholics', *Belfast Telegraph*, 14 August 1969.
[18] LHL NIPC P577: *Violence and Civil Disturbances in Northern Ireland in 1969: Report of Tribunal of Inquiry* (Belfast: HMSO, 1972).
[19] 'Two committees to foster peace', *The Irish Times*, 1 December 1970.

In Belfast, the closest that clergy came to overtly supporting republicans in 'the '68 years' was a temporary alliance with the CCDC. An umbrella group of local grassroots committees guarding their areas against police and loyalist incursions, the CCDC included republicans in their number. When armed republicans repelled a loyalist attack on the nationalist enclave of Short Strand in July 1970, clergy, CCDC members, and the fledgling Provisional republican movement jointly celebrated the 'defence' of St Matthew's Church. The building became a symbol of community resistance. CCDC chairman Tom Conaty and two Belfast clergymen met Provisionals days after the gunfight. Father Patrick Toner, secretary to Bishop Philbin of Down and Connor, praised the nascent PIRA's role.[20]

However, concord between clergy, Catholic vigilantes, and Provisional republicans was short-lived. By late 1970, when the PIRA shifted from defenderism and escalated its offensive, the CCDC and its supporters implored republicans to stop. Republicans rejected these demands, arguing that the CCDC's moderation ignored the Catholic community's continual suffering. When the CCDC called for a PIRA ceasefire in November 1970, a republican press statement claimed that the CCDC had lost credibility with the Belfast public after the British imposed a curfew on the Falls Road and killed a Catholic civilian, Daniel O'Hagan. In a televised interview on 9 November 1970, CCDC representative Father Murphy admitted that popular confidence in his organisation had declined during the previous year.[21]

Through subsequent months, Belfast's leading churchmen remained hopeful that publicising Catholic grievances would undercut the burgeoning republican campaign. Accordingly, priests aligned with the CCDC. As popular support for republicanism mounted, especially after the introduction of internment in August 1971, the likelihood of alleviating Catholic alienation declined. Conaty and Father Murphy worked with the Minority Rights Association and met representatives of the Republic of Ireland government in September 1971 to advise that a 'settlement package' in Northern Ireland needed to abolish internment and reform the RUC.[22]

Politically engaged clergy in the late 1960s and early 1970s had more enduring ties with the Catholic Ex-Servicemen's Association (CESA) than with republicans. The CESA mobilised former British military service personnel to

---

[20] LHL NIPC P13526: *Freedom Struggle by the Provisional IRA* (Dublin: Irish Republican Publicity Bureau, 1973).
[21] LHL NIPC P13526: *Freedom Struggle by the Provisional IRA* (Dublin: Irish Republican Publicity Bureau, 1973).
[22] NAI TSCH/2002/8/483: 'Memorandum of meeting with Fr. Murphy and Mr. Conaty' (24 September 1971).

staff barricades during civil rights marches – and some clergy joined. Keen to dispel any suggestion that the CESA or the civil rights movement constituted a nationalist conspiracy, Derry CESA members proposed to carry a union flag on a NICRA march in January 1969. According to Belfast CESA organiser Phil Curran, the CESA would cooperate with the British Army and Ulster Defence Regiment to protect Catholic areas. So close was the CESA's connection to the Church that its members sought Cardinal Conway's blessing to form a new defensive organisation in November 1972.[23]

Marianne Elliott has evoked the founding Provisionals' 'right-wing, pious nationalism'.[24] For Mark Ryan and Graham Spencer, the early Provisional movement was similarly close to the Catholic Church's political morality. Ryan argued that the PIRA's founders were 'staunchly anti-communist, even devoutly Catholic' and deferential to 'religious reaction'.[25] Spencer endorsed journalist Ed Moloney's depiction of the early Provisionals' 'traditional conservative, republican values'.[26] Today, such perspectives intermesh with liberal criticisms of Sinn Féin's longstanding ambiguity on social politics. But while 'new Sinn Féin' has not committed wholesale to, for example, a woman's right to abortion,[27] neither have Provisional republicans historically simply acquiesced in clerical edicts.

Several of the Provisional movement's founders were devout Catholics whose politics were infused with Catholic morality. Yet they also criticised theocracy and limited the Church's political authority. Interviewed in January 1972, Belfast PIRA leader Joe Cahill identified as a practising Catholic but criticised clerical 'interference' in Irish politics. Cahill advocated a secular state and lambasted the CCDC for including 'too many priests for my liking'.[28] The outlook of the first

---

23 John O'Neill, '"Fourth force": The Catholic ex-servicemen's association' (15 December 2016) https://treasonfelony.wordpress.com/2016/12/15/fourth-force-the-catholic-ex-servicemens-association/ (accessed 7 September 2017).

24 Marianne Elliott, *The Catholics of Ulster: a history* (London: Allen Lane – Penguin Press, 2000), p. 419.

25 Mark Ryan, *War and peace in Ireland: Britain and the IRA in the new world order* (London: Pluto Press, 1994), pp. 36, 75.

26 Spencer, *From armed struggle*, 47.

27 In May 2018, Sinn Féin's new leader Mary Lou McDonald endorsed pro-choice positions, but stipulated this was a matter of individual conscience in the party. The following month, at the party's *ard fheis*, delegates supported a leadership motion that women should have access to abortions within 'a limited gestational period'. Several prominent northern party representatives do not share McDonald's views, and more than 20 party *cumainn* demanded a free conscience vote. 'Unity in abortion laws needed across Ireland says Sinn Féin leader', *The Irish News*, 25 May 2018; John Manley, 'Sinn Féin votes to liberalise party abortion policy', *The Irish News*, 18 June 2018.

28 Christopher Macy, 'Sinn Fein and the IRA's: 1' and 'Sinn Fein and the IRA's: 2', *Humanist*, Volume 87, Number 1, Ulster Special Issue (January 1972).

PIRA Chief of Staff, Seán Mac Stíofáin, was similarly complex. Mac Stíofáin positioned himself as 'radically left-wing in everything, except religion'. Only his interpretation of Marxism as inherently irreligious prevented Mac Stíofáin from identifying as a Marxist. He opposed abortion and only 'reluctantly' accepted arguments for liberalising divorce legislation. Yet he held that if Christ's teachings were applied, 'you'd have no need for revolutionary movements'.[29] Sinn Féin's founding president Ruairí Ó Brádaigh also combined personal faith with distaste for the Church's political doctrine. He opposed abortion but considered contraception a matter of conscience, wanted a 'pluralistic' society, and criticised the Church's political interventions.[30]

Simultaneously, in public the Provisionals accepted the Catholic Church as an arbiter on republicans' moral, if not political, declarations. Eoin Ó Broin's assessment of founding Provisionals espousing 'Christian socialism' accurately reflects how senior Provisionals presented their programme as compatible with Catholicism.[31] In February 1970, promoting the *Comhar na gComharsan* (neighbours' cooperation) economic programme, *An Phoblacht* accentuated the 'Christian values' that underpinned this 'social order'.[32] To confer legitimacy on their campaign, Provisional propagandists occasionally pointed to sympathetic clergy: in 1973, publicity celebrated Father Seán McManus of Macken, County Fermanagh, who had declared 'the Six-County state... illegal'.[33]

Cognisant of the Church's social and institutional influence, the Provisional grassroots also highlighted those clerics who seemed sympathetic. In a letter to the *Ulster Herald* in September 1971, Provisional supporter Aidan Corrigan cited Catholic theologians who held that the rebels of 1916 were saints in heaven. Corrigan invoked 'Natural Law', the Bible, and Catholic teaching to justify a Provisional campaign of defence against 'British colonialism'.[34]

---

[29] Seán Mac Stíofáin interview with Robert W. White, 1990. Robert W. White, *Out of the ashes: an oral history of the Provisional Irish republican movement* (Newbridge: Merrion, 2017), pp. 45–46.

[30] John Rooks, 'Sinn Féin president talks to unionists', *Belfast Telegraph*, 28 July 1971.

[31] Eoin Ó Broin, *Sinn Féin and the politics of left republicanism* (London: Pluto Press, 2009), p. 233. Kevin Bean and Mark Hayes have argued similarly that 'underlying social Catholicism' informed *Éire Nua*, the Provisionals' socioeconomic programme in the early 1970s. Kevin Bean & Mark Hayes, 'Sinn Féin and the new republicanism in Ireland: electoral progress, political stasis, and ideological failure', *Radical History Review*, 104 (2009), p. 133.

[32] LHL NIPC P13526: *Freedom Struggle by the Provisional IRA* (Dublin: Irish Republican Publicity Bureau, 1973).

[33] LHL NIPC P13526: *Freedom Struggle by the Provisional IRA* (Dublin: Irish Republican Publicity Bureau, 1973).

[34] Aidan Corrigan, 'Persistent vitriolic attacks by Erne Sense', *Ulster Herald*, 18 September 1971.

Provisionals tended to distinguish between a supposedly aloof Catholic hierarchy and more socially attuned parish priests. Bishops were cast as ignorant, whereas clergy embedded in those troubled districts were supposedly more aware of the grievances that inspired republican insurgency. In 1973, a Catholic sympathiser wrote an open letter to Bishop Cahal Daly asking why bishops 'who only speak when they can help the Establishment' refused to condemn British Army behaviour in Northern Ireland. The writer implied that clerics on the ground who supported 'down-trodden Catholics' would maintain 'the Faith' while bishops acquiesced in British rule.[35] Bishops were held to account for their lofty dismissals of republicanism: at a meeting of Sinn Féin's North-West Executive in January 1972, the party's Ulster organiser, Maurice Conway, challenged the absent Bishop Anthony McFeely of Raphoe to a public debate.[36]

As the armed struggle escalated through 1971 and 1972, public disputations between senior churchmen and middle-ranking republicans mounted. Provisional publicists carefully distinguished between personal faith and Catholic institutional leadership: the former compatible with republicanism; the latter remote and politically unqualified. In January 1971, after Bishop Philbin of Down and Connor condemned rioters and republicans, *An Phoblacht* editor Seán Ó Brádaigh challenged Philbin to justify British rule in Ireland by Catholic moral teaching.[37] Addressing a public meeting in August 1971, Niall Fagan of Sinn Féin's Dublin *Comhairle Ceantair* promoted a secular state and portrayed the Catholic hierarchy as an obstacle to national unity. Fagan insisted that his position was consonant with Christianity.[38]

Leading Provisionals dismissed their most senior clerical critics as a haughty elite oblivious to reality. After Cardinal Conway urged Provisionals to declare a ceasefire or concede demands to the British in 1972, Ruairí Ó Brádaigh portrayed Conway as unqualified to comment:

> Did [Conway] at any time visit the men [in Long Kesh] or in Magilligan or Crumlin Road, or on board the Maidstone? Did he ever make the few minutes walk['] from Ara Coeli to Armagh Jail to visit the young women serving up to 12 years there?[39]

[35] Michael Dawson, 'Open letter to Dr. Daly, Bishop of Ardagh', *Republican News*, 16 February 1973.

[36] 'Republicans challenge bishop to public debate', *Donegal Democrat*, 7 January 1972.

[37] 'Sinn Fein letter to Bishop', *The Times*, 25 January 1971.

[38] 'S.F. calls for guns and strikes', *The Irish Press*, 11 August 1971.

[39] LHL NIPC P1355: P1355: Ruairí Ó Brádaigh, *Our People, Our Future: What Éire Nua Means* (Dublin: Sinn Féin, 1973).

In a statement in 1973, the Provisional leadership blamed Pope Paul VI's 'advisors' for papal edicts encouraging Irish Catholics to accept the Special Powers Act and internment. Provisional publicity accepted the Pope as undisputed head of the Church, but insisted that his supremacy did not 'give him the right or the authority to ask Irish Catholics to accept the morally unacceptable'. Papal advisors were 'far removed from the present thinking of the Irish people'.[40]

However, bishops and cardinals were not alone in condemning republicanism. Many parish priests, even in the most deprived areas of Belfast and Derry, lambasted the republican campaign from the pulpit. Locally, Provisional responses ranged from outright dismissals to more restrained insistences that politics were beyond a priest's rightful purview. After Father Patrick Gallagher of Ballyshannon, County Donegal, criticised the PIRA in 1971, the Provisionals' North-West Executive unequivocally accused Gallagher of 'ignorance' and 'bigotry'.[41] By contrast, in 1972, when a parish priest in Ardoyne claimed Provisionals were intimidating the local population, local republicans expressed gratitude for spiritual guidance, but asserted that his political views 'do not interest us'.[42] Ardoyne Provisionals were more vituperative towards the Church leadership, defiantly announcing that 'no amount of condemnation from the Catholic Heirarchy [sic]... shall sway us from our ideals'.[43]

Having clashed with Church authorities repeatedly over the armed campaign, leading Provisionals were not inclined to broach social politics in the 1970s. The movement's ambiguous stance on divorce and contraception reflected its unease concerning the Catholic Church's moral authority. In 1973, a Derry Provisional scorned the movement's awkwardness around social politics, and implored the leadership to repudiate Catholic theocracy. Identifying the 'Christian and Socialist' movement as a curious combination of 'humanitarians, christians, socialists and Irishmen', the republican correspondent anticipated disinterest, or even hostility, from comrades: 'many people will say, "what has Irish unity to do with contraception and divorce?"' Defying the taboo of overt anticlericalism, the Derry republican urged the movement's hierarchy to oppose the Republic's 'repressive laws' against contraception and divorce.[44]

Republican retrospectives recast intergenerationally the Provisional movement's past interactions with religious authority. Especially for Provisionals born in the 1950s and early 1960s and close to Gerry Adams's generation and

[40] 'Who is advising the Pope on Ireland?', *Republican News*, 19 May 1973.
[41] 'Ballyshannon priest criticised I.R.A. methods', *Ulster Herald*, 1 January 1972.
[42] Frank Burton, *The politics of legitimacy: struggles in a Belfast community* (London: Routledge & Kegan Paul, 1978), pp. 94, 97, 103.
[43] EHI: 'We have the right', *Ardoyne Freedom Fighters: Freedom 1972 Bulletin*.
[44] 'Divorce in Ireland', *Volunteer: North West Republican* (April 1973).

trajectory, Sinn Féin's 1970s leadership was unhealthily close to the Church. Séanna Walsh, born in Belfast in 1956, describes a 'hangover of religion' among an older generation of Provisionals.[45] Eamonn MacDermott, born in Derry in 1957, remembered Billy McKee and his founding PIRA comrades as 'a Catholic movement'. By contrast, MacDermott remembered his milieu as emphatically 'not a Catholic movement. We didn't see ourselves as fighting for *Catholic Ireland*.'[46] For Conor Murphy, born in south Armagh in 1963, 'the older brigade, the mature republicans... had more of a Catholic outlook'. A younger cadre 'superseded' the original leadership. The new leaders and their supporters incorporated practising Catholics, 'but Catholic thinking didn't dominate'.[47]

Today, general hostility towards the Catholic Church's historical political agency is one of the few points of concord between Sinn Féin supporters and 'dissenting' republicans alike. For a founding member of the PIRA in west Belfast who broke with the Provisionals in the 1980s, the Church was inherently hidebound and would 'accept any government' that complied with its own institutional interests.[48] Another founding member of the PIRA from north Belfast argued that the Church's leadership had for centuries acquiesced in nationalists' subjugation.[49]

In the early 1970s, Official republican propagandists and prisoners excoriated the Church as an international bastion of reactionary social politics and capitalist exploitation. Derry Officials promoted a 'secular' republicanism that would 'destroy' the Catholic Church's privileged position, 'one of the curses of this area'.[50] Writing in a series of pamphlets historicising and elaborating republican politics, leading Official ideologue Eoin Ó Murchú positioned the 'Catholic Hierarchy' as 'the staunchest defender' in Ireland of the 'English... capitalist system'.[51]

Officials' 'stageist' revolutionary strategy informed their critique of a conservative Church. Especially after the OIRA ceasefire in May 1972, the movement prioritised working-class unity as a precondition for national reunification. Observing increasingly unfavourable conditions amid a polarising conflict, portrayed Provisional republicans and the Church conniving to fuel sectarianism and division. Writing in their prisoners' journal in 1975, one Official accused the Catholic Church of cynically obstructing ecumenicism and maintaining a 'shameful sectarian' education system.[52] Similar ideas suffuse

---

45 Séanna Walsh interview with Jack Hepworth. Belfast, 12 August 2015.
46 Eamonn MacDermott interview with Jack Hepworth. Derry, 17 September 2015.
47 Conor Murphy interview with Jack Hepworth. Newry, 16 September 2015.
48 Kevin Hannaway interview with Jack Hepworth. Belfast, 6 December 2017.
49 Francie McGuigan interview with Jack Hepworth. Belfast, 6 December 2017.
50 'Communism, the Church and the IRA', *Starry Plough* (Derry: n.d. [1972]).
51 LHL NIPC P1481: Eoin Ó Murchú, *Culture and Revolution in Ireland* (Dublin: Repsol Pamphlet Number 2, July 1971).
52 'An Irish Church or a British pawn?', *An Eochair: A Bulletin of the Irish Republican*

Official memory today: a former internee described the Church and Provisionals colluding in the early 1970s to 'reinforce' hostile portrayals of the Officials' supposedly 'foreign ideologies'.[53]

PD's class politics from 1969 similarly censured the Church. But PD activists also charged NICRA and the Provisionals with compromising politically to suit Catholic social teaching. NICRA's reluctance to criticise the Church contributed to PD's final withdrawal from the mainstream civil rights movement in 1971.[54] PD's 'faceless committee' determined to make no such concessions to religious opinion: its founding programme in 1969 lambasted religious schools' 'indoctrination of pupils'.[55] The group's figurehead, Michael Farrell, suggested that the Provisionals encouraged sectarianism by assuming their newspaper's readership was uniformly Catholic: Farrell counterposed PD's cross-community engagement with the Shankill Development Association in west Belfast. For Farrell, the Provisionals were incapable of 'developing class consciousness among Protestant workers'.[56]

However, even for some cadres of this radical organisation, outside the main urban centres religious sensitivities remained taboo. In April 1969, practising Catholics among Fermanagh PD refused to join a cross-border march promoting liberalised contraception and divorce laws.[57] Negotiating the Church's socio-political authority challenged even the theoretically secular politics of radicals '68ers in Northern Ireland.

Republican socialism, prison protests, and the Catholic Church, c.1974–1981

The IRSP was formed in December 1974, and its military wing, the INLA, soon followed. From 1976, protests against the criminalisation of republican prisoners – culminating in the hunger strikes of 1980 and 1981 – led republican socialists in the IRSP-INLA and PD, alongside sections of the Provisional movement, into increasingly acute conflict with the Church. Prison protests transformed many republicans' interactions with religion.

Movement, Long Kesh, 9 (n.d. [1975]).

[53] Former Official republican internee interview with Jack Hepworth. Belfast, 31 March 2016.
[54] Brian Hanley & Scott Millar, *The lost revolution: the story of the Official IRA and the Workers' Party* (Dublin: Penguin Ireland, 2009), p. 206.
[55] 'Where we stand', *P.D. Voice: The Newspaper of People's Democracy*, Number 1 (June 1969).
[56] 'Socialist's view on the North', *The Irish Press*, 16 March 1971.
[57] Peter Cosgrove, 'People's Democracy member 1969: Part 1' (6 October 2014). Available at https://irishrepublicanmarxisthistoryproject.wordpress.com/2014/10/06/peoples-democracy-member-1969/ (accessed 15 February 2017).

Because the IRSP emerged as a split from the Official republican movement, many of its founding members mirrored Officials' explicit hostility towards not only the Catholic hierarchy, but clergy in general. The IRSP's foundational manifesto in May 1975 aspired to a 'secular' society.[58] INLA Chief of Staff Seamus Costello condemned the 'sectarian' Irish education system.[59]

When the republican socialist movement was forming, the Provisional high command was engaged with clergy in peace talks at Feakle, County Clare. Perceiving clergy as British collaborators, the IRSP denounced the Church's 'peace at any price lobby'.[60] When PIRA prisoner Frank Stagg died on hunger strike in 1976, one republican socialist prisoner decried the 'Irish Catholic hierarchy' that 'sided with the British Repression Machine'.[61] Self-styled aloofness from the Church's social influence remained important to the republican socialist movement. Interviewed more than a decade later, a leading volunteer emphasised that 'God didn't get a mention' when an individual was sworn into the INLA.[62]

INLA volunteers on the ground welcomed confrontation with the Church. In 1982, an IRSP member branded the 'sectarian' Catholic Church the British government's 'staunchist [sic] ally in Ireland'.[63] After two priests disarmed INLA volunteers during a riot, the Derry INLA threatened clergy: 'Under no circumstances will this type of partisan behaviour be tolerated.'[64] The warning contrasted sharply with the PIRA's response when an Andersonstown parish priest compromised a planned bomb attack on the nearby British Army barracks. After the hunger strikes of 1981, the Provisionals had their own disputes with the Catholic leadership, but the Belfast Brigade deferred to perceived community sentiment on this occasion:

Contrary to our stated position of dealing severely with touts, no action was taken against this priest as we felt that, at that time, people would not have fully understood the necessity for action *against this particular person*.[65]

Present-day IRSP perspectives on the Catholic Church historicise its political agency as institutionally malign, but also consider more nuanced challenges to

---

[58] 'IRSP *ard fheis*', *The Starry Plough/An Camchéachta*, Volume 1, Number 3 (June 1975).
[59] LHL NIPC P7004: *I owe my allegiance only to the working class: selected writings and speeches of Seamus Costello* (San Francisco: Irish Republican Socialist Committees of North America, 1995).
[60] 'Church split?', *The Starry Plough/An Camchéachta*, Volume 1, Number 4 (July 1975).
[61] Tony Cosgrove, 'Bishop Daly gave Brits licence to kill', *The Starry Plough/An Camchéachta*, Volume 1, Number 11 (February 1976).
[62] 'Rebel with a cause', *In Dublin*, 14 May 1987.
[63] 'St. Joseph's and St. Mary's reject Chilvers', *The Starry Plough/An Camchéachta* (April 1982).
[64] 'Bishop hits INLA threats to priests', *The Irish Press*, 12 May 1981.
[65] 'Informers warned', *Iris*, 6 (July 1983). Italics added.

the Church's ideological hegemony. Surveying the Church's role in the conflict, veteran IRSP member Fra Halligan argued that the Catholic hierarchy was consistently determined 'to subdue republicanism'.[66] Yet some former INLA prisoners remember relishing the opportunity to challenge clergy on history, politics, and morality. Peadar Lagan recalled that in the mid-1990s, a small number of his rural comrades attended Mass in jail – a right enshrined in the movement's prison charter. According to Lagan, republican socialists enjoyed the combative sociability of interactions with a visiting priest. Lagan himself supported religious schools on the grounds of strong academic reputation.[67] Don Browne remembered that PIRA and INLA prisoners alike enjoyed bombarding a 'novice priest' with philosophical and spiritual questions each Easter. These exchanges bolstered republicans' sense of truculent critical inquiry towards dominant social powers.

> We asked him what he thought the soul meant, and what does that mean intellectually, the soul is something you can – and we says, *Well how can you go to a child and ask them to take first communion and them have a full understanding of what that means? You're sitting there, a novice priest, you can't tell me.* Those types of conversations were going on.[68]

Especially after the Eighth Amendment to the Republic of Ireland constitution in 1983, PD militants strove to dismantle the Church's political influence. In this schema, the Catholic Church's influence in conservative social politics vindicated an anti-imperialist revolutionary impulse across the entire island. Belfast PD councillor John McAnulty abhorred the 'church-dominated neo-colony in the 26 counties'.[69] Dismissively reviewing the New Ireland Forum of 1983 and 1984, PD's National Committee portrayed Bishop Cahal Daly and SDLP leader John Hume conspiring 'from their respective pulpits' to 'collaborate with British imperialism'.[70] A PD pamphlet published in 1987 argued that the border consolidated the Republic's major 'colonial feature': the Church's 'insuperable' and 'archaic' political dominance.[71] These all-Ireland framings echoed James Connolly, who anticipated a 'carnival of reaction both North and South' when partition was mooted in 1914.[72]

---

[66] Fra Halligan interview with Jack Hepworth. Belfast, 15 September 2015.
[67] Peadar Lagan interview with Jack Hepworth. Bellaghy, 11 December 2017.
[68] Don Browne interview with Jack Hepworth. Derry, 12 December 2017.
[69] 'Irish National Congress: A way forward?', *An Reabhloid*, Volume 5, Number 1 (n.d.).
[70] 'Alienation! Daly's code for collaboration!', *Socialist Republic: Paper of People's Democracy*, Volume 8, Number 2 (March–April 1985).
[71] LHL NIPC P6570: PD, *Women in Struggle* (Dublin: PD, 1987).
[72] Writing in March 1914, Connolly dismissed suggestions that partitioning the island

As Scull has argued, the hunger strikes of 1980 and 1981 were turning points for many grassroots Provisionals' interpretations of the Catholic Church.[73] Even some of the more religious Provisionals considered the Church's actions during the hunger strikes to be inadequate, or even detrimental, to the republican prisoners' cause.

During the 1970s, Father Denis Faul of Dungannon, County Tyrone, repeatedly called for the Provisionals to end their armed campaign, and unsuccessfully attempted to broker a ceasefire in 1977. He also authored several meticulously researched polemics against internment, prison conditions, and British Army conduct. Unionist critics caricatured the cleric as a 'Provo priest'.[74]

However, from 1981, increasingly explicit Provisional anti-clericalism centred upon Father Faul's complicated role in protracted negotiations between prisoners, their families, the republican movement, and the British government. At a public meeting in west Belfast in September 1981, relatives of two PIRA hunger strikers accused Faul of undermining the strike. The NHBAC, in which Provisionals held substantial influence, criticised senior churchmen for exhorting hunger strikers to abandon their fast.[75] When the hunger strike ended a month later, the Andersonstown H-Block & Armagh Committee's public relations officer blamed priests for 'callous manipulation' of prisoners' families and 'sowing seeds of despair and division with outright lies and double talk'.[76]

Publicly, during and after the momentous breach with the Church in 1981, Provisional leaders were stridently anti-clerical. For Gerry Adams, Bishop Edward Daly's opposition to the hunger strike was 'completely irrelevant' since

could facilitate Home Rule: 'The recent proposals of Messrs. Asquith, Devlin, Redmond and Co. for the settlement of the Home Rule question deserve the earnest attention of the working class democracy of this country... Such a scheme as that agreed to by Redmond and Devlin, the betrayal of the national democracy of industrial Ulster would mean a carnival of reaction both North and South, would set back the wheels of progress, would destroy the oncoming unity of the Irish Labour movement and paralyse all advanced movements whilst it endured.' James Connolly, 'Labour and the proposed partition of Ireland', *Irish Worker*, 14 March 1914, quoted in Shaun Harkin (ed.), *The James Connolly reader* (Chicago, Illinois: Haymarket Books, 2018), p. 363.

[73] Scull, *Catholic church and the Northern Ireland troubles*, 89.

[74] 'Monsignor Denis Faul', *The Independent*, 1 April 2009.

[75] Liam Clarke, *Broadening the battlefield: the H-blocks and the rise of Sinn Féin* (Dublin: Gill & Macmillan, 1987), p. 198; NHBAC statement (8 September 1981) cited in PRONI CENT/1/10/62: A. K. Templeton, 'Northern Ireland Office: protests and second hunger strike' (10 September 1981).

[76] 'Andersonstown H-Block & Armagh Committee', *Andersonstown News*, 10 October 1981.

1 Official IRA volunteers parade in Downpatrick, County Down, Easter Sunday 1974.
Credit: Image bh010930, Bobbie Hanvey Photographic Archives, John J. Burns Library, Boston College.

2 Provisional IRA Chief of Staff Dáithí Ó Conaill addresses journalists at a safe house in the Republic of Ireland, 18 July 1974.
Credit: Peter Denton.

3 Provisional IRA mural at Islandbawn Street, west Belfast, 1982.
Credit: Jeff Sluka.

4 Republicans in Sinn Féin offices in Belfast, 1984.
Credit: Kaveh Kazemi.

5 RUC officers hand INLA Chief of Staff Dominic McGlinchey to Gardaí on the Irish border at Killeen, County Armagh, 11 October 1985.
Credit: Image bh010831, Bobbie Hanvey Photographic Archives, John J. Burns Library, Boston College.

6 Provisional IRA volunteers at a training camp in County Donegal, August 1986.
Credit: Kaveh Kazemi.

7 Bloody Sunday Justice Demonstration, Derry City, 1994.
Credit: Rory Nugent.

8 A Provisional IRA volunteer preparing for an operation near the border in
south Armagh, 1994.
Credit: Rory Nugent.

republicans derived their mandate and motivation from the people.[77] Interviewed shortly after the hunger strike ended, Sinn Féin director of publicity Danny Morrison identified the movement as 'a secular organisation' opposed to the Catholic Church's 'special place' in southern politics.[78] During a televised debate in February 1983, Morrison posited that republicans' lived experiences mediated clerical authority. For Morrison, republicans might

> take their religion from Rome, but they take their politics from their hard experience on the ground, and that's the way it should be.[79]

Sinn Féin's *ard fheis* appeared to endorse Morrison's claim, amending the party's objectives, having declined to do so three years earlier. From 1983, the Provisionals' 'social principles' officially supplanted their founders' 'Christian principles'.[80]

From 1981, Sinn Féin's Education Department promulgated increasingly hostile positions against the Catholic Church. Party members were encouraged to criticise the Church internationally and historically. The revised education programme of 1981 explicitly denounced a Church that supported 'corrupt, dictatorial and anti-Christian' regimes.[81] Another Education Department lecture highlighted the Catholic Church's 'divisive' role during the United Irishmen rebellion of 1798, and its subsequent support for the Act of Union.[82]

PIRA volunteers and their families largely shared the leadership's heightened distaste for the Church from 1981. An anonymous volunteer who joined the Provisionals in 1981 reflected the following year that she had discovered the 'hypocrisy of the Catholic hierarchy... immediately' during the hunger strike.[83] In May 1982, when Father Faul implored the republican community to give

---

[77] Maev-Ann Wren, 'H-Block group priest opposes hunger-strike', *The Irish Times*, 3 March 1981.

[78] Bob Rowthorn, 'Ireland's intractable crisis: interviews with the UDA and the Provisional IRA', *Marxism Today* (December 1981).

[79] HVA D00570 Tape 37: *Counterpoint* (3 February 1983).

[80] Richard Davis, 'The convergence of orange and green socialism: the Marxist quagmire', in Alan O'Day (ed.), *Terrorism's laboratory: the case of Northern Ireland* (Aldershot: Dartmouth Publishing, 1995), p. 184.

[81] LHL NIPC P938: Sinn Féin Education Department, *Nationalism and Socialism* (Dublin: Sinn Féin, 1981).

[82] LHL NIPC Tom Hartley Collection PH441: Sinn Féin Education Department, *History of Republicanism, Part 2* (Dublin: Sinn Féin, 1981).

[83] 'A people's army', *Iris*, 4 (November 1982).

information to the security forces, Belfast Provisionals and Derry prisoners' relatives attacked Britain's 'unwitting allies' among Catholic clergy.[84]

Religion had provided consolation for some imprisoned republicans enduring blanket protests and hunger strikes in 1980 and 1981. Irrespective of individual spirituality, Catholicism had also represented an assertion of collective identity. During the hunger strike of 1980, senior Belfast Provisional Brendan Hughes attended Mass seeking 'solace'.[85] Bobby Sands's diaries recorded prisoners reciting the Rosary in unison every evening to raise morale and antagonise prison warders.[86]

However, recriminations after the hunger strike ended in October 1981 truncated Catholicism's functions as a repository of consolation and community in the jail. By 1982, republicans told Father Faul to stop visiting, and Mass attendance declined sharply.[87] Eamonn MacDermott, imprisoned from 1977 to 1992, remembered that although there had been

> a lot of religion during the blanket [protests]... by the mid-eighties, Catholicism within the movement would have been very weak... Once the blanket was over, religion had no big part.[88]

Across the north, Faul became a focal point for republicans' wrath: in 1986, a Sinn Féin *cumann* in Newry dismissed Faul's 'deliberately misleading' and 'predictable' public criticisms.[89]

Anger with the Church endured viscerally in former prisoners' memories. In 1986, PIRA volunteer Mairéad Farrell opined that when Faul had urged hunger strikers to abandon their fast five years earlier, the Church had shown its 'true colours'.[90] Some two decades after the hunger strikes, ex-prisoners Laurence McKeown, John Pickering, and Peadar Whelan condemned the Church's position. For Whelan, Father Faul was as culpable as Margaret Thatcher for the hunger strikers' deaths.[91]

---

[84] "'Withdraw from IRA and INLA", priest appeals', *Ulster Herald*, 11 December 1982.

[85] Brendan Hughes interview with Laurence McKeown. Laurence McKeown, *Out of time: Irish republican prisoners in Long Kesh, 1972–2000* (Belfast: Beyond the Pale Publications, 2001), p. 77.

[86] Bobby Sands, *Writings from prison* (Cork: Mercier, 1998), p. 75.

[87] Anonymous PIRA prisoner, 'Jail history' (n.d. [*c*.1996]). Copy in author's possession.

[88] Eamonn MacDermott interview with Jack Hepworth. Derry, 17 September 2015.

[89] 'Sinn Fein reply to Father Faul', *Newry Reporter*, 23 October 1986.

[90] Jenny McGeever, 'A woman's place is in the struggle: An interview with Mairead Farrell', *Spare Rib*, 204 (August 1989).

[91] Brian Campbell, Laurence McKeown, & Felim O'Hagan (eds.), *Nor meekly serve my time: the H-block struggle, 1976–1981* (Belfast: Beyond the Pale Publications, 1994), pp. 244, 258, 265.

Father Faul's controversial agency remains pervasive in republican testimonies. Reflecting more than 30 years later, Kevin Lynch, a former PIRA volunteer from Donagh, County Fermanagh, remembered that he was religious when he was imprisoned in 1980, but 'in '81... the priests would condemn [republicans]... We sort of boycotted Father Faul.'[92] Séanna Walsh recalled that after Bobby Sands was elected as MP for Fermanagh-South Tyrone in April 1981, Faul 'changed' and 'embarked on a one-man band operation to do whatever he could to bring down the IRA'.[93]

Mindful of the growing rancour, republicans who retained personal faith afforded clerical politics reduced credence. As Jeffrey Sluka's embedded research in west Belfast suggested, the republican grassroots carefully filtered Church politics. In his study of Divis Flats in 1981 and 1982, Sluka found popular conceptions of the Church's salvific and political functions were increasingly polarised. Some 58.9 per cent of Sluka's sample thought clergy should be 'listened to and their advice heeded' but it was ultimately 'not essential' to follow their directives. A slight majority (54.5 per cent) thought it 'not very important' to follow a priest's advice.[94]

Yet even among republicans who theoretically disdained religious authority, there remained a tendency to look to the Church to legitimise political positions. Reflecting three years after the death of her brother, INLA hunger striker Mickey Devine, one Derry republican argued that if priests had exhorted their congregations to support the protests, the British government might have granted republican prisoners their five demands.[95] Bernadette Devlin's rupture with Catholic authority originated at Queen's University Belfast in the late 1960s, but only in May 1981 did Devlin perceive priests' 'last vestige of betrayal'. Awaiting news of Bobby Sands's imminent death, Catholics across the north prayed in the streets. Devlin recalled the parish priest in Coalisland, County Tyrone

> warned people in the church to be careful of whom they stood with, who they prayed with lest their prayers be construed as political support for terrorism.[96]

---

[92] Fáilte Cluain Eois, *Their prisons, our stories* (Castleblayney: Fáilte Cluain Eois, 2015), p. 71.

[93] Séanna Walsh interview with Jack Hepworth. Belfast, 12 August 2015.

[94] Jeffrey A. Sluka, *Hearts and minds, water and fish: support for the IRA and INLA in a Northern Irish ghetto* (Greenwich, Connecticut: JAI Press, 1989), p. 248.

[95] Eileen Fairweather, Róisín McDonough, & Melanie McFadyean, *Only the rivers run free: Northern Ireland – the women's war* (London: Pluto Press, 1984), p. 107.

[96] LHL NIPC P5935: *Freedom Only Comes if You Take It! A Speech by Bernadette Devlin McAliskey* (New York: H-Block/Armagh Committee, 1981).

Despite their anti-clerical rhetoric, senior Provisionals continually expected Catholic leaders to cohere local communities and publicise grievances with British rule. Through the 1980s, Provisionals repeatedly awaited Church involvement in broad-based campaigns against security forces, supergrass trials, and strip-searching in prisons. Danny Morrison invited Bishop Cahal Daly to meet the Provisionals in the early 1980s, but received no reply.[97] In 1983, Provisional writer Peter Hayes criticised the 'Catholic hierarchy' for inaction over 'shoot-to-kill' controversies.[98] An editorial in Provisional organ *Iris* the same year condemned Bishop Cahal Daly's 'studious silence' during supergrass trials.[99]

Many republicans still implicitly valued churchmen's categories of probity and legitimacy. In an open letter in 1985, Gerry Adams implored Bishop Cahal Daly to pronounce whether the British presence was 'morally justified'.[100] Even when attacking Father Faul, Provisional publicity cited Sandinista priest Ernesto Cardenal as evidence of clerics' capacity to engage radical politics.[101] In the columns of a local newspaper, Fermanagh Sinn Féin's public relations officer Pádraig Ó Manacháin insisted that 'well-known Catholic authorities' and theologians had demonstrated that 'the Just War theory is quite valid'.[102]

Expectations that the Church hierarchy would at least validate republican grievances were commonplace throughout the Provisional movement in the 1980s. Speaking after being released from custody when a 'supergrass' withdrew evidence in 1983, Belfast Provisional Eddie Carmichael said it was 'up to... the like of the established churches' to protest against supergrass trials.[103] Recognising the Church's societal influence, in 1985 PIRA prisoners from Strabane, County Tyrone implored the town's population to support a new local group pressurising anti-republican clergy to denounce strip-searching.[104] The social roles Provisionals projected on the Church recall Antonio Gramsci's conceptions of subaltern agency and 'organic intellectuals'. Republicans broadly

---

[97] Danny Morrison interview with Jack Hepworth. Belfast, 11 August 2015.

[98] Peter Hayes, 'Shoot to kill: the unchanging face of repression', *Iris*, 5 (March 1983).

[99] 'Catholic hierarchy: propping up the Orange State', *Iris*, 6 (July 1983).

[100] Ó Fiaich Library and Archive NP2/5: Gerry Adams, 'Open letter to Cahal Daly, Bishop of Down & Connor' (1 February 1985).

[101] Sluka, *Hearts and minds*, 259–261.

[102] 'Fermanagh Sinn Fein's claims', *Fermanagh Herald*, 13 December 1980.

[103] Eddie Carmichael quoted in British Universities Film & Video Council: 'Released IRA man claims RUC attempted bribery' (22 October 1983). Available at http://bufvc. ac.uk/tvandradio/lbc/index.php/segment/0016800322002 (accessed 22 September 2017).

[104] Strabane Republican POW's, '"Catholics for Justice" supported', *Strabane Chronicle*, 20 April 1985.

understood Catholic intellectuals as 'functionaries' of the ruling class. Yet parish priests' class- and place-based connections to the oppressed signalled their social importance.[105]

Loath to risk insulting the Catholic community en masse, Provisional leaders were selective in their iconoclastic pronouncements. Criticisms frequently targeted an ignorant Catholic 'hierarchy', rather than the entire Church body. An internal Sinn Féin document written in 1981 exhorted party representatives 'at all levels' to 'facilitate religion' since Christianity was 'part of the Irish culture'.[106] At an Easter commemoration in 1984, Sinn Féin's new president, Gerry Adams, pinpointed his ire towards Cahal Daly, and not the faithful more broadly. Daly, Adams argued, personified a 'long and inglorious tradition of Irish Church leaders' who consistently condemned 'any radical, separatist, or republican organisation'.[107]

Tensions between radical political theory, personal faith, individual priests, and the Church's institutional influence were complex, especially during the 1980s. Consequently, practising Catholics among the republican grassroots forged political positions increasingly independent of, and sometimes in spite of, clergy. The mother of Belfast PIRA volunteer Jimmy McMullen sympathised with the Pope's stated desire for exclusively non-violent political action. However, her experiences of the blanket protests informed her criticisms of priests with whose politics she disagreed.[108] As the mother of internees and PIRA blanket protesters, Fitzsimmons from north Belfast thought the Church hierarchy had 'sided with the establishment'. Fitzsimmons maintained her faith but would 'ignore' the Church's political pronouncements.[109] Increasingly, Catholic laity protested against perceived anti-republican sermons. In February 1992, at the funeral of PIRA volunteers Kevin Barry O'Donnell and Sean O'Farrell in Coalisland, Monsignor Liam McEntaggart said senior activists should examine their consciences before sending young volunteers on operations. More than 200 mourners walked out in protest.[110]

[105] Antonio Gramsci, *Selections from the prison notebooks of Antonio Gramsci* (ed. and transl. Quentin Hoare and Geoffrey Nowell Smith) (London: Lawrence & Wishart, 1971), pp. 150–151, 365, 368–369.

[106] LHL NIPC P982: Sinn Féin, *Towards a Policy on Culture/Dréacht pholasaí ar chultúr* (Dublin: Sinn Féin, 1981).

[107] 'The bishops and Sinn Fein', *Derry People & Donegal News*, 5 May 1984.

[108] Tim Pat Coogan, *The H-block story* (Dublin: Ward River Press, 1980), p. 89.

[109] Catherine Shannon, 'Catholic women and the Northern Irish troubles', in Yonah Alexander & Alan O'Day (eds.), *Ireland's terrorist trauma: interdisciplinary perspectives* (Hemel Hempstead: Harvester Wheatsheaf, 1989), p. 239.

[110] '200 walk out over priest's plea at Provo funeral', *Irish Independent*, 21 February 1992.

Today, among Provisionals and 'dissenters' alike, oral histories generally claim that republicans have always bifurcated the Church's religious and political authority. Conor Murphy, imprisoned from 1981 to 1984 and now an elected Sinn Féin representative, remembered his mother – 'a very devout Catholic' and daily communicant, with a brother and two sons imprisoned for republican activities – 'had her own sense and didn't look to the Church for her political leadership'.[111] Similarly, former Belfast PIRA volunteer Nuala Perry argued that Catholic republicans tended to divorce their personal faith from their political conscience. Where religiosity and politics were concerned, 'it was as if the two never really met'.[112]

As the previous chapter demonstrated, from the late 1980s many PIRA prisoners formulated feminist positions on social policy and reproductive rights. Anti-clericalism underpinned these critiques – especially targeting the perceived theocracy in the Republic of Ireland. Provisional feminists, including members of Sinn Féin's Women's Department, were not inclined to disaggregate the Church's political agency. Instead, they lambasted a uniformly archaic institution impeding women's emancipation. In 1988, Maghaberry PIRA prisoners accused the Church of malign complicity in closing abortion information centres and clinics and promoting 'medieval morality' and 'so-called "therapy sessions"' instead.[113] Writing in 1993, PIRA prisoner Pamela Kane condemned the Church's positions on contraception and divorce and positioned the Church alongside the state and judiciary as Ireland's 'biggest bastions of patriarchy'.[114]

The feminist strand of republican hostility to the Church hierarchy was especially uncompromising, perceiving little potential for political change in Catholic institutions. The Derry branch of Sinn Féin's Women's Department identified 'the Churches' with 'Thatcherism' among a right-wing 'emerging coalition' in the late 1980s.[115] In 1995, PIRA prisoner Mary McArdle dismissed Pope John Paul II's apology to women. For McArdle, the papacy had balefully presided over the Catholic Church's domination of Irish politics, and the Pope's words were patronising.[116]

---

[111] Conor Murphy interview with Jack Hepworth. Newry, 16 September 2015.

[112] Nuala Perry interview with Jack Hepworth. Belfast, 30 March 2016.

[113] Women Republican POWs Maghaberry Gaol, 'Defend the clinics campaign', *Iris Bheag*, 7 (February 1988).

[114] Pamela Kane, 'Fighting back!', *Women in Struggle/Mna I Streachilt*, Volume 4 (n.d. [1993]).

[115] 'The role of women in Sinn Fein', *Iris Bheag*, 11 (June 1988).

[116] Mary McArdle correspondence with Philomena Gallagher, 1995. Philomena Gallagher, 'An oral history of the imprisoned female Irish Republican Army', MPhil (Trinity College Dublin, 1995), p. 54.

Occasionally, personal affinities between Provisionals and individual priests survived the turbulent context. Clergy who accentuated humanitarian commitments, especially concerning prisoners, were sometimes spared the hostility that generally defined interactions between republicans and priests. At Christmas 1975, when a parochial house in Riverstown, County Sligo fell into disrepair, local Provisionals demanded the diocese rehouse the 'quiet, friendly, understanding' parish priest.[117] When Cardinal Ó Fiaich died in 1990, PIRA prisoner John McComb, serving a 16-year sentence in Durham's Frankland Prison, wrote a eulogy. In a letter to a clerical friend, McComb claimed Ó Fiaich had 'never lost contact with his people'. Even the 'many' prisoners who had 'given up religion' still regarded Ó Fiaich highly, McComb insisted.[118] Paul Stitt, imprisoned for PIRA activities in 1994, praised three Belfast priests who joined republican prisoners for 'good and energetic debates' in Long Kesh through the 1990s.[119] Raymond McCartney, who spent 17 years in prison, remembered friendships between republicans and priests overcoming political differences:

> In Long Kesh there'd be priests coming in to say Mass, and some of them would detect it, and would have said, *you know, because the Church called something wrong, doesn't mean you're not part of the Church.*[120]

'Provo priests': radical clergy and liberation theology, *c.*1968–1994

Throughout the conflict, a minority of clergy moved beyond merely acknowledging lay Catholic grievances, and supported physical-force republicanism more overtly. As Marianne Elliott has argued, such instances were uncommon.[121] Yet despite their numerical minority, clerical fellow-travellers command attention as a particular and unusual strand of Irish republicanism. Understanding how and why a small number of churchmen sympathised with republicanism illuminates the breadth of subjective meanings attached to the struggle.

Republican clergy situated the campaign for Irish unity in a tradition that spanned centuries and enacted God's justice. Father Seán McManus from County Fermanagh was fined in August 1971 for obstructing an RUC officer

---

[117] 'Parish priest lives in squalor', *Riverstown News* (Nollaig '75).
[118] Ó Fiaich Library and Archive NP5/24: Letter from John McComb, Frankland Prison (14 May 1990).
[119] Paul Stitt, *Republican outcast: the Paul Stitt story* (Belfast: Justice Press, 2006), p. 52.
[120] Raymond McCartney interview with Jack Hepworth. Derry, 18 September 2015.
[121] Marianne Elliott, *Catholics of Ulster*, 471.

during an anti-internment rally in Enniskillen. Father McManus told the court that the 'colonial' northern state violated divine law, and 'sympathy' was 'too weak a word' for his support for republican guerrillas.[122] Priestly republicanism coupled tenets of national sovereignty and cultural heritage with religiously inflected conceptions of equality, justice, and agricultural and industrial stewardship. In the early 1970s, Canon James McDyer of Glencolumbkille, County Donegal lauded the Provisionals' Éire Nua proposals as an emblem for national sovereignty. McDyer's 'firm belief in God and Ireland' informed his republican hostility to the EEC. McDyer led the 'Save the West' movement, which championed farmers' cooperatives and industrial development in west Donegal.[123]

Priests' declarations of support for the Provisional movement of the 1970s rested heavily upon historical legitimacy. Writing for *Republican News* in 1973 and 1974, Father Art O'Neill located the 'honest' PIRA downstream of Pádraig Pearse's visionary nationalism in 1916. For O'Neill, clergy who celebrated the revolutionary period of the early twentieth century but castigated the Provisionals were hypocrites.[124] Father Piaras Ó Dúill served four years' imprisonment in Belfast between 1957 and 1961 during the IRA's Operation Harvest. He later chaired the NHBAC in the early 1980s, and was a veteran Irish language activist. For Ó Dúill, 'love of country' was 'part of the love of God'.[125] He framed the PIRA campaign as a continuation of the War of Independence of 1919 to 1921.[126]

In the 1970s, most of the few republican clergy resided in isolated or rural parishes. Some even joined republican guerrilla movements. Substantial evidence suggests that Father James Chesney, a curate in the rural parish of Cullion, County Derry, was involved with the PIRA's bombing of the nearby village of Claudy in 1972.[127] Henry McDonald has cited cases of three priests involved with the PIRA in the north Antrim countryside in the early 1970s.[128] In 1980,

---

[122] 'Six Counties Redemptorist "in sympathy with IRA"', *Irish Independent*, 7 September 1971.

[123] 'An ordinary guy', *The Irish Press*, 28 March 1972; 'Canon McDyer', *Saoirse*, 9 (January 1988).

[124] Father Art O'Neill, 'The duties of priests towards republicans', *Republican News*, 6 April 1974.

[125] Love of country', *Republican News*, 13 July 1974; 'Bundoran call to fight extradition', *Saoirse*, 5 (September 1987).

[126] Liam Ó Cuinneagáin, 'An Chaora Dhubh ag Innilt ar an Uiagneas (Spléachadh ar an Athair Piaras Ó Dúill)', *Comhar*, Volume 44, Number 3 (March 1985).

[127] Rosie Cowan, '"It became obvious Father Chesney was south Derry's answer to Bonnie and Clyde"', *The Guardian*, 21 September 2002.

[128] Henry McDonald, 'Three more IRA priests in Claudy link', *The Observer*, 22 December 2002.

Father Vincent Forde, with a parish in the village of Castlewellan, County Down, was convicted of an INLA armed bank robbery.[129]

The majority of republican churchmen were relatively low-ranking in the priesthood. Those on society's margins who were not detailed to a specific parish were among the Provisionals' supporters in the early 1970s. In May 1972, two Cistercian monks in Belfast admitted aiding prisoners who had absconded from Crumlin Road Jail.[130] The same year, monks at Portglenone Abbey in County Antrim published Christmas cards for the Ardoyne Relief Committee, with proceeds donated to internees and their dependants.[131]

Clergy who sympathised with republican objectives in the 1970s were usually active at the intersection of local community politics and civil disobedience. These networks' concentric circles were most apparent in County Fermanagh, where in 1973 republicans and committed civil rights activists alike celebrated 'many clergymen... who are actively supporting our cause'. For one member of the Fermanagh Civil Disobedience Committee, campaigning for the 'poor and oppressed' defined 'what Christianity is all about'. Local collective memory lionised rebel priests of the early twentieth century's revolutionary period: the mention of Canon Maguire and Canon Coyle drew a standing ovation at a civil disobedience meeting.[132] Boundaries between anti-unionist protest and militant republicanism were blurred.

Across the north, personal connections and kinship ties underscored a degree of republicanism among clergy who privately supported bereaved families. After PIRA hunger striker Martin Hurson died in 1981, his brother Brendan recalled priests from the farming communities of south Armagh visiting the family home to offer support.[133] After PIRA volunteer Antoine Mac Giolla Bhrighde was killed by the Special Air Service (SAS) in December 1984, his mother received consoling letters from several priests in south Derry, commending Mac Giolla Bhridghde as a 'committed soldier' and 'good Christian'. Mac Giolla Bhridghe belonged to the religiously devout minority among the Provisionals.[134]

Republicans known to clergy were sometimes spared the condemnation that usually emerged from the Catholic hierarchy. Patrick Kelly was one of eight PIRA volunteers killed by the SAS during an operation in Loughgall,

---

[129] 'Priest held in Eire swoop', *Daily Telegraph*, 12 January 1980.

[130] 'The past two weeks', *Fortnight*, 40 (25 May 1972).

[131] IEL: Ardoyne Relief Committee Christmas greeting card (1972). Copy in author's possession.

[132] 'Many clergy and religious support resistance campaign to oppression', *Concerned: Official Organ of Fermanagh Civil Disobedience Committee*, Number 85 (5 May 1973).

[133] Padraig O'Malley, *Biting at the grave: the Irish hunger strikes and the politics of despair* (Boston: Beacon Press, 1990), pp. 268, 271.

[134] Susan McKay, *Bear in mind these dead* (London: Faber & Faber, 2008), p. 121.

County Armagh, in May 1987. At Kelly's funeral Mass, Father Brian McNiece commended Kelly as 'an upright and truthful man who loved his family, his Irish culture, his faith and his country'.[135]

Republican clergy formed an oppositional strand within their Church, and echoed Provisional criticisms of the Catholic hierarchy. Dissenting priests accused a moralising leadership of being oblivious to injustices facing Northern Ireland's Catholic laity. Particular opprobrium was reserved for bishops who condemned republicans and blithely called for 'reconciliation'.

Individual priests felt isolated, even ostracised, within the Church. Yet these deracinated churchmen often responded defiantly. In west Belfast, Father Des Wilson resigned his ministry in June 1975 after charging his superior, Bishop Philbin, with ignoring British Army brutality.[136] Father Joe McVeigh, from rural Lisbellaw, County Fermanagh, authored many pamphlets advocating a British withdrawal and detailing the state's role in human rights abuses.[137] McVeigh was similarly critical of the Church: interviewed in the early 1990s, he expressed admiration for only four radical priests nationwide. Murray noticed that outspoken activists were often banished to missionary work abroad: 'My bags are always packed.'[138]

Republican clergy such as Desmond Wilson and Piaras Ó Dúill contradicted other priests' positions at contentious moments. In 1980, three west Belfast churches barred from their grounds the coffin of PIRA volunteer Kevin Delaney. Delaney died when a bomb he was transporting exploded prematurely on a train, killing two civilians. Wilson defied the hierarchy's orders and held funeral Mass in Delaney's home.[139] Ó Dúill's partisan position on the hunger strike of 1981 rejected hostile Catholic commentary. For Ó Duill, Sands and his comrades made 'the ultimate sacrifice for others' in acts 'very different from the mind and mentality of a suicide'.[140]

In 1983, when Father Faul implored Catholics to supply the security forces with information, Wilson branded Faul's remarks 'ill-advised and damaging'.[141] Addressing the first meeting of the Donegal Anti-Extradition Committee in September 1987, Wilson said a Church that failed to oppose 'immoral'

---

[135] 'MP slams comment by funeral priest', *Tyrone Constitution*, 14 May 1987.

[136] 'Church split?', *The Starry Plough/An Camchéachta*, Volume 1, Number 4 (July 1975).

[137] See, for example, LHL NIPC P4475: Father Joe McVeigh, *Tackling the Root Causes: The Only Way to Peace* (Omagh: Community for Justice, 1991).

[138] Rory Nugent, 'Inside the IRA', *Spin*, August 1994.

[139] 'Volunteer Dee Delaney laid to rest', *An Phoblacht/Republican News*, 26 January 1980.

[140] LHL NIPC Sinn Féin Boxes: 'Statement by Fr. Piaras Ó Dúill – Chairman National H-Block/Armagh Committee' (5 May 1981).

[141] 'Confidentiality and the clergy', *Iris*, 6 (July 1983).

extradition merited nobody's allegiance.[142] The following year, when a parish priest in Maghera, County Derry contravened veteran republican and former NICRA chair Kevin Agnew's wishes for Father Piaras Ó Dúill to conduct his funeral service, Ó Dúill condemned the Church's 'arrogance'.[143]

After acrimonious arguments with the Church in Ireland, many PIRA prisoners studied liberation theology in the early 1980s and looked to Central and South America for an idealised version of clerical activism.[144] Discovering liberation theology more than a decade after it had emerged from the Medellín conference of 1968, Provisional prisoners celebrated its leading exponents, not least Peruvian priest Gustavo Gutiérrez. This counter-cultural cleric championed 'the right of the poor to think out their own faith' and become 'active agents of their own destiny'.[145] Gutiérrez's radical gospel coupled counter-hegemonic pedagogy with campaigns against poverty and human rights abuses.

For PIRA prisoners, liberation theology connoted the didacticism and internationalist leftism that influenced republican prison communities. It also offered qualified compatibility with the Church. As Gerry MacLochlainn put it, this radical nexus appealed especially, although not exclusively, to 'some of the people who would have been very Catholic... starting to make their way towards socialism'.[146] PIRA prisoner Jim McVeigh researched liberation theology for the Provisional movement's internal education programme in the mid-1980s. For McVeigh, the inspiration of radical clergy in Central and South America empowered prisoners' internal discussions and anti-elitism. In Long Kesh, liberation theology legitimised leftists' disillusionment with the Irish Catholicism's particularly 'conservative ethos'.[147]

The work of Brazilian-born cleric Paolo Freire was central to republican prisoners' education programmes and cultural interests through the 1980s. After his exile to Chile in 1964, Freire lobbied for agrarian reforms and coordinated

---

[142] 'F. F. supporters to be pressed on extradition', *Donegal Democrat*, 18 September 1987.

[143] 'Funeral of Kevin Agnew', *Saoirse*, 22 (February 1989).

[144] Official republicans had engaged with international liberation theology a decade earlier than their Provisional counterparts. In 1973, an anonymous Official from Derry pinpointed Colombian national liberation militant Camilo Torres as the revolutionary cleric *par excellence*. Torres, a 'Third World hero', exemplified the activist-priest, committed to socialism, pedagogy, and revolutionary 'inspiration for the down trodden [*sic*]. 'The revolutionary priest', *The Starry Plough: Derry's Own Republican Newspaper*, Volume 2, Number 5 (n.d. [*c*.1973]).

[145] Gustavo Gutiérrez, *A theology of liberation: history, politics, and salvation* (London: SCM Press, 1988), p. xix.

[146] Gerry MacLochlainn interview.

[147] Jim McVeigh, 'The Irish Church and republicanism: The need for liberation theology', *The Furrow*, 50 (January 1999).

adult education programmes. He elucidated his political and pedagogical philosophy in *Pedagogy of the oppressed* (1968), which was first translated into English in 1970. Freire advocated open discussions of political ideas, strategy, and internal education programmes within a radical movement and its community base. He cautioned against the risk of leadership ossifying or drifting towards authoritarianism. To counteract these tendencies, Freire implored the 'student' to achieve critical consciousness.[148]

Freire's approach to education, more than his theology per se, inspired the Provisionals' prison regime. Former prisoner Micheál Mac Giolla Ghunna remembered how Freire's writings underpinned the Provisionals' internal education from 1981, spanning Irish language classes, poetry, crafts, creative writing, and music. In 1995, PIRA prisoners drew upon Augusto Boale's related concept of the 'theatre of the oppressed' to adapt and perform Bobby Sands's writings on the stage.[149]

Liberation theology's radical class politics scarcely registered with Catholic clergy in Northern Ireland. However, its radical implications appealed to those few republican priests, including Father Joe McVeigh. In 1978, McVeigh quoted José Porfirio Miranda and Paulo Freire on the Church's responsibility to address socioeconomic and political problems. McVeigh argued that political violence could be justified to 'the kind of radical changes that we believe are necessary',[150] and imagined an 'Irish or Celtic Theology of Liberation' or 'Church of the Poor' replacing Ireland's 'authoritarian' Church.[151] McVeigh recognised that he was a distinct minority among Ireland's Catholic clergy. Yet as this chapter has posited, this radical cleric's career highlighted the religiopolitical complexities of a heterogeneous republican movement.

Conclusion

Ethnic Catholics of devout faith and none alike participated in the Irish republican struggle: republicans' perspectives on organised religion contrasted markedly. Throughout the conflict, republicans differed as to how far they would accommodate Catholic opinion and morality. How republicans interpreted

---

[148] Paulo Freire, *Pedagogy of the oppressed* (transl. Myra Bergman Ramos) (Harmondsworth: Penguin Books, 1972), pp. 11, 42, 54, 68, 97.

[149] Micheál Mac Giolla Ghunna, *Cultural Struggle and a Drama Project* (1995). Copy in author's possession.

[150] LHL NIPC P5080: Father Joe McVeigh, *Thoughts on the Liberation of Ireland* (Monaghan: Borderline Press, 1978).

[151] Joseph McVeigh, 'A liberation theology', *Socialist Republican: Quarterly Publication of the Socialist Republican Collective*, Volume 1, Issue 1 (n.d. [1988]).

Catholicism – as both a political and philosophical institution, and as a contentious ethno-national identity – informed how they historicised, spatialised, and explained their campaign.

Irish republicanism's complex relationship with Catholicism casts in sharp relief the similarities and differences between Ireland and Europe in the decades that succeeded 1968. In their wide-ranging study, Robert Gildea, James Mark, and Anette Warring situated secularisation and radical Catholic activism as paramount legacies of Europe's '68 years.[152] By contrast to events in Poland and Italy, for instance, Ireland experienced relatively little radical action *within* the Catholic Church.[153] Unlike nationalist movements in El Salvador and East Timor, for example, Irish republicans enjoyed no support from senior members of the Catholic Church.[154] Whereas many clergy joined revolutionary movements in Nicaragua and El Salvador in the 1970s and 1980s,[155] Irish republicans received scant, and often heavily qualified, sympathy from clergy.

Nevertheless, in Northern Ireland and in pockets of the Republic of Ireland, substantial sections of the Catholic population, practising or lapsed, supported militant organisations drawn predominantly from their ethno-national community. For many Catholics in Northern Ireland, confessional allegiance was an essential signifier of a profoundly politicised collective identity.

The few priests who sympathised with republican politics framed the struggle for Irish independence as a centuries-long crusade. Father Joe McVeigh traced Irish Catholics' subjugation through 'centuries' in which the Church had stood with the 'politically and socially powerful'.[156] Sympathetic churchmen framed British rule as an emblem of injustice and human rights abuses. The majority of this select group of clergy were connected to republicanism through kinship ties, or served in rural parishes with a substantial local republican base. Father Brian McCreesh, originally from Camlough, County Armagh, with a parish in republican east Tyrone, supported his brother, PIRA volunteer Ray McCreesh, through the hunger strike of 1981.[157] Republican

---

[152] Robert Gildea, James Mark, & Anette Warring (eds.), *Europe's 1968: voices of revolt* (Oxford: Oxford University Press, 2013), pp. 212, 218.

[153] Rebecca Clifford & Nigel Townson, 'The church in crisis: Catholic activism and "1968"', *Cultural and Social History*, 8 (2011), p. 531.

[154] Kenneth Medhurst, 'Politics and religion in Latin America', in George Moyser (ed.), *Politics and religion in the modern world* (London: Routledge, 1991), p. 199; Chris Lundry, 'From passivity to political resource: the Catholic church and the development of nationalism in East Timor', *Asian Studies*, 38 (2002), pp. 12–13, 26.

[155] Bahman Bakhtiari, 'Revolution and the church in Nicaragua and El Salvador', *Journal of Church and State*, 28 (1986), pp. 20, 28–29.

[156] Joe McVeigh, 'Reflecting on the Irish Catholic Church', *The Furrow*, 61 (May 2010).

[157] 'Mrs. Thatcher replies to telegram', *Irish Examiner*, 21 May 1981.

clergy narrated patriotism as a form of divine obligation. When the SAS killed PIRA volunteer Colm McGirr in December 1983, Father McCreesh denounced the 'violation of the law of nature' when 'Irishmen [were] struck down... in their own ancestral fields'.[158]

Republicans often distinguished within the Church's structures. Although clerical sympathies with republicanism were few and far between, leading Provisional republicans carefully ascribed opposition only to individual members of the 'Catholic hierarchy'. Nuanced interpretations of 'the Church' endure today. Narrating the origins of the peace process, veteran Belfast republican Kevin Hannaway credited 'individuals' such as Fathers Alec Reid and Gerry Reynolds, 'not the Church itself', with courageous cross-community initiatives.[159] As another founding member of the Provisional movement put it: 'I don't class the hierarchy as the Catholic Church: I think they're two separate things.'[160]

Grassroots Provisionals studiously separated the Church's spiritual and political espousals, and filtered these positions accordingly. These bifurcations became especially important after the Provisional movement en masse condemned the Church's contentious role in the hunger strike of 1981. Every time parish priest Father Mullan, presiding at Bobby Sands's funeral, implored republicans to end their armed struggle, an octogenarian mourner repeatedly interjected that only a 'just peace' would suffice.[161] When PIRA volunteer Martin McCaughey from Cappagh, County Tyrone was killed in 1990, his father warned the local churchman that the family would bring republican symbols into the chapel and bury McCaughey with full military honours irrespective of the cleric's wishes.[162]

The founding Provisionals were not entirely deferential to Church authority. Nevertheless, successive Provisional leaderships were consistently pragmatic, selectively co-opting Catholic categories of morality. In the early 1970s, senior Provisionals framed their ideology as compatible with Catholic teaching. To discredit their Official republican rivals, Provisionals also appealed to popular disdain for Soviet atheism.

Even into the mid-1980s, after the tumult of the hunger strikes, Provisionals expected the Church to vindicate protests against British rule. The movement faced the challenge of maintaining a considerable proportion of practising

---

158 'Volley as two killed by SAS are buried', *The Irish Press*, 7 December 1983.
159 Kevin Hannaway interview with Jack Hepworth. Belfast, 6 December 2017.
160 Francie McGuigan interview with Jack Hepworth. Belfast, 6 December 2017.
161 'The funeral of Bobby Sands', *An Phoblacht/Republican News*, 9 May 1981.
162 'IRA Volunteers Dessie Grew & Martin McCaughey' (2012). Available at https://www.youtube.com/watch?v=5RdoXpWDPQc (accessed 22 September 2017).

Catholics among their supporters. As late as 1984, one Sinn Féin strategist suggested party education events should include Church representatives on discussion panels and encourage debates about the relationship between the Church and the republican struggle.[163]

By contrast, from the late 1960s, the Officials, PD – and, from the mid-1970s, the IRSP-INLA – opposed the Church more systematically, theoretically, and internationally. All three organisations branded the Provisionals socially conservative Catholics. In Ireland as in contemporary Italy, interactions between Catholicism and radicalism were hotly contested. Catholic youth groups constituted a major bloc among Italian student radicals in the late 1960s.[164] By contrast, in Ireland, young radicals broke more decisively with the Church: PD students such as Margaret Ward and Bernadette Devlin campaigned for reproductive rights and denounced the perceived hypocrisy of Catholic morality.[165] Other PD members flouted the Republic of Ireland's Church-backed censorship laws by marching across the border bearing banned books in 1969.[166]

Publicly, republicans looked to religious authority to legitimise grievances in the eyes of the Catholic population; privately, some activists found consolation in religion. However, to many republicans, the Catholic Church in Ireland was at best irrelevant, and at worst detrimental, to their struggle. Unlike post-war France and Belgium, Northern Ireland had no tradition of worker-priests.[167] Irish radical clergy did not establish ecclesiastical base communities, the likes of which propelled liberation theology in Central and South America after the Medellín conference of 1968.[168]

Unlike Nicaragua's Sandinistas, who proclaimed Catholicism at the 'cornerstone' of their nationality in October 1978,[169] Provisionals shared Cuban revolutionaries' vision of eliminating the Church's hidebound political influence. Yet most republicans also acknowledged the Church's societal standing and

[163] LHL NIPC P3885: Sinn Féin, *Republican Education: What We Need to Know to Win* (Dublin: Sinn Féin, 1985).

[164] Luisa Passerini, *Autobiography of a generation: Italy, 1968* (Hanover: Wesleyan University Press, 1996), p. 86.

[165] Margaret Ward, 'From civil rights to women's rights', in Michael Farrell (ed.), *Twenty years on* (Dingle: Brandon, 1988), p. 122; Bernadette Devlin, *The price of my soul* (London: Pan Books, 1969), p. 74.

[166] Paul Arthur, *The People's Democracy, 1968–1973* (Belfast: Blackstaff, 1974), p. 54.

[167] Joseph Rutte, 'The worker-priest archetype', *Psychological Perspectives: A Quarterly Journal of Jungian Thought*, 60 (2017), p. 447.

[168] Daniel H. Levine, 'Assessing the impacts of liberation theology in Latin America', *Review of Politics*, 50 (1988), pp. 248, 250–251, 258–259.

[169] Bakhtiari, 'Revolution and the church', 23.

the devout believers among their own radical ranks.[170] Religion constituted a curious political hurdle for republicans: Catholicism implied the contested ethnonational identity with which republicans identified, yet its institutions were overwhelmingly hostile.

---

[170] Siegel, *The meek and the militant*, 259, 264–265.

'The Age-Old Struggle'

Conclusion

Examining republicanism

As this book has demonstrated, examining the dynamic heterogeneity of Irish republicanism since 1968 is central to understanding republicanism's evolution. Differences within republicanism had profound impacts on the Northern Ireland conflict, as social movement theorists Robert W. White, Niall Ó Dochartaigh, Lorenzo Bosi, and Gianluca de Fazio have shown.[1] Such analysis requires attention both to centripetal and centrifugal forces within the movement. For different reasons, republicanism's opponents and leaders have historically presented republicanism as monochrome and unified. Yet these portrayals conceal a more complicated reality.

In 2013, Paul Gill and John Horgan analysed a dataset of 1,240 former PIRA volunteers. With up to 39 data-points on each individual, their statistical prosopography recorded, inter alia, roles within the movement, age at first identifiable activity, connections to place, and occupation. This analysis suggested the nuanced micro-dynamics of place and class in the PIRA, beyond reductive dichotomies of urban and rural, young and old, unskilled and professional. Gill and Horgan evoked a movement that was largely working-class, but spanned skilled and unskilled, specialised and unspecialised workers; which was chiefly

---

[1] Robert W. White, 'Structural identity theory and the post-recruitment activism of Irish republicans: persistence, disengagement, splits, and dissidents in social movement organizations', *Social Problems*, 57 (2010), pp. 341–370; Lorenzo Bosi & Niall Ó Dochartaigh, 'Armed activism as the enactment of a collective identity: the case of the Provisional IRA between 1969 and 1972', *Social Movement Studies*, 17 (2018), pp. 35–47; Gianluca de Fazio, 'Intra-movement competition and political outbidding as mechanisms of radicalisation in Northern Ireland, 1968–1969', in Lorenzo Bosi, Chares Demetriou, & Stefan Malthaner (eds.), *Dynamics of political violence: a process-oriented perspective on radicalisation and the escalation of political conflict* (Farnham: Ashgate, 2014), pp. 115–136.

urban, but constituted almost as much in small towns or villages with fewer than 10,000 inhabitants as in the larger cities of population above 100,000.[2] This book has sought qualitative embellishment and explanation to Gill's and Horgan's detailed quantitative investigation.

Thematic analysis of republican subjectivities risks essentialising every republican as uniformly politicised, reflective, and participant in intra-republican debates. A corrective is required. At one level, during their campaign, republicans were unified only by the overarching objectives of forcing a British withdrawal. Maintaining unity within their campaign was an obvious imperative. The themes and questions this book probes would often have appeared abstract or even irrelevant for individuals engaged in guerrilla war.

Appreciating republicanism's complex dynamics is integral to understanding political processes today. Furthermore, this research eschews the polarising rhetoric that would perpetuate division and deliberately frustrate attempts to understand ideas and actions across society. Researching republicanism negotiates ethical, legal, and methodological challenges, and all participants – activists, interviewees, academics, commentators, archivists, and funding bodies – must be safeguarded in the spirit of academic freedom and inquiry. As Marisa McGlinchey has stated, 'academic research should never be an information-gathering exercise for the security forces or the state'.[3]

While navigating censorious impulses, research at the intersection of the controversial past and contested present should not disown its challenging nature. On the contrary, the multifaceted difficulty of such work confirms its importance. Irrespective of political subjectivities and sensitivities, researching contentious politics promises to enhance mutual understanding and engagement. Detailed critical analysis of a polyvocal past does not lead to one singular or consensual position in the present day. Instead, thorough engagement with

---

[2] Gill and Horgan found PIRA members typically became active in their mid-twenties: the average age of first identifiable PIRA activity was 24.99 years. Although 34.1 per cent of their sample operated in a town or city with a population of 100,000 or more, a significant minority of PIRA activity took place in villages and small towns: some 39.1 per cent were active in villages and towns with a population of 10,000 or fewer. Gill and Horgan recorded a 'broad spectrum of occupation types' among 422 volunteers. Overall, almost two-thirds (63.4 per cent) of this sample of 422 worked in construction, services, or the industrial sector, and these ranks were fairly evenly balanced between specialists (61 per cent of construction workers; 42 per cent of industrial/services workers), and non-specialists. Paul Gill & John Horgan, 'Who were the volunteers? The shifting sociological and operational profile of 1240 PIRA members', *Terrorism and Political Violence*, 25 (2013), pp. 435–456.

[3] Marisa McGlinchey, *Unfinished business: the politics of 'dissident' Irish republicanism* (Manchester: Manchester University Press, 2019), p. 214.

the past contributes to a meaningful ongoing conversation today about the motivations, ideas, and perceptions that underpin acts and deeds.

A heterogeneous tradition

The preceding chapters have elaborated Ronnie Munck's critique of the republicanism's internal composition since 1968. For Munck, simplistic binaries of intra-republican difference – young and old, left and right, politicos and militarists – overlook seismic changes within republicanism.[4] This book posits three interconnected explanatory forces for understanding republican variation: dynamic networks between 'orthodox' and 'pragmatic' republicans, experiences of place, and political formulations of class. These forces remain relevant surveying republican fragmentation two decades after the Good Friday Agreement.

Especially after 1969, networks within republicanism usually formed what this book terms 'pragmatic' and 'orthodox' milieux. The distinction between these networks was more fluid and contingent than fixed categories of generation, geography, or rank within the movement. Especially at moments of crisis or heightened debate within republicanism, pragmatists were more open to tactical adaptation, perceiving new political opportunities. Their degree of readiness to alter course usually correlated with confidence in the movement's leaders. By contrast, orthodox republicans stressed the political authority of tradition in 'the age-old struggle'. In fractious circumstances, orthodox republicans branded their critics as 'splitters' dividing the movement; conversely, pragmatists scorned 'theological' republicans as outmoded and inflexible.

Historically, these contentious categories were important for how republicans interpreted boundaries and arguments within their movement. Yet these networks were always dynamic: many self-styled republican pragmatists in the 1970s and 1980s were deliberately appropriating the language of orthodoxy by the 1990s. For example, through much of the 1970s and 1980s, peaking with the Sinn Féin *ard fheis* of November 1986, Gerry Adams and his milieu criticised the founding Provisional republican leadership around Ruairí Ó Brádaigh. For pragmatic Adamsites advocating tactical innovation and strategic review, Ó Brádaigh's refusal to countenance taking seats in the Dáil was outmoded orthodoxy. By contrast, by the late 1990s, Adamsites brokering republican engagement with the peace process insisted upon their own orthodoxy: for Adams and McGuinness,

---

[4] Ronnie Munck, 'Irish republicanism: containment or new departure', in Alan O'Day (ed.), *Terrorism's laboratory: the case of Northern Ireland* (Aldershot: Dartmouth Publishing, 1995), p. 165.

republicans who opposed the PIRA ceasefires and the Good Friday Agreement were 'dissidents' and 'traitors to Ireland'.

Republican networks continue to fluctuate, and their volatility informs their contemporary significance. Successive moments of intra-movement fracture have made impossible a consensual narrative of the republican past. Among older generations of dissenting republicans – active during the conflict but now opposed to Sinn Féin's constitutional strategy – longstanding ties with like-minded comrades are vital. These affinities offer a stable connection to a past struggle whose meaning has been upended by ongoing political processes. Equally, for veteran republicans elected to office as Sinn Féin representatives, parallel networks essentially affirm a shared journey. Ongoing disputes within republicanism today revolve around questions of historical legitimacy and strategic evolution.

Examining republicanism across the past five decades, this book has suggested the significance of generational cohorts. Broadly, three 'generations' defined diachronic shifts in Irish republicanism. First, the senior republicans of the late 1960s before the movement split – including Ruairí Ó Brádaigh (born 1932) and Tomás Mac Giolla (1924) – proceeded to the founding leaderships of the Provisional and Official movements respectively. This generation had experienced earlier republican campaigns, and observed British imperial decline.

A 'second generation' emerged around Gerry Adams (1948) and Martin McGuinness (1950). Having been active in republicanism since the late 1960s and early 1970s, this cadre rose to the Provisional leadership in the early 1980s. Parallels in the IRSP-INLA include those at the centre of the organisation's feuds in the late 1980s, most notably Jimmy Brown (1956), Ta Power (1954), and Gerard Steenson (1957). This generational cohort played pivotal roles in intra-republican debates about tactics, strategy, and revolution theory from the 1980s, as Chapter 2 showed. This 'second' generation led the Provisional movement for several decades. As recently as January 2017, Adams remained Sinn Féin president, and McGuinness served as Northern Ireland's Deputy First Minister.

Finally, a 'third' generation born around or after the outbreak of conflict in 1968 joined republican organisations from the mid-1980s, but seldom reached leadership roles before 1998. Some of these republicans were associated with the Provisional movement in the 1990s before becoming prominent critics of the Good Friday Agreement after 1998, including John Connolly (1976) from County Fermanagh, Colin Duffy (1968) from Lurgan, County Armagh, Davey Jordan (1971) from Donaghmore, County Tyrone, and Carl Reilly (1975) from Belfast.[5]

---

[5] Connolly left the Provisionals in 1997 and was jailed in 2000, later becoming leader of the Real IRA prisoners in Maghaberry. Connolly cut ties with republican groups on his release in 2007. Duffy received a life sentence in 1995 but was acquitted

However, generations only go so far in explaining republican heterogeneity. While Adams and McGuinness defined republican leadership from the early 1980s, multiple currents existed beneath the surface of this ostensibly disciplined movement. Republicans from different places, class backgrounds, networks, and personal trajectories participated in the struggle, through the middle-ranks and grassroots of Provisional republicanism – to say nothing of other groups in this multi-organisational field.

The gulf between republican networks should not be overstated. Milieux frequently blur, and interactions are not uniformly acrimonious. Some republicans accentuate shared experience and hardships, and express differences with former comrades in measured terms. Former INLA prisoner Seamus McHenry recalled past republican schisms but insisted that he would never 'crucify' or 'condemn' other organisations: 'there's a lot of good volunteers lying dead now'.[6] A Provisional for more than 30 years, Albert Allen explained why he had never joined Sinn Féin:

> I found myself – and not only myself, but loads of other volunteers, we have never been a part of Sinn Féin, although we're all politically aware, we could've, could've. But I made a decision at the time that I would not join Sinn Féin, and I wouldn't go that way and the direction that I took then was more of a community-based effort. I've been involved in the residents' group round here and been involved for years. And before that I was instrumental in setting up the ex-prisoners' [organisation], I was instrumental in the memorial gardens, I'm still the chairperson of that, but I don't, I don't go that way [Sinn Féin]. I don't have a grievance against anybody who does, do you know what I mean, but that was my particular view of the time... But I would never go out and condemn [Sinn Féin]... and I would be against them, but I wouldn't be able to go out my way to

the following year. Jordan was imprisoned in the early 1990s and was elected as Saoradh's national chair in September 2016. Reilly joined the PIRA in 1993 but later left the Provisionals and chaired Republican Network for Unity. 'Former Real IRA commander: Even cameras on masts would be seen as "spy posts" in border regions', *thejournal.ie*, 18 February 2019. Available at https://www.thejournal.ie/real-ira-brexit-border-john-connolly-4495704-Feb2019 (accessed 20 February 2019); Carmel Robinson, 'Murder appeal will focus on evidence of jailed UVF man', *The Irish Times*, 16 May 1996; Connla Young, 'New "revolutionary" republican party Saoradh launched', *The Irish News*, 26 September 2016; Rogelio Alonso, *The IRA and armed struggle* (Abingdon: Routledge, 2007), p. 60; Andrew Norfolk, 'Terrorism keeps Belfast charity in business', *The Times*, 21 August 2018.

6 Seamus McHenry interview with Jack Hepworth. Belfast, 7 December 2017.

condemn them, because at the end of the day it's happened, it's gone; you're not gonna fix it. They're going to go down this route anyway, and it'll always be that way now... But again, it doesn't mean to say that Sinn Féin have the only voice for republicans. There's other people with different opinions that have other ideas.[7]

Place remains salient among republicans, informing identities within the movement and continually reframing the conflict's legacies. Place-based variations within republicanism distinguished rural townlands from urban strongholds, north from south, county from county. Experiences of the conflict differed across the north and shaped place-based variations in republicanism: between densely populated working-class west Belfast, and the rural hinterland of south Armagh; between the 'peace walls' and urban interfaces of Lurgan and Portadown, and the staunchly republican villages of Cappagh and Carrickmore; between the everyday encounters with the British Army, RUC, and Ulster Defence Regiment in Northern Ireland; and, just a short distance away, the curious political environment of border areas of the Republic of Ireland. Fraught experiences of crossing the border often reinforced republican grievances: in 1982, Michael McMahon, chair of a Sinn Féin *cumann* in Bundoran, County Donegal, complained that republicans returning to Fermanagh and Tyrone after a day trip to the Republic were routinely detained for several hours at Ulster Defence Regiment checkpoints.[8]

How republicans positioned themselves within the movement corresponded to how they spatialised their struggle differently, between local, regional, national, and international ideological formulations. Even since 1998, ongoing disputes over marches, flags, and commemorations have buttressed the continual contestation of public space in Northern Ireland. Through the 2010s, social transformation projects repeatedly stalled. In 2013, First Minister and Deputy First Minister respectively, Peter Robinson and Martin McGuinness, envisaged removing all of Northern Ireland's so-called 'peace walls' by 2023,[9] yet more than 100 barriers remained in December 2018.[10]

Republican collective identities were multi-layered and contingent. Some defined themselves in international terms as anti-imperialists or leftists, while others were more emphatically *Irish* republicans. Identities were reconstituted

---

[7] Albert Allen interview with Jack Hepworth. Belfast, 13 December 2017.

[8] 'Check-point "delays" condemned', *Ulster Herald*, 14 August 1982.

[9] Gerry Moriarty, 'Robinson and McGuinness want "peace walls" down within 10 years', *The Irish Times*, 10 May 2013.

[10] Rebecca Black, 'Progress on transforming Northern Ireland's peace walls "slowed by lack of government"', *Belfast Telegraph*, 10 December 2018.

dynamically. In prison communities, or when writing collectively to a local newspaper, republicans might identify as a Fermanagh republican, or even more specifically as a Divis Flats or Kilwilkie republican. Organisational identity could overlap with locality: South Derry Erps, for example, or East Tyrone Provos. Republican testimonies around place and class linked the individual to their networks. Narrating subjective conceptions of community and identity, the language of place mediated political class consciousness.

Republicans' networks and communities declared de facto autonomy and sovereignty, eluding state authority. In 1969, attacks by state forces and loyalists on civil rights marches and Catholic areas of west Belfast and Derry produced acutely localised defence committees. These groups contained the kernel of a renascent militant republicanism, including experienced veterans such as Billy McKee (born 1921) and Joe Cahill (1920), as well as legions of younger foot-soldiers born in the late 1940s and early 1950s. Once the old republican movement split in late 1969 and early 1970 amid disputes about 'August '69', the Provisionals quickly mobilised across large parts of Northern Ireland and the Republic's border counties. This movement would dominate republicanism, numerically and politically, throughout the following three decades.

The republican split of 1969 reflected different interpretations of the unfolding crisis. Yet it also mapped broader diversity in how individuals and networks strategised and spatialised republicanism. For Provisional republican founders Ó Brádaigh and Ó Conaill, Ireland's struggle was relatively isolated from developments elsewhere; they emphasised the national context, and often particular local dynamics.

Place profoundly coloured variations in republicanism. For example, civil rights and republican politics interacted particularly closely in Fermanagh and Tyrone, less so in Derry or south Armagh. In 1988, when Provisionals established '68 Committees to harness the civil rights legacy, they targeted 'places of memory' in the civil rights struggle such as Coalisland, Dungannon, and Enniskillen.[11] Even as their repertoires of contention diversified, the Provisionals remained attuned to the zeitgeist of local communities in Ireland. Addressing a campaign meeting in rural south Armagh in 1999, Sinn Féin's European election candidate Mitchel McLaughlin accentuated his credentials to represent Ireland's 'small farmers' on the 'international stage'.[12]

---

[11] Pierre Nora defined a *lieu de mémoire* as 'any significant entity, whether material or nonmaterial in nature, which by human will or the work of time has become a symbolic element of the memorial heritage of any community'. Pierre Nora, *Realms of memory: the construction of the French past – volume 1: conflicts and divisions* (New York: Columbia University Press, 1996), p. xvii.

[12] 'Confident start to campaign', *South Armagh Scéal*, 8 (20 May 1999).

The depth of Provisionals' engagement with their host community from 1970 set them apart in republicanism's multi-organisational field. As we have seen, the movement's nascent grassroots engagement commenced with street defence committees, neighbourhood cooperatives, and community vigilantism from the early 1970s. Especially from the early 1980s, Sinn Féin's electoral machine and urban activism fastened the movement's local credentials in communities across the north. By this juncture, within working-class Catholic communities, the Provisionals broadly constituted what the Italian Marxist Antonio Gramsci termed a 'hegemonic group'. For Gramsci, such an institution would

> propagate itself throughout society – bringing about not only a unison of economic and political aims, but also intellectual and moral unity.[13]

Local complexities in republicanism evaded leaders' representations of a singular 'national' struggle. Provisionals in Derry City, for example, consistently defied the movement's official line on feminism from the mid-1980s, criticising its stance on abortion and treatment of women within its ranks. Most of the few clergy who openly supported republican aspirations, and even sympathised with their methods, resided in isolated, rural parishes in majority-community areas.

Outside the Provisional movement, the IRSP-INLA and PD enjoyed a degree of popular support, but their leftism was relatively doctrinaire. In contrast, more pragmatic Provisionals expanded their base through the 1980s and diversified their conception of republicanism. In the process, they alienated some of their own militants, who considered Sinn Féin's expansion and the pliable politics of pan-nationalism a diversion from a specific political programme and disciplined armed campaign.

Republican experiences of class and interactions with socialism undergirded the movement's complex ecology. Formulations of place and collective memory are oriented around class as a lived experience. Leftism and internationalism complicated republicanism during the conflict. Today, disenchanted republicans often invoke the Provisionals' acquiescence not only in state structures, but the socioeconomic status quo. Many 'dissenting' and 'dissident' republicans highlight inequalities as they observe ongoing socioeconomic plight in Northern Ireland, where unemployment and poverty remain acute. The left-republicanism of organisations such as Saoradh, IRSP, and the 1916 Societies decries economic hardship across a partitioned island.

---

[13] Antonio Gramsci, *Selections from the prison notebooks of Antonio Gramsci* (ed. and transl. Quentin Hoare and Geoffrey Nowell Smith) (London: Lawrence & Wishart, 1971), p. 406.

In the broader context of the global '68, republicanism defies straight-forward categorisation. Through the 1960s, the repression of civil rights protests bequeathed multifaceted opposition to the unionist regime. Dissension spanned liberal unionists, constitutional nationalists, socialist revolutionaries, and militant republicans. In 1969, Belfast's student radicals founded PD, whose interna-tionalist leftism and provocative tactics frequently collided with the wider civil rights movement across Northern Ireland.

Republicanism's composition and strategies differed considerably from those of the 'terrorist' afterlives of '68 in Western Europe. Compared to West Germany's Rote Armee Fraktion, Italy's Brigate Rosse, and France's Gauche Prolétarienne, republicans, especially the PIRA, were:

- more numerous, and unified in fewer organisations rather than multitudinous underground cells;
- more working class in membership, whereas Europe's 'terrorists' included greater numbers of students, radical workers, and intellectuals;
- more integrated in their host society, enjoying a greater degree of community support;
- more formally and publicly politicised, especially through Sinn Féin from the 1980s;
- more theoretically eclectic and ambiguous, compared to doctrinaire leftists, anarchists, and Maoists in Europe.

Republicans waged consistent, 'low-intensity' guerrilla warfare in an ethno-nationalist campaign to corrode the British government's will to remain in Northern Ireland. By contrast, Europe's terrorists favoured 'spectacular' acts of violence to provoke state repression and stir the masses against injustice and oppression worldwide.[14]

Situating Irish republicanism as a strand of post-'68 radicalism highlights differences in how republicans formulated political ideas and interacted with revolutionary politics beyond Ireland. In the early 1970s, Official republican leaders such as Tomás Mac Giolla and Seán Garland framed the republican campaign globally among Third World anti-imperialist movements. By contrast, socialism was a secondary concern for senior Provisionals such as Ruairí Ó Brádaigh and Dáithí Ó Conaill. Instead, they identified a particularly Irish

---

[14] Kay Schiller, 'Political militancy and generation conflict in West Germany during the "red decade"', *Debatte: Journal of Contemporary Central and Eastern Europe*, 11 (2003), p. 29.

revolutionary tradition, which usually harked back to the rebellion of 1798, or the period from 1912 to 1923.

Within Ireland, class politics infused complex republican attitudes towards the Catholic Church. Left-wing republicans – spanning radical Provisionals, as well as members of the IRSP-INLA and PD – condemned church institutions as bastions of social conservatism. Conversely, although the founding Provisionals did not entirely defer to Catholic authority, they pragmatically insisted their politics were compatible with religious teaching. During the early 1970s, leading Provisionals such as Ruairí Ó Brádaigh lambasted their Official republican rivals as irreligious. Yet even practising Catholics among the Provisionals were not averse to challenging the Church hierarchy's political pronouncements.

Where their politics interacted with socialism, feminism, and internationalism, republicans' political priorities differed. For example, for early Provisionals such as Seán Mac Stíofáin, republicanism's purpose was simply to end British rule in Ireland: thereafter, the Irish populace would determine the independent nation's direction. By contrast, leftist republicans such as Tomás Mac Giolla and Seamus Costello considered the national question just one element of a wider social revolution. The resulting upheaval would transform class relations and liberate the working class.

In their critical analyses of republican metamorphosis, Mark Ryan and Kevin Bean characterised Irish republicanism as 'deeply influenced by the changes taking place in world politics' and 'susceptib[le] to the ideological pull of external forces'.[15] These assessments are truer for some sections of republicanism than for others. Although some Provisionals aligned their campaign with international radicalism, others isolated Ireland.

Contrasting perspectives on global class politics map broader divisions among Provisionals. Republicans interacted with the radical left in different ways for different ends. Official republican publicity identified explicitly with leftist national liberation movements, especially those receiving support from the USSR. Through the 1970s and 1980s, left-wing theoreticians in PD studied working-class struggles from Britain to sub-Saharan Africa, from Central America to south-east Asia. By contrast, Provisional leaders Ó Brádaigh and Adams instrumentalised anti-imperialist struggles elsewhere. In their framework, political upheavals in Poland, Nicaragua, Zimbabwe, and Honduras provided basic encouragement for republicans in struggle. Whereas Officials in the early 1970s situated Ireland's struggle in a global succession of socialist

---

[15] Mark Ryan, 'From the centre to the margins: the slow death of Irish republicanism', in Chris Gilligan & Jon Tonge (eds.), *Peace or war? Understanding the peace process in Northern Ireland* (Aldershot: Ashgate, 1997), p. 73; Kevin Bean, *The new politics of Sinn Féin* (Liverpool: Liverpool University Press, 2007), p. 74.

revolutions, senior Provisionals tended to treat Ireland as a place apart that could draw only vaguely upon international anti-imperialism.

For republican leftists – especially in the Official movement in the early 1970s and the theoretically minded wing of the IRSP-INLA from the mid-1970s – revolutionary struggles worldwide were about more than nebulous inspiration. For these republican radicals – including PD and the LCR in the late 1980s – studying anti-imperialism and class politics internationally rendered their own strategy and credo. They read international politics and revolutionary theory with considerable acuity and critical enquiry.

Especially during imprisonment, many republicans studied international politics and revolutionary theory. Cognisant that such tendencies could spark internal critique, the leaderships of Sinn Féin and the PIRA studiously avoided doctrinaire leftism. Instead, republican leaders preferred more general rhetoric around redistributive and cooperative economics in 'the new Ireland'. Almost inversely, the IRSP *Ard Comhairle* asserted control of its military wing, the INLA, and attempted to codify the movement's republican socialism. Militarists such as Gerard Steenson resisted this direction and the movement split catastrophically.

By the late 1980s, leftist Provisionals perceived their movement compromising with moderate nationalism and drifting towards reformism and clientelism. Socialism and internationalism also bled into feminist critiques of the Adams leadership. PIRA women in Maghaberry subverted their own movement's attempts to contain women's subjugation as a specifically Irish issue. Female prisoners internationalised patriarchy and connected with feminist anti-imperialists in Britain and beyond. Similarly, leftist PIRA men in Long Kesh harnessed radical pedagogy and considered their movement uncommitted to women's liberation and socialist revolution.

For successive Provisional leaderships, socialism and feminism within their movement had the potential to distort a unifying republican position. To contain feminism within republican orthodoxy, Ó Brádaigh and Adams alike accentuated women's agency in the republican past. In theory at least, for Official republicans and members of PD and the IRSP-INLA, women's liberation was integral to the social revolution they envisaged. Adams framed women's repression specifically as a product of British rule; IRSP and PD representatives situated patriarchy in tandem with advanced capitalism and imperialism worldwide.

The crisis of the international left from 1989 barely affected Provisional republican strategy in any immediate sense. As the 'new world order' crystallised after the Cold War, the republican campaign endured. International radical opposition to globalisation and neoliberal democratisation after 1989 barely registered with the Provisional leadership. While Mexico's Zapatistas issued their First Declaration and Revolutionary Laws in January 1994 – a symbolic protest against the North American Free Trade Agreement – republicans continued a low-intensity armed struggle and discussed the Downing Street Declaration.

In the early 1990s, only leftist margins of the Provisional movement lamented the rise of neoliberal regimes in the former Soviet Union. Into the mid-1990s, South Africa's conflict transformation was far more influential in senior Provisionals' international politics. Relatively detached from the vicissitudes of the new world order, many republicans remained optimistic as the twenty-fifth anniversary of 1969 approached. Until discussions about prison releases began in late 1994, the PIRA's rank-and-file scarcely addressed peace processes elsewhere, instead confident that a British withdrawal would soon occur leaving republicans to shape the 'new Ireland'.

Keeping the movement together

Exploring republicanism's internal dynamics, there is an epistemological danger of overstating difference and divergence. Addressing this dilemma requires attention to the centripetal forces that cohered republican organisations and maintained a remarkable degree of functional unity. As one republican veteran put it, reflecting over several decades of conflict: 'My idea at that time was: keep everybody together. That was the main thing: keep the movement together.'[16]

In a political tradition encompassing thousands of activists and supporters, yet navigating extremely hostile external conditions, 'keeping the movement together' was inevitably a priority. Yet while this objective was implicit throughout republican ranks – even within groups much smaller than the Provisional movement – some republicans were more attuned than others to the diversity of their tradition.

The further republicans interrogated the dynamics of their movement and reviewed their tactics, strategies, and priorities, the more fractures appeared. Leaders and middle-ranks organisers faced the practical imperative of maintaining internal unity and projecting cohesion for practical functionality and public consumption. This process usually entailed marginalising introspective questions and superficially imagining an integrated movement.

Broadly speaking, republican organisations and their communities cohered an enduring movement with remarkable success. Considering republicanism's diversity, the degree to which the Provisional movement in particular sustained internal unity merits attention. Even when the movement experienced internal dissension, the 'salami effect' preserved its leadership: the rate of breakaway was sufficiently gradual and numerically minor – and, crucially, usually included

---

[16] Albert Allen interview.

only a few leaders – for the Provisionals to retain their de facto leadership of the self-styled 'republican movement'.

The strength of individual commitment to an organisational identity was a crucial factor in maintaining unity. Pathways to, and through, mobilisation navigated the individual's cognitive, collective, and affective senses of themselves, their community, and their struggle.[17] As Sidney Tarrow argued, an activist negotiates multi-layered considerations, combining including individual rationale and group dynamics.[18]

Individual pathways in republicanism steered around several complicating factors, deepening ties to comrades. There was a cognitive level, at which the individual considered their position relative to the movement – although this is necessarily complicated by social identity and group membership. There were the individual's networks of kinship and friendship, intimately connected to place and lived experience. Additionally, a conjunctural element of particular circumstance at a given historical moment shaped activist careers.

The decision to leave an organisation was not taken lightly: many republicans persisted within their movement irrespective of concerns about the direction of the struggle. Brian Kenna from Crumlin, County Dublin, was released from Portlaoise in 1995 after serving five years' imprisonment for his role in a PIRA robbery. Reflecting more than 20 years later, as chair of socialist-republican party Saoradh, Kenna recalled his protracted, even reluctant, break with the Provisionals. Kenna had remained in Sinn Féin after 1998, even standing in local elections, despite growing concerns about the peace process:

> Like all republicans at that time, I did [support the peace initiatives], and I had a certain amount in belief in it. I was led to believe that it would lead us to a united Ireland. But over the years, I realised that this was not going to happen.[19]

---

[17] These components recall Henri Tajfel's conception of individual social identity within a movement. For Tajfel, group membership had cognitive, evaluative, and emotional dynamics: as part of an activist network, the individual derived interpretive frameworks, a positive or negative value, and a sense of selfhood and relationality within the wider group. Henri Tajfel, 'The achievement of group differentiation', in Henri Tajfel (ed.), *Differentiation between social groups: studies in the social psychology of intergroup relations* (London: Academic Press, 1978), pp. 27-60.

[18] Sidney Tarrow, 'Social movements in contentious politics: a review article', *American Political Science Review*, 90 (1996), p. 880.

[19] Brian Kenna interview with Dieter Reinisch, 2018. Dieter Reinisch, 'Interview with new Saoradh chairperson Brian Kenna' (1 December 2018). Available at https://me.eui.eu/dieter-reinisch/blog/interview-kenna/ (accessed 12 December 2018).

Competing organisational identities also bolstered republican groups' internal cohesion. 'Othering' alternative networks strengthened sentiments of belonging. Differences between republican organisations were of varying importance at particular times and through groups' strata. Organisation leaderships espoused varying class politics, revolutionary strategies, and different versions of the 'new Ireland'. Organisational identity shaped individual networks, inside and outside prison: members of a particular republican group mostly encountered their closest comrades. Recalling his decision to refuse Belfast republicans' invitations to join the PIRA in the late 1980s, former INLA prisoner Seamus McHenry put it plainly: 'I could never be a Provisional.'[20]

Especially when republican leaders from diverse traditions and organisations collaborated – in the National H-Block/Armagh Committee in the early 1980s, for example – group identity acquired additional significance. Nevertheless, this book has broadly suggested that in the lower echelons of republican organisations, political ideas and identities overlapped and blurred. Differences between early OSF leader Tomás Mac Giolla and founding Sinn Féin president Ruairí Ó Brádaigh are easily identified. In the late 1980s, left-leaning PIRA volunteers in Long Kesh and their INLA counterparts had far more in common. Nevertheless, to this day, the politics of republican identity remain loaded: some members of Sinn Féin reject the label 'Provisional' on the grounds that it supposedly gives undue credence to alternative groups.

The diachrony of republican heterogeneity is key to understanding how organisations configured loyalty within their ranks. In the Provisional movement, the piecemeal quality of tactical experimentation, and the almost millenarian enthusiasm that often accompanied it, generally prevented potentially major schisms. The Provisionals experienced considerable dissent within their movement from the late 1980s, but internal criticisms were largely contained, and splits were limited and sporadic. Maintaining a notable degree of unity relied upon two chief conventions. First, the movement had traditionally entrusted major decisions to its leadership. Second, from the early 1990s, Provisional middle ranks played increasingly important roles, informing and consulting the membership around piecemeal changes. Irrespective of whether the leadership privately predetermined its route, the movement's internal liaisons galvanised trust and a sense of shared authority among vital networks.

Under Adams's leadership from 1983, Sinn Féin's electoral turn became a paradigmatic shift in Irish republicanism. To unify the movement, Adamsites presented changes as tactical experiments, as distinct from seismic strategic changes. Over the following two decades, adaptations and trials morphed into

---

[20] Seamus McHenry interview with Jack Hepworth. Belfast, 7 December 2017.

more profound realignments, culminating ultimately in 'exclusively democratic' methods by 2005.

To a certain extent, the Provisional high command reciprocated the trust it enjoyed. Middle ranks in Sinn Féin and the PIRA were informed of decisions, and consulted increasingly through the 1980s. Especially during debates within republicanism, the cachet of 'veteran' status commanded respect. Pragmatists and orthodox alike vied for senior republicans' hallowed approval. Meanwhile, active volunteers were occupied mainly with prosecuting the armed struggle, devoting greater attention to strategic and theoretical concerns only after capture and imprisonment.

Years of staunch commitment to absolutist and contentious objectives meant that republican activism became a key, often defining, aspect of an individual's life and identity. Investing energy and making sacrifices to be part of the movement inevitably meant that republicans were loath to break with their comrades. Consequently, some Provisionals displaced their personal misgivings in the name of unity and staying 'on the one road'.

Interviewed in 1997, a PIRA veteran candidly admitted that defeat would be difficult even to contemplate. As was the case for many republicans, Gerard Hodgins's perspectives on the peace process oscillated as events unfolded in the mid-1990s. Hodgins remembered feeling 'very despairing' when, in February 1996, he learned that the PIRA had broken its 18-month ceasefire. The following year, with the ceasefire renewed, Hodgins was slightly more positive. Asked whether the war was over, he replied hopefully:

> We're not going to surrender. Everybody's invested too much in this struggle and lost too much. I would hope maybe in a year if you ask me the same question I could say, *yes, the war is over.*[21]

Hodgins was not alone in expressing acute trepidation at the thought that the struggle might not achieve its central objective.

Analytical categories such as 'militarists' and 'politicos', or 'hawks' and 'doves' serve an indicative purpose, inasmuch as they highlight points of friction within the movement. Yet they miss the complexity and processual dynamics of individual subjectivities. As this book has shown, many militarily active republicans ostensibly supported Sinn Féin's electoral experimentation in the 1980s, despite personal misgivings. According to his brother Peter, PIRA volunteer Martin McCaughey was reluctant when local republicans asked him to become a Sinn Féin councillor in east Tyrone. Nevertheless, McCaughey

---

[21] Gerard Hodgins quoted in *Provos: The IRA and Sinn Fein – Episode 4: Endgame* (BBC1, broadcast 14 October 1997).

agreed and served on Dungannon Council for several months, before he was hospitalised in Dublin after being shot in a gun battle with the British Army.[22] In October 1990, while collecting rifles from an arms dump, he was shot dead by undercover soldiers.

Even senior Sinn Féin figures were not insulated from doubts about the electoral turn. Derry elected representative Mitchel McLaughlin wondered whether Sinn Féin lost its grassroots relevance when its representatives entered Northern Ireland's council chambers. Interviewed in 1989, McLaughlin, a councillor in his native city, outlined some unintended consequences of moving into official political roles:

> We have to become more active politically on the streets... One aspect of the electoral strategy that was concerning me was we were getting a bit ring-rusty in terms of street politics. An unforeseen aspect of getting so many elected representatives was that our own grassroots organisations started to channel their energies through their elected representatives. We want them to be the interface between the community in the way they used to be.[23]

Republican organisations' internal policing also contributed to silencing sections of potential dissent. Marginalising critics took several forms. Many republicans whose criticisms of the movement were relatively muted were ostracised or shunned in their community. Leftist Provisionals Micky McMullan and Tommy McKearney experienced a degree of social isolation from their former comrades in Long Kesh in the 1980s. More extremely, former PIRA prisoner Paddy Fox from east Tyrone received death threats from republicans after he spoke against the Good Friday Agreement in 1998.[24]

Divisions within the IRSP and INLA unfolded more publicly and bloodily through the 1980s. The republican socialist movement was riven with disagreement over the fundamental question of whether the party or the army would be the movement's centre of gravity. Volatile factionalism publicly scarred the organisation from its foundations in the mid-1970s.

---

[22] Cllr. Martin McCaughey, Sinn Fein, Cappagh, 'A Republican view on the GAA match', *Ulster Herald*, 21 April 1990; 'IRA Volunteers Dessie Grew & Martin McCaughey', YouTube (2012). Available at https://www.youtube.com/watch?v=5RdoXpWDPQc (accessed 22 September 2017).

[23] '"It's a counter-insurgency policy"', *the next step: Revolutionary Communist Party Weekly*, 13 October 1989.

[24] Henry McDonald, 'I spoke against peace so now they want to kill me', *The Observer*, 31 January 1999.

Republican transformation

The Good Friday Agreement was a threshold moment in Irish republicanism. Prior to 1998, internally disciplined organisations cohered thousands of militants and sustained low-intensity struggle. Yet these organisations also included diverse individuals who historicised, spatialised, and strategised their struggle differently. Since the PIRA's armed campaign ended in 2005, mainstream commentary has presented militarism as the sole divider within republicanism. This book has suggested that republicanism's mosaic quality was, and is, more complicated, spanning class politics, place, and networks of orthodox and pragmatic republicans.

For more than a century, Irish republicanism's strategic and definitional positions have been contested inside and outside the movement. Repeatedly, a powerful strand within Irish republicanism has portrayed militarism as radicalism's apotheosis. In this schema, the forcefulness of the methods – epitomised by armed struggle – corresponds to the radicalism of the activists. Here, the national question marginalises all other considerations: 'politics' becomes a pejorative metonym for the compromises that split republicanism in 1921. Yet the dichotomy between 'politics' and 'armed struggle' has never been static or fixed. For many republicans, 'politics' ceased to be an unwelcome cipher for reformism during long prison sentences.

Assessing changes within Irish republicanism over three decades, Tarrow's theoretical model of social movement demobilisation is worth recalling. Tarrow posited four key factors undermining protest movements: regime repression; activist exhaustion; contenders' claims being satisfied; and activist groups becoming incorporated and institutionalised in orthodox politics.

   i.   Regime repression did not drive changes in republican activism. Republicans faced consistent repression between the late 1960s and late 1990s. The most catastrophic military reverses the Provisionals experienced renewed revolutionary succour among their grassroots.[25] Throughout these decades, the PIRA and INLA alike experienced major military reverses, but sustained

---

[25] For example, after the PIRA lost eight volunteers in an SAS ambush at Loughgall, County Armagh in May 1987 – the movement's single greatest loss – a Strabane republican whose brother had been killed in similar circumstances two years earlier asserted that such reverses only intensified the will to struggle. As Catriona Breslin put it: 'You can't take foreign guns and foreign armies coming into your country and shooting you down. It just makes you more determined.' Joan Phillips, 'Assassins: SAS shoot-to-kill at Loughgall', *the next step: Revolutionary Communist Party Weekly*, 15 May 1987.

    low-intensity warfare. On the contrary, shifting political opportunity structures, particularly around Sinn Féin's growing electoralism in the 1980s, broadened the republican campaign.

ii.   Activist exhaustion affected the Provisional leadership more than its prisoners and rank-and-file. Adamsites in the late 1980s advocated talks with the SDLP and a 'pan-nationalist' alliance, partly as a response to a perceived military impasse. However, many Provisionals' confidence in their armed campaign endured through the 1990s.

iii. Contenders' claims being satisfied did not directly drive republican demobilisation. Fundamentally, the British government did not withdraw and did not relinquish the principle of consent within Northern Ireland. Nevertheless, although Provisional supporters of the Adams leadership shifted their repertoires of contention, they did so in the belief that doing so would expedite their objectives.

iv. Activist groups becoming incorporated and institutionalised in orthodox politics rings true for the Provisional movement, which committed to exclusively constitutional methods by 2005. However, this book has argued that this institutionalisation was an outcome, rather than a cause, of shifting strategies from the 1980s.

How individuals interpreted 'legitimacy' and political priorities emerged as a central difference among republicans in the 1980s. Commemorations of 1968 in 1978 and 1988 highlighted how activists historicised their radical pasts amid ongoing struggle. The historical contexts of 1916 and the legacies of James Connolly were particularly pliable, offering adamant militarists and revolutionary socialists alike a touchstone for their political heritage. Where international struggles were concerned, some republicans looked to revolutionary processes elsewhere for basic inspiration against an imperialist power. Others studied in greater detail, seeking to extract strategic lessons.

In the late 1980s, strategic innovators in the Provisional leadership redefined the republican campaign as a rights-based struggle for 'pan-nationalist' self-determination. New departures bled into electoral tactics, council work, and grassroots activism, and exposed divisions within the movement. Leftist republicans criticised Adamsites for compromising with moderate nationalism. An older guard including Ruairí Ó Brádaigh and Dáithí Ó Conaill complained that electoralism desecrated historical legitimacy and undermined armed struggle.

Provisional republicanism's shifting strategies stemmed from two interlinking factors: first, moments of crisis in the republican struggle amid limited political opportunities; second, and perhaps paradoxically, republican perceptions of regime vulnerability at particular opportune moments. Having diagnosed weakness in the movement, the PIRA adopted a cell structure geared for a 'long war' of attrition in the late 1970s. Speaking with the Army Council's authority in 1978, a senior Provisional explained framed internal reorganisation as a response to informer infiltration and a mistaken ceasefire from February 1975 to January 1976.[26] Similarly, in the late 1980s, Adamsites in the leadership diagnosed impasse in their campaign and initiated a pan-nationalist front to develop the republican base and explore constitutional avenues after two decades of guerrilla war.

Yet Provisional new departures were also experimental responses to leaders' perceptions of weaknesses in the state's authority – even if these moments were transitory and largely unanticipated. Through the 1980s, the Provisionals adapted their tactics incrementally as new political opportunities appeared. These changes later evolved into more profound, strategic change. In 1981, having endured five years of British criminalisation policy, the hunger strikers' election campaigns garnered widespread publicity. Simultaneously surprised and encouraged by these developments, Provisional leaders subsequently determined to pursue further experiments.

Comparably, the Anglo-Irish Agreement of November 1985 provoked unionist ire and inadvertently created new political opportunities for Provisionals. Abused by unionist councillors, Sinn Féin appealed to a growing nationalist constituency and substituted insistence on 'armed struggle' for the more consensual bandwidth of civil rights. Meanwhile, the movement harnessed the radical potential of grassroots activism in besieged Catholic working-class communities. The Provisional movement's career from the early 1980s fits David A. Snow's and David A. Benford's argument that new injustice frames prompt tactical innovation.[27]

Republicanism today

Contemporary debates about republican fragmentation profoundly colour subjective representations of the past. Interviewees who have remained in an organisation throughout their activist career tend to collapse time and republican heterogeneity. They stress an essential version of republicanism from which they have not wavered.

---

[26] *Magill*, Volume 1, Number 11 (August 1978), pp. 14, 16.
[27] David A. Snow & David A. Benford, 'Master frames and cycles of protest', in Aldon C. Morris & Carol McClurg Mueller (eds.), *Frontiers in social movement theory* (New Haven, Connecticut: Yale University Press, 1992), p. 146.

Conversely, republicans who have experienced schisms and left their previous groups, or who are disillusioned with the outcomes of the struggle, often present a greater degree of difference within republicanism. They emphasise points of fissure within republicanism, and the seeming contradictions of former comrades.

The wide-ranging reflections of Jim McCrystal – a former Provisional from Lurgan, County Armagh – emblematised those dismayed by the direction of their erstwhile movement. Interviewed by Marisa McGlinchey in 2013, McCrystal, who had been imprisoned with Gerry Adams in the 1970s, contrasted a heroic past with his assessment of republican decline, or even defeat:

> I think in my own mind we could have achieved it… had we not succumbed to the British government. I think we were on the verge of something…[28]

Speculating as to what 'might have been', McCrystal's testimony echoed what Alessandro Portelli called the 'uchronic moment'. For Portelli, oral history interviewees' 'uchronic dreams' reflected on aspirations for transformations that did not materialise. Remembering a past 'that could have gone differently', these memories assert historical agency by asserting the potential of past activism.[29]

Today, 'dissenting' and 'dissident' republicans frame the Provisionals' expanding repertoires of contention since the 1980s as a catalogue of errors acquiescing in British statecraft. Republican fragmentation today risks obscuring the profound confidence among the majority of Provisionals throughout the 1990s that British withdrawal was either imminent, or inevitable in the longer term. Even during the PIRA ceasefires of the mid-1990s, many Provisionals continually perceived their movement as the commanding authors of the embryonic peace process.

'Dissenters' and 'dissidents' tend to erase the gradualism of the Provisionals' tactical and strategic changes. Claims that Adamsites determined decades ago to manipulate the movement towards exclusive constitutionalism overlook the

---

[28] Jim McCrystal interview with Marisa McGlinchey, August 2013. McGlinchey, *Unfinished business*, 79.

[29] Alessandro Portelli, 'Uchronic dreams: working class memory and possible worlds', in Raphael Samuel & Paul Thompson (eds.), *The myths we live by* (London: Routledge, 1990), pp. 147–155. Jonna Katto found similar patterns in oral testimonies of economically marginalised former Frelimo militants in Mozambique, who were disillusioned with the revolution's outcomes. Jonna Katto, 'Landscapes of belonging: female ex-combatants remembering the liberation struggle in urban Maputo', *Journal of Southern African Studies*, 40 (2014), pp. 539–557; Jonna Katto, 'Emotions in protest: unsettling the past in ex-combatants' personal accounts in northern Mozambique', *Oral History*, 46 (2018), pp. 53–62.

incremental and unpredictable qualities of those processes. Critique of Adams's leadership is on firmer ground when it recognises the profound power vested in the Provisionals' upper echelons. The Provisional movement had a long history of entrusting major strategic decisions to its leaders. Consequently, when the movement altered its repertoires of contention – through electoralism in the 1980s or peace negotiations in the 1990s, for example – the grassroots specifically identified these innovations with 'the leadership'.

The ebb and flow of Northern Ireland's peace process has added new layers of complexity in republicanism's internal composition. In the twenty-first century, the ideas and strategies of republicans inside and outside Sinn Féin have shifted markedly. Among those who argue regretfully that Irish unification has never been more unlikely, there is a distinct lack of consensus on how to transform the situation.

In 2019, a former senior member of the PIRA's East Tyrone Brigade reflected on republicanism's transformation during his lifetime. Frankie Quinn, who was sentenced to 16 years' imprisonment in 1988, remembered arguments in Long Kesh at the time of the PIRA ceasefire in 1994. Some of those republicans who had opposed the ceasefire then, Quinn claimed, were now among Sinn Féin's most vocal advocates.

Some 25 years on, Quinn's life in east Tyrone reflected multivalent commitment to the republican community: he was a founder member of the 1916 Societies, a cultural and political dissenting republican network, and coordinated a support group for ex-prisoners in Dungannon. Yet Quinn had no sympathy with those erstwhile Provisionals who advocated renewing a military campaign: 'My view on armed struggle at this stage is that it's pointless, it's not going to achieve anything.' Alluding to 'dissident' republicans killing journalist Lyra McKee during riots in Derry City in April 2019, Quinn emphasised his point:

> Irish unity wasn't achieved by armed struggle. Is a bomb that takes a bit of concrete out of a gate post, is the shooting of an innocent young girl going to achieve Irish unity? I don't think so.[30]

Similarly, among some sections of those have remained in the Provisional movement for decades, there is an undercurrent of impatience. By early 2017, Gerry Adams and Martin McGuinness had been at the apex of Sinn Féin for more than three decades. Their detractors were not necessarily crypto-dissenters who would accuse Adams and McGuinness of 'selling out' or capitulating: more

---

[30] Freya McClements, "'Armed struggle is pointless. It's not going to achieve anything'", *The Irish Times*, 31 August 2019.

moderate critics simply called for a change of leadership. Aged 67, Thomas McNulty could reflect on a lifelong republican career, from imprisonment in Portlaoise alongside McGuinness in the 1970s to the chair of a Sinn Féin *cumann* in County Cavan almost five decades later. McNulty's past attested an enduring commitment to one organisational expression of republicanism, throughout its tactical and strategic changes.

However, by 2016, McNulty demanded reinvigoration of the leadership. McNulty lauded Adams's achievements, crediting the Sinn Féin president with 'steer[ing] the republican movement from conflict to peace... A great debt of gratitude is due to Mr Adams.' But for McNulty, a younger generation was now responsible for building upon those foundations. Invoking past threshold moments in the struggle, including the historic Sinn Féin *ard fheis* of 1986 that confirmed Adams's ascendancy in the movement, McNulty urged the president to step aside: 'just as there was a time for change in 1986, there is a time for change again in 2016'.[31]

Especially since the global financial crash of 2008, the Good Friday Agreement and the unfolding political initiatives in 'post-conflict' Northern Ireland have been subject to renewed criticism. Analysts and scholars such as Eric Kaufmann, Amanda Hall, and Seán Byers have connected ongoing socioeconomic deprivation in the north with the peace process's unfulfilled promises.[32] These analyses highlight enduring political and residential polarisation in Northern Ireland. On all sides of the conflict, 'whataboutery' remains ubiquitous in a contemporary political scene that appears decreasingly prepared to address the difficult past. Invoking 'negative peace', Hall captured the sense of halting in a process that was once celebrated internationally: 'violence is managed or reduced, but the conflict has yet to be transformed'.[33]

Some three years without a power-sharing government in Northern Ireland, from January 2017 to January 2020, reinforced diagnoses of crisis in the peace process. Contemporary critiques are inextricably linked to a broader discourse around consociationalism. A substantial political science literature has posited that consociationalism undercuts the most militant opposition to the status quo but risks fixing ethnic and social division and segregation.[34]

---

[31] John Manley, 'Gerry Adams told to step down by Sinn Féin cumann chairman', *The Irish News*, 16 July 2016.

[32] Eric Kaufmann, 'The Northern Ireland peace process in an age of austerity', *Political Quarterly*, 83 (2012), pp. 203–209; Amanda Hall, 'Incomplete peace and social stagnation: shortcomings of the Good Friday Agreement', *Open Library of Humanities*, 4 (2018), pp. 1–31; Seán Byers, 'Northern Ireland's deeper crisis', *Tribune* (24 January 2019). Available at https://tribunemag.co.uk/2019/01/northern-irelands-deeper-crisis# (accessed 1 February 2019).

[33] Hall, 'Incomplete peace and social stagnation', 3.

[34] Rick Wilford, 'Inverting consociationalism? Policy, pluralism, and the post-modern',

If consociationalism perpetuates macro-divisions across society, it also necessarily neglects internal micro-divisions *within* communities – and even within specific and contested elements, such as republicanism. The architects of the Good Friday Agreement (1998) and St Andrews Agreement (2006) could justifiably claim to have transformed formal political practice in Northern Ireland. A major component of their work was to marginalise the militants who had been at the forefront of the war for 30 years.

Yet the diplomatic initiatives of the early twenty-first century conceived of monolithic community blocs that were never, of course, homogenous. As this book has demonstrated, republicanism was historically a variegated politics, and its mosaic quality endures today – despite centralising tendencies in republican organisations. Correspondingly, republican interpretations of the peace process have been wide-ranging.

These responses are geographically, socially, and politically complex and continue to unfold today. For example, those who founded Saoradh in 2016 spanned veteran former Provisionals who had been politically 'homeless' for many years, alongside younger republicans belonging to the so-called ceasefire generation. Speaking prior to Saoradh's formation in 2016, Nuala Perry said she knew 'at least twenty or thirty other independent republicans who feel very isolated because they don't belong to a certain group'.[35] As Marisa McGlinchey has shown, even among that section of republicans who broadly criticise Sinn Féin's direction since the 1980s, there have been many moments of rupture.[36]

By implication, there are many different republican positions outside Sinn Féin today. Competing republican versions of the past further complicate the last three decades. Those outside Sinn Féin today often readily admit that moments they now repudiate in Sinn Féin's historical trajectory were not immediately apparent. Among those who now criticise the Provisionals' direction, several factors of memory intermesh: grievances around class politics; the absence of a promised 'peace dividend'; and the ostracisation of formerly prominent republicans who became 'dissenters'.

As we have seen, republicanism's historical and dynamic heterogeneity contributes powerfully to the complexity of collective memory today. As Molly

in Brigid Hadfield (ed.), *Northern Ireland: politics and the constitution* (Buckingham: Open University Press, 1992), pp. 29–46; James Anderson & James Goodman (eds.), *Dis/agreeing Ireland: contexts, obstacles, hopes* (London: Pluto Press, 1998); Paul Dixon, 'The politics of antagonism: explaining McGarry and O'Leary', *Irish Political Studies*, 11 (1996), pp. 130–141. Marie Breen-Smyth, 'Hierarchies of pain and responsibility: victims and war by other means in Northern Ireland', *Trípodos*, 25 (2009), pp. 27–40.

[35] Marisa McGlinchey interview with Nuala Perry. McGlinchey, *Unfinished business*, 58.

[36] McGlinchey, *Unfinished business*, 24, 50.

Andrews concluded in her seminal study of activism throughout the life course, for veterans of a social movement

> activism is not merely something which the respondents do, nor even just a part of them. It is them. During their long, accumulated years of engagement, they have come to define themselves through their activism.[37]

The extent to which historical activism continually shapes identities informs the sensitivity of contested memory. Consequently, attempts to redefine past struggle can provoke considerable anguish and anger within and without republicanism.

After the Real IRA claimed responsibility for killing two British soldiers at Massereene Barracks in Antrim in March 2009, disparate republican responses revealed disorientation and fragmentation. Sinn Féin representatives unequivocally condemned the 'dissidents', employing incendiary language that caused discomfiture among wider sections of the republican base, far beyond the 'dissidents' themselves.

For two disillusioned former PIRA prisoners from east Tyrone, mainstream republicans lambasting 'dissidents' implicitly called into question the struggle that had spanned decades. Brian Arthurs and Peter McCaughey had left Sinn Féin in 2008 after a major split in County Tyrone, when five *cumainn* resigned. For Arthurs and McCaughey, Martin McGuinness could not condemn republican actions in 2009 without casting aspersions on the movement of 1969. Reviewing the intervening decades, Arthurs said:

> No one can deny that there have been changes in the North but it is an equality agenda being pursued. People did not die, they did not take up arms, for equality. They did so for Irish freedom.[38]

Both Arthurs and McCaughey had lost brothers in the conflict, in 1987 and 1990 respectively. For McCaughey, the memory of the republican dead was indivisible from contemporary politics:

> Was my brother a 'conflict junkie', a 'neanderthal' or a 'traitor to the island of Ireland'? That is what Martin McGuinness would call him

---

[37] Molly Andrews, *Lifetimes of commitment: aging, politics, psychology* (Cambridge: Cambridge University Press, 1991), p. 164.

[38] 'Arthurs attacks SF leadership', *Irish Republican News*, 28 October 2010. Available at https://republican-news.org/current/news/2010/10/arthurs_attacks_sf_leadership. html (accessed 15 July 2019).

if he was killed on active service today. My brother was a freedom fighter. He fought for a united Ireland. That goal is still there and remains deeply cherished by republicans in Tyrone. We were disgusted when Martin McGuinness stood at the gates of Stormont with the chief constable of the PSNI after Massereene and demonised republicans. He did not speak for us.[39]

The complex ecology of the republican past indelibly marks Northern Ireland today. Republicanism remains divided socially, geographically, strategically, and, for many of its adherents, personally. Republican legacies remain contested among ex-combatants and across society more broadly. Contrary to popular usage, there is no singular 'republican movement'. Its breadth has alternately strengthened and strained Irish republicanism, and continues to do so today.

---

[39] 'Arthurs attacks SF leadership', *Irish Republican News*, 28 October 2010. Available at https://republican-news.org/current/news/2010/10/arthurs_attacks_sf_leadership. html (accessed 15 July 2019).

Appendix I

Key Actors

Gerry Adams: Born Belfast, 1948; interned, 1972, 1973–1976; president, Sinn Féin, 1983–2018; Sinn Féin MP, Belfast West, 1983–1992, 1997–2011; TD, Louth, 2011–present.

Seamus Costello: Born Bray, County Wicklow, 1939; joined SF and IRA, 1955; imprisoned, 1957–1960; founding member of IRSP and INLA, 1974; INLA Chief of Staff, 1974–1976; killed by OIRA, 1977.

Bernadette Devlin: Born Cookstown, County Tyrone, 1947; founding member of People's Democracy, 1968; MP, Mid-Ulster, 1969–1974; joined IRSP, 1974; joined Independent Socialist Party, 1977; founding member of South Tyrone Empowerment Programme, 1997.

Máire Drumm: Born Newry, 1919; joined NICRA; joined *Cumann na mBan*; vice-president, Sinn Féin; killed by Red Hand Commando, 1976.

Mairéad Farrell: Born Belfast, 1957; PIRA prisoner, 1976–1986; OC PIRA in Armagh Jail; killed on PIRA active service, 1988.

Seán Garland: Born Dublin, 1934; joined IRA, 1953; imprisoned, 1957–1959; founding member of OSF and OIRA, 1970; elected general secretary, OSF, 1977; died, 2018.

Brendan Hughes: Born Belfast, 1948; joined PIRA, 1969; PIRA prisoner, 1974–1986; OC PIRA in Crumlin Road Jail, 1974–1975; OC PIRA in Long Kesh, 1977–1978, 1978–1980; died, 2008.

Seán Lynch: Born Enniskillen, County Fermanagh, 1954; PIRA prisoner, 1986–1998; Vice OC PIRA in Long Kesh, 1992–1994; OC PIRA in Long

Kesh, 1994–1996; Sinn Féin councillor, Fermanagh County Council, 2011; Sinn Féin MLA, Fermanagh-South Tyrone, 2011–present.

Tomás Mac Giolla: Born Nenagh, County Tipperary, 1924; joined IRA, 1950; president, Sinn Féin, 1962–1970; founding member of Official republican movement, 1970; TD, The Workers' Party, Dublin West, 1982–1992; died, 2010.

Seán MacManus: Born Blacklion, County Cavan, 1950; Secretary, County Sligo Anti-H-Block Committee, 1980; joined Sinn Féin Ard Comhairle, 1982; National Chairperson, Sinn Féin, 1984–1990; Sinn Féin councillor, Sligo County Council, 1994–2017.

Seán MacStíofáin: Born London, 1928; joined IRA, 1948; imprisoned, 1953–1959; founding member of PIRA, 1969; PIRA Chief of Staff, 1970–1972; imprisoned, 1972–1973; resigned from Sinn Féin, 1982.

Martin McGuinness: Born Derry, 1950; OC PIRA in Derry City, 1972; PIRA prisoner, 1973, 1974; Sinn Féin Assembly representative, Derry, 1982–1986; Sinn Féin vice-president; Sinn Féin MP, Mid-Ulster, 1997–2013; Sinn Féin MLA, Mid-Ulster, 1998–2016; Sinn Féin MLA, Foyle, 2016–2017; Deputy First Minister, Northern Ireland, 2007–2017; died, 2017.

Anthony McIntyre: Born Belfast, 1957; PIRA prisoner, 1974-1975, 1976-1993; left Provisional movement, 1998. In 1999, McIntyre gained his PhD for a thesis entitled 'A Structural Analysis of Modern Irish Republicanism: 1969–1973'. He is the author of *Good Friday: the death of Irish republicanism* (New York: Ausubo Press, 2008), and co-founded *The Blanket*, an online magazine critically analysing the peace process. McIntyre was later lead researcher on the Boston College oral history project.

Billy McKee: Born Belfast, 1921; joined IRA, 1939; imprisoned, 1940–1946; founding member of PIRA, 1969; OC Belfast Brigade PIRA, 1970–1971, 1974; imprisoned, 1971–1974; joined RSF, 1986; died, 2019.

Ruairí Ó Brádaigh: Born Longford, County Longford, 1932; joined SF, 1950; joined IRA, 1951; imprisoned, 1956–1958; IRA Chief of Staff, 1958–1959; imprisoned, 1959–1960; founder member of Sinn Féin, 1970; president, Sinn Féin, 1970–1983; founder member of RSF, 1986; president, RSF, 1986–2009; died, 2013.

Dáithí Ó Conaill: Born Cork, 1938; joined IRA, 1955; founding member of PIRA, 1970; imprisoned, 1975–1977; founding member of RSF, 1986; died, 1991.

Rita O'Hare: Born Belfast; joined Provisional movement, c.1971; PIRA prisoner, 1976–1979; founding leader of Sinn Féin Women's Department, 1979; editor, *An Phoblacht/Republican News*, 1985–1990; Sinn Féin director of publicity, 1990–1998; Sinn Féin representative to North America, 1998–2019; Sinn Féin general secretary, 2007–2009.

Gerard Steenson: Born Belfast, 1957; joined OIRA, 1972; joined INLA, 1974; founder member of Irish People's Liberation Organisation, 1986; killed in feud, 1987.

Appendix II

Interviewees

Albert Allen: Born Belfast, 1954; joined Na Fianna Éireann, 1969; joined OIRA, 1970; joined PIRA, 1971; interned, 1971–1972; PIRA prisoner, 1976, 1977–1978, 1978–1986; OC PIRA in Crumlin Road Jail, 1978.

Mickey Brady: Born Newry, 1950; Sinn Féin MLA, Newry & Armagh, 2007–2015; Sinn Féin MP, Newry & Armagh, 2015–present.

Don Browne: Born Derry, 1959; joined OIRA; joined INLA; republican prisoner, 1985–1998; resigned from INLA, 1986.

Charlie Casey: Born Newry; Sinn Féin councillor, Newry, 2001–present.

Gerry Foster: Born Belfast, 1963; joined INLA, 1982; INLA prisoner, 1982–1988, 1992–1994.

Fra Halligan: Born Belfast, 1968; joined IRSP, 1984.

Kevin Hannaway: Born Belfast, 1947; joined PIRA, 1969; interned, 1971; imprisoned 2018.

Peadar Lagan: Born Magherafelt, County Derry, 1974; INLA prisoner, 1993–1996.

Eamonn MacDermott: Born Derry, 1957; PIRA prisoner, 1977–1992. Since 1996, Eamonn has worked as a journalist.

Gerry MacLochlainn: Born Derry, 1954; republican prisoner, 1980–1983; Sinn Féin representative in London, 1984–1994.

Patrick Magee: Born Belfast, 1951; joined PIRA, 1972; interned, 1973–1975; PIRA prisoner, 1985–1999. During his incarceration, Patrick wrote a doctoral thesis on representations of republicans in fiction. He later developed this into a book: *Gangsters or guerrillas? Representations of Irish republicans in 'troubles fiction'* (Belfast: Beyond the Pale Publications, 2001). Patrick's memoir *Where grieving begins: building bridges after the Brighton bomb* was published by Pluto Press in 2021.

Raymond McCartney: Born Derry, 1954; joined PIRA, 1972; interned, 1972–1974; PIRA prisoner, 1977–1994; OC PIRA in Long Kesh, 1989–1991; Sinn Féin MLA, Foyle, 2004–2020.

Francie McGuigan: Born Belfast, 1947; joined PIRA, 1969; left Provisional movement, 1990s.

Seamus McHenry: Born Belfast; joined OIRA; joined IRSP-INLA, 1974; INLA prisoner.

Tommy McKearney: Born Lurgan, County Armagh, 1952; joined PIRA, 1971; republican prisoner, 1977–1993; founding member of League of Communist Republicans, 1986. Tommy's book *The Provisional IRA: from insurrection to parliament* was published by Pluto Press in 2011.

Danny Morrison: Born Belfast, 1953; Sinn Féin Director of Publicity, 1979–1990; Sinn Féin Assembly representative, Mid-Ulster, 1982–1986; imprisoned, 1990–1995. Danny is the author and editor of eight books, including the novels *West Belfast* (1989; republished Coesfeld: Elsinor Verlag, 2015) and *The wrong man* (Cork: Mercier, 1997). Danny's prison letters formed the basis of *Then the walls came down: a prison journal* (Cork: Mercier, 1999).

Conor Murphy: Born Camlough, County Armagh, 1963; imprisoned, 1981–1984; Sinn Féin councillor, Newry and Mourne District Council, 1989–1997; Sinn Féin MLA 1998-present; Sinn Féin MP, Newry and Armagh, 2005–2015; Finance Minister, 2020–present.

Nuala Perry: Born Belfast, 1958; joined *Cumann na mBan*; joined PIRA, 1975; PIRA prisoner, 1975–1977, 1981–1982; left Provisional movement, late 1990s; founder member of Saoradh, 2016.

Séanna Walsh: Born Belfast, 1956; PIRA prisoner, 1973–1976, 1976–1984, 1988–1998; Sinn Féin councillor, Belfast City Council, 2016–present.

Appendix III

A Note on the Photographs

I am extremely grateful to the photographers who agreed for their work to be reproduced in this book: Peter Denton, Bobbie Hanvey, Kaveh Kazemi, Rory Nugent, and Dr Jeff Sluka. I am additionally thankful to the Burns Library at Boston College for their permission to reproduce work from the monumental Bobbie Hanvey Archive.

Of course, each tremendously evocative photograph has its own, often fascinating, story: this Appendix sketches some of these contextual scenes. In doing so, it exhorts readers to follow some of the links that emerge from this select body of work.

As a television journalist and researcher, **Peter Denton** worked closely with acclaimed documentary-maker Peter Taylor on the Northern Ireland conflict. This photograph dates from Peter's work on the current affairs programme *This Week* in 1974. With Peter Taylor, he was preparing a documentary for Thames TV marking the first five years of 'the Troubles' in Northern Ireland. Securing the contribution of the most wanted man in Britain and Ireland, PIRA Chief of Staff Dáithí Ó Conaill, was a considerable achievement.

Peter Denton is on the right of the frame, opposite Dáithí Ó Conaill. The image captures Ó Conaill during a break in filming in a safe house at an unknown location outside Dublin. As Peter remembers: 'Someone in the TV crew had a stills camera, and Ó Conaill didn't object. For me, this was a defining journalistic moment: I'd been assiduously working towards this interview for months, without any sure indication that I would get anywhere near this moment.' Now retired, Peter is an accomplished amateur photographer, who shares his wide-ranging work through Flickr: www.flickr.com/people/peterdenton/

Born in Brookeborough, County Fermanagh in 1945, **Bobbie Hanvey** is an award-winning photographer and radio broadcaster. In an acclaimed career, Bobbie won Northern Ireland Provincial Press Photographer of the Year three times in the 1980s. In 1985 and 1986, Bobbie won Northern Ireland's award for Best People Picture. His first photographic book, *Merely players* (Colourpoint Books, 1999) comprised portraits of Northern Ireland's politicians and personalities since the 1970s. Bobbie's *The last days of the RUC* (Local Press, 2005) traced the transformation of policing in Northern Ireland.

Bobbie's photographs here are among approximately 19,000 negatives digitised by Boston College. The J. J. Burns Library holds 80,000 of Bobbie's negatives and happily many of these images are being digitised and can be accessed online: bc-primo.hosted.exlibrisgroup.com/primo-explore/ collectionDiscovery?vid=bclib_new&collectionId=81517036850001021

Reconstructions: the Troubles in photographs and words (Merrion, 2018) is a celebrated collaboration between Bobbie and his son, the artist and musician Steafán Hanvey, combining Bobbie's photography with Steafán's poetry.

Born in Iran in 1952, **Kaveh Kazemi**'s wide-ranging career as a photojournalist has taken him to the former Yugoslavia several years before its breakup, Lebanon, Nicaragua, Cuba, Syria, Cyprus, and far beyond. Kaveh's work has featured in many prominent outlets, including *Time*, *Newsweek*, *The New York Times*, *Geo*, and *Der Spiegel*. Kaveh's photography from the Iran–Iraq War and the first Gulf War has been the subject of particular acclaim. His celebrated *Revolutionaries: the first decade* (Nazar Publishing, 2017) documents his native Iran ten years after the revolution.

In 1985, Kaveh chose Northern Ireland for his first self-commissioned assignment. His photograph of three republicans in Sinn Féin's Belfast office dates from his first visit to Ireland. In November of that year, while photographing loyalist protests against the Anglo-Irish Agreement, Kaveh approached republicans to ask permission to visit a PIRA training camp. Some nine months later, republicans granted Kaveh's request and amid tight security he was escorted, masked and hooded, to an unknown location in County Donegal, where he photographed trainee volunteers.

Kaveh's extraordinary photographs from his visits to Northern Ireland in the mid-1980s form his major recent book *My days in troubled Ireland* (Nazar Publishing, 2019). Kaveh dedicated this work 'to the people of Ireland for their warm hospitality and generosity of spirit during some of the hardest days in their history'. Further information about Kaveh's work can be found at www.kavehkazemi.com

New York-born **Rory Nugent** was on the staff of American music magazine *Spin* when he travelled to Ireland in December 1993 to write a feature on the PIRA. A writer, photojournalist, and explorer, Rory spent four months in Ireland, during which time he interviewed many republicans. Rory's portrait presents a PIRA volunteer preparing for an operation near the border in south Armagh. Rory's photograph of the Bloody Sunday march in Derry in 1994 depicted 'a crowd of thousands that represented just about every socio-economic and age bracket of Northern Ireland'.

Rory's feature article 'Inside the IRA' – published in *Spin* in August 1994 – was a remarkable insight into the republican movement on the eve of the PIRA ceasefire. Rory reflects on the questions that underpinned his unique experiences: 'First, what goes through the volunteers' heads from the time they kiss the kids goodnight and a few minutes later start handling an Armalite and focusing on the op ahead? Second, if the IRA was, as the leadership told me, ready to push the pause button and suspend ops, ready to declare a ceasefire and willing to prioritize the ballot over the bullet, could they actually deliver the goods? Was the army as a whole, as well as individual volunteers, strong enough to deconstruct both the myth and reality that they had spent a lifetime writing, producing and enacting and take up a rather banal routine of being an out of work parent like their friends? For many, their skill set involved aspects of guerrilla warfare and little else.'

Rory later undertook an assignment in Iran and Iraq during 2001 and 2002. He remains a full-time writer, and his most recent book, *Down at the docks*, was published by Pantheon in 2009.

A political anthropologist, Dr **Jeff Sluka** took his PhD from the University of California, Berkeley, and spent the 1981/1982 academic year living in west Belfast's republican communities. His experiences and observations formed the basis of Jeff's detailed ethnographic study *Hearts and minds, water and fish: support for the IRA and INLA in a Northern Irish ghetto* (JAI Press, 1989). A world-leading expert on the cultural dimensions of political violence and ethnonationalist conflicts, he is now Professor of Social Anthropology at Massey University, New Zealand.

Bibliography

Interviews by the author

Albert Allen – Belfast, 13 December 2017
Mickey Brady – Newry, 15 September 2015
Don Browne – Derry, 12 December 2017
Charlie Casey – Newry, 15 September 2015
Gerry Foster – Belfast, 13 August 2015
Fra Halligan – Belfast, 15 September 2015
Kevin Hannaway – Belfast, 6 December 2017
Peadar Lagan – Bellaghy, 11 December 2017
Eamonn MacDermott – Derry, 17 September 2015
Gerry MacLochlainn – Derry, 12 December 2017
Patrick Magee – Belfast, 13 August 2015
Raymond McCartney – Derry, 18 September 2015
Francie McGuigan – Belfast, 6 December 2017
Seamus McHenry – Belfast, 7 December 2017
Tommy McKearney – Armagh, 15 September 2015; Moy, 8 December 2017
Danny Morrison – Belfast, 11 August 2015
Conor Murphy – Newry, 16 September 2015
Nuala Perry – Belfast, 30 March 2016 and 13 December 2017
Séanna Walsh – Belfast, 12 August 2015
Former Official republican internee: Belfast, 31 March 2016
Former Armagh republican prisoner: County Armagh, 2017
Former Provisional republican internee: Belfast, December 2017
Former Provisional republican internee: Belfast, December 2017
Former Provisional republican activist: Lurgan, March 2016
Former Provisional republican activist: County Donegal, April 2017

Group interview A: Newry, 15 September 2015
Group interview B: Belfast, 6 December 2017

Printed primary sources

Newspapers
An Phoblacht
An Phoblacht/Republican News
Andersonstown News
The Anglo-Celt
Belfast News Letter
Belfast Telegraph
The Cork Examiner
Daily Mail
The Daily Telegraph
Derry Journal
Derry People & Donegal News
Donegal Democrat
Drogheda Argus and Leinster Journal
Drogheda Independent
Dundalk Democrat
Evening Herald
Fermanagh Herald
The Guardian
Impartial Reporter
The Independent
The Independent on Sunday
Irish Examiner
Irish Independent
The Irish News
The Irish Press
The Irish Times
Leinster Express
Leitrim Observer
Lurgan Mail
Mid-Ulster Mail
The Munster Express
The New York Times
Newry Reporter
the next step: Revolutionary Communist Party Weekly
The Observer
Offaly Independent
Palatinate
Republican Bulletin: Iris Na Poblachta
Republican News
Saoirse: Irish Freedom

The Sligo Champion
The Starry Plough/An Camchéachta
The Starry Plough: Derry's Own Republican Newspaper
Strabane Chronicle
Sunday Independent
Sunday Tribune
The Times
Tyrone Constitution
Tyrone Courier
Ulster Herald
Unfree Citizen: Newspaper of the People's Democracy
United Irishman
Western People
Workers Press: Weekly Paper of the Workers Revolutionary Party

Periodicals
Eileen Hickey Irish Republican History Museum, Belfast
An Guth
Iris: The Republican Magazine
The Irish People/An Choismhuintir
Irish Prisoners of War
Lagan Valley Bulletin
Saoirse: Newspaper of the Irish Republican Socialist Party

Northern Ireland Political Collection, Linen Hall Library, Belfast
Ainriail: A Belfast Anarchist Bi-Monthly
An Eochair: A Bulletin of the Irish Republican Movement, Long Kesh
An Reabhloid: Journal of Peoples Democracy
An Troid: The Turf's Own Republican Newssheet
Anarchy
Ballymurphy News
Barricade Bulletin
Beansaor/Free Woman: Journal of Women Against Imperialism
The Captive Voice/An Glór Gafa
Concerned: Official Organ of the Fermanagh Civil Disobedience Committee
Congress '86
The Fermanagh Nationalist
Fortnight
Fourthwrite: The Journal of the Irish Republican Writers Group
Gralton
Hibernia
International Socialism
Iris Bheag

Irish Freedom: Bulletin of the Irish Freedom Movement
Magill
Marxism Today
Na Madraí: The Newssheet of the Seamus Burns/Charlie Hughes Sinn Féin Cumann
New Left Review
New Statesman
The Northern Star
Patriot Bulletin
P.D. Voice: The Newspaper of People's Democracy
The Plough
The Plough: South Down/South Armagh's Own Republican Paper
Rebel
Riverstown News
Socialist Republic: Paper of People's Democracy
Socialist Republican: Quarterly Publication of the Socialist Republican Collective
Socialist Worker Review
South Armagh Scéal
Sovereign Nation
Spare Rib
The Times Literary Supplement
Trouble & Strife
A Woman's Voice
Women in Struggle/Mna I Streachilt

Ex-Prisoners' Outreach Programme, Derry
Volunteer: North West Republican

Irish Left Archive <clririshleftarchive.org>
The Blanket: A Journal of Protest and Dissent
The Furrow
LookLeft
WeeklyWorker

Working Class Movement Library, Salford
Living Marxism

Pamphlets
Northern Ireland Political Collection, Linen Hall Library, Belfast
Irish Republican Socialist Party Boxes 1–4
Provisional Sinn Féin Boxes 1–21

P1001: PD, *Prisoners of Partition: H-Block/Armagh* (Belfast: PD, 1980)

P1008: PD, *H-Block Struggle: Irish Revolution on the March* (Belfast: PD, 1980)

P1012: Michael Farrell, *The Battle for Algeria* (Belfast: PD, 1973)

P1016: Joe Quigley, *Common Market, Common Enemy* (Belfast: PD, 1971)

P10175: Sinn Féin, *Presidential Address of Ruairí Ó Brádaigh to 79th Ard-Fheis* (Dublin: Sinn Féin, 1983)

P1026: CCDC, *Northern Ireland: The Black Paper – The Story of the Police* (Belfast: CCDC, 1973)

P10294: RSF, *Éire Nua: A New Democracy* (Dublin: RSF, 2000)

P1052: NICRA, *Proposals for Peace: Democracy and Community Reconciliation* (Belfast: NICRA, 1973)

P10559: Colombia Broadcasting System, *The Informer: An Interview with Sean O'Callaghan for* 60 Minutes (1997)

P10564: *An Interview with Martin McGuinness* (Derry: publisher unknown, 1991)

P1060: Robert Heatley, *Direct Rule: Civil Rights NOT Civil War* (Belfast: NICRA, 1972)

P10631: Jim McVeigh, *Republican Roll of Honour and Statement on the Day the Last Prisoners Were Released, 28th July 2000* (2000)

P1071: North Derry Civil Rights Association, *Northern Ireland: There is Only One Way!* (Belfast: North Derry Civil Rights Association, 1971)

P1073: NICRA, *True Facts: Martial Law Declared* (Belfast: NICRA, 1972)

P1074: NICRA, *Massacre at Derry* (New York: National Association for Irish Freedom, 1972)

P11112: Greater Clonard Ex-Prisoners' Association, *Clonard Martyrs Memorial Garden: In Memory of Our Dead* (Belfast: Greater Clonard Ex-Prisoners' Association, 2001)

P11325: Short Strand 1980–1981 Committee, *Prison Letters on the 1981 Hunger Strike* (Belfast: Short Strand 1980–1981 Committee, 2001)

P11477: Loughgall Truth and Justice Campaign, *The Unequal Victims* (Newtownabbey: Island Publications, 2001)

P11677: Sinn Féin, *The Hillsborough Deal: Stepping Stone or Mill-Stone?* (Dublin: Sinn Féin Publicity Department, 1985)

P12164: Community of the Peace People, *Assembly of the Peace People, October 6th–8th 1978* (Belfast: Community of the Peace People, 1978)

P13096: IRSP, *Memories of 1981: The Story of the 1981 Hungerstrike as Told by Relatives, Friends and Comrades of the Prisoners* (Derry: Celebration of Resistance 1981–2001, 2001)

P1331: Father Desmond Wilson & Father Joe McVeigh, *British Occupation in the North of Ireland: Two Priests Speak Out!* (Belfast: Published by the authors, 1982)

P1337: Republican Clubs, *Torture: The Case of the Beechmount Three* (Belfast: Belfast Executive of the Republican Clubs, 1976)

P1341: OSF, *Ard Fheis Report 1973* (Dublin: OSF, 1973)

P1346: *Inside the IRA: Interviews with Cathal Goulding* (Philadelphia, Pennsylvania: Recon Publications, Volume 3, Number 1, January 1975)

P1348: Tomás Mac Giolla, *The Making of the Irish Revolution: A Short Analysis* (Dublin: OSF, 1975)

P13526: *Freedom Struggle by the Provisional IRA* (Dublin: Irish Republican Publicity Bureau, 1973)

P1355: Ruairí Ó Brádaigh, *Our People, Our Future: What Éire Nua Means* (Dublin: Sinn Féin, 1973)

P1418: OSF, *The I.R.A. Speaks* (Dublin: OSF, 1973)

P1420: OSF, *Why Sinn Féin Says No to the Common Market* (Dublin: OSF, 1971)

P1461: McKelvey Republican Club, *Freedom manifesto for the seventies* (n.d. [1970])

P1476: Irene Brennan, *Northern Ireland: A Programme for Action* (London: Communist Party of Great Britain, 1975)

P1480: Tomás Mac Giolla, *Where We Stand: The Republican Position* (Belfast: OSF, 1972)

P1508A: Communist Party of Ireland, *Unite – Defeat Unionism!* (Belfast: Communist Party of Ireland, 1970)

P1573: Mervyn Dane, *The Fermanagh 'B' Specials* (Enniskillen: W. Trimble Ltd, 1970)

P1588: Gerry Foley, *Ireland in Rebellion: Including Interviews with Cathal Goulding, Chief of Staff, Irish Republican Army, and Tomás Mac Giolla, President, Sinn Féin* (New York: Pathfinder Press, 1971)

P16288: *Why We Ended the Hunger-Strike: The Full Text of the H-Block Blanket Men's Statement Announcing the End of the Hunger-strike* (Belfast: Sinn Féin, 1981)

P1638: Irish Communist Organisation, *Why a Workers Defence Force is Needed* (Belfast: Irish Communist Organisation, 1969)

P16410: Fionnbarra O'Dochartaigh, *A Woman's Place? Pairtí Poblachtacht Soisalach na hÉireann, Doire colmcille Discussion Document* (Derry: IRSP, 1984)

P16456: IRSP, *A Fighting Voice for Socialism: Ten Years of the IRSP* (Belfast: IRSP, 1984)

P1656A: Sinn Féin, *Ard Fheis '85: Clár agus Rúin* (Dublin: Sinn Féin, 1985)

P1716A: Irish Independence Party, *Irish Dialogue: The First Step* (Belfast: Irish Independence Party, 1977)

P1722: Wolfe Tone Society, *Gerry Adams Presidential Address* (London: Wolfe Tone Society Publications, 1985)

P17590: *Women Speak Out: British Counterinsurgency, Armed Struggle and the Mass Movement – Interview with Bernadette Devlin McAliskey and Martha McClelland* (Washington, DC: Counterspy, 1983)

P179: Sinn Féin, *The Informers: A Sinn Féin Publication* (Dublin: Sinn Féin, 1983)

P1798: Sinn Féin Publicity Department, *Do Not Extradite the H-Block Escapees* (Belfast: Sinn Féin, 1986)

P2009: Sinn Féin Education Department, *Election Interventions – Historical & Contemporary* (Dublin: Sinn Féin, 1983)

P2010: *Ballot and Bullet: Interview with Danny Morrison, Sinn Féin Director of Publicity* (Publisher unknown, 1983)

P2028: Brighton Troops Out Movement, *Sinn Fein Speaks in Brighton: Text of a Speech by Daisy Mules, S.F. Trade Union Department* (Brighton: Brighton Troops Out Movement, 1986)

P2043A: *Bodenstown '86: Text of Oration to the Annual Commemoration at the Graveside of Theobald Wolfe Tone* (London: Wolfe Tone Society Publications, 1986)

P2091: Gerry MacLochlainn, *The Irish Republican and Juche Conceptions of National Self-dignity are One and the Same* (London: Mosquito Press, 1985)

P2112: OSF, *Ard-Fheis '72 Report* (Dublin: OSF, 1972)

P2135: Lynda Edgerton & Pat Brown, *Must We Be Divided for Life?* (Belfast: Northern Ireland Women's Rights Movement, 1983)

P2275: *The Politics of Revolution: The Main Speeches and Debates from the 1986 Sinn Fein Ard-Fheis, Including the Presidential Address of Gerry Adams* (Belfast & Dublin: Republican Publications, 1986)

P2303: Sinn Féin, *Ard-Fheis '86: Clár agus Rúin* (Dublin: Sinn Féin, 1986)

P2766: RSF, *Republican Diary 1988: Dialann Poblachtach* (Dublin: RSF, 1987)

P2771: Sinn Féin, *Setting the Criteria: Tackling Discrimination – Sinn Féin's Analysis and Proposals* (Dublin: Sinn Féin, 1987)

P2872: Sinn Féin, *Presidential Address of Ruairí Ó Brádaigh to 76th Ard-Fheis* (Dublin: Sinn Féin, 1980)

P2886: Scopoli, *The Hooded Men and the Science of Torture* (Derry: IRSP, 1978)

P2896: Ta Power, *An Historical Analysis of the I.R.S.P.: Its Past Role, Root Cause of its Problems and Proposals for the Future* (Dublin: IRSP, 1987)

P3080A: *Armed Struggle: The Communist Party's Open Letter to the Provisional IRA and the Complete and Unedited Contributions to the Debate that Appeared in the Party's Press Irish Socialist and Unity* (Dublin: Communist Party of Ireland, 1988)

P3097: Barra Mac Giolla Dhuibh, *Republican Politics: A 'Rural' Six-Counties Perspective* (Omagh: Published by the author, 1988)

P3195: Desmond Wilson & Oliver Kearney, *West Belfast: The Way Forward?* (Belfast: Concerned Community Groups, 1988)

P3196: Desmond Wilson & Oliver Kearney, *West Belfast: Liberation or Oppression?* (Belfast: Published by the authors, 1988)

P3331: Sinn Féin, *Ard Fheis 1989: Clár agus Rúin* (Dublin: Sinn Féin, 1989)

P3396: Sinn Féin, *The Sinn Féin/SDLP Talks, January–September 1988* (Dublin: Sinn Féin Publicity Department, 1989)

P3417: Sinn Féin, *Manifesto: Local Government Election May 1989* (Belfast: Tom Hartley, Sinn Féin Director of Elections, 1989)

P3600: League of Communist Republicans, *From Long Kesh to a Socialist Ireland* (Shannon: League of Communist Republicans, 1988)

P367: PD, *A Woman's Place is on the Barricades* (Belfast: PD, 1984)

P3690: Sinn Féin, *Ard Fheis Political Report 1989–1990* (Dublin: Sinn Féin, 1990)

P3884: Sinn Féin Education Department, *Loyalism: Part 2* (Dublin: Sinn Féin, 1984)

P3885: Sinn Féin, *Republican Education: What We Need to Know to Win* (Dublin: Sinn Féin, 1985)

P3886: Sinn Féin Education Department, *History of Republicanism, Part 1* (Dublin: Sinn Féin, 1981)

P3887: Sinn Féin Education Department, *Economic Resistance* (Dublin: Sinn Féin, 1984)

P3888: Sinn Féin Education Department, *Women in Ireland* (Dublin: Sinn Féin, 1984)

P397: Sinn Féin Education Department: *Social Agitation* (Dublin: Sinn Féin, 1984)

P4037: Bogside Community Association, *Report of Policing Committee* (Derry: Bogside Community Association, 1975)

P4181: Sinn Féin, *Ard Fheis 1990* (Dublin: Sinn Féin, 1990)

P4203: CCDC, *Stop! Stop! Stop!* (Belfast: CCDC, 1970)

P447A: British and Irish Communist Organisation, *Imperialism* (Belfast: British and Irish Communist Organisation, 1975)

P4475: Father Joe McVeigh, *Tackling the Root Causes: The Only Way to Peace* (Omagh: Community for Justice, 1991)

P4616: Sinn Féin, *Political Report 86ú Ard Fheis 1990–1991* (Dublin: Sinn Féin, 1991)

P4634: Sinn Féin, *Ard Fheis 1991: Speeches* (Dublin: Sinn Féin, 1991)

P4640: SDLP, *Election Special: Let's Do It Again* (Newry: Frank Feely, 1987)

P4641: Sinn Féin, *Ard Fheis 1979: Clár agus Rúin* (Dublin: Sinn Féin, 1979)

P4643: Sinn Féin, *Ard Fheis 1976: Clár agus Rúin* (Dublin: Sinn Féin, 1976)

P4805: C. Desmond Greaves, *Civil Rights in Northern Ireland: Opening Speech by the Conference Chairman, C. Desmond Greaves* (London: National Consultative Conference, 1969)

P5071: Movement for a Socialist Republic, *The Autonomy of the Women's Movement* (Dublin: Movement for a Socialist Republic, 1977)

P5080: Father Joe McVeigh, *Thoughts on the Liberation of Ireland* (Monaghan: Borderline Press, 1978)

P5183: Sinn Féin Foreign Affairs Bureau, *Republican Prisoners and the Prison Struggle in Ireland* (Belfast: Sinn Féin Foreign Affairs Bureau, 1991)

P5219: *Fianna Éireann Handbook/Lámhleabhar Fianna Éireann* (Dublin: Fianna Éireann, 1988)

P5630: Clergy for Justice, *What is Britain's Role in Ireland?* (Dublin: Clergy for Justice, 1993)

P5681: Sinn Féin, *Ard Fheis 1994* (Dublin: Sinn Féin, 1994)

P5935: *Freedom Only Comes if You Take It! A Speech by Bernadette Devlin McAliskey* (New York: H-Block/Armagh Committee, 1981)

P5966: *His Name was Joe MacManus: A Sligo Tribute* (Sligo: publisher unknown, date unknown [1993?])

P6015: National Graves Association, *Belfast Graves* (Dublin: National Graves Association, 1994)

P6121: *Presidential Address of Ruairí Ó Brádaigh to the 84th Ard-Fheis* (Dublin: RSF, 1988)

P6125: RSF, *Ard Fheis 1990: Clár agus Rúin* (Dublin: RSF, 1990)

P6126: *Presidential Address of Ruairí Ó Brádaigh to the 86th Ard-Fheis of Sinn Féin in the Spa Hotel, Lucan, County Dublin, 27–28 October 1990* (Dublin: RSF, 1990)

P6192: *The Church and the Irish Struggle: A Discussion with Gary Mac Eoin, Bernadette McAliskey and Des Wilson* (Belfast: Joe McVeigh, 1994)

P6409: Sinn Féin Education Department, *Republican Ideology* (Belfast: Sinn Féin, 1990)

P6534: *Communication to NICRA Members from Bríd Rodgers, John Donaghy, and Conn McCluskey* (Published by the authors, 1970)

P6570: PD, *Women in Struggle* (Dublin: PD, 1987)

P7004: *I Owe My Allegiance Only to the Working Class: Selected Writings and Speeches of Seamus Costello* (San Francisco: Irish Republican Socialist Committees of North America, 1995)

P769: John Darby, *Intimidation in Housing* (Belfast: Northern Ireland Community Relations Commission, 1974)

P7890: Sinn Féin Women's Department, *Towards a Lasting Peace: Sinn Féin Women's Manifesto* (Belfast: Sinn Féin Women's Department, 1992)

P7992: Community of the Peace People, *The H Block: The Hunger Strike in the Maze Prison* (Belfast: Community of the Peace People, 1980)

P808: Communist Party of Ireland, *For Unity and Socialism: Manifesto of the Communist Party of Ireland* (Dublin: Communist Party of Ireland, 1970)

P8117: Sinn Féin, *Éire Nua: The Social and Economic Programme of Sinn Féin* (Dublin: Sinn Féin, 1974)

P8279: Derry Citizens Defence Association, *Meeting of Derry Citizens Defence Association: Celtic Park, 10 August 1969* (Derry: Publisher unknown, 1969)

P8307: Sinn Féin, *Speech by Martin McGuinness on London–Dublin Talks: Sinn Féin Ard Fheis 1985* (Dublin: Sinn Féin, 1985)

P872: *Battle of Bogside* (Derry: Bogside Republican Appeal Fund, 1969)

P881B: *Notes for Revolutionaries* (Belfast: Republican Publications, 1983)

P8852: Community of the Peace People, *The H-Block Protest: Hunger Strikes and Emergency Laws* (Belfast: Community of the Peace People, 1981)

P938: Sinn Féin Education Department, *Nationalism and Socialism* (Dublin: Sinn Féin, 1981)

P941: Sinn Féin, *Ard Fheis 1980: Clár agus Rúin* (Dublin: Sinn Féin, 1980)

P942: Sinn Féin, *Ard Fheis 1978: Clár agus Rúin* (Dublin: Sinn Féin, 1978)

P943: Sinn Féin, *Ard Fheis 1977: Clár agus Rúin* (Dublin: Sinn Féin, 1977)

P949: Republican Press Centre, *Readings from Fintan Lalor* (Belfast: Republican Press Centre, 1975)

P952: Sinn Féin, *Mining and energy: the Sinn Féin policy* (Dublin: Elo Press, 1974)

P957: Sinn Féin Education Department, *The Split* (Dublin: Sinn Féin, 1979)

P958: Sinn Féin Education Department, *Where Sinn Féin Stands* (Dublin: Sinn Féin, 1979)

P959: Sinn Féin Education Department, *Loyalism: Part 1* (Dublin: Sinn Féin, 1984)

P9601: Martina Anderson, *25th Anniversary Ethel Lynch Inaugural Memorial Lecture* (Publisher unknown, 1999)

P961: Clonard Housing Association, *Clonard: Death of a Community* (Belfast: Clonard Housing Association, 1976)

P982: Sinn Féin, *Towards a Policy on Culture/Dréacht pholasaí ar chultúr* (Dublin: Sinn Féin, 1981)

P985: Sinn Féin, *Éire Nua: The Social, Economic and Political Dimensions* (Dublin: Sinn Féin, 1979)

P998: PD, *Internment '71, H-Block '81: The Same Struggle* (Belfast: PD, 1981)

PA0142A and PA0142B: Gerry Adams letter from Long Kesh to *Irish News* in response to 'Protestant Socialist' letter (1977)

PA0144: H6 resolutions for the Sinn Féin Ard-Fheis, 8 October 1981 (1981)

PA0147: H-block prison comm from PRO for the 1983 hunger strike commemoration (1983)

PH2922: Father Denis Faul, *Women in Jail in Northern Ireland* (Published by the author, 1978)

PH2927: Father Piaras Ó Dúill, *Hunger Strike: The Children of '69* (Published by the author, 1981)

PPO0306: Sinn Féin Belfast Executive, *Éire Nua* (Belfast: Sinn Féin, 1979)

PPO0483: People's Democracy, *Fight! Don't Vote!* (Belfast: PD, 1974)

PPO0492: NICRA, *A Bill of Rights Now* (Belfast: NICRA, 1975)

PPO1241: *Release Joe Cahill* (Belfast: Sinn Féin, 1973)

PPO2223: *Support the Struggle for Liberation in South Africa and Namibia* (Belfast: Northern Ireland Women's Rights Movement, 1986)

Oversize P8377: Denis Donaldson, *Éire Nua and the Peoples' Councils* (1977)

Oversize P8801: Sinn Féin, *Sinn Féin Explained* (Belfast: Sinn Féin, 1979)

Tom Hartley Collection PH1545: Relatives Action Committee, *An information Sheet from the Relatives Action Committee of South Derry and East Antrim* (1978)

Tom Hartley Collection PH1571: Sinn Féin Education Department, *New Members Course: Notes for Sinn Féin Education Officers* (Belfast: Sinn Féin, 1981)

Tom Hartley Collection PH1640: Sinn Féin Department of Women's Affairs, *Abortion Ireland* (Dublin: Sinn Féin Department of Women's Affairs, 1981)

Tom Hartley Collection PH1687: *Hunger Strike in H-Block, Long Kesh, 1981* (1986)

Tom Hartley Collection PH2168: Two Traditions Group, *Northern Ireland and the Two Traditions in Ireland* (Belfast: Two Traditions Group, 1984)

Tom Hartley Collection PH2284: Wolfe Tone Society, *The 1981 Hunger Strikes: Biographical Sketches* (London: Wolfe Tone Society, 1982)

Tom Hartley Collection PH441: Sinn Féin Education Department, *History of Republicanism, Part 2* (Dublin: Sinn Féin, 1981)

Tom Hartley Collection PH504: Sinn Féin, *Ard Fheis 1982: Clár agus Rúin* (Dublin: Sinn Féin, 1982)

Official reports

Northern Ireland Political Collection, Linen Hall Library, Belfast

P175: *Principal Conclusions and Overall Assessment of the Bloody Sunday Inquiry* (London: Stationery Office, 2010)

P205: *Disturbances in Northern Ireland: Report of the Commission under the Chairmanship of Lord Cameron Appointed by the Governor of Northern Ireland* (Belfast: HMSO, 1969)

P377: New Ireland Forum, *The Cost of Violence Arising from the Northern Ireland Crisis Since 1969* (Dublin: The Stationery Office, 1983)

P577: *Violence and Civil Disturbances in Northern Ireland in 1969: Report of Tribunal of Inquiry* (Belfast: HMSO, 1972)

Other

Irish Left Archive <clririshleftarchive.org>

James Gallagher, *Our Orientation to the Republican Movement* (10 November 1984)

PRO Republican POWs, Portlaoise Prison, *Volunteer Jim Lynagh Lecture 1994: Peace strategy debated in Portlaoise*

Ó Fiaich Library and Archive, Armagh

NP2/5: Gerry Adams, 'Open letter to Cahal Daly, Bishop of Down & Connor' (1 February 1985)

NP5/24: Letter from John McComb, Frankland Prison (14 May 1990)

Secondary sources

Books

Gerry Adams, *Cage eleven* (Dingle: Brandon, 1990)

Gerry Adams, *Selected writings* (Dingle: Brandon, 1997)

Yonah Alexander & Alan O'Day (eds.), *Ireland's terrorist trauma: interdisciplinary perspectives* (Hemel Hempstead: Harvester Wheatsheaf, 1989)

Yonah Alexander & Alan O'Day (eds.), *Terrorism in Ireland* (London: Croom Helm, 1983)

Rogelio Alonso, *The IRA and armed struggle* (Abingdon: Routledge, 2007)

James Anderson & James Goodman (eds.), *Dis/agreeing Ireland: contexts, obstacles, hopes* (London: Pluto Press, 1998)

Terry H. Anderson, *The movement and the sixties: protest in America from Greensboro to Wounded Knee* (New York: Oxford University Press, 1995)

Molly Andrews, *Lifetimes of commitment: aging, politics, psychology* (Cambridge: Cambridge University Press, 1991)

Begoña Aretxaga, *Shattering silence: women, nationalism and political subjectivity in Northern Ireland* (Princeton, New Jersey: Princeton University Press, 1997)

Paul Arthur, *The People's Democracy, 1968–1973* (Belfast: Blackstaff, 1974)

Attack International, *The spirit of freedom: the war in Ireland* (London: Attack International, 1989)

Arthur Aughey & Duncan Morrow (eds.), *Northern Ireland politics* (Harlow: Longman, 1996)

Joost Augusteijn (ed.), *The Irish revolution, 1913–23* (Basingstoke: Palgrave Macmillan, 2002)

Thomas Bartlett, *Ireland: a history* (Cambridge: Cambridge University Press, 2011)

Jenny Beale, *Women in Ireland: voices of change* (Basingstoke: Macmillan, 1986)

Kevin Bean, *The new politics of Sinn Féin* (Liverpool: Liverpool University Press, 2007)

Kevin Bean & Mark Hayes, *Republican voices* (Monaghan: Seesyu Press, 2001)

Sally Belfrage, *Living with war: a Belfast year* (New York: Viking, 1987)

Geoffrey Bell, *The British in Ireland: a suitable case for withdrawal* (London: Pluto Press, 1984)

J. Bowyer Bell, *The secret army: the IRA, 1916–1979* (Dublin: Poolbeg, 1989)

Walter Benjamin, *Illuminations: essays and reflections* (New York: Schocken Books, 1977)

David Beresford, *Ten men dead: the story of the 1981 Irish hunger strike* (London: HarperCollins, 1994) [First edition London: Grafton, 1987]

P. Berresford Ellis, *A history of the Irish working class* (London: Victor Gollancz, 1972)

Paul Bew, Peter Gibbon, & Henry Patterson, *Northern Ireland, 1921–1996: political forces and social classes* (London: Serif, 1996)

Paul Bew & Henry Patterson, *The British state and the Ulster crisis: from Wilson to Thatcher* (London: Verso, 1985)

Patrick Bishop & Eamonn Mallie, *The Provisional IRA* (London: Heinemann, 1987)

Lorenzo Bosi & Gianluca de Fazio (eds.), *The troubles in Northern Ireland and theories of social movements* (Amsterdam: Amsterdam University Press, 2017)

J. Bowyer Bell, *The IRA, 1968–2000: analysis of a secret army* (London: Frank Cass, 2000)

Gerry Bradley & Brian Feeney, *Insider: Gerry Bradley's life in the IRA* (Dublin: O'Brien Press, 2009)

Evelyn Brady, Eva Patterson, Kate McKinney, Rosie Hammill, & Pauline Jackson, *In the footsteps of Anne: stories of republican women ex-prisoners* (Belfast: Shanway Press, 2011)

Tim Brannigan, *Where are you really from? Kola Kubes and gelignite, secrets and lies – the true story of an extraordinary family* (Newtownards: Colourpoint Creative, 2010)

Steve Bruce, *Religion in modern Britain* (Oxford: Oxford University Press, 1995)

Dominick Bruno & Matthew Costello (eds.), *Éire Nua: a new beginning* (Belfast: Cumann Na Saoirse Náisiúnta, 2012)

Thomas Paul Burgess (ed.), *The contested identities of Ulster Catholics* (London: Palgrave Macmillan, 2018)

Edward Burke, *An army of tribes: British Army cohesion, deviancy and murder in Northern Ireland* (Liverpool: Liverpool University Press, 2018)

Frank Burton, *The politics of legitimacy: struggles in a Belfast community* (London: Routledge & Kegan Paul, 1978)

Sarah Buscher & Bettina Ling, *Máiread Corrigan and Betty Williams: making peace in Northern Ireland* (New York: The Feminist Press, 1999)

Anne Cadwallader, *Lethal allies: British collusion in Ireland* (Cork: Mercier, 2013)

John Callaghan, *The far left in British politics* (Oxford: Basil Blackwell, 1987)

Brian Campbell, Laurence McKeown, & Felim O'Hagan (eds.), *Nor meekly serve my time: the H-block struggle, 1976–1981* (Belfast: Beyond the Pale Publications, 1994)

Sarah Campbell, *Gerry Fitt and the SDLP: 'In a minority of one'* (Manchester: Manchester University Press, 2015)

Kenneth Christie, *Political protest in Northern Ireland: continuity and change* (Reading: Link Press, 1992)

Liam Clarke, *Broadening the battlefield: the H-blocks and the rise of Sinn Féin* (Dublin: Gill & Macmillan, 1987)

Liam Clarke & Kathryn Johnston, *Martin McGuinness: from guns to government* (Edinburgh: Mainstream, 2001)

John Conroy, *War as a way of life: a Belfast diary* (London: Heinemann, 1987)

Kieran Conway, *Southside Provisional: from freedom fighter to the Four Courts* (Blackrock: Orpen Press, 2014)

Tim Pat Coogan, *1916: the mornings after* (London: Head of Zeus, 2015)

Tim Pat Coogan, *The H-block story* (Dublin: Ward River Press, 1980)

Tim Pat Coogan, *The IRA* (London: Fontana, 1980) [First edition London: Pall Mall Press, 1970]

Tim Pat Coogan, *The troubles: Ireland's ordeal 1966–1995 and the search for peace* (London: Hutchinson, 1995)

Mary S. Corcoran, *Out of order: the political imprisonment of women in Northern Ireland, 1972–1998* (Cullompton: Willan Publishing, 2006)

Ingo Cornils & Sarah Waters (eds.), *Memories of 1968: international perspectives* (Oxford: Peter Lang, 2010)

Joe Craig, John McAnulty, & Paul Flannigan, *The real Irish peace process* (Belfast: Socialist Democracy, 1998)

Austin Currie, *All hell will break loose* (Dublin: O'Brien Press, 2004)

P. M. Currie & Max Taylor (eds.), *Dissident Irish republicanism* (New York: Continuum, 2011)

Jennifer Curtis, *Human rights as war by other means: peace politics in Northern Ireland* (Philadelphia, Pennsylvania: University of Pennsylvania Press, 2017)

John Darby, *Intimidation and the control of conflict in Northern Ireland* (Dublin: Gill & Macmillan, 1986)

Margaretta D'Arcy, *Tell them everything* (London: Pluto Press, 1981)

Síle Darragh, *'John Lennon's dead': stories of protest, hunger strikes and resistance* (Belfast: Beyond the Pale Publications, 2011)

Nicholas Davies, *Dead men talking: collusion, cover-up and murder in Northern Ireland's Dirty War* (Edinburgh: Mainstream, 2004)

Graham Dawson, *Soldier heroes: British adventure, empire and the imagining of masculinities* (London: Psychology Press, 1994)

Graham Dawson, Jo Dover, & Stephen Hopkins (eds.), *The Northern Ireland troubles in Britain: impacts, engagements, legacies and memories* (Manchester: Manchester University Press, 2017)

Ciarán de Baroid, *Ballymurphy and the Irish war* (London: Pluto Press, 1990)

Bernadette Devlin, *The price of my soul* (London: Pan Books, 1969)

Mario Diani & Ron Eyerman (eds.), *Studying collective action* (London: Sage, 1992)

Martin Dillon, *God and the gun: the church and Irish terrorism* (London: Orion, 1997)

Paul Dixon & Eamonn O'Kane, *Northern Ireland since 1969* (Abingdon: Routledge, 2014)

Brian Dooley, *Black and green: the fight for civil rights in Northern Ireland and black America* (London: Pluto Press, 1998)

Karen Dubinsky, Catherine Krull, Susan Lord, Sean Mills, & Scott Rutherford (eds.), *New world coming: the sixties and the shaping of global consciousness* (Toronto: Between the Lines, 2009)

Marianne Elliott, *The Catholics of Ulster: a history* (London: Allen Lane – Penguin Press, 2000)

Marianne Elliott, *When God took sides: religion and identity in Ireland – unfinished history* (Oxford: Oxford University Press, 2009)

Richard English, *Armed struggle: the history of the IRA* (London: Pan Books, 2012) [First edition London: Macmillan, 2003]

Richard English, *Does terrorism work? A history* (Oxford: Oxford University Press, 2016)

Richard English, *Irish freedom: the history of nationalism in Ireland* (London: Pan Macmillan, 2006)

Fáilte Cluain Eois, *Their prisons, our stories* (Castleblayney: Fáilte Cluain Eois, 2015)

Eileen Fairweather, Róisín McDonough, & Melanie McFadyean, *Only the rivers run free: Northern Ireland – the women's war* (London: Pluto Press, 1984)

Michael Farrell, *Northern Ireland: the orange state* (London: Pluto Press, 1980)

Michael Farrell (ed.), *Twenty years on* (Dingle: Brandon, 1988)

Seán Farren, *The SDLP: the struggle for agreement in Northern Ireland* (Dublin: Four Courts Press, 2000)

Marie-Therese Fay, Mike Morrissey, & Marie Smyth, *Northern Ireland's troubles: the human costs* (London: Pluto Press, 1999)

John M. Feehan, *Bobby Sands and the tragedy of Northern Ireland* (Cork: Mercier, 1983)

Brian Feeney, *Sinn Féin: a hundred turbulent years* (Madison, Wisconsin: University of Wisconsin Press, 2002)

Diarmaid Ferriter, *The border: the legacy of a century of Anglo-Irish politics* (London: Profile Books, 2019)

Carole Fink, Philipp Gassert, & Detlef Junker (eds.), *1968: the world transformed* (Cambridge: Cambridge University Press, 1998)

Daniel Finn, *One man's terrorist: a political history of the IRA* (London: Verso, 2019)

Martyn Frampton, *The long march: the political strategy of Sinn Féin* (Basingstoke: Palgrave Macmillan, 2008)

Paulo Freire, *Pedagogy of the oppressed* (transl. Myra Bergman Ramos) (Harmondsworth: Penguin Books, 1972)

Philomena Gallagher & Paul McGlinchey, *Truth will out* (n.p.: Philomena Gallagher & Paul McGlinchey, 2017)

Philipp Gassert & Alan E. Steinweis (eds.), *Coping with the Nazi past: West German debates on Nazism and generational conflict, 1955–1975* (New York: Berghahn, 2006)

Carlo Gébler, *The glass curtain: inside an Ulster community* (London: Abacus, 1992) [First edition London: Hamish Hamilton, 1991]

Ian Geldard & Keith Craig, *IRA, INLA: foreign support and international connections* (London: Institute for the Study of Terrorism, 1988)

Tony Gifford, *Supergrasses: the use of accomplice evidence in Northern Ireland* (London: Cobden Trust, 1984)

Robert Gildea, James Mark, & Anette Warring (eds.), *Europe's 1968: voices of revolt* (Oxford: Oxford University Press, 2013)

Raymond Gilmour, *Dead ground: infiltrating the IRA* (London: Little, Brown, 1998)

Antonio Gramsci, *Selections from the prison notebooks of Antonio Gramsci* (ed. and transl. Quentin Hoare and Geoffrey Nowell Smith) (London: Lawrence & Wishart, 1971)

Kenneth Griffith & Timothy E. O'Grady, *Curious journey: an oral history of Ireland's unfinished revolution* (London: Hutchinson, 1982)

Che Guevara, *Guerrilla warfare: a method* (Beijing: Foreign Languages Press, 1964)

Gustavo Gutiérrez, *A theology of liberation: history, politics, and salvation* (London: SCM Press, 1988)

Desmond Hamill, *Pig in the middle: the army in Northern Ireland, 1969–1984* (London: Methuen, 1985)

Carrie Hamilton, *Women and ETA: the gender politics of radical Basque nationalism* (Manchester: Manchester University Press, 2007)

Brian Hanley, *The impact of the troubles on the Republic of Ireland, 1968–1979: boiling volcano?* (Manchester: Manchester University Press, 2018)

Brian Hanley & Scott Millar, *The lost revolution: the story of the Official IRA and the Workers' Party* (Dublin: Penguin Ireland, 2009)

Shaun Harkin (ed.), *The James Connolly reader* (Chicago, Illinois: Haymarket Books, 2018)

Toby Harnden, *'Bandit country': the IRA and south Armagh* (London: Hodder & Stoughton, 1999)

Aidan Hegarty, *Kevin Lynch and the Irish hunger strike* (Belfast: Camlane Press, 2006)

Thomas Hennessey, *The evolution of the troubles, 1970–1972* (Dublin: Irish Academic Press, 2007)

Stephen Hopkins, *The politics of memoir and the Northern Ireland conflict* (Liverpool: Liverpool University Press, 2013)

Human Rights Watch, *Human rights in Northern Ireland* (New York: Human Rights Watch, 1991)

John Hume, *Personal views: politics, peace and reconciliation in Ireland* (Dublin: Town House, 1996)

Martin Ingram & Greg Harkin, *Stakeknife: Britain's secret agents in Ireland* (Dublin: O'Brien Press, 2004)

Irish Freedom Movement, *The Irish war* (London: Junius, 1987) [First edition London: Junius, 1983]

Cynthia L. Irvin, *Militant nationalism: between movement and party in Ireland and the Basque country* (Minneapolis, Minnesota: University of Minnesota Press, 1999)

Alvin Jackson, *Ireland, 1798–1998: war, peace and beyond* (Oxford: Oxford University Press, 2010)

Alvin Jackson (ed.), *The Oxford handbook of Irish history* (Oxford: Oxford University Press, 2014)

Neil Jarman, *Material conflicts: parades and visual displays in Northern Ireland* (Oxford: Berg, 1997)

Kumari Jayawardena, *Feminism and nationalism in the third world* (London: Zed Books, 1986)

Peniel E. Joseph (ed.), *The black power movement: rethinking the civil rights–black power era* (London: Routledge, 2006)

Kevin Kelley, *The longest war: Northern Ireland and the IRA* (London: Zed Press, 1982)

Liam Kennedy, *Out of history: Ireland, that 'most distressful country'* (Belfast: Institute of Irish Studies, 1996)

Caroline Kennedy-Pipe, *The origins of the present troubles in Northern Ireland* (Harlow: Longman, 1997)

Brian Kenny, *Tony Heffernan: from Merrion Square to Merrion Street* (Published by the author, 2013)

Martin Klimke, Jacco Pekelder, & Joachim Scharloth (eds.), *Between Prague Spring and French May: opposition and revolt in Europe, 1960–1980* (New York: Berghahn, 2011)

Martin Klimke & Joachim Scharloth (eds.), *1968 in Europe: a history of protest and activism, 1956–1977* (Basingstoke: Palgrave Macmillan, 2008)

Peter Leary, *Unapproved routes: histories of the Irish border, 1922–1972* (Oxford: Oxford University Press, 2016)

John Lindsay (ed.), *Brits speak out: British soldiers' impressions of the Northern Ireland conflict* (Derry: Guildhall Press, 1998)

Marie-Violaine Louvet, *Civil society, post-colonialism and transnational solidarity: the Irish and the Middle East conflict* (Basingstoke: Palgrave Macmillan, 2016)

F. S. L. Lyons, *Ireland since the famine* (London: Fontana, 1985) [First edition London: Weidenfeld & Nicolson, 1971]

Eileen MacDonald, *Shoot the women first* (London: Fourth Estate, 1991)

Patrick Magee, *Gangsters or guerrillas? Representations of Irish republicans in 'troubles fiction'* (Belfast: Beyond the Pale Publications, 2001)

Agnès Maillot, *New Sinn Féin: Irish republicanism in the twenty-first century* (Abingdon: Routledge, 2004)

Laurence Marley, *Michael Davitt: freelance radical and frondeur* (Dublin: Four Courts Press, 2010)

Laurence Marley (ed.), *The British Labour Party and twentieth-century Ireland: the cause of Ireland, the cause of labour* (Manchester: Manchester University Press, 2016)

Nell McCafferty, *The Armagh women* (Dublin: Co-op Books, 1981)

Nell McCafferty, *Peggy Deery: an Irish family at war* (Dublin: Attic Press, 1988)

Barry McCaffrey, *Alex Maskey: man and mayor* (Belfast: Brehon Press, 2003)

Eamonn McCann, *War and an Irish town* (London: Pluto Press, 1993) [First edition Harmondsworth: Penguin, 1974]

Martin J. McCleery, *Operation Demetrius and its aftermath: a new history of the use of internment without trial in Northern Ireland, 1971–1975* (Manchester: Manchester University Press, 2015)

Conn McCluskey, *Up off their knees: a commentary on the civil rights movement in Northern Ireland* (Dungannon: Conn McCluskey & Associates, 1989)

Henry McDonald, *Gunsmoke and mirrors: how Sinn Féin dressed up defeat as victory* (Dublin: Gill & Macmillan, 2008)

Henry McDonald & Jack Holland, *INLA: deadly divisions* (Dublin: Poolbeg, 2010) [First edition Dublin: Torc Books, 1994]

Fearghal McGarry, *Rebels: voices from the Easter rising* (London: Penguin, 2011)

Martin McGartland, *Dead man running: the true story of a secret agent's escape from the IRA and MI5* (Edinburgh: Mainstream, 1998)

Marisa McGlinchey, *Unfinished business: the politics of 'dissident' Irish republicanism* (Manchester: Manchester University Press, 2019)

Cillian McGrattan, *Memory, politics and identity: haunted by history* (Basingstoke: Palgrave Macmillan, 2013)

Cillian McGrattan, *Northern Ireland, 1968–2008: the politics of entrenchment* (Basingstoke: Palgrave Macmillan, 2010)

John McGuffin, *The guineapigs* (Harmondsworth: Penguin, 1974)

Maria McGuire, *To take arms: a year in the Provisional IRA* (Basingstoke: Macmillan, 1973)

Anthony McIntyre, *Good Friday: the death of Irish republicanism* (New York: Ausubo Press, 2008)

Susan McKay, *Bear in mind these dead* (London: Faber & Faber, 2008)

Tommy McKearney, *The Provisional IRA: from insurrection to parliament* (London: Pluto Press, 2011)

Ciaran McKeown, *The passion of peace* (Belfast: Blackstaff, 1984)

Laurence McKeown, *Out of time: Irish republican prisoners in Long Kesh, 1972–2000* (Belfast: Beyond the Pale Publications, 2001)

David McKittrick & David McVeigh, *Making sense of the troubles* (London: Penguin, 2001)

Thomas Anthony McNulty, *Exiled* (Dublin: TMN Publications, 2013)

Robert Lee Miller, Rick Wilford, & Freda Donoghue, *Women and political participation in Northern Ireland* (Aldershot: Avebury, 1996)

Ed Moloney, *A secret history of the IRA* (London: Penguin, 2002)

Ed Moloney, *Voices from the grave: two men's war in Ireland* (London: Faber & Faber, 2010)

Aldon C. Morris & Carol McClurg Mueller (eds.), *Frontiers in social movement theory* (New Haven, Connecticut: Yale University Press, 1992)

Danny Morrison, *Then the walls came down: a prison journal* (Cork: Mercier, 1999)

Peter Morton, *Emergency tour: 3 Para in south Armagh* (Wellingborough: William Kimber & Co., 1989)

Caroline O. N. Moser & Fiona C. Clark (eds.), *Victims, perpetrators or actors? Gender, armed conflict and political violence* (London: Zed Books, 2001)

David Moss, *The politics of left-wing violence in Italy, 1969–1985* (Basingstoke: Macmillan, 1989)

Chantal Mouffe (ed.), *Gramsci and Marxist theory* (London: Routledge & Kegan Paul, 1979)

George Moyser (ed.), *Politics and religion in the modern world* (London: Routledge, 1991)

Marc Mulholland, *The longest war: Northern Ireland's troubled history* (Oxford: Oxford University Press, 2002)

Patrick Mulroe, *Bombs, bullets and the border: policing Ireland's frontier – Irish security policy, 1969–1978* (Newbridge: Irish Academic Press, 2017)

Gareth Mulvenna, *Tartan gangs and paramilitaries: the loyalist backlash* (Liverpool: Liverpool University Press, 2016)

Gerard Murray, *John Hume and the SDLP: impact and survival in Northern Ireland* (Dublin: Irish Academic Press, 1998)

Gerard Murray & Jonathan Tonge, *Sinn Féin and the SDLP: from alienation to participation* (London: Hurst & Company, 2005)

Raymond Murray, *State violence in Northern Ireland, 1969–1997* (Cork: Mercier, 1998)

Jörg Neuheiser & Stefan Wolff (eds.), *Peace at last? The impact of the Good Friday Agreement on Northern Ireland* (New York: Berghahn, 2002)

Pierre Nora, *Realms of memory: the construction of the French past – volume 1: conflicts and divisions* (New York: Columbia University Press, 1996)

Brendan O'Brien, *The long war: the IRA and Sinn Féin* (Dublin: O'Brien Press, 1999)

Eoin Ó Broin, *Sinn Féin and the politics of left republicanism* (London: Pluto Press, 2009)

Eimear O'Callaghan, *Belfast days: a 1972 teenage diary* (Sallins: Merrion, 2014)

Alan O'Day (ed.), *Terrorism's laboratory: the case of Northern Ireland* (Aldershot: Dartmouth Publishing, 1995)

Niall Ó Dochartaigh, *From civil rights to Armalites: Derry and the birth of the Irish troubles* (Cork: Cork University Press, 1997)

Malachi O'Doherty, *The trouble with guns: republican strategy and the Provisional IRA* (Belfast: Blackstaff, 1998)

Shane O'Doherty, *The volunteer: a former IRA man's true story* (London: Fount, 1993)

Gearóid Ó Faoleán, *A broad church: the Provisional IRA in the Republic of Ireland, 1969–1980* (Newbridge: Irish Academic Press, 2019)

Des O'Hagan, *Letters from Long Kesh* (Dublin: Citizen Press, 2012)

Cornelius O'Leary, Sydney Elliott, & R. A. Wilford, *The Northern Ireland assembly, 1982–1986: a constitutional experiment* (London: C. Hurst & Co., 1988)

Padraig O'Malley, *Biting at the grave: the Irish hunger strikes and the politics of despair* (Boston: Beacon Press, 1990)

Liam O'Ruairc, *The League of Communist Republicans, 1986–1991* (Published by the author, 2001)

Luisa Passerini, *Autobiography of a generation: Italy, 1968* (Hanover: Wesleyan University Press, 1996)

Henry Patterson, *Ireland since 1939: the persistence of conflict* (Dublin: Penguin, 2006)

Henry Patterson, *Ireland's violent frontier: the border and Anglo-Irish relations during the troubles* (Basingstoke: Palgrave Macmillan, 2013)

Henry Patterson, *The politics of illusion: republicanism and socialism in modern Ireland* (London: Hutchinson Radius, 1989)

Robert Perry, *Revisionist scholarship and modern Irish politics* (Farnham: Ashgate, 2013)

Norman Porter (ed.), *The republican ideal: current perspectives* (Belfast: Blackstaff, 1998)

Simon Prince, *Northern Ireland's '68: civil rights, global revolt and the origins of the troubles* (Dublin: Irish Academic Press, 2007)

Simon Prince & Geoffrey Warner, *Belfast and Derry in revolt: a new history of the start of the troubles* (Dublin: Irish Academic Press, 2011)

Bob Purdie, *Politics in the streets: the origins of the civil rights movement in Northern Ireland* (Belfast: Blackstaff, 1990)

Gerd Rainer-Horn & Padraic Kenney (eds.), *Transnational moments of change: 1945, 1968, 1989* (Lanham, Maryland: Rowman & Littlefield, 2004)

F. Stuart Ross, *Smashing H-block: the rise and fall of the popular campaign against criminalisation, 1976–1982* (Liverpool: Liverpool University Press, 2011)

Kristin Ross, *May '68 and its afterlives* (Chicago: University of Chicago Press, 2002)

Paul Routledge, *John Hume: a biography* (London: HarperCollins, 1997)

Mark Ryan, *War and peace in Ireland: Britain and the IRA in the new world order* (London: Pluto Press, 1994)

Chris Ryder, *The Ulster Defence Regiment: an instrument of peace?* (London: Mandarin, 1992)

Rosemary Sales, *Women divided: gender, religion and politics in Northern Ireland* (London: Routledge, 1997)

Andrew Sanders, *Inside the IRA: dissident republicans and the war for legitimacy* (Edinburgh: Edinburgh University Press, 2012)

Andrew Sanders, *The long peace process: the United States of America and Northern Ireland, 1960–2008* (Liverpool: Liverpool University Press, 2019)

Bobby Sands, *Writings from prison* (Cork: Mercier, 1998)

Kay Schiller, 'Political militancy and generation conflict in West Germany during the "red decade"', *Debatte: Journal of Contemporary Central and Eastern Europe*, 11 (2003), pp. 19–38

Margaret M. Scull, *The Catholic church and the Northern Ireland troubles* (Oxford: Oxford University Press, 2019)

Timothy Shanahan, *The Provisional Irish Republican Army and the morality of terrorism* (Edinburgh: Edinburgh University Press, 2009)

Paul N. Siegel, *The meek and the militant: religion and power across the world* (Chicago, Illinois: Haymarket Books, 2005)

Jeffrey A. Sluka, *Hearts and minds, water and fish: support for the IRA and INLA in a Northern Irish ghetto* (Greenwich, Connecticut: JAI Press, 1989)

Evan Smith & Matthew Worley (eds.), *Against the grain: the British far left from 1956* (Manchester: Manchester University Press, 2014)

M. L. R. Smith, *Fighting for Ireland? The military strategy of the Irish republican movement* (London: Routledge, 1995)

Marie Smyth & Marie-Therese Fay (eds.), *Personal accounts from Northern Ireland's troubles: public conflict, private loss* (London: Pluto Press, 2000)

Graham Spencer, *From armed struggle to political struggle: republican tradition and transformation in Northern Ireland* (London: Bloomsbury, 2015)

Jennifer E. Spreng, *Abortion and divorce law in Ireland* (Jefferson, North Carolina: McFarland & Company, 2004)

Jonathan Stevenson, *'We wrecked the place': contemplating an end to the Northern Irish troubles* (New York: Free Press, 1996)

Paul Stitt, *Republican outcast: the Paul Stitt story* (Belfast: Justice Press, 2006)

Sean Swan, *Official Irish republicanism, 1962–1972* (Belfast: Lulu Press, 2006)

Robert Taber, *The war of the flea: guerrilla warfare theory and practice* (St Albans: Paladin, 1970)

Sidney G. Tarrow, *Power in movement: social movements and contentious politics* (Cambridge: Cambridge University Press, 2011)

Peter Taylor, *Brits: the war against the IRA* (London: Bloomsbury, 2001)

Peter Taylor, *Provos: the IRA and Sinn Féin* (London: Bloomsbury, 1997)

Peter Taylor, *States of terror: democracy and political violence* (Harmondsworth: Penguin, 1993)

Charles Tilly, *Contentious performances* (Cambridge: Cambridge University Press, 2008)

Charles Tilly & Lesley J. Wood, *Social movements, 1768–2012* (Boulder, Colorado: Paradigm Publishers, 2013)

Vladimir Tismaneanu (ed.), *Promises of 1968: crisis, illusion and utopia* (Budapest: Central European University Press, 2011)

Colm Tóibín, *Bad blood: a walk along the Irish border* (London: Picador, 2010) [First edition, as *Walking along the border*, London: Queen Anne Press, 1987]

Kevin Toolis, *Rebel hearts: journeys within the IRA's soul* (London: Picador, 1995)

Charles Townshend, *Political violence in Ireland: government and resistance since 1848* (Oxford: Clarendon Press, 1983)

Matt Treacy, *Building a tunnel to the moon: the end of the Irish Republican Army* (Belfast: Lulu Press, 2017)

Matt Treacy, *The IRA, 1956–1969: rethinking the republic* (Manchester: Manchester University Press, 2011)

Leon Trotsky, *Marxism and terrorism* (New York: Pathfinder Press, 1995)

Mao Tse-tung, *On guerrilla warfare* (transl. Samuel B. Griffith II) (Champaign, Illinois: University of Illinois Press, 2000 [1937])

Bryan S. Turner, *Religion and social theory* (London: Sage, 1991)

Mark Urban, *Big boys' rules: the SAS and the secret struggle against the IRA* (London: Faber & Faber, 1992)

Marcel van der Linden, *Western Marxism and the Soviet Union: a survey of critical theories and debates since 1917* (Leiden: Brill, 2007)

Xavier Vigna, *L'insubordination ouvrière dans les années 68: essai d'histoire politique des usines* (Rennes: Rennes University Press, 2007)

Anna von der Goltz (ed.), *'Talkin' 'bout my generation': conflicts of generation building and Europe's '1968'* (Göttingen: Wallstein Verlag, 2011)

Pat Walsh, *From civil rights to national war: Northern Ireland Catholic politics, 1964–1974* (Belfast: Athol Books, 1989)

Margaret Ward (ed.), *A difficult dangerous honesty: ten years of feminism in Northern Ireland* (Belfast: Women's Book Collective, 1986)

Lachlan Whalen, *Contemporary Irish republican prison writing: writing and resistance* (Basingstoke: Palgrave Macmillan, 2007)

Robert W. White, *Out of the ashes: an oral history of the Provisional Irish republican movement* (Newbridge: Merrion, 2017)

Robert W. White, *Provisional Irish republicans: an oral and interpretive history* (Westport, Connecticut: Greenwood Press, 1993)

Robert W. White, *Ruairí Ó Brádaigh: the life and politics of an Irish revolutionary* (Bloomington, Indiana: Indiana University Press, 2006)

S. A. Whiting, *Spoiling the peace? The threat of dissident republicans to peace in Northern Ireland* (Manchester: Manchester University Press, 2015)

John Whyte, *Interpreting Northern Ireland* (Oxford: Clarendon Press, 1990)

Sabine Wichert, *Northern Ireland since 1945* (Harlow: Longman, 1991)

Des Wilson, *An end to silence* (Cork: Mercier, 1985)

Simon Winchester, *In holy terror: reporting the Ulster troubles* (London: Faber & Faber, 1974)

Joanne Wright, *Terrorist propaganda: the Red Army Faction and the Provisional IRA, 1968–1986* (Basingstoke: Macmillan, 1991)

Journal articles

Rogelio Alonso, 'The modernisation in Irish republican thinking toward the utility of violence', *Studies in Conflict and Terrorism*, 24 (2001), pp. 131–144

Rogelio Alonso, 'Terrorist skin, peace-party mask: the political communication strategy of Sinn Féin and the Provisional IRA', *Terrorism and Political Violence*, 28 (2016), pp. 520–540

Joost Augusteijn, 'Political violence and democracy: an analysis of the tensions within Irish republican strategy, 1914–2002', *Irish Political Studies*, 18 (2003), pp. 1–26

Paul Badham, 'The contribution of religion to the conflict in Northern Ireland', *International Journal on World Peace*, 5 (1988), pp. 45–67

Bahman Bakhtiari, 'Revolution and the church in Nicaragua and El Salvador', *Journal of Church and State*, 28 (1986), pp. 15–42

Laia Balcells, Lesley-Ann Daniels, & Abel Escribà-Folch, 'The determinants of low-intensity intergroup violence: the case of Northern Ireland', *Journal of Peace Research*, 53 (2016), pp. 33–48

Stephen W. Beach, 'Social movement radicalization: the case of the People's Democracy in Northern Ireland', *Sociological Quarterly*, 18 (1977), pp. 305–318

Kevin Bean, 'The new departure? Recent developments in republican strategy and ideology', *Irish Studies Review*, 10 (1995), pp. 2–6

Kevin Bean & Mark Hayes, 'Sinn Féin and the new republicanism in Ireland: electoral progress, political stasis, and ideological failure', *Radical History Review*, 104 (2009), pp. 126–142

Mia Bloom, Paul Gill, & John Horgan, 'Tiocfaidh ár mná: women in the Provisional Irish Republican Army', *Behavioral Sciences of Terrorism and Political Aggression*, 4 (2012), pp. 60–76

Mia Bloom & John Horgan, 'Missing their mark: the IRA's proxy-bomb campaign', *Social Research*, 75 (2008), pp. 579–614

Lorenzo Bosi, 'Explaining pathways to armed activism in the Provisional Irish Republican Army, 1969–1972', *Social Science History*, 36 (2012), pp. 347–390

Lorenzo Bosi & Niall Ó Dochartaigh, 'Armed activism as the enactment of a collective identity: the case of the Provisional IRA between 1969 and 1972', *Social Movement Studies*, 17 (2018), pp. 35–47

Richard Bourke, 'Languages of conflict and the Northern Ireland troubles', *Journal of Modern History*, 83 (2011), pp. 544–578

J. Bowyer Bell, 'The escalation of insurgency: the Provisional Irish Republican Army's experience, 1969–1971', *Review of Politics*, 35 (1973), pp. 398–411

Marie Breen-Smyth, 'Hierarches of pain and responsibility: victims and war by other means in Northern Ireland', *Trípodos*, 25 (2009), pp. 27–40

Steve Bruce, 'Victim selection in ethnic conflict: motives and attitudes in Irish republicanism', *Terrorism and Political Violence*, 9 (1997), pp. 56–71

Anna Bryson, '"Whatever you say, say nothing": researching memory and identity in mid-Ulster, 1945–1969', *Oral History*, 35 (2007), pp. 45–56

Jeffrey James Byrne, 'Beyond continents, colours, and the Cold War: Yugoslavia, Algeria, and the struggle for non-alignment', *International History Review*, 37 (2015), pp. 912–932

Colm Campbell & Ita Connolly, 'A model for the "war against terrorism"? Military intervention in Northern Ireland and the 1970 Falls curfew', *Journal of Law and Society*, 30 (2003), pp. 341–375

Sarah Campbell, '"We shall overcome"? The Good Friday/Belfast Agreement and the memory of the civil rights movement', *Open Library of Humanities*, 4 (2018), pp. 1–25

Rebecca Clifford & Nigel Townson, 'The church in crisis: Catholic activism and "1968"', *Cultural and Social History*, 8 (2011), pp. 531–550

Gordon Clubb, 'Selling the end of terrorism: a framing approach to the IRA's disengagement from armed violence', *Small Wars & Insurgencies*, 27 (2016), pp. 608–635

Clara Connolly, 'Communalism: obstacle to social change', *Women: A Cultural Review*, 2 (1991), pp. 214–219

Anthony Coughlan, 'C. Desmond Greaves, 1913–1988: an obituary', *Saothar*, 14 (1989), pp. 5-15

Colin Coulter, '"British rights for British citizens": the campaign for equal citizenship for Northern Ireland', *Contemporary British History*, 29 (2015), pp. 486–507

Michael Cox, 'Bringing in the "international": the IRA ceasefire and the end of the Cold War', *International Affairs*, 73 (1997), pp. 671–693

W. Harvey Cox, 'Who wants a united Ireland?', *Government and Opposition*, 20 (1985), pp. 29–47

Tony Craig, 'From backdoors and back lanes to backchannels: reappraising British talks with the Provisional IRA', *Contemporary British History*, 26 (2012), pp. 97–117

Tony Craig, 'Monitoring the peace? Northern Ireland's 1975 ceasefire incident centres and the politicisation of Sinn Féin', *Terrorism and Political Violence*, 26 (2014), pp. 307–319

Tony Craig, 'Sabotage! The origins, development and impact of the IRA's infrastructural bombing campaigns, 1939–1997', *Intelligence and National Security*, 25 (2010), pp. 309–326

Liam Cullinane, '"A happy blend"? Irish republicanism, political violence and social agitation, 1962–1969', *Saothar*, 35 (2010), pp. 49–65

Michael Cunningham, 'The political language of John Hume', *Irish Political Studies*, 12 (1997), pp. 13–22

Graham Dawson, 'Trauma, place and the politics of memory: Bloody Sunday, Derry, 1972–2004', *History Workshop Journal*, 59 (2005), pp. 151–178

Paul Dixon, 'The politics of antagonism: explaining McGarry and O'Leary', *Irish Political Studies*, 11 (1996), pp. 130–141

C. J. M. Drake, 'The Provisional IRA: a case study', *Terrorism and Political Violence*, 3 (1991), pp. 43–60

Richard Dunphy & Stephen Hopkins, 'The organisational and political evolution of the Workers' Party of Ireland', *Journal of Communist Studies*, 8 (1992), pp. 91–118

Aaron Edwards, '"A whipping boy if ever there was one"? The British Army and the politics of civil–military relations in Northern Ireland, 1969–1979', *Contemporary British History*, 28 (2014), pp. 166–189

Richard English, 'Socialism and republican schism in Ireland: the emergence of the Republican Congress in 1934', *Irish Historical Studies*, 27 (1990), pp. 48–65

Jocelyn Evans & Jonathan Tonge, 'Northern Ireland's third tradition(s): the Alliance Party surveyed', *British Elections & Parties Review*, 11 (2001), pp. 104–118

Jocelyn A. J. Evans, Jonathan Tonge, & Gerard Murray, 'Constitutional nationalism and socialism in Northern Ireland: the greening of the Social Democratic and Labour Party', *British Elections and Parties Review*, 10 (2000), pp. 117–132

Gearóid Ó Faolean, 'The Ulster Defence Regiment and the question of Catholic recruitment, 1970–1972', *Terrorism and Political Violence*, 27 (2015), pp. 838–856

Antony Field, 'The hollow hierarchy: problems of command and control in the Provisional IRA', *Journal of Terrorism Research*, 8 (2017), pp. 11–23

Daniel Finn, 'The point of no return? People's Democracy and the Burntollet march', *Field Day Review*, 9 (2013), pp. 4–21

Daniel Finn, 'Republicanism and the Irish left', *Historical Materialism*, 24 (2016), pp. 181–197

Martyn Frampton, 'Sinn Féin and the European arena: "ourselves alone" or "critical engagement"?', *Irish Studies in International Affairs*, 16 (2005), pp. 235–253

Martyn Frampton, '"Squaring the circle": the foreign policy of Sinn Féin, 1983–1989', *Irish Political Studies*, 19 (2004), pp. 43–63

Michael Frisch, 'Oral history and Hard Times: a review essay', *Oral History Review*, 7 (1979), pp. 70–79.

Christine Anne George, 'Archives beyond the pale: negotiating legal and ethical entanglements after the Belfast Project', *American Archivist*, 76 (2013), pp. 47–67

Paul Gill & John Horgan, 'Who were the volunteers? The shifting sociological and operational profile of 1240 PIRA members', *Terrorism and Political Violence*, 25 (2013), pp. 435–456

Paul Gill, John Horgan, & James A. Piazza, 'Counterterrorism killings and Provisional IRA bombings, 1970–1998', *Terrorism and Political Violence*, 28 (2016), pp. 473–496

Paul Gill, Jeongyoon Lee, Karl R. Rethemeyer, John Horgan, & Victor Asal, 'Lethal connections: the determinants of networks in the Provisional IRA, 1970–1998', *International Interactions*, 40 (2014), pp. 52–78

Gordon Gillespie, 'The Sunningdale Agreement: lost opportunity or an agreement too far?', *Irish Political Studies*, 13 (1998), pp. 100–114

Niall Gilmartin, 'Feminism, nationalism and the re-ordering of post-war political strategies: the case of the Sinn Féin Women's Department', *Irish Political Studies*, 32 (2017), pp. 268–292

Niall Gilmartin, 'Negotiating new roles: Irish republican women and the politics of conflict transformation', *International Feminist Journal of Politics*, 17 (2015), pp. 58–76

Stephen C. Greer, 'Supergrasses and the legal system in Britain and Northern Ireland', *Law Quarterly Review*, 102 (1986), pp. 198–249

Amy E. Grubb, 'Microlevel dynamics of violence: explaining variation in violence among rural districts during Northern Ireland's troubles', *Security Studies*, 25 (2016), pp. 460–487

Adrian Guelke, 'The peace process in South Africa, Israel and Northern Ireland: a farewell to arms?', *Irish Studies in International Affairs*, 5 (1994), pp. 93–106

Adrian Guelke & Jim Smyth, 'The ballot bomb: terrorism and the electoral process in Northern Ireland', *Terrorism and Political Violence*, 4 (1992), pp. 103–124

Claire Hackett & Bill Rolston, 'The burden of memory: victims, storytelling and resistance in Northern Ireland', *Memory Studies*, 2 (2009), pp. 355–376

Amanda Hall, 'Incomplete peace and social stagnation: shortcomings of the Good Friday Agreement', *Open Library of Humanities*, 4 (2018), pp. 1–31

Carrie Hamilton, 'On being a "good" interviewer: empathy, ethics and the politics of oral history', *Oral History*, 36 (2008), pp. 35–43

Brian Hanley, '"Agitate, educate, organise": the IRA's *An tOglach*, 1965–1968', *Saothar*, 32 (2007), pp. 51–62

Brian Hanley, '"I ran away"? The IRA and 1969 – the evolution of a myth', *Irish Historical Studies*, 38 (2013), pp. 671–687

Brian Hanley, '"Moderates and peacemakers": Irish historians and the revolutionary centenary', *Irish Economic and Social History*, 43 (2016), pp. 113–130

John A. Hannigan, 'The armalite and the ballot box: dilemmas of strategy and ideology in the Provisional IRA', *Social Problems*, 33 (1985), pp. 31–40

Peter Hart, 'The social structure of the Irish Republican Army, 1916–1923', *Historical Journal*, 42 (1999), pp. 207–231

Bernadette C. Hayes & Ian McAllister, 'British and Irish public opinion towards the Northern Ireland problem', *Irish Political Studies*, 11 (1996), pp. 61–82

Bernadette C. Hayes & Ian McAllister, 'Sowing dragon's teeth: public support for political violence and paramilitarism in Northern Ireland', *Political Studies*, 49 (2001), pp. 901–922

Kevin Hearty, 'The malleability of memory and Irish republican memory entrepreneurship: a case study of the "Loughgall martyrs"', *Ethnopolitics*, 14 (2015), pp. 1–19

Jack Hepworth, '"We're getting the victory we fought for", we were told': retrospective subjective analysis in oral histories of Irish republicanism', *Oral History*, 48 (2020), pp. 68–79

Christopher Hewitt, 'Catholic grievances, Catholic nationalism and violence in Northern Ireland during the civil rights period: a reconsideration', *British Journal of Sociology*, 32 (1981), pp. 362–380

Paddy Hoey, 'Dissident and dissenting republicanism: from the Good Friday/Belfast Agreement to Brexit', *Capital & Class*, 43 (2018), pp. 1–24

Stephen Hopkins, 'The life history of an exemplary Provisional republican: Gerry Adams and the politics of biography', *Irish Political Studies*, 33 (2018), pp. 259–277

Stephen Hopkins, '"Our whole history has been ruined!" The 1981 hunger strike and the politics of republican commemoration and memory', *Irish Political Studies*, 31 (2016), pp. 44–62

Stephen Hopkins, 'Sinn Féin, the past and political strategy: the Provisional Irish republican movement and the politics of "reconciliation"', *Irish Political Studies*, 30 (2015), pp. 79–97

John Horgan & Max Taylor, 'Proceedings of the Irish Republican Army General Army Convention, December 1969', *Terrorism and Political Violence*, 9 (1997), pp. 151–158

Paul Howard, 'The Long Kesh hunger strikers: 25 years later', *Social Justice*, 33 (2006), pp. 69–91

James M. Jasper & Jane D. Poulsen, 'Recruiting strangers and friends: moral shocks and social networks in animal rights and anti-nuclear protests', *Social Problems*, 42 (1995), pp. 493–512

Erin Jessee, 'The limits of oral history: ethics and methodology amid highly politicised research settings', *Oral History Review*, 38 (2011), pp. 287–307

Jonna Katto, 'Emotions in protest: unsettling the past in ex-combatants' personal accounts in northern Mozambique', *Oral History*, 46 (2018), pp. 53–62

Jonna Katto, 'Landscapes of belonging: female ex-combatants remembering the liberation struggle in urban Maputo', *Journal of Southern African Studies*, 40 (2014), pp. 539–557

Eric Kaufmann, 'The Northern Ireland peace process in an age of austerity', *Political Quarterly*, 83 (2012), pp. 203–209

James Allison King, '"Say nothing": silenced records and the Boston College subpoenas', *Archives and Records*, 35 (2014), pp. 28–42

Colin Knox, 'The 1989 local elections in Northern Ireland', *Irish Political Studies*, 5 (1990), pp. 77–84

Rachel Caroline Kowalski, 'The role of sectarianism in the Provisional IRA campaign, 1969–1997', *Terrorism and Political Violence*, 28 (2016), pp. 658–683

Fintan Lane, 'Labour lives: Miriam Daly', *Saothar*, 27 (2002), pp. 101–102

Daniel H. Levine, 'Assessing the impacts of liberation theology in Latin America', *Review of Politics*, 50 (1988), pp. 241–263

Matthew Lewis & Shaun McDaid, 'Bosnia on the border? Republican violence in Northern Ireland during the 1920s and 1970s', *Terrorism and Political Violence*, 29 (2017), pp. 635–655

Christina Loughran, 'Armagh and feminist strategy: campaigns around republican women prisoners in Armagh Jail', *Feminist Review*, 23 (1986), pp. 59–79

Christina Loughran, 'Writing our own history: organising against the odds – 10 years of feminism in Northern Ireland', *Trouble & Strife*, 11 (Summer 1987), pp. 48–54

Malvern Lumsden, 'Peace by peace? Socio-economic structures and the role of the Peace People in Northern Ireland', *Current Research on Peace and Violence*, 1 (1978), pp. 41–52

Chris Lundry, 'From passivity to political resource: the Catholic church and the development of nationalism in East Timor', *Asian Studies*, 38 (2002), pp. 1–33

Brendan Lynn, 'Revising northern nationalism, 1960–1965: the Nationalist Party's response', *New Hibernia Review*, 4 (2000), pp. 78–92

Laura E. Lyons & Mairead Keane, '"At the end of the day": an interview with Mairead Keane, national head of Sinn Fein Women's Department', *boundary 2*, 19 (1992), pp. 260–286

Gregory M. Maney, 'The paradox of reform: the civil rights movement in Northern Ireland', *Research in Social Movements, Conflicts and Change*, 34 (2012), pp. 3–26

Deborah Martin & Byron Miller, 'Space and contentious politics', *Mobilization*, 8 (2003), pp. 143–156

Ian McAllister, 'Political attitudes, partisanship and social structures in Northern Ireland', *Economic and Social Review*, 14 (1983), pp. 185–202

Ian McAllister, 'Political opposition in Northern Ireland: the National Democratic Party, 1965–1970', *Economic and Social Review*, 6 (1975), pp. 353–366

Ian McAllister, 'Social contacts and political behaviour in Northern Ireland, 1968–1978', *Social Networks*, 5 (1983), pp. 303–313

Ian McBride, 'The shadow of the gunman: Irish historians and the IRA', *Journal of Contemporary History*, 46 (2011), pp. 686–710

Martin McCleery & Aaron Edwards, 'The 1988 murders of Corporal David Howes and Corporal Derek Wood: a micro dynamic analysis of political violence during the Northern Ireland conflict', *Critical Military Studies* (2017), pp. 1–19

Anne McClintock, 'Family feuds: gender, nationalism and the family', *Feminist Review*, 44 (1993), pp. 61–80

Kieran McEvoy & Anna Bryson, 'Justice, truth and oral history: legislating the past "from below" in Northern Ireland', *Northern Ireland Legal Quarterly*, 67 (2016), pp. 67–90

Kieran McEvoy, David O'Mahony, Carol Horner, & Olwen Lyner, 'The home front: the families of politically motivated prisoners in Northern Ireland', *British Journal of Criminology*, 39 (1999), pp. 175–197

Cillian McGrattan, 'Dublin, the SDLP, and the Sunningdale Agreement: maximalist nationalism and path dependency', *Contemporary British History*, 23 (2009), pp. 61–78

Anthony McIntyre, 'Modern Irish republicanism: the product of British state strategies', *Irish Political Studies*, 10 (1995), pp. 97–122

Michael McKinley, '"Dangerous liaisons"? The Provisional Irish Republican Army, Marxism, and the communist governments of Europe', *History of European Ideas*, 15 (1992), pp. 443–449

Peter John McLoughlin, '"It's a united Ireland or nothing"? John Hume and the idea of Irish unity, 1964–1972', *Irish Political Studies*, 21 (2006), pp. 157–180

Rachel Monaghan, 'An imperfect peace: paramilitary "punishments" in Northern Ireland', *Terrorism and Political Violence*, 16 (2004), pp. 439–461

Rachel Monaghan, 'The return of "Captain Moonlight": informal justice in Northern Ireland', *Studies in Conflict & Terrorism*, 25 (2002), pp. 41–56

John F. Morrison, 'Copying to be different: violent dissident Irish republican learning', *Studies in Conflict & Terrorism*, 40 (2017), pp. 586–602

John F. Morrison, '"Trust in me": allegiance choices in a post-split terrorist movement', *Aggression and Violent Behaviour*, 28 (2016), pp. 47–56

Hazel Morrissey, 'Betty Sinclair: a woman's fight for socialism, 1910–1981', *Saothar*, 9 (1983), pp. 121–132

Marc Mulholland, 'Irish republican politics and violence before the peace process, 1969–1994', *European Review of History*, 14 (2007), pp. 397–421

Marc Mulholland, 'Northern Ireland and the far left, *c.*1965–1975', *Contemporary British History*, 32 (2018), pp. 542–563

Ronnie Munck, 'The making of the troubles in Northern Ireland', *Journal of Contemporary History*, 27 (1992), pp. 211–229

Joane Nagel, 'Masculinity and nationalism: gender and sexuality in the making of nations', *Ethnic and Racial Studies*, 21 (1998), pp. 242–269

John Nagle, 'Sites of social centrality and segregation: Lefebvre in Belfast – a "divided city"', *Antipode*, 41 (2009), pp. 326–347

Sabelo J. Ndlovu-Gatsheni, 'Making sense of Mugabeism in local and global politics: "So Blair, keep your England and let me keep my Zimbabwe"', *Third World Quarterly*, 30 (2009), pp. 1139–1158

Niall Ó Dochartaigh, '"Everyone trying": the IRA ceasefire, 1975 – a missed opportunity for peace?', *Field Day Review*, 7 (2011), pp. 50–77

Niall Ó Dochartaigh, 'The longest negotiation: British policy, IRA strategy and the making of the Northern Ireland peace settlement', *Political Studies*, 63 (2015), pp. 202–220

Catherine O'Donnell, 'The Sunningdale communiqué (1973) and bipartisanship in the Republic of Ireland', *Working Papers in British-Irish Studies*, 81 (2007), pp. 1–16

Mervyn O'Driscoll, 'A "German invasion"? Irish rural radicalism, European integration, and Irish modernisation, 1958–1973', *International History Review*, 38 (2016), pp. 527–550

Brendan O'Duffy, 'Violence in Northern Ireland, 1969–1994: sectarian or ethno-national?', *Ethnic and Racial Studies*, 18 (1995), pp. 740–772

Gearóid Ó Faoleán, 'Ireland's Ho Chi Minh trail? The Republic of Ireland's role in the Provisional IRA's bombing campaign, 1970–1976', *Small Wars & Insurgencies*, 25 (2014), pp. 976–991

Denis O'Hearn, 'Repression and solidary cultures of resistance: Irish political prisoners, past and present', *American Journal of Sociology*, 115 (2009), pp. 491–526

Brendan O'Leary, 'Mission accomplished? Looking back at the IRA', *Field Day Review*, 1 (2005), pp. 217–246

Ted Palys & John Lowman, 'Defending research confidentiality "to the extent the law allows": lessons from the Boston College subpoenas', *Journal of Academic Ethics*, 10 (2012), pp. 271–297

Connal Parr, 'Ending the siege? David Ervine and the struggle for progressive loyalism', *Irish Political Studies*, 33 (2018), pp. 202–220

Henry Patterson, 'The border security problem and Anglo-Irish relations, 1970–1973', *Contemporary British History*, 26 (2012), pp. 231–251

Henry Patterson, 'The Provisional IRA, the Irish border, and Anglo-Irish relations during the troubles', *Small Wars and Insurgencies*, 24 (2013), pp. 493–517

Henry Patterson, 'Sectarianism revisited: the Provisional IRA campaign in a border region of Northern Ireland', *Terrorism and Political Violence*, 22 (2010), pp. 337–356

Robert Perry, 'Revisionism: the Provisional republican movement', *Journal of Politics and Law*, 1 (2008), pp. 43–53

Robert Perry, 'Revisionist Marxism in Ireland: the party', *Critique*, 36 (2008), pp. 457–477

Simon Prince, 'The global revolt of 1968 and Northern Ireland', *Historical Journal*, 49 (2006), pp. 851–876

Simon Prince, 'Mythologising a movement: Northern Ireland's '68', *History Ireland*, 16 (September–October 2008), pp. 26–29

Simon Prince & Geoffrey Warner, 'The IRA and its rivals: political competition and the turn to violence in the early troubles', *Contemporary British History*, 27 (2013), pp. 271–296

Bob Purdie, 'Was the civil rights movement a republican/communist conspiracy?', *Irish Political Studies*, 3 (1988), pp. 33–42

Dieter Reinisch, '*Cumann na mBan* and women in Irish republican paramilitary organisations, 1969–1986', *Estudios Irlandeses*, 11 (2016), pp. 149–162

Dieter Reinisch, 'Women's agency and political violence: Irish republican women and the formation of the Provisional IRA, 1967–1970', *Irish Political Studies*, 34 (2019), pp. 420–443

Kacper Rekawek, 'How terrorism does not end: the case of the Official Irish Republican Army', *Critical Studies on Terrorism*, 1 (2008), pp. 359–376

Kacper Rekawek, '"Their history is a bit like our history": comparative assessment of the Official and Provisional IRAs', *Terrorism and Political Violence*, 25 (2013), pp. 688–708

Chris Reynolds, 'Beneath the troubles, the cobblestones: recovering the "buried" memory of Northern Ireland's 1968', *American Historical Review*, 123 (2018), pp. 744–748

Chris Reynolds, 'The collective European memory of 1968: the case of Northern Ireland', *Études Irlandaises*, 36 (2011), pp. 1–17

Chris Reynolds, 'Northern Ireland's 1968 in a post-troubles context', *Interventions*, 19 (2017), pp. 631–645

Briege Rice, '"Hawks turn to doves": the response of the postrevolutionary generation to the 'new' troubles in Ireland, 1969–1971', *Irish Political Studies*, 30 (2015), pp. 238–254

Anthony Richards, 'Terrorist groups and political fronts: the IRA, Sinn Fein, the peace process and democracy', *Terrorism and Political Violence*, 13 (2001), pp. 72–89

Bill Rolston, 'Politics, painting and popular culture: the political wall murals of Northern Ireland', *Media, Culture and Society*, 9 (1987), pp. 5–28

Bill Rolston, 'Prison as a liberated zone: the murals of Long Kesh, Northern Ireland', *State Crime*, 2 (2013), pp. 149–172

F. Stuart Ross, 'Between party and movement: Sinn Féin and the popular movement against criminalisation, 1976–1982', *Irish Political Studies*, 21 (2006), pp. 337–354

Carmel Roulston, 'Women on the margin: the women's movement in Northern Ireland, 1972–1988', *Science and Society*, 53 (1989), pp. 219–236

Joseph Ruane & Jennifer Todd, 'Diversity, division and the middle ground in Northern Ireland', *Irish Political Studies*, 7 (1992), pp. 73–98

Joseph Rutte, 'The worker-priest archetype', *Psychological Perspectives: A Quarterly Journal of Jungian Thought*, 60 (2017), pp. 445–464

Ignacio Sànchez-Cuenca, 'The dynamics of nationalist terrorism: ETA and the IRA', *Terrorism and Political Violence*, 19 (2007), pp. 289–306

Andrew Sanders, 'Problems of class, religion and ethnicity: a study of the relationship between Irish republicans and the Protestant working class during the Ulster "troubles", 1969–1994', *Irish Political Studies*, 24 (2009), pp. 89–105

Margaret M. Scull, 'The Catholic Church and the hunger strikes of Terence MacSwiney and Bobby Sands', *Irish Political Studies*, 31 (2016), pp. 282–299

Peter Shirlow & Lorraine Dowler, '"Wee women no more": female partners of republican political prisoners in Belfast', *Environment and Planning*, 42 (2010), pp. 384–399

Andrew Silke, 'Rebel's dilemma: the changing relationship between the IRA, Sinn Féin and paramilitary vigilantism in Northern Ireland', *Terrorism and Political Violence*, 11 (1999), pp. 55–93

Richard Sinnott, 'The north: party images and party approaches in the Republic', *Irish Political Studies*, 1 (1986), pp. 15–32

M. L. R. Smith & Peter R. Neumann, 'Motorman's long journey: changing the strategic setting in Northern Ireland', *Contemporary British History*, 19 (2005), pp. 413–435

Lee A. Smithey, 'Social movement strategy, tactics, and collective identity', *Sociology Compass*, 3 (2009), pp. 658–671

David A. Snow, Louis A. Zurcher, & Sheldon Ekland-Olson, 'Social networks and social movements: a microstructural approach to differential recruitment', *American Sociological Review*, 45 (1980), pp. 787–801

Graham Spencer, 'Sinn Féin and the media in Northern Ireland: the new terrain of policy articulation', *Irish Political Studies*, 21 (2006), pp. 355–382

Rachel Stevenson & Nick Crossley, 'Change in covert social movement networks: the "inner circle" of the Provisional Irish Republican Army', *Social Movement Studies*, 13 (2014), pp. 70–91

Benjamin Stidworthy, '"Double oppression": homosexuality and the Irish republican movement', *Historical Discourses: The McGill Undergraduate Journal of History*, 27 (2012–2013), pp. 152–164

Tim Strangleman, 'Deindustrialisation and the historical sociological imagination: making sense of work and industrial change', *Sociology*, 51 (2017), pp. 466–482

Scott Sullivan, 'From theory to practice: the patterns of violence in Northern Ireland, 1969–1994', *Irish Political Studies*, 13 (1998), pp. 76–99

Henri Tajfel, 'Social identity and intergroup behaviour', *Social Science Information*, 13 (1974), pp. 65–93

Sidney Tarrow, 'Inside insurgencies: politics and violence in an age of civil war', *Perspectives on Politics*, 5 (2007), pp. 587–600

Sidney Tarrow, 'Social movements in contentious politics: a review article', *American Political Science Review*, 90 (1996), pp. 874–883

Jennifer Todd, 'Northern Irish nationalist political culture', *Irish Political Studies*, 5 (1990), pp. 31–44

Jonathan Tonge, 'From Sunningdale to the Good Friday Agreement: creating devolved government in Northern Ireland', *Contemporary British History*, 14 (2000), pp. 39–60

Jonathan Tonge, '"No-one likes us; we don't care": "dissident" Irish republicans and mandates', *Political Quarterly*, 83 (2012), pp. 219–226

Jonathan Tonge, 'The political agenda of Sinn Féin: change without change?', *Contemporary Political Studies*, 2 (1997), pp. 750–760

Jonathan Tonge, 'Sinn Féin and "new republicanism" in Belfast', *Space & Polity*, 10 (2006), pp. 135–147

Jonathan Tonge, '"They haven't gone away, you know": Irish republican "dissidents" and the armed struggle', *Terrorism and Political Violence*, 16 (2004), pp. 671–693

Charles Townshend, 'Religion, war, and identity in Ireland', *Journal of Modern History*, 76 (2004), pp. 882–902

Michael von Tangen Page & M. L. R. Smith, 'War by other means: the problem of political control in Irish republican strategy', *Armed Forces & Society*, 27 (2000), pp. 79–104

Margaret Ward & Marie-Thérèse McGivern, 'Images of women in Northern Ireland', *The Crane Bag*, 4 (1980), pp. 66–72

Geoffrey Warner, 'The Falls Road curfew revisited', *Irish Studies Review*, 14 (2006), pp. 325–342

Lachlan Whalen, '"Our barbed wire ivory tower": the prison writings of Gerry Adams', *New Hibernia Review*, 10 (2006), pp. 129–139

Leo J. Whelan, 'The challenge of lobbying for civil rights in Northern Ireland: the Committee on the Administration of Justice', *Human Rights Quarterly*, 14 (1992), pp. 149–170

Robert W. White, 'The 1975 British-Provisional IRA truce in perspective', *Éire-Ireland*, 45 (2010), pp. 211–244

Robert W. White, 'From peaceful protest to guerrilla war: micromobilisation of the Provisional Irish Republican Army', *American Journal of Sociology*, 94 (1989), pp. 1277–1302

Robert W. White, 'The Irish Republican Army: an assessment of sectarianism', *Terrorism and Political Violence*, 9 (1997), pp. 20–55

Robert W. White, 'Provisional IRA attacks on the UDR in Fermanagh and south Tyrone: implications for the study of political violence and terrorism', *Terrorism and Political Violence*, 23 (2011), pp. 329–349

Robert W. White, 'Structural identity theory and the post-recruitment activism of Irish republicans: persistence, disengagement, splits, and dissidents in social movement organizations', *Social Problems*, 57 (2010), pp. 341–370

Andrew Wilson, 'The conflict between Noraid and the Friends of Irish Freedom', *Irish Review*, 15 (1994), pp. 40–50

Benjamin R. Young, 'Hammer, sickle, and the shamrock: North Korea's relations with the Workers' Party of Ireland', *Journal of Northeast Asian History*, 12 (2015), pp. 105–130

Book chapters

Paul Arthur, 'Republican violence in Northern Ireland: the rationale', in John Darby, Nicholas Dodge, & A. C. Hepburn (eds.), *Political violence: Ireland in a comparative perspective* (Ottawa: University of Ottawa Press, 1990), pp. 48–63

D. George Boyce, '"Can anyone here imagine?": southern Irish political parties and the Northern Ireland problem', in Patrick J. Roche & Brian Barton (eds.), *The Northern Ireland question: myth and reality* (Aldershot: Avebury Press, 1991), pp. 173–188

Tom Boylan, Chris Curtin, & Michael Laver, 'A changing society: Ireland since the 1960s', in Thomas Bartlett, Chris Curtin, Riana O'Dwyer, & Gearóid Ó Tuathaigh (eds.), *Irish studies: a general introduction* (Dublin: Gill & Macmillan, 1988), pp. 192–220

Callum G. Brown, 'A revisionist approach to religious change', in Steve Bruce (ed.), *Religion and modernization: sociologists and historians debate the secularization thesis* (Oxford: Clarendon, 1992), pp. 31–58

Sarah Campbell, 'Power sharing and the Irish dimension: the conundrum for the SDLP in Northern Ireland', in David McCann & Cillian McGrattan (eds.), *Sunningdale, the Ulster Workers' Council strike and the struggle for democracy in Northern Ireland* (Manchester: Manchester University Press, 2017), pp. 127–140

Eduardo Canel, 'New social movement theory and resource mobilization theory: the need for integration', in M. Kaufman & H. Dilla Alfonso (eds.), *Community power and grassroots democracy: the transformation of social life* (London: Zed Books, 1997), pp. 198–221

Mary Corcoran, 'Mapping carceral space: territorialisation, resistance and control in Northern Ireland's women's prisons', in Scott Brewster, Virginia Crossman, Fiona Beckett, & David Alderson (eds.), *Ireland in proximity: history, gender, space* (London: Routledge, 1999), pp. 157–172

Carol Coulter, 'Feminism and nationalism in Ireland', in David Miller (ed.), *Rethinking Northern Ireland: culture, ideology and colonialism* (London: Longman, 1998), pp. 160–178

Gianluca de Fazio, 'Intra-movement competition and political outbidding as mechanisms of radicalisation in Northern Ireland, 1968–1969', in Lorenzo Bosi, Chares Demetriou, & Stefan Malthaner (eds.), *Dynamics of political violence: a process-oriented perspective on radicalisation and the escalation of political conflict* (Farnham: Ashgate, 2014), pp. 115–136

Donatella della Porta, 'In-depth interviews', in Donatella della Porta (ed.), *Methodological practices in social movement research* (Oxford: Oxford University Press, 2014), pp. 228–261

Donatella della Porta, 'Introduction: on individual motivations in underground political organizations', in Donatella della Porta (ed.), *Social movements and violence: participation in underground organizations* (Greenwich, Connecticut: JAI Press, 1992), pp. 3–28

Richard Dunphy, 'The contradictory politics of the Official Republican movement, 1969–1992', in Richard Dunphy (ed.), *Les républicanismes Irlandais* (Rennes: Presses Universitaires de Rennes, 1997), pp. 117–138

Daniel Finn, 'The British radical left and Northern Ireland during the "troubles"', in Evan Smith & Matthew Worley (eds.), *Waiting for the revolution: the British far left from 1956* (Manchester: Manchester University Press, 2017), pp. 201–217

Tony Garvin, 'The north and the rest: the politics of the Republic of Ireland', in Charles Townshend (ed.), *Consensus in Ireland: approaches and recessions* (Oxford: Clarendon, 1988), pp. 95–109

Adrian Guelke, 'Loyalist and republican perceptions of the Northern Ireland conflict: the UDA and Provisional IRA', in Peter H. Merkl (ed.), *Political violence and terror: motifs and motivations* (Berkeley, California: University of California Press, 1986), pp. 91–122

Adrian Guelke, 'Policing in Northern Ireland', in Brigid Hadfield (ed.), *Northern Ireland: politics and the constitution* (Buckingham: Open University Press, 1992), pp. 94–109

Andre Gunder Frank & Barry K. Gills, 'The 5,000-year world system: an interdisciplinary introduction', in Andre Gunder Frank & Barry K. Gills (eds.), *The world system: five hundred years or five thousand?* (London: Routledge, 1993), pp. 3–58

Brian Hanley, 'The rhetoric of republican legitimacy', in Fearghal McGarry (ed.), *Republicanism in modern Ireland* (Dublin: University College Dublin Press, 2003), pp. 167–177

Richard Jenkins, 'Bringing it all back home: an anthropologist in Belfast', in Colin Bell & Helen Roberts (eds.), *Social researching: politics, problems, practice* (London: Routledge & Kegan Paul, 1984), pp. 147–164

Chris Lundry, 'From passivity to political resource: the Catholic church and the development of nationalism in East Timor', *Asian Studies*, 38 (2002), pp. 1–33

Anthony McIntyre, 'Provisional republicanism: internal politics, inequities, and modes of repression', in Fearghal McGarry (ed.), *Republicanism in modern Ireland* (Dublin: University College Dublin Press, 2003), pp. 178–198

Monica McWilliams, 'Women in Northern Ireland: an overview', in Eamonn Hughes (ed.), *Culture and politics in Northern Ireland, 1960–1990* (Milton Keynes: Open University Press, 1991), pp. 81–100

Edward P. Moxon-Browne, 'Alienation: the case of Catholics in Northern Ireland', in Martin Slann & Bernard Schechterman (eds.), *Multidimensional terrorism* (Boulder, Colorado: Lynne Rienner Publishers, 1987), pp. 95–110

Henry Patterson, '1974 – year of liberty'? The Provisional IRA and Sunningdale', in David McCann & Cillian McGrattan (eds.), *Sunningdale, the Ulster Workers' Council strike and the struggle for democracy in Northern Ireland* (Manchester: Manchester University Press, 2017), pp. 141–158

Alessandro Portelli, 'Uchronic dreams: working class memory and possible worlds', in Raphael Samuel & Paul Thompson (eds.), *The myths we live by* (London: Routledge, 1990), pp. 147–155

Michael Poole, 'The geographical location of political violence in Northern Ireland', in John Darby, Nicholas Dodge, & A. C. Hepburn (eds.), *Political violence: Ireland in a comparative perspective* (Ottawa: University of Ottawa Press, 1990), pp. 64–82

Dieter Reinisch, 'Performing resistance: sport and Irish republican identity in internment camps and prisons', in Dittmar Dahlmann, Gregor Feindt, & Anke Hilbrenner (eds.), *Sport under unexpected circumstances: violence, discipline, and leisure in penal and internment camps* (Göttingen: Vandenhoeck & Ruprecht, 2018), pp. 245–266

Bill Rolston, 'Alienation or political awareness? The battle for the hearts and minds of northern nationalists', in Paul Teague (ed.), *Beyond the rhetoric: politics, the economy and social policy in Northern Ireland* (London: Lawrence & Wishart, 1987), pp. 58–80

Bill Rolston, 'Community politics', in Liam O'Dowd, Bill Rolston, & Mike Tomlinson (eds.), *Northern Ireland: between civil rights and civil war* (London: CSE Books, 1980), pp. 148–177

Bill Rolston, 'The limits of trade unionism', in Liam O'Dowd, Bill Rolston, & Mike Tomlinson (eds.), *Northern Ireland: between civil rights and civil war* (London: CSE Books, 1980), pp. 68–94

Bill Rolston, 'Music and politics in Ireland: the case of loyalism', in John P. Harrington & Elizabeth J. Mitchell (eds.), *Politics and performance in contemporary Northern Ireland* (Amherst, Massachusetts: University of Massachusetts Press, 1999), pp. 29–56

Mark Ryan, 'From the centre to the margins: the slow death of Irish republicanism', in Chris Gilligan & Jon Tonge (eds.), *Peace or war? Understanding the peace process in Northern Ireland* (Aldershot: Ashgate, 1997), pp. 72–84

M. L. R. Smith, 'Fin de siècle, 1972: the Provisional IRA's strategy and the beginning of the eight-thousand-day stalemate', in Alan O'Day (ed.), *Political violence in Northern Ireland: conflict and conflict resolution* (Westport, Connecticut: Praeger, 1997), pp. 15–32

Jim Smyth, 'Moving the immovable: the civil rights movement in Northern Ireland', in Linda Connolly & Niamh Hourigan (eds.), *Social movements and Ireland* (Manchester: Manchester University Press, 2006), pp. 106–123

Henri Tajfel, 'The achievement of group differentiation', in Henri Tajfel (ed.), *Differentiation between social groups: studies in the social psychology of intergroup relations* (London: Academic Press, 1978), pp. 27–60

William Thompson & Barry Mulholland, 'Paramilitary punishments and young people in west Belfast: psychological effects and the implications for education', in Liam Kennedy (ed.), *Crime and punishment in west Belfast* (Belfast: The Summer School, 1995), pp. 51–66

Mike Tomlinson, 'Housing, the state, and the politics of separation', in Liam
O'Dowd, Bill Rolston, & Mike Tomlinson (eds.), *Northern Ireland: between
civil rights and civil war* (London: CSE Books, 1980), pp. 119–147

Max Travers, 'Qualitative interviewing methods', in Maggie Walter (ed.), *Social
research methods* (Oxford: Oxford University Press, 2013), pp. 227–253

Dawn Walsh & Eoin O'Malley, 'The slow growth of Sinn Féin: from minor
player to centre stage?', in Liam Weeks & Alistair Clark (eds.), *Radical
or redundant? Minor parties in Irish politics* (Dublin: History Press Ireland,
2012), pp. 203–218

Margaret Ward, '"Ulster was different"? Women, feminism and nationalism
in the north of Ireland', in Yvonne Galligan, Eilís Ward, & Rick Wilford
(eds.), *Contesting politics: women in Ireland, north and south* (Boulder,
Colorado: Westview Press, 1999), pp. 219–239

Rick Wilford, 'Inverting consociationalism? Policy, pluralism, and the
post-modern', in Brigid Hadfield (ed.), *Northern Ireland: politics and the
constitution* (Buckingham: Open University Press, 1992), pp. 29–46

Unpublished theses
David F. Fanning, 'Irish republican literature, 1968–1998: "standing on the
threshold of another trembling world"', PhD (Ohio State University, 2003)

Philomena Gallagher, 'An oral history of the imprisoned female Irish
Republican Army', MPhil (Trinity College Dublin, 1995)

Index